CHURCH AND STATE IN CANADA WEST, 1841-1867

CANADIAN STUDIES IN HISTORY AND GOVERNMENT

A series of studies edited by G. S. French, sponsored by the Canadian Social Science Research Council, and published with financial assistance from the Canada Council.

1. *Church and State in Canada West, 1841–1867.* By J. S. Moir.

2. *The French Shore Problem in Newfoundland.* By F. F. Thompson.

3. *Alignment of Political Groups in Canada, 1841–1867.* By P. G. Cornell.

4. *The Private Member of Parliament and the Formulation of Public Policy.* By R. N. Kelson.

5. *The San Juan Water Boundary Question.* By J. O. McCabe.

6. *The Mark of Honour.* By H. C. Mathews.

7. *The Political History of Newfoundland, 1832–64.* By G. E. Gunn.

8. *Upper Canada's Clergy Reserves.* By A. Wilson.

9. *The Franchise and Politics.* By J. Garner.

10. *The Land Policies of Upper Canada.* By L. F. Gates.

11. *The Jesuits' Estates Question, 1760–1888.* By R. C. Dalton.

Church and State in Canada West

THREE STUDIES IN THE RELATION
OF DENOMINATIONALISM AND
NATIONALISM, 1841-1867

BY

JOHN S. MOIR

UNIVERSITY OF TORONTO PRESS

Printed in the United States of America

TO JACQUELINE

FOREWORD

THIS is the first volume in the series, Canadian Studies in History and Government, sponsored by the Canadian Social Science Research Council and similar in general character and purpose to the companion series, Canadian Studies in Economics, already being published for the Council. The intention is to make available works of scholarly research which have rather specialized content. The series is meant to be wide in its scope, comprising works done in Canada on history and government, instead of works solely on Canadian history and government, and interpreting "government" broadly to cover studies in politics or in related aspects of community life. In fact, the first criterion for the inclusion of a volume will be the worth of the contribution which it makes to Canadian scholarship in this general field, rather than any precise qualification as to its content.

J. M. S. CARELESS
General Editor

CONTENTS

INTRODUCTION   xi

1. THE FIRST AND FOURTH ESTATES IN CANADA WEST   3
2. THE CLERGY RESERVES, 1839-1849: THE COMPROMISE THAT FAILED   27
3. THE CLERGY RESERVES, 1849-1857: SECULARIZATION AND COMPENSATION   52
4. THE UNIVERSITY QUESTION, 1840-1849: IN SEARCH OF A SYSTEM   82
5. THE UNIVERSITY QUESTION, 1850-1867: A PATTERN ESTABLISHED   106
6. RELIGION AND ELEMENTARY EDUCATION, 1841-1851: PROTECTION FROM
        INSULT   129
7. RELIGION AND ELEMENTARY EDUCATION, 1852-1867: THE WAR OF TOTAL
        SEPARATION   150

RETROSPECT   181

APPENDIXES   183

  I. Denominational Growth in Canada West   185
 II. Development of the Presbyterian Churches   186
III. Development of the Methodist Churches   187
 IV. Statistics of the Clergy Reserves Fund, Canada West   188
  V. Statistical Growth of Separate Schools in Canada West   189
 VI. The Settlement of the Rectories Question   190

BIBLIOGRAPHIC NOTE   193

NOTES   197

INDEX   217

INTRODUCTION

THE PROBLEM of the relationship of the Christian Church to the state is as old as Christianity itself. The relation of the two bodies cannot properly be defined as an article of faith, yet it is an integral factor in the Christian religion. Although several statements by Christ on this problem are recorded in the New Testament, the guiding principle of render unto Caesar the things of Caesar, and unto God the things of God, does little to clarify or explain what that relationship should be in matters of detail. Every age since Christ has sought and developed its own solution to the problem, but because the problem is part of Christianity, it must, like Christianity, be eternal, and each generation must face it anew. Theocracy was tried in Geneva, Erastianism in England, and complete separation of church and state in the United States of America; and time has found each solution wanting in some respect. In Canada West between 1841 and 1867 the opposed ideals of established state-churchism and complete separation fought for recognition. The solution then was found in a compromise nominally favourable to the forces of complete separation of church and state.

The contest in Canada West was deeply influenced by the contemporary religious developments in Europe, and particularly those in Britain. The growth of Puseyism or Tractarianism as part of the Oxford Movement in the 1840's, the disruption of the Church of Scotland in that same decade, the "Papal Aggression" controversy which raged in the early fifties, and the renewed vigour of the Church of Rome under Pius IX, in a Europe torn by revolution and the growth of nationalism—each of these developments in turn was reflected in the religious and political life of Canada West after 1841.

Here, in the former Upper Canada, now the western half of the newly created United Province of Canada, the problem of the relation of church and state was far from new. The attempt to found a little England complete with an established church had met with strong opposition in the frontier community of Upper Canada, and had been a contributing cause of the recent abortive Rebellion of 1837. But after the Union of Upper and Lower Canada the problem took on a new appearance, in part as a result of the Rebellion itself, in part as a result of the contemporary events in Europe. To the older force of North American frontierism, and its corollary of complete separation of church and state, was added the leaven of nationalism. The full implications of this change did not become evident until the Union was almost a decade old.

Admittedly, the concept of a pre-Confederation Canadian nationalism—a sense of geographic, political and social identity—requires qualification, for only national interests can create a national spirit. It is a commonplace of Canadian historians to date the birth of Canadian nationalism from the War of 1812-14, which drew both French- and English-speaking Canadians together in defence of their home or native land, but the growth of a true national sentiment was severely retarded by the sense of exile, as voiced in "The Canadian Boat Song," by the stark reality of colonial status, and by the indigenous parochialism and regionalism of a scattered population in a broad land. Only when Canadian statesmen faced national responsibilities after the achievement of responsible government, and after the railways and telegraph had provided isolated areas with the means of rapid communication, could the parts be welded into a whole. Confederation provided only a framework for political and economic nationalism —the psychological sense of identity was slow in following the flag and trade. "Canadian nationalism differs from the nationalism of the Old World in this, that while they draw their inspiration largely from the past, it draws its inspiration mainly from the future." [1] (Significantly, Troeltsch and Niebuhr describe this forward-looking attitude also as being one mark of the sect,[2] and religious sects played a lively part in Canada West.)

Nevertheless the seeds of nationalism were already planted in the Canadian Union of 1841. Lord Durham's abortive plan for a confederation of British North America had been accepted by many leading Canadians and his famous Report held out this idea of wider union as "the only means of fostering such a national feeling . . . as would effectively counterbalance whatever tendencies may now exist toward separation [from the mother country]."[3] This "means" was not adopted until 1867, but signs of national feeling are not lacking during the Union period. In spite of, and at times because of, all the sectional practices and divisions which grew up to compromise the Union of the Canadas, their union was the necessary precursor to Confederation. In fact Reformers demanded the end of the existing union in the very name of political nationalism and all that term connotes. Thomas D'Arcy McGee repeatedly advocated a "Canadian nationality" without any limiting prefix, and other journalists called upon new immigrants to forget Old World feuds and differences, such as those of Orange and Green, and to become truly Canadians. Similarly, the ideal educational system was regularly defined by most Upper Canadians, and particularly those of Reform politics, as "national schools" and "national university."

The conjunction of political and religious radicalism in Canada West was not accidental, as the groundwork had been well laid during the half-century existence of Upper Canada. The fact that the overwhelming majority of Loyalists and post-Loyalist American settlers who first entered the colony were not members of the Church of England, from the start practically nullified the plan to make this an established church. Even the possibility of maintaining the preferred position of a political or "territorialized" church,[4] which the Church of England held until the 1830's, must have appeared to its staunchest adherents as a doubtful chance at best. After Union that doubtful chance became a definite disadvantage in the eyes of many Anglicans. External opposition to Anglican supremacy came from two sources: from the Church of Scotland, which claimed equal rights as a co-establishment in the empire, and from the voluntarists, who demanded the complete separation of state and church in the name of Christianity. Voluntarism in theory denotes the free will of the individual. In practical terms it means voluntary membership and the reliance of churches on the financial and moral support of their adherents, in contradistinction to support or aid from the civil authorities. By its opponents it has been described as "ecclesiastical free trade." It implies by necessity the complete separation of the affairs of religion and politics. The ideal is clearly put in the lines of Dr. Isaac Watts,

> Let Caesar's due be ever paid to Caesar and his throne,
> But consciences and souls were made to be the Lord's alone.

The sole duty of the civil magistrate towards Christianity is then the protection of religious liberty.

The force of voluntarism in Canada West was a reflection of its important rôle in the "North American way of life."[5] The strongest supporters of the voluntary principle were, and are, the Baptists. In Canada West voluntarism was an ideal of the majority of Protestant churches—Baptist, Congregational, Methodist, and Presbyterian. The obvious exceptions were the Churches of England and Scotland. The Quakers and other Plain Folk were rendered passive voluntarists by their faith. The Church of Rome, traditionally favourable to establishment, was restricted in its influence by its numerical inferiority in Canada West. It could not hope for ascendancy; it must make the best of its opportunities in a predominantly Protestant province, but, thanks to the Union of 1841, those opportunities were greatly enhanced by the political support which the numerically superior Roman Catholics of Canada East could give their co-religionists in Canada West.

The conflict between the forces of voluntarism and church-statism in Canada West centred largely on two issues—establishment and education. Establishment, in a circumscribed form, was represented by the Clergy Reserves, the forty-four Rectories, and government grants of land and money to a few denominations. In the field of education, church-statism was apparent in the public funds given to denominational colleges and in the existence of denominational separate elementary schools. Those churches which advocated a closer connection with the state demanded special privileges and rights at the expense of the state and other religious bodies. Voluntarists rejected these claims in the name of religious equality. Paradoxically the voluntarists found their strongest ally in the concept of a non-religious statism. For purposes of education the state should be a "collective parent," and for purposes of religion the churches should depend on the voluntary support of their members. These are specific examples of what Niebuhr terms "idealizing the cause of the state" on the part of the denominations and sects.[6]

Thus, within the body politic of Canada West, it might be said that two antithetical tendencies were at work. On the one hand was *centrifugal denominationalism*—the tendency of the largest churches to claim a special privileged and protected status as the religious counterpart of the civil authority. On the other hand was *centripetal nationalism*—a force which in Canada West sought to equate all creeds by separating them completely from the world of politics. The exposition of this thesis—the conflict between centrifugal denominationalism and centripetal nationalism—has been confined to the three major topics, namely, Clergy Reserves, the University question, and religion in elementary education. In each study the same pattern, a change coinciding with the Great Ministry, is discernible.

In the history of Canada West the period of the Great Ministry of Baldwin and Lafontaine marks a watershed in the development of the relations of church and state. In 1840 the passing of a new Clergy Reserves Act to divide the bulk of the proceeds among a few denominations created a sort of plural establishment, which pleased no one, but which was generally acquiesced in for the sake of peace. The continuing existence of the endowed Anglican Rectories seemed to ensure the quasi-ascendancy of the Church of England. The growth of denominational colleges in the forties led to demands for the sharing of the endowment of the provincial University. This was matched by the voluntarists' demand for the nationalization of King's College which was monopolizing that ample endowment. At the same time provision for separate Roman Catholic or Protestant elementary schools, as protection from insult, had been made in the educational system which Egerton Ryerson was busy constructing. The claims of the Church of England to have its own schools had been rejected, as had the Church of Scotland's demand for compulsory use of the Bible in classrooms. But extreme voluntarists were not satisfied with decentralized elementary education, and were loudly demanding the abolition of separate schools of all kinds, and total state control of the educational system.

During the decade after Union the resentment of voluntarists and nationalists steadily increased against what they believed to be the growing influence of denominationalism. When the Reform party won the general election of December, 1847, the hopes of religious as well as political reformers rose. At last the opportunity had come to establish by constitutional means that civil and religious equality of which they had dreamed so long, and which William Lyon Mackenzie had failed to gain by force of arms. The realization that their party leaders were in fact conservatives at heart came slowly. Grumbling at the slowness of reform mounted steadily, and soon produced the Clear Grit group of advanced reformers. After the retirement of Baldwin and Lafontaine the process of disintegration within the party was hastened by the popular distrust of Francis Hincks, and of his "combination" with certain former Clear Grits.

Considerations, both constitutional and political, frustrated the popular cry for secularization of the Clergy Reserves and abolition of the Rectories for six years. At last, in 1854, the Reserves were secularized; not, however, by Reformers, but by the new Liberal-Conservative party. Centripetal nationalism did not gain a complete victory, for provisions were included, protecting the vested rights of incumbents, which were in essence a compromise with denominationalism. However much this solution disappointed the extremists on both sides, at least it did settle finally this long-vexed problem to the satisfaction of the majority in Canada West. The case of the Rectories was less of a victory for nationalism, because the existing Rectories were permanently maintained, though no new ones could be legally created.

The Great Ministry acted more positively in the matter of University reform. The "National Endowment" for higher education was in fact nationalized, and every inducement and pressure was used to reduce denominational rivals of the provincial University. Once more thoroughgoing Reform hopes failed of complete realization, for the denominational institutions continued to exist as equals of the state institutions, to receive some government aid, and actually to increase in numbers. The fulfilment of the compromise between denominationalism and nationalism in higher education was not reached in Canada West before Confederation, but the developments after 1850 ensured that neither force would exclude the other from the field. The acceptance of the co-existence of both national and denominational colleges in the province was the first step towards the present solution of general grants and affiliation at Toronto.

Yet only in the field of elementary education did centripetal nationalism suffer a really serious reverse. Here the demand for denominational schools, which the Church of England had brought forward in the forties, was taken up with considerably more success by the Roman Catholics in the fifties and sixties. Thanks to the tremendous influx of Irish Roman Catholics after the potato famine, and to the presence in the United Legislature of the virtually solid Roman Catholic representation from Canada East, the Church of Rome was able to push beyond the original provisions for protection from insult in the elementary schools. Claiming its own denominational schools as a right, the Church of Rome established bit by bit its own system of elementary education. This process was stopped just short of complete educational dualism by the compromise written into the British North America Act, by which Roman Catholic separate schools were placed under the same ultimate control as the common schools of this province. This settlement has been accepted, at least by Protestants, as a final compromise between nationalism and denominationalism in elementary education.

Behind these developments lay a community of outlook on problems of religion and morality which embraced practically all Protestants of Canada West. Generally speaking, the attitude towards such subjects as temperance and Sabbath labour transcended denominational lines, although there was a closer connection of religious reform with political reform than with political conservatism. "Almost all men who are right on the liquor law question," wrote one Reformer, "are also right on the Clergy Reserves question." [7] The end of the Clergy Reserves marked the removal of the last major barrier to this Protestant unity of outlook, and paved the way for the development of a sort of omnibus Protestant denomination, which was not an organization but an attitude.[8] The process of union among the Protestant churches of Ontario began soon after Confederation, and though organic union is still incomplete, the "Protestant outlook" exists today even more certainly than it did in Canada West.

CHURCH AND STATE IN CANADA WEST, 1841-1867

CHAPTER ONE

THE FIRST AND FOURTH ESTATES IN CANADA WEST

CANADIAN HISTORIANS are only beginning to explore the religious history of their country. Isolated monographs and articles have from time to time appeared dealing with particular aspects of Canada's social history in the widest sense of that term. With a few notable exceptions, however, the story of the Christian denominations especially in relation to political problems has been left untold by both secular and religious scholars. The few books devoted to religious history are of the most general nature, and the little that has been written of state-church relations is more usually chronicle or contemporary propaganda than history. E. H. Oliver's *Winning of the Frontier* (Toronto, 1930) is one brilliant though brief exception. Likewise, with the exception of C. B. Sissons' *Egerton Ryerson* (2 vols., Toronto, 1937, 1947) there have been no significant modern biographies of the religious leaders of Upper Canada before Confederation. The older biographical works in this field are almost invariably poor specimens of scholarship and literature. Nor are there any denominational histories, old or new, of more than one volume except Carroll's invaluable series, *Case and his Cotemporaries* (5 vols., Toronto, 1867-77). It is a peculiar fact that the Methodists alone should have recorded their acts for posterity, while other churches both larger and smaller have ignored their pasts.

Too often the lay historian has been discouraged from approaching the field of Canada's religious history by the privacy of church archives and an *odium theologicum* which asserts that only men of the cloth are sufficiently competent, and sympathetic, to be trusted with such work. It is not surprising, therefore, that of the thirty-one individuals immortalized as *Makers of Canada* only two are ecclesiastics. The natural inference that religion has played no significant part in our national development is the antithesis of truth. These studies are offered as a partial proof of the important rôle of Christian denominations in the history of Canada, and specifically in the political history of Canada West.

It is not the intention of this chapter to tell the full story of each of these churches. Such a task must await the combined efforts of many researchers, and the unearthing of records as yet unavailable to the investigator. Instead, the first part of the chapter attempts to outline briefly the historical development of the major religious bodies in Canada West, and to note their individual attitudes on the more significant problems of church-state relations. The second part describes the major areas of conflict between Cross and Crown, and between various churches or groups of churches, but deliberately excludes any lengthy reference to those two issues which form the body of this study, namely church establishment and religious education.

I

THE CHURCH OF ENGLAND

The Church of England was the largest and most influential Christian denomination in Canada West before Confederation.[1] Under the leadership of John

Strachan, whose episcopate (1839-67) corresponds almost exactly with the period of this study, the Church of England continued to take a prominent part in the political life of the province, as it had in Upper Canada, seeking to obtain or retain the peculiar privileges which it claimed by virtue of orthodoxy and establishment in England. But its opponents during the Union were numerous. Dissenters had, since the 1820's, been jealous of its privileged position. Although this position was severely circumscribed at the time of Union, Protestants outside the pale of the "Establishment" still clamoured for religious equality, either separately as denominations or collectively as the "underprivileged." To the Church's fear and distrust of Dissent was added an unmitigated horror and hatred of the Church of Rome, a sentiment generally shared by all Protestant bodies of that day.

The other external force of opposition to the Church of England was that of the would-be secularizationists, the radicals of Canada West and their willing allies, the Whigs at Westminster. The influence of these two groups rose and fell with the tide of politics. But one source of opposition to Strachan's dreams of ecclesiastical supremacy which only rose, never fell, was much closer to the Bishop's Palace. Within the Church itself a large body of liberal-minded clergy and laity doubted the wisdom of many of John Toronto's policies. Generally speaking, these people were Low Church and Church of Ireland, and their numbers and influence grew rapidly in the late forties as a result of the Oxford Movement and of the increased immigration to Canada. Their stronghold was the peninsula of western Ontario, but they were also to be found throughout the rest of the diocese.

The conflict of Irish Low Churchism *versus* English High Churchism began to appear in the mid-forties and by the time of the founding of Trinity College it had become open warfare. Puseyism and Tractarianism had rent several congregations, and in the field of education Low Churchmen openly opposed Strachan's demand for parochial schools and his control of the "Church University." Both Huron and Wycliffe Colleges were established as Low Church rivals of Trinity. And on the score of establishment most of the Low Church element actually favoured secularization. Thus Low Churchmen could generally be classed as Reformers and advanced Conservatives, hardly ever as Tories.

Strachan's diocese as defined in 1839 comprised all Canada West, but its physical magnitude led him as early as 1850 to seek a three-way partition.[2] That move was delayed until 1857, the year after the Church had obtained self-government in Canada West.[3] In 1851 Strachan had called lay representatives to his triennial visitation of the clergy with the intention of strengthening the Church's disputed hold on its share of the Clergy Reserves.[4] By provincial enactment this lay participation in church government was formalized in 1856 when laymen were included in the diocesan Synod of Toronto, the first such body to meet in the British Empire.[5]

The following year the internal strife reached a climax when Low and High Church elements openly contested the election of a bishop for the newly-created Huron Diocese.[6] The Low Church triumphed over Strachan by rejecting his nominee, Archdeacon A. N. Bethune, in favour of Benjamin Cronyn, a graduate of Trinity College, Dublin. The same issue arose at Kingston when the See of Ontario was created. Here Francis Hincks had been compaigning secretly on behalf of his younger brother, Thomas, a cleric in Ireland, and he had used every political means at his disposal to assure the enthroning of a Hincks.[7] Strachan's favourite, Bethune, was again defeated after a contest which rocked and split the Church even more deeply than the Huron election. But the choice of J. T. Lewis as Bishop was a compromise which favoured the Low Church only inasmuch as Lewis was another graduate of Trinity College, Dublin.[8]

The rapidly expanding need for increased personnel and finances had most serious consequences for the Church of England during the period of the Union. The fact that the Church was not indigenous (it augmented its clergy largely by importing young Englishmen) was complicated by the refusal of the lay immigrants to support their ministers,[9] and by the increasing reluctance of the industrialized mother country to subsidize the Church particularly in a colony whose separation from the mother country was the topic of popular discussion.[10] At the same time the Church of England in Canada lost its share of the Clergy Reserves. The only solution was to adopt the disagreeable practice of voluntarism, which once accepted proved to be the Church's salvation in Canada. The secularization of the Clergy Reserves and the creation of synodical self-government for the Church of England marks the end of its colonial dependence and the beginning of its development as a purely Canadian denomination. The Old World heritage of monopoly was finally abandoned of necessity, in favour of a policy of competition.[11]

Apart from the difference of opinion on liturgy, education, and voluntarism, the Low and High Church groups assumed distinctive social attitudes. The Low Church was at one with dissenters in its abhorrence of gambling, drinking, and all similar sins of the flesh.[12] The mouthpiece of such sentiments, the *Echo and Protestant Episcopal Recorder*, was founded in 1851, and was openly and avowedly anti-Puseyite and anti-Romanist. Strachan's official paper, the *Church*, had suffered from incompetent editors, financial reverses, and popular reaction against its High Churchism ever since its inception in 1837. The *Patriot*, an entirely secular journal, proved in the long run to be a more effective and vocal partisan of Toryism and High Churchism.

After the passing of the *Church* in 1856 (during 1852–3 it was called *Canadian Churchman*) the Anglicans had no official journal. This development coincided with the waning of popular interest in the exclusive claims of the Church. From time to time other Church of England periodicals were established but all met with indifferent success. The *Canadian Church Press* and the *Ecclesiastical Gazette* both confined themselves exclusively to religious news. Only the *Echo* continued to discuss openly the various problems concerning church and state relations.

THE CHURCH OF SCOTLAND AND OTHER PRESBYTERIANS

The Church of Scotland had long claimed the privileged position of being an established church in Upper Canada, but unlike the Church of England it had failed to gain Imperial recognition before the Union.[13] True, it had received a measure of government assistance, but the collusion of Strachan and successive Lieutenant-Governors had excluded it from any share of the Clergy Reserves. But despite the fact that they were fewer in number than the Anglicans, the men of the Kirk held an equally important place in the councils and affairs of the province.

In the 1830's a movement for the union of the Church of Scotland and the much smaller Synod of the United Secession Church (generally called the United Synod) had begun, but only the chance of sharing in the division of the

Clergy Reserves in 1840 finally brought the two bodies together. The Reverend William Smart, leading member of the United Synod, told William Morris, lay spokesman for the Kirk, that although the two churches had at last agreed to unite, "I should have felt better if the courtship had not been quite so long, and if the Marriage had taken place when our feelings were youthful and warm, however, as the Union or Marriage has now taken place, it only remains for the parties themselves, and their friends to make it as happy & prosperous as they can." [14] Three years later Smart and another minister left the union because of its continuing connection with the mother Church of Scotland. "I am not aware," wrote Smart, "that any good has resulted from the connexion so formed in 1840, and . . . I do not see any in prospect." [15] But their action in withdrawing smacks strongly of that independent spirit which possessed both individuals and congregations of Scottish Presbyterian ancestry.

If there was one tendency which marked all Presbyterians in Canada more than any other it was their strong individualistic, anti-clerical and anti-sacerdotal tradition. The power of the laity in church affairs rose from the congregation through the presbytery to the annual synod meeting where the laity were most vocal in defending their freedom from all priestly presumptions. The control of church property was always a focal point for this clash of lay and clerical authority. Thus the creation of Queen's University led to such a struggle within its Board of Trustees, and was followed soon after by a similar conflict over the management of the Kirk's share of the Clergy Reserves. [16]

But the attempt of certain ministers in 1843 to obtain a Temporalities Act favourable to themselves precipitated a major revolt of the laity. Congregations met to denounce the "iniquitous and insidious" scheme of their own clergy and petitioned the Governor General and Parliament against its enactment. [17] "This ought to prove a lesson to the Synod," wrote Hugh Scobie, editor of the *British Colonist*. [18] So it may have done, for never again did the ministers of the Church of Scotland in Canada dare to make such a bare-faced grab for temporal power.

Even while the Church of Scotland in Canada was being disturbed by the Temporalities Bill, its parent church in Britain was torn asunder by Chalmer's non-intrusionist Free Church movement. In Scotland the peculiar principle of non-intrusion—that the state should acknowledge God's sovereignty and endow the church, but thereafter maintain a hands-off policy—had been abused, and schism was in the air. In Canada the arguments employed for and against non-intrusion had no relevance, but being recent exiles from their fathers' land, the Scots of this province took a lively interest in the division of the mother church. Sympathy for these newest secessionists from the "auld Kirk" was first awakened in Canada West by the Reverend John Bayne who had been in Edinburgh seeking new ministers when the discussion preceding the disruption occured in 1842. [19] Many Canadian members saw a direct connection between the deceased Temporalities Bill and "intrusion"—a connection neither accidental nor innocent in their eyes—for both were supported by like-minded parties. [20] During the next year a deputation from the Free Church toured Canada West laying a firm foundation for provincial disruption, even to the extent of alienating six of the seven theological students at Queen's University. [21]

In 1843 the Canadian Synod of the Kirk declared it had no interest in the Scottish problem, but expressed its sympathy for the distressed body. [22] Its undefined "connexion" with the mother church was not satisfactory to some ministers, and at the next meeting of the Synod, in 1844, one group demanded complete separation from the Kirk in Scotland, the creation of an autonomous Canadian church, and the explicit rejection of any state-church relation other than perfect ecclesiastical independence. Less than this would be "treason to Christ." [23]

The defence of the "Connexionists" in Canada consisted of a declaration of the Synod's virtual independence. The jurisdiction of the Scottish Synod did not extend beyond "the quay of Greenock." [24] It is noteworthy that this rebuttal was not signed by any minister west of Kingston, and of the twenty-three ministers (one-quarter of the whole body of clergy) who retired to form the Free Church (Synod of the Presbyterian Church of Canada), thirteen were west of Hamilton, and seventeen west of Kingston. [25] Thus the pattern of religious radicalism in the Kirk parallels that of the Anglican Low Church both geographically and ideologically.

If the disruption in Canada seemed to have no just cause, at least it had motives. Many laymen saw in the Free Church an escape from submission to "clerical pretensions," an alternative which would strengthen their position in the Kirk. To Isaac Buchanan, who had referred to his spiritual advisers as "Vile Ecclesiastics," the disruption was a golden opportunity. [26] "Scotchmen when they dont [sic] like or differ with their Ministers will have an alternative besides going to the Episcopalians & losing all his [sic] moral weight or to sects who are in too many cases little more than political dissenters." [27] Buchanan personally offered £50 to any Free Church congregation providing the trustees retained control of all property. [28] Small wonder that the Reverend William Rintoul complained that the Scots of Chinguacousy were "pretty well imbued with an Ecclesiastic-phobia." [29]

Less evident at this early stage of the Free Church's history was that voluntarist sentiment which later became its distinguishing battle flag. Non-intrusion was accepted without question as the principle of church-state relations for the new church, and both clergy and laity were distressed to find that the disruption had cost the "protestants" their share of the government financial support which they had got in the Kirk. Thus in fact the Free Church became voluntarist, whatever it might be in theory, and after disruption the influence of George Brown and his father, Peter, through their newspapers, was largely responsible for establishing the voluntarist idea in the hearts of Free Kirkmen over the opposition of some of its ministers. In the wake of the disruption, Thomas Liddell, the perspicacious principal who had opened Queen's, wrote: "For a long time past I have been convinced that, especially considering the *native unpopularity* of the principle of Establishments in this country, unless the Synod take measures, & that immediately to defend herself, by means of the press, & thro' her influential Lay Members, & also perambulate the country, to discover who are her adherents, & to strengthen their hands—the country may be given up into the hands of the voluntaries and non Government men." [30] But voluntarism was not directly involved in the disruption, nor was it universally accepted even in the Free Church as late as the 1850's.

The disruption of 1844 marked the turning of the tide of fortune for the Church of Scotland in Canada West. Thereafter the influence and members of that denomination declined in inverse ratio to the success of the Free Church. Not until the eve of Confederation did the Church of Scotland have the number of clergy it possessed before 1844, [31] and not until 1852 could it boast a native-born clergyman. So rapidly did the Free Church expand that in less than seven years it had far outstripped the "Residuary Church" in size, and with its advocacy of national education, religious equality, and "Protestant principles," it assumed the rôle of leadership among dissenters vacated by the Wesleyan Methodists between 1834 and 1838. It also tended to show an affinity with political reformism.[32]

The only other Presbyterian group of any consequence was the United Presbyterian Church, relatively small in numbers and containing more Irish- and American-born adherents than Scottish. Overtures for union with the Free Church had been offered and received by the United Presbyterians in 1844 but came to naught until 1861, when seventy United Presbyterian ministers joined 163 of the Free Church, together being more than double the number of Church of Scotland ministers.[33] The major cause of the seventeen-year delay in forming this union was, as always among the Presbyterians, the issue of church-state relations rather than any doctrinal difference. The United Presbyterians were voluntarists and denied Christ's Headship over the nations. The Free Church asserted that Christ was Head and could command the civil magistrates' support. By 1861 the Free Church was completely voluntarist in sentiment and the problem of Christ's Headship was solved with one of those typically Canadian compromise resolutions which meant whatever both parties believed it did.[34]

Unlike other Christian denominations of Canada West the Church of Scotland never had an official journal of its own. Before the disruption Peter Brown's *Banner* claimed to represent the Kirk's opinion, and after 1844 the *British Colonist* stood in an ever vaguer relationship as long as its editor, Hugh Scobie, lived. The Free Church on the other hand believed religiously in the power of the press, and in addition to the *Banner* (which died in 1848), it had from the time of disruption an official voice in the monthly *Ecclesiastical and Missionary Record*, more popularly known simply as the *Record*. The *United Presbyterian Magazine* was not started until 1860 and like the denomination it spoke for, it had little to say about politics.

THE WESLEYANS AND OTHER METHODISTS

Of all the Christian denominations in Canada West the Wesleyan Methodists are probably the best known, because they are the most written about. Originally organized as part of the Genesee Conference in New York State, they had achieved complete independence in 1829 under the name of Methodist Episcopal Church. At the instigation of the Colonial Office, the British Wesleyans began in the early 1830's to expand their operations from Lower Canada into Upper Canada with the specific objective of acting as an eradicator of (or at least a strong deterrent to) the supposed radical and "republican" tendencies of North American Methodism.[35] To forestall this political manœuvre and prevent the duplication of work by rival organizations, the Canadian body entered into union with the British Conference in 1833. But a minority of the Canadians, correctly sensing some ulterior motive behind the British influx, refused to join and organized another church which retained the name and many of the distinctive features of the Methodist Episcopals.

The union of the British Wesleyans and Canadians into the Wesleyan Methodist Church proved to be an unhappy arrangement because of their differing attitudes regarding the relations of church and state. The Canadians had for years been the most vocal opponents of Anglican supremacy and the advocates of equal religious liberty, whereas the British group retained their traditional deference towards the "Establishment." This difference of outlook became most embarrassing during the Rebellion and finally caused an open rupture when the Clergy Reserves question was revived in 1840. As a result of the British Wesleyans' desire for a share of the Clergy Reserves money the union was dissolved by the British Conference at the very moment when the two Canadas were being reunited. The position of the Canadian body was explained by Lord Sydenham to Lord John Russell, "The Upper Canada Conference is the most powerful body in the Province, and does the greatest possible good, for which is has been very badly treated. It is thoroughly Whig—with your Government, whilst the other is bitterly opposed to you in England, and the Leaders, for they have few followers, will do everything against mine here, because I won't persecute the Catholics." [36]

After six years of the most violent internecine war, during which time both parties were excluded from participation in the Clergy Reserves funds, a new and lasting union was negotiated. This reunion had been influenced by the growth of Tractarianism and Millerism, and by the example of the Evangelical Alliance in England, but the opponents of Methodism credited it to the desire to obtain state aid.[37] Thereafter, though the two parties might not see eye to eye on such problems as state endowments and religious education, they did manage to keep their differences repressed, and to present a seemingly united front on public issues. But the heyday of political radicalism among the Wesleyans passed with the first union in 1834, and after the Union of the Canadas they held to the straight and narrow path of a neutrality which verged into conservatism. Only on the University question did they become involved in politics, but this problem, they insisted, was primarily a religious one and thus they justified their partisanship.

The recurrent drift of both laity and clergy from the Wesleyan Methodists to the Church of England was partly a desire for ritualistic service and partly a revolt against the puritanical morality of Methodism, especially in the matter of temperance. Occasionally, too, the Wesleyan clergy faced strong lay reaction against the "political intermeddling" of some ministers, and during the Metcalfe crisis laymen in Toronto even founded a newspaper in opposition to Ryerson's public involvement in that controversy. But the official journal of the Wesleyans, the *Christian Guardian,* contrived to stay aloof from such political scrapes despite the efforts of parties outside the denomination to use or abuse its power.

Although Canadian Methodists of all descriptions were essentially voluntarists, the Wesleyans did accept state aid for their educational institutions, much to the disgust of all other branches of Methodism. The policy was inherently self-contradictory and the Wesleyans were never able to find a logical solution to their dilemma. They did, however, maintain with all other Methodists a common attitude on other social problems, being strong advocates of temperance, and sabbatarianism.

Of the other Methodist bodies, the largest was always the Methodist Episcopal Church, about one-third the size of the Wesleyans. The circuit-rider tradition of frontier democracy, lay participation in church management, and militant evangelism were maintained by the Episcopals long after their Wesleyan brethren had been "corrupted" with the formalism and respectability of bourgeois urbanization. The other Methodist churches—Bible Christian, New Connexion, and Primitive—were separately insignificant in numbers and influence, and tended to follow the lead of the Methodist Episcopals in their political ideas. The close connection between the left-wing Methodist groups and the anti-Clergy Reserves movement, for instance, is an indisputable fact. Generally speaking, it may be said that all the non-Wesleyan Methodists were inclined to political as well as religious radicalism. Numerically they equalled the Wesleyans, and it is an error to overlook their influence, to equate them with the Wesleyans, or to treat them simply as camp-followers of the Wesleyans by ignoring their differences of opinions. In organization these bodies copied the efficient circuit —district—Conference system of the Wesleyans, and like the Presbyterians, the main *raison d'être* of every Methodist body was its distinctive approach to the problem of church-state relations.

The official paper of the Wesleyan Methodists was the *Christian Guardian*, founded in 1829, the same year as Upper Canada Academy. It was a purely denominational paper, its editor being elected at each annual Conference. For the first dozen years of its existence, during which Egerton Ryerson usually occupied the editorial chair, the *Guardian* was a power to be reckoned with in provincial politics. But after 1840 it was deliberately transformed into a strictly religious periodical, almost devoid of politically controversial material. The British Wesleyans established the *Wesleyan* after the separation of 1841, and a dissident element within the Canadian body founded the *Toronto Periodical Journal* at the height of the Metcalfe controversy. Both papers were intended to counterbalance the *Guardian,* but neither lived long nor provided any strong opposition to the official Canadian Wesleyan Methodist publication.

The *Canada Christian Advocate* was begun in 1845 as a private venture but was taken over officially by the Methodist Episcopal Church in 1847. The *Advocate* was loud, bellicose, and radical, parrotting much that the *Globe, Banner,* and *Examiner* said, and could always be found in the forefront of the battle when denominational privileges were being demanded by its adversaries. The *Evangelist* was published intermittently as a monthly by the Primitive Methodist Church from 1848 to 1851, at which time it was turned into a weekly paper. Neither the *Evangelist* nor its successor the *Christian Journal* which began in 1857 showed much interest in the affairs of this world, but on rare occasions they did express strong voluntarist sentiments, and generally agreed with the policies of the *Canada Christian Advocate.* These remarks also apply to the *Christian Messenger* which was begun by the New Connexion Methodists as early as 1844. It was elevated from a monthly journal into a weekly in 1847, but died of poor circulation just three years later. In its place there immediately arose the *Watchman,* though it spoke only unofficially for that denomination. The *Watchman's* avowed principle was Protestantism, especially "*dissent* or non-conformity," and to this ideal it remained militantly true, upholding national education, separation of church and state, and voluntarism against any and all opponents. (A later paper of the same name was not denominational, but Orange.)

In conclusion it may be said that there existed a unity of outlook among all the non-Wesleyan Methodists, and that their attitudes were shared by many Canadian Wesleyans. But union with the British Wesleyans and urbanization had modified and compromised the Wesleyan Methodist attitude on the relations of church and state since the era of Upper Canada, and this denomination was to be found in the conservative *via media* during the period of the Union, desperately maintaining a position of neutrality to prevent internal divisions.

THE BAPTIST, CONGREGATIONALIST,
AND SMALLER PROTESTANT CHURCHES

Despite their relative paucity of numbers, the Baptists of Canada West were unquestionably the most militant, dogmatic, and vocal denomination in a province where these attributes were common property. As the majority of Baptists were of Scottish descent they had much in common with the Free Church, while at the same time they shared with the Congregationalists the traditions and the ideals of English nonconformity. Yet their influence, which probably was greater than their numerical strength would suggest, was seriously vitiated by their strong individualism and two internal lines of division. The Baptist congregations of the Ottawa Valley were usually missions organized from Montreal under strong "old country" influence, whereas the churches in the western peninsula were dominated and closely allied to the United States Baptists.[38] Across these national lines the issue of open *versus* closed communion cut like a knife, and though the east tended to be open and the west closed, this was only a tendency, not a rule.

The strong individualism which prevented co-operation between these chequered groups also infested particular congregations. Internal dissension was rife within congregations as it was within communions, and the power of the purse was most effectively wielded against any preacher or cause which did not please individual members. A weak union of the congregations of Canada West collapsed in 1849 after six years of futile effort to combine these autonomous units.[39] The immediate cause of this disruption was the issue of open communion, but even the Regular (or closed communion) Baptists of Quebec and Ontario found co-operation impossible until 1888. Even today the Baptist communion remains divided by the subtlest points of faith.

Regardless of this balkanizing tendency among the Baptists, they were completely of one mind on the question of the relation of church and state. Their stand in favour of national education, voluntarism, religious equality, and absolute separation of church and state was uncompromised for more than a century after the Union of the two Canadas, and they yielded first place to none in the advocacy of these ideals.

Baptist newspapers were numerous, particularist and short-lived. The *Evangelical Pioneer*, despite its pugnacious editorials, lasted only three years (1847-50) because it spoke solely for the Regular Baptists. The *Canada Baptist Magazine and Missionary Register* (1837-49) became a weekly in 1843, but the *Register* was closed when the Regular Baptist Union collapsed. The *Christian Messenger*, founded at Brantford and later renamed the *Canadian Baptist*, seems to have come closer to being a truly denominational journal than any of its predecessors, simply because it stressed the points of agreement rather than the differences of the several divisions in the communion. It perpetuated and amplified the tradition of the *Register* for fearless and outspoken criticism on public affairs

The history of the Congregationalists of the province has not yet been written, probably because of the scarcity of primary source material. They received no missionary aid from abroad and practically no increase in numbers as a result of immigration. Nevertheless they played a prominent rôle in the politico-religious disputes of the period.[40] Though less rigid in their theology than the Baptists, the Congregationalists held the same basic belief in the separation of church and state, and their laymen and clergy were always prominent in the activities of

such organizations as the Anti-Clergy Reserves Association. Their only newspaper, the *Canadian Independent*, appeared as a monthly beginning in 1853-4. It
seldom touched on political matters except sectarian education, and confined
itself for the most part to religious news.

Closely allied to the Baptists in theology and to the Baptists, Congregationalists,
and non-Wesleyan Methodists in politics were several small denominations such
as the Disciples of Christ, and the Christians. Each of these two bodies had two
newspapers at different times—the *Witness of Truth* and the *Banner of Faith*
belonging to the Disciples and the *Christian Luminary* and *Christian Offering*
belonging to the Christians. But as none of these journals concerned itself with
the affairs of the province and as the combined numbers of the two groups
mentioned probably did not exceed a thousand, they can be dismissed by lumping
them with the other larger voluntarist denominations.

Yet another grouping of denominations comprises the Mennonites, Tunkers,
and Quakers. For the purpose of these studies they can be ignored since their
faith precluded their participation in politics. Being non-jurors and pacifists
they were virtually disfranchised, although their sympathies undoubtedly lay
with the aggregation of voluntarists. Finally, mention should be made of the
Lutherans whose numbers approximately equalled those of the Congregationalists. Lacking any newspaper to express their views and usually unacquainted
with the English language, the Lutherans were as quiet as the Quakers. Traditionally they favoured a close connection between religion and the state, and
on at least one occasion, by applying for a share of Clergy Reserves funds, they
proved themselves untouched by their voluntarist milieu.

THE CHURCH OF ROME

The Roman Catholic Church in Canada West at the time of Union was smaller
than either the Church of England or the Church of Scotland, and about equal
to the combined strength of the British and Canadian Wesleyan Methodists.
By 1867 the Church of Rome was second to the Church of England, thanks to
the great influx of Irish after the potato famine, and was considerably more
influential than any other Christian denomination. This power, however, arose
not so much from the increased membership in the upper province as from the
close religious and political connection with the large Roman Catholic population
in Canada East.

Although Upper Canada was predominantly and deliberately a Protestant province, the Roman Catholics had received the same magnanimous treatment there
as had the French Canadians after the Conquest. At a time when their religion
was proscribed in Britain, Roman Catholics in Upper Canada were receiving
financial assistance from the state and denominational privileges which were
denied to the dissenters. Yet their inferior status in the Imperial connection
limited their power to demand further favours. They could and did receive
willingly any emoluments offered by the government, but they could not ask as
much as they probably would have desired. After Union, however, the alliance
with their co-religionists along the lower St. Lawrence and the sudden and
gigantic flood from Ireland greatly improved the political bargaining position of
that church. The flood-tide of immigration also necessitated a more extensive
and effective organization of the Roman Church in Canada West and the number
of sees was repeatedly increased after 1850.

Despite its great size and huge political potential the Church of Rome maintained a posture and attitude of relative neutrality in the affairs of state in the upper province. It took money from the Protestant Clergy funds when it was offered, but it did not interfere officially with the popular demand for the secularization of the Reserves. Similarly it stood by as a disinterested observer while the Protestant denominations fought for control of the provincial University endowment. On one major public issue, however, the Church of Rome did stand forth adamantly in demanding what was considered a sacred right. That issue was the separate schools question.

Lest it be mistakenly presumed that there was no other source of friction between the Roman Catholics and Protestants in Canada West than that of sectarian control of elementary education, it must be added at once that the existence of Orangism and a general Protestant antipathy to Rome accentuated by the "Papal Aggression" controversy provided a fertile and seemingly eternal source of irritations and petty conflicts for both parties of Christians. But this was more a chronic condition breaking out intermittently as the result of some particular incident, and despite the troubles lurking just below the surface, it was mostly sound and fury signifying little of major importance to the main religio-political problems of Canada West.

No newspaper spoke officially for the Church of Rome in Canada West after the demise of that most yellow weekly, the *Catholic* of Kingston, during the forties. From 1837 onwards the *Mirror* was published at Toronto and though its politics were anti-Orange and moderate reform, it managed for at least a generation to avoid sectarian discussion. In 1854 the *Catholic Citizen* was founded at Toronto as a belligerently Irish journal which sought first, foremost, and solely the advancement of its faith and its nationality. The *Citizen* failed in 1858 and was immediately replaced by the *Canadian Freeman*, liberal, Irish, anti-Orange, and uncompromisingly the advocate of separate schools and political independence for the Roman Catholics. The *Freeman* was intended to be the Upper Canadian counterpart of the Montreal *True Witness* but the stormy political career of their idol, Thomas D'Arcy McGee, soon drove a wedge between these two papers which seriously damaged their denominational influence. The most notable feature of the journalistic efforts of Roman Catholics in Canada West was a strong tendency to feud with one another in the best Donnybrook style, and to change political horses as often as the whim struck them.

II

It has already been suggested that the reign of the Great Ministry from 1848 to 1851 forms a watershed in the history of the relations of church and state in Canada West. This applies particularly to establishment and education but it also is true of other aspects of the religio-political problem in the province. The change can best be described, however inadequately, as a shift in emphasis from interdenominational rivalry to a struggle between nationalism and denominationalism, and to a lesser degree a struggle between Roman Catholic and Protestant. These last two aspects are not mutually inclusive. Neither Roman Catholics nor Protestants, nor even particular denominations, thought, acted, or voted *en bloc* on the various religious issues involving the power and position of the state. With this obvious reservation in mind, however, the general conclusions seem valid.

The history of Upper Canada in the 1830's had been filled with the clash of church and state, and the attitudes assumed by the denominations then were perpetuated after Union. In fact the response to Durham, his mission, and his Report gave a sure foretaste of the religious divisions on public issues during the 1840's. Durhamism had brought together the strong reform tendencies of Roman Catholics, Methodists, and Presbyterians, while the Tory party continued in Sydenham's day and later to be closely identified in policy and personnel with the Church of England. Legislative Councillors Archdeacon Strachan and Chief Justice Robinson had strenuously opposed Durham's policies and union.[41] To Strachan it seemed that union would inevitably place both Canadas under papist control.[42] "In this country as at home," wrote one Anglican, "with the help of our liberal & infidel Government the Roman Church is likely to raise its head again." [43]

Other denominations did not share this phobia with the Anglicans. The Wesleyan Methodists saw union as the only alternative to a colonial despotism.[44] Their admiration of Durham approximated hero-worship, and the support offered to his successor was no less enthusiastic. The *Christian Guardian* was happy to defend Thomson, a "Whig Radical," against the attacks of the *Church* and its echo, the Cobourg *Star*. Jonathan Scott, the *Guardian's* editor, boasted to the *Church* of his conversion to moderate reformism. Yet at the same time he rejected the radical *Examiner's* condemnation of the Governor General's choice of W. H. Draper as an Executive Councillor. No-party government was as much the ideal of the Wesleyan Methodists as it was of Lord John Russell or C. P. Thomson.

The same persuasive influence which Thomson wielded over the Wesleyan Methodists even won over some of the staunchest Tory Anglicans, such as John Macaulay, much to the disgust of John Strachan. The old "loyal party" (self-styled) was prostrated, and never fully recovered after Union. Conservatives were resigned to the inevitability of progress. The Union Act and a Clergy Reserves Bill were easily arranged by the Governor General with the help of "dissatisfied Scotch and Methodists." [45] The *Christian Guardian* accepted whole-heartedly Russell's restricted interpretation of responsible government.[46] Small wonder that Thomson referred to that journal as "the only decent paper in both Canadas." [47] With such wide support in the upper province he could afford to ignore the opposition of the old Tory guard. Canada got peace and prosperity, and Thomson got his baronage.

The tragic death of Sydenham in 1841 was a blow to the Imperial reconstruction programme for Canada. It was also viewed as a personal loss by many colonists. "I have lost a Friend" was the eulogy composed by Egerton Ryerson on Canada's behalf for the *Christian Guardian* of September 29, but he was undoubtedly speaking for himself as well. Stanley carefully explained the religious situation and Sydenham's policy in the instructions to the new Governor General. "The habits and opinions of the People of Canada are, in the main, averse from the absolute predominance of any single Church. . . ." Though the Churches of England and Scotland were legally established and endowed, the Church of Rome was also recognized by law, and "the cooperation of Wesleyan Methodists and Protestant dissenters is not to be refused or discouraged by the Executive." [48] Bagot took this advice to heart, and the stable relations between church and state which Sydenham had established were sucessfully maintained. The colony continued to work unitedly for prosperity under Bagot, yet the resentment of the Church of England against its reduced position after the Union and Clergy Reserves Acts did not entirely disappear. When Bagot died the *Church* did not deign to notice his passing except by the briefest reference in its editorial column.

From the moment of Lord Metcalfe's arrival, however, the religious situation seemed to take a turn for the worse from which it never recovered during the life of the Union. Orangism was once more openly identified with Toryism and Anglicanism, and Reformers, especially Roman Catholics, were forcibly reminded of its politico-religious ideals. The union of Orange and Green had long since dissolved, and now in 1843 a series of riots occured in which the causes of the British connection and Protestant ascendancy were combined. In support of this revived Tory truculence, John Toronto called for a strong party organization to oppose "Papists, Radicals & Rebels." [49] The governmental reaction to this politico-religious threat was the Secret Societies Bill which would have outlawed the Loyal Orange Order. But the Orangemen were prepared for this eventuality which never occured. Their plans to go underground were being laid when the Baldwin-Lafontaine Ministry resigned.[50] The provincial Parliament did, however, pass the Party Processions Act during that session, and for seven years the Order was effectively barred from its disturbing celebrations of the Glorious Twelfth. The part played by the Secret Societies Bill in bringing about the fall of the Reform Government is uncertain. Probably it was of no more immediate consequence than the ill-starred University Bill. But it required no prophet to foresee active Orange participation in the defence of Lord Metcalfe on the hustings.

The entrance of Egerton Ryerson as champion of the Governor General in the political affray caused by the "Metcalfe controversy" nearly wrecked the Wesleyan Methodist Church. It also threatened to complicate still further the tangled political situation by adding to it the elements of a denominational dispute. The editor of the *Christian Guardian* had definite reform sympathies, yet tried to maintain the neutral position of that journal against Ryerson's demand that his political articles be printed.[51] That the *Colonist* was then opened to Ryerson suggests that many in the Church of Scotland held the same conservative views as "Leonidas." Scott's reluctance to allow Ryerson the use of the *Guardian* cost him not only Ryerson's friendship but also his job as editor.[52] But many Wesleyan Methodists especially in Toronto were equally opposed to Ryerson's course,[53] and the pressure brought to bear by the *Toronto Periodical Journal* forced the Wesleyan Methodist Conference to avow publicly its neutrality regardless of the opinions of individual clergymen.[54] The upshot of this crisis for that demomination was the loss of twenty-two hundred members within two years.[55]

Meanwhile the *Church* was boasting of Anglican unity in support of the Queen's representative, forgetful of its late opposition to Lord Sydenham and Bagot. Cynical editors suggested that this support would soon disappear if Lord Metcalfe kept his promises to other denominations. The *Examiner* accused the Governor General of giving charitable gifts to the various churches as bribes for the purchase of popular influence, an imputation indignantly denied by the recipients. The *Catholic* did not attempt to hide its support for the ministerial cause, thus offering the Orangemen a further incentive for organizing political opposition to Reform. A widely circulated rumour that the Roman Catholics were about to rise in another St. Bartholomew's Massacre was given a surprising amount of credence in rural areas.[56] But Stanley enjoined the Governor General to depend on measures rather than men to win Canada West. He also suggested, even less idealistically, that the French Roman Catholic clergy might and ought to be used to influence their parishioners against the rising tide of "Ultra Democratic principles." [57]

In the end the triumph of Lord Metcalfe's supporters at the polls was hailed by the *Church* as a victory for state-churchism, and the thirty-five Anglicans elected to the Assembly were urged to uphold the "best of causes," namely the established position of their own denomination. Bishop Strachan went so far as to support the request of the Reverend Edward Osler for two hundred acres with the assertion that the good "social and political effects" of his teaching were responsible for the re-election of W. B. Robinson, sometime Inspector General.[58]

Between the time of the Metcalfe controversy and the election of the Great Ministry in 1848, the major politico-religious issues in Canada West were the Clergy Reserves and the University question. A minor issue was an amendment to the Act for the Independence of the Legislative Assembly passed in 1844 with little fuss in Parliament. The purpose of the amendment was to disfranchise clergymen, but it was repealed the following year after bitter criticism by the affected parties. Aside from this minor incident, there was little to disturb the churches of the province or to bring them into conflict with the state.

When the next general election was called in the last month of 1847, denominational and national interests became entangled once more. For the Churches of England and Scotland and for the Wesleyan Methodists the main issue was not responsible government but John A. Macdonald's University Endowment Division Bill in which they were named as beneficiaries. Although the Roman Catholics also held a potential stake in the University endowment, for them the election meant an opportunity to avenge Orange insults by returning their traditional friends, the Reformers. In some places Roman Catholic priests were accused of using religious threats to regiment the parochial vote in the right direction, a charge denied, naturally enough, with much vehemence.[59] But the close connection of religion and political reformism was never more evident than in the election of 1847. The reasons are obvious. The twin pole stars of the Reform party in Canada West were responsible government and complete separation of church and state.

The year 1848 passed without any reference to religious affairs. Indeed it was one of the quietest years of the Union in every way. By contrast, 1849 was one of political turmoil and violence. Yet the events connected with the Rebellion Losses Bill and the annexation movement had little connection with religion. The Tories who attacked Lord Elgin and burned the Parliament buildings may have been, as it was claimed, mostly Orangemen, but their hatred was directed against the rebels rather than against French-Canadian Roman Catholics, and it was noted by one editor that the signers of the Annexation Manifesto could not be identified with any one party or sect.[60]

Both the University and Clergy Reserves questions were once more before the public during that hectic year, but these will be discussed separately. A change of attitude, or rather of tempo, was becoming apparent in Reform circles with a growing demand for an end to denominational privileges. That demand was made in the name of nationalism, the same force that had just rocked the political structures of Europe. But in Canada West the issue which really gave the succeeding decade the title of the "fiery fifties" was one which began in England with the reconstitution of the Roman Catholic hierarchy in that country.

The "Papal Aggression" controversy which followed was mirrored and magnified in Canada, inflaming both Roman Catholic and Protestant feelings to an extent beyond modern imagination. It also cut across the political lines in Canada West, and thereby appreciably weakened the Reform party and its aims.

The reaction of the Church of England to "Papal Aggression" was as violent in Canada as it was in England.[61] The appointment of Bishop de Charbonnel to the Roman Catholic See of Toronto was viewed as a serious affront by John Strachan and his church,[62] though no offence had been taken to Michael Power, De Charbonnel's predecessor. The Wesleyan Methodists were similarly disturbed by the resurgence of Romanism, but they did support De Charbonnel's claim to the title of Bishop of Toronto. The aggression issue was widely agitated throughout the upper province for many months, and as a result of a famous challenge George Brown became the most prominent champion of "Protestant Ascendancy."[63] Sober minds on both sides deprecated the agitation, warning that Protestants and Roman Catholics alike would be injured by the feelings evoked. Nevertheless before the elections of 1851 were held it was apparent that many ridings in Canada West would be won or lost through the influence of the religious question.

By 1851, however, the Reform party was already split by the revolt of the Clear Grits, and also its most powerful press supporter, the *Globe*, had been "kicked out" for its anti-Catholic stand and its opposition to Francis Hincks.[64] When two Grits, Rolph and Cameron, were enticed back to the Reform Government, the *Globe* of November 4 announced that "The Anti-State Church cause has been sold into the hands of the enemy. . . ."[65] It was not simply the aggression issue that was involved but the Coalition Government's whole policy of currying denominational favour. Although the *rapprochement* between the Grits and George Brown was delayed for three more years, Brown was destined to become the acknowledged leader of both Grits and anti-state church men, and state-churchism became the *cause célèbre* of political differences in the United Province.

The one body which Brown could not lead was the Orange Order. Although Orangism was at one with Brown in its opposition to French papist domination, it remained basically a Tory political machine rather than a religious cult. The number of Orangemen in Canada West more than doubled with each decade after Union, from about twenty thousand in 1840 to forty-five thousand around 1850, and was up to one hundred thousand by 1860. The Orange Order, like the Church of Rome, favoured sectarian education, and was ready even in the 1850's to unite temporarily with Roman Catholics for ends antithetical to many of Brown's political principles.

The ferment of "Papal Aggression" had just begun to abate when the tragic Gavazzi riots and the Montreal Massacre occured to throw Canada West once more into an anti-Catholic fit. A demonstration at Quebec prevented Gavazzi (a priest who had left the Church of Rome and now was lecturing against Romanism) from speaking there. A near-riot at Montreal had more tragic consequences when regular troops, who had been called out to preserve order, unaccountably fired into the crowd dispersing after the lecture, killing almost a score. The bloodshed of the Gavazzi incident was the result of transplanted Irish nationalism and human error as much as it was religious hatred. But Protestants could see only an infringement of freedom of speech and conscience, and evidence of the terrible tales they had been told about Romanism. The riots were caused, it was said, by "an ignorant and superstitious people, instigated by wicked and bigoted priests."[66] Upper Canadian editors insisted that the Church of Rome had encouraged the outrages, and disclaimers by respectable Roman Catholics were dismissed as a pretence of innocence.[67] When no scapegoats were found by the authorities, Protestants were sure that no justice could be had by Protestants in Canada East, and one paper ominiously reported that "fabulous numbers" of Orangemen had been made in a single night at Montreal.[68] Roman Catholic papers replied with a general denunciation of Gavazzi as a "Red Republican," and of the Protestant press as a "yelping pack of curs." [69]

Roman Catholic sentiment was solidifying in response and reaction to the attacks of George Brown and the ultra-Protestants. At the beginning of 1854 a new Roman Catholic journal, the *Catholic Citizen*, appeared and took up a more militant and sectarian position than the *Mirror*. In its first number, on January 5, the *Citizen* asked its readers how long two hundred thousand Roman Catholics in Canada West would be ruled by men who could not appreciate the value of Roman Catholic institutions. "Our answer is, NO LONGER THAN WE, CATHOLICS, ARE WILLING TO ADMIT OUR INFERIORITY BY A TAME SUBMISSION." [70] Its editor agreed with the *True Witness* that the Roman Catholic party had won responsible government, but warned that all Canadian Protestants hated the Church of Rome.[71] In the eyes of the *Catholic Citizen* it therefore behoved all Roman Catholics not to vote for any camp-follower of Gavazzi or any Protestant who forced Roman Catholic children to attend the irreligious common schools. Roman Catholics must not identify themselves with any political party until politicians proved their friendliness to the Church of Rome by active measures.[72]

Many Protestants were similarly opposed to Brown's attempt to identify the Reform party with a particular religious attitude. At the same time the non-denominational Protestant Alliance at Toronto spoke out in favour of church union as a defence against Roman Catholicism.[73] This statement was underlined by the case of Sarah Bolster (a Protestant girl supposedly enticed into a nunnery by priestly wiles), which excited many newspapers in Canada West during 1855. The Bolster case was soon dropped and for a year and a half afterwards the upper province was spared any major religious disturbance beyond the excitement attending the secularization of the Clergy Reserves.

In the last days of 1855, however, there occured the most serious incident in a decade marked by violent religious crises. The horrible murder at St. Sylvestre of Robert Corrigan, a convert to Protestantism, was entirely the result of Irish religious passions translated to the New World. But the brutality of the killers and their immunity from justice inflamed every part of Canada West and nearly destroyed the Conservative Government in the bargain. The outrage at St. Sylvestre was first blamed on a lodge of Ribbonmen, and the seeming inability of the police and Government to apprehend the murderers led to wild charges of Government duplicity. "How long," demanded the *Globe*, "are Protestants to be killed like dogs and the Government to be permitted to shield their murderers? Are men who support such a Government to receive the votes of Protestants?"[74] For once the *Globe* had the backing of almost every Upper Canadian newspaper, and Roman Catholic attempts to keep the incident in its true perspective served only to incite rather than mollify Protestant feelings.

The partisan charge of Judge Duval to the Roman Catholic jury and the subsequent acquittal of the accused men was the last straw to most people in Canada West. "The farce of a trial" was over, announced the *Christian Guardian* of March 5, 1856. "The killing of a Protestant is not murder, and therefore no crime!!!!!!!" "A murder of a Protestant with impunity—whose only offence was Protestantism, will pave the way to other butcheries," said the usually moderate *News of the Week*.[75] Against this miscarriage of justice J. H. Cameron raised his voice in the Assembly, demanding that the Ministry produce Judge Duval's charge.

The Government threatened to resign in the face of this combined Orange-radical move, and made the vote on Cameron's motion a ministerial one. Even so the motion passed by a vote of 48 of 44, only four Upper Canadians supporting the Government and no less than ten Conservatives voting against the ministers. The Government managed to nullify the effects of this political crisis by obtaining a vote of confidence. But the Corrigan murder marked the beginning of a process of disintegration for the MacNab-Taché Ministry, a process which ended a session of chronic crisis with the revival of the seat of government question and the deposing of Upper Canada's own "Gallant Knight" as leader of the Conservatives in Canada West. When Hogan, the last of Corrigan's accused murderers, was acquitted early in 1857, some Upper Canadians expressed astonishment, but most viewed this as the inevitable consequence of papist domination. "The Pope rules Canada," remarked the rabidly Protestant Bowmanville *Statesman*, "and why not St. Sylvester?"[76] Orangemen, it added, supported the very Government "which protects Judge Duval, whilst clearing Papal murderers from Protestant justice." The Orange Order had never officially voiced an opinion on the Corrigan outrage, but J. H. Cameron had acted, not without personal motives, as the Orange spokesman in the Legislature.

Numerous incidents of religious violence followed closely in the wake of Corrigan's murder. Placards appeared throughout Toronto calling on Protestants to prevent any "Dogan" parades and to prepare to wreak vengeance for St. Sylvestre by trusting God and keeping their powder dry.[77] The death of a Roman Catholic at the hands of an Orangeman during the municipal elections in Nepean Township was represented by Roman Catholic papers as a parallel of the Corrigan case. At Fergus one man was stabbed in the midst of an Orange—Roman Catholic argument. Orangemen returning to Guelph from a "Dogan-trampling" march at Rockwood on the Glorious Twelfth were attacked by railroad navvies. Superintendent of Education Ryerson dismissed one of these Orangemen from his teaching post as a person unfit to guide the minds of children.

"Protestantism," said the *News of the Week* on July 18, 1856, when reporting another Orange parade, "may be said to be the genius of Upper Canada. The success of Orangism is the best proof that it is the spirit of the age."[78] But the Guelph *Advertiser*, striking an early note of nationalism, advised Irishmen to leave their quarrels at home. "When they come to Canada, let them become Canadians."[79] The end of these religious battles was not, however, in sight. The *Mirror*, which continually identified the cry of "Protestant Ascendancy" with the Church of England, generously blamed the anti-Orange editorials of the Montreal *True Witness* for perpetuating the discord in Canada West. Roman Catholics in that section of the province were a minority, the *Mirror* added, and any violence on their part would be worse than useless. The Brampton *Times* agreed with the *Mirror*'s strong disapproval of Governor General Head's action in receiving an Orange address on the twelfth of July. The *Times* insisted that the Orange Society was a political party: "Religion and Protestantism are merely secondary objects of their lines of ambition."[80] The *Mirror*, however, was willing to make allowances for the Governor General because, as the tool of the Ministry, he was not personally responsible for his actions.

An attempt by J. H. Cameron in the same session of 1856 to get an Orange Incorporation Act which would make the Order simply a benevolent society had antagonized many militant Orangemen. It had also failed to gain his re-election as Grand Master. The *Mirror* was now convinced that a Catholic party was an impossibility in Canada, that Roman Catholics must work through existing political organizations to obtain such denominational rights as separate schools.[81] This announcement coincided in time with rumours that both J. S. Macdonald and George Brown were courting the French vote in hopes of ousting the Coalition Government, and Brown was reported to be ready to settle religious differences honestly and amicably.[82]

The first Legislative Council elections, held late in that year, were marked by appeals for a united Protestant vote. The *Globe* asserted that each candidate's religion must be a test of his political fitness. Moderate liberals rejected this trend as a sort of declaration of war on the Roman Catholics and generally deprecated the linking of "Rep. by Pop." with the religious question. Great Protestant demonstrations were held at various points throughout Canada West, variously described by the *Mirror* as petty village celebrations or evidences of rampant Anglicanism, but the net result seems to have been negligible in terms of returning ultra-Protestant Councillors.[83]

The anniversary of the Battle of the Boyne was celebrated more peaceably in 1857. Robert Wallace, speaking to the assembled Orangemen of Oxford County, stated that the Order's numbers had risen to approximately one hundred thousand as a result of Roman Catholic demands for the public endowment of their schools and institutions at the expense of Protestants who paid most of the taxes.[84] The only reported violence occured at Toronto when an attack on an off-duty police-man wearing Orange colours developed into a rock-throwing street fight. But the relative quiet of 1857 was only the calm before the storm. The full tide of religious animosity in Canada West was reached in 1858.

As prelude to a year of unprecedented violence the general elections held in December of 1857 saw the cry of "no popery" raised by Orange Conservatives and Grits alike. But the Orange Order was split by internal dissension and twenty-one of its candidates were defeated.[85] Moderate liberals, however, regretted the loss of some advocates of religious toleration who had fallen victims of "the 'no popery' howl ... that most stupid of shams." [86] Every conceivable trick had been employed with fair success to divide and conquer by religious appeals. In the name of Vinegar Hill Roman Catholics were called on to assert their independence against "grunting Methodists," "canting Presbyterians," and "humbug Temperance societies." [87] However much the *Mirror* might deprecate this "Green Card" trick, its editor was prepared to use his journalistic influence to defeat the "Covenanters." But when the returns came in they proved that the religious question had wrought its devastation in the ranks of both liberals and conservatives.

Early in 1858 William Miller was acquitted at Guelph by a Protestant judge and Orange jury in the death of John Farrell, a Roman Catholic, despite a coroner's jury return of "wilful murder." Immediately the cry of "no justice" was raised by the Roman Catholic journals just as it had been sounded two years before by Protestant papers when Hogan was released. A St. Patrick's Day parade at Toronto turned into a riot in which one Roman Catholic, Matthew

Sheedy, was killed. This was followed the same night by an attack on the National Hotel where a predominantly Protestant Irish dinner was being held only yards from where Sheedy had fallen. Toronto Irish Roman Catholics petitioned Parliament for a special commission to investigate the Farrell and Sheedy cases and for an Act to exclude both Orangemen and Roman Catholics from juries sitting at trials where religion was involved. The petition was accompanied by a threat to arm in self-defence if Roman Catholics were not protected.[88]

Four Roman Catholics were tried and three convicted of assault in the St. Patrick's Day riots. Only one Protestant was charged, and he was acquitted. This action was hailed by the *Catholic Citizen* as a triumph for mob law. "Every Orangeman indicted, has been acquitted!—every Catholic found guilty!"[89] Obviously Orangemen would protect their brethren even at the expense of justice, and Roman Catholics must use violence in self-defence. The *Mirror* of April 23, 1858, listed four victims of Orange murderers in Canada West and warned that a bloody march was planned for the twelfth of July. Jury-packing by the Orange Order had sent Lount and Matthews to the gallows. Now justice for Roman Catholics had become a farce in Canada West thanks to these same bigots.

The *crescendo* of violent feelings continued. Roman Catholic clergy preached special sermons against all secret societies. With two exceptions the Roman Catholic newspapers were united now in their opposition to "Cromwellianism and Orangeism."[90] The two exceptions were the *Irishman,* edited by McGee who was considered a traitor to his race and his religion, and the *True Witness,* which was "ignorant of colonial politics." Peaceful coexistence of Orange and Green would not be permitted by the interested parties.

The annual Orange parades in 1858 seemed open invitations to civil war. But the crisis passed without bloodshed, except of course at Toronto. There a Roman Catholic was shot by an Orangeman, but no arrests were made by the "Orange police" because the Roman Catholic had stabbed the Orangeman before the shooting. The good effects of the restraint shown on both sides in the province was undone by Governor General Head's "gracious" reception of another Orange address. To Roman Catholic eyes it seemed that Head had not learned his lesson in 1857, and the only recourse from such public insults seemed to be petition for his recall. Further incidents of violence occurred late in the year, in Mornington Township and in the neighbourhood of Arthur. In each instance the magistrates were accused of abetting and protecting the culprits. To the *Canadian Freeman* it seemed that the "scoundrels . . . have received a *carte blanche* from the Orange Attorney General West."[91]

Viewed in retrospect the unhappy incidents of 1858 seem indeed to indicate at least a want of firmness on the part of the Government in dealing with the two opposing factions. But the Government in 1858 was not in a strong position where it could take a firm stand. The Irish Roman Catholic vote was wavering in the balance, undecided in its support of the Conservatives, who were partly Orange, yet openly fearful of the consequences of a Grit success. On the other hand there were definite indications that the Conservative apathy towards Orange incorporation was driving that body into the open arms of George Brown. At least these latter parties shared the common ground of "broad Protestant principles," whereas Orangeman John A. Macdonald had been notoriously successful to date in obtaining French Roman Catholic co-operation in the Legislature.

The rise and fall of the Grit two-day Ministry was a case in point illustrating the fluctuating state of religio-political party alignments. The *Canadian Freeman* was pleased with the fall of Macdonald's Government.[92] The only fly in the new ministerial ointment was the presence of George Brown. But the *Freeman* was even willing to postpone judgment on him until his "panacea" and "programme" were known. Both the *Mirror* and the *Daily Colonist* on the other hand rejoiced in the collapse of the Brown-Dorion Government.[93] To the *Colonist*, the Grit attempt to form a ministry was proof "that the 'Dogan' cry of December last was merely a sort of election farce." The Free Church had bent in submission to prelacy, it was said, and thereby had assured the anti-sectarian Conservatives of eventual triumph. When the ousted ministers returned to their constituents for re-election, the *Canadian Freeman* supported George Brown against J. H. Cameron as the lesser of two evils. It noted sarcastically that Orange sympathy for the Roman Catholics was lavished only at elections.[94] It was "silly" of Cameron, said the *Freeman*, to expect Roman Catholics not to vote for Brown. But the *British Tribune* warned the Roman Catholics whose votes had returned Brown that they must accept the full responsibility for his future actions.[95]

The tide of conflict between Orange and Green seemed past its high-water mark after 1858. Perhaps it was only the quiescence of exhaustion. In any case feelings of religious animosity never again ran so high during the remaining years of the Union. In 1859 only three incidents disturbed the religious situation in Canada West. The "abduction" of a Miss Starr into a convent was another Sarah Bolster case, in which the Church of Rome might well plead that *volenti non fit injuriam*. The light sentence imposed on an Orangeman, after a charge of attempted murder was laid following another brawl, led the *Canadian Freeman* on November 11, 1859, to accuse Chief Justice Robinson of "partisan conduct," and to aver once more that "trial by jury, as far as Catholics are concerned, is mere bagatelle." But the most serious episode of the year was the riot accompanying Father Chiniquy's attempt to denounce Romanism to the inhabitants of Canada East. Protestant papers remembered that freedom of speech had also been denied to Gavazzi, but the *Mirror* pointed out with the logic of a Schoolman that, as Chiniquy was neither a Roman Catholic nor a Protestant, he was outside the protection of the law as much as any mediaeval criminal.[96]

The year 1860 might well have passed with equal serenity if the Duke of Newcastle had not attended His Royal Highness, the Prince of Wales, on the latter's visit to Canada. Before the Imperial heir had even sighted the soil of Canada West the groundwork for the "Orange affair" had been laid. To the *Globe*'s complaints (and the *Globe* was not the only dissatisfied party) that prelates of the Churches of England and Rome got preferential treatment in being presented to the Prince, the *Canadian Freeman* replied on August 30 that the dissenters of Canada West were only "locusts," "mostly minor fry" unworthy to precede a divinely appointed bishop. The *Freeman* then hailed the imbroglio at Kingston as a "bloodless victory" over the "Orang (Outang) Association." Newcastle's actions, it added, were "an example of English Statemanship."[97]

English statesmanship it may have been, or even Anglo-Irish, but it was not Upper Canadian statesmanship. The Protestant press of Canada West was almost unanimous in its condemnation of Newcastle and its exculpation of the Orangemen. When *La Minèrve* suggested that the Order should be suppressed in Canada, the *Globe* remarked sagely that it would require the services of an army to enforce such a law if the Orangemen decided to oppose it.[98]   The

Protestant press had the last laugh at the expense of the *Freeman* and the *Mirror* when Grand Master J. H. Cameron personally presented the Address of the Orange Grand Lodge to the Queen in 1861.

The "Orange affair" of 1860 could have had serious repercussions for the Ministry at the general elections due the following summer if John A. Macdonald's speaking tour of the upper province had not dragged much of the Conservatives' fat out of the Orange fire. Even so the Orangemen of Macdonald's own constituency were conspicuously to the fore in Oliver Mowat's daring challenge for the seat of Kingston.[99] Grits and Orangemen were using the old religious question at the polls, but their influence was not proportional to their hatred, nor were they united. Orange papers denounced the Grits as traitors to Protestantism, but the Order itself was still divided on the question of allegiance to the Conservatives, and the division cost them some seats. The Reformers had lost the support of the *Canadian Freeman* because of the *Globe*'s abuse of Roman Catholicism and its praise of the Orange action in 1860. Brown was defeated in Toronto by the Irish Roman Catholic vote, and the *Freeman* boasted that Brown's fate would be a salutary lesson to a demagogue and outcast. Roman Catholics had supported Brown in 1858 because he was opposed by J. H. Cameron. Now, according to the *Freeman*, they showed their independence and their dislike of Brown by electing his opponent.[100]

"The politico-religious politician has grown to be a regular roadster on our political highways," remarked the *Ontario Observer* of October 17, 1861. But the days of the politico-religious politician were numbered. A reaction against the hoaxes perpetrated in the name of Protestantism or Roman Catholicism was becoming apparent. True, the Roman Catholic journals still rejected Rouge and Grit alike as anti-clerical and anti-religious. For such papers the only remaining issue was, which party would offer more in the way of support for separate schools? But the Whitby *Chronicle* noted at the Legislative Council elections of 1862 that "The no-popery cry of '57 is no longer a trump card for the political ranter; nor can the high Protestant horse be trotted out to deluded admirers." [101] The Protestants at least were learning the lessons of the two-party system, however belatedly.

The last throes of the politico-religious question in Canada West before Confederation centred around the separate school question and Fenianism. The latter issue was raised late in 1864 when the *Watchman*, an Orange paper, announced the existence of a Fenian plot to murder all Protestants.[102] This statement was given an air of plausibility when the Irish brotherhood wrecked an Orange hall in Toronto, desecrating the Bible, the flag, and the Queen's picture to boot. The *Canadian Freeman* was now put on the defensive, and indignantly denied the *Globe*'s charge that Irish Catholics were necessarily Fenians, and that they planned to extirpate Protestants.[103] Widespread alarm had followed these rumours of impending massacre, and guilt by association was wildly charged against all Roman Catholics.

When no incidents occurred during 1865 to excite Fenian-phobia among the Protestants of Canada West, the *Freeman* regained some of its old bellicosity. Scurrilously abusive articles appeared in its columns condemning such varied bodies as England, Bible societies, and Protestants. The mere proximity of Fenians on the Niagara border may have emboldened its editor. The woes of Ireland became its theme song. But its tone soon changed again to injured innocence when the Fenian threat became a reality and when the Canadian militiamen showed their determination to defend the province against the enemies of Britain. Volunteers marching past Bishop Lynch's palace shouted "To Hell with the Pope." [104] Protestant papers accused the *Freeman* of sedition. The temper of the times had changed once more, and not without some reason where the *Freeman* was concerned.

The *Freeman* admitted its error as soon as the Fenian invasion occurred at Lime Ridge. [105] The editor denounced the incursion as an outrage and confessed, rather ambiguously, that he had always believed the Fenians to be too sensible to attack Canada. McGee, who had hitherto been a *persona non grata* because of his alliance with Brown, now became the *Freeman's* hero, the rallying point for all Irishmen in the province. The *Freeman's* conversion seemed genuine and lasting, though it and other papers were soon complaining with good reason of a "social persecution" by insult and violence conducted by some Protestants who insisted on equating Roman Catholicism with Fenianism and disloyalty. [106]

Three problems in the relations of church and state which have purposely been reserved for discussion at this point are sabbatarianism, temperance, and ecclesiastical corporations. All of these problems were raised particularly in the last two decades of the Union, and all three bore directly on the politics of the day to some extent. Temperance and sabbatarianism were issues accentuated by the growing industrialization of the province, and ones which had their counterparts a generation earlier in the United States. The problem of incorporating religious bodies was a relatively simple legal one which could and should have been solved at an early date in the province's history.

The general objection to ecclesiastical corporations was the ancient question of mortmain. In a colony so acutely conscious of the land and its utilization, any measure which would remove property permanently from the open market beyond the reach of the independent yeomen was naturally suspect. In Canada the problem was kept perpetually before the public because no general Act governing such incorporations existed, and each case had to be heard by the Legislature and there accepted or rejected, not solely on its own merits, but in the light of current political exigencies.

The row within the Church of Scotland caused by the attempt to get a Temporalities Bill has already been mentioned. A similar storm occured among the Wesleyan Methodists when incorporation of their benevolent societies was sought in 1851. The controversy took on the appearance of a struggle between lay and clerical elements, with outside parties encouraging the former by talk of a grab for "clerical power." [107] The church authorities denied that the request for incorporation was hasty, secretive or unseemly, or that it was dictated by ulterior motives. [108] The Church of England had incorporated its Church Societies in 1843 specifically to assist with the management of the Church's share of the Clergy Reserves funds. A Temporalities Bill was proposed by P. B. de Blaquière in 1851, but it met with Strachan's strong disapproval because it restricted clerical power. One year later a more acceptable Act was obtained, but only after it had gone through the formality of being reserved by the Governor General.

That such incorporations were an absolute necessity for the business of the denominations was obvious, but the opposition arose primarily because of the numerous enactments in favour of Roman Catholic communities which enabled them to hold land. No less than twenty-one such Bills were introduced at the single session of 1849. Popular opinion seemed to favour a general incorporation Bill in 1853, but none was passed. Three years later one was introduced which put specific limits on the mortmain holdings of incorporated religious bodies by providing that gifts of land must be sold within six months. This short period aroused Roman Catholic opposition and with French Canadian assistance the term was extended to two years. Needless to say, Protestant papers complained that this arrangement left too much power in the hands of the priests and that the passing of the Bill was an imposition on Canada West. The whole problem was solved in 1859 by a general Act when the laws were consolidated at that time.

Closely allied to Acts of Incorporation was one particular controversy which excited the upper province to extremes of language. Roman Catholic residents of Three Rivers requested an Act to tax themselves for the rebuilding of their cathedral. Protestant papers of course credited the scheme to the minds of greedy priests, and false rumours were circulated that Protestants too would be taxed. Much of the opposition was directed simply against the Church of Rome, but some arose from hatred of the Hincks-Morin Coalition Government. Basically the protest was against taxation for religious purposes, inspired by the fear that the Three Rivers' cathedral might be the thin edge of the wedge regardless of the fact that in this instance the Act had been demanded by the taxpayers themselves.

Sabbatarianism, the strictest interpretation of God's Third Commandment, is an aspect of puritanism which has been a hallmark of Ontario life for over a century, and one which was long a source of self-congratulation to its inhabitants. Deeply influenced by contemporary movements in both Britain and the United States, the agitation in Canada West against "Sunday profanation" during the fifties was directed especially against labour on the canals and railways, and in the post-office. John Strachan even pronounced himself in favour of a five or five and a half day work week, but added that the Sabbath should be happy, not blue.[109] Sabbatarianism was a widespread movement which embraced most denominations except the Roman Catholics, who were prone to deride it as the Covenanters' "hobby." In 1853 petitions for closing the post-offices and canals on Sundays came to Parliament from almost 17,500 people in Upper Canada, but from only 3,000 in Lower Canada.[110] The *Colonist* objected that any such legislation, though it had been proposed by a Select Committee of the Assembly, would actually contravene the principle of separation of church and state.[111] Bills for this purpose were presented almost every year by George Brown and others, but never got the support of a majority of the Legislature.

Temperance movements were not new to Upper Canada but the example of the famous Maine Law seemed to stimulate renewed interest. In the 1850's popular opinion supported a campaign for complete prohibition. Moderates objected, not to temperance, but to compulsory sobriety which they termed a form of socialism. But the Methodists and Baptists especially threatened at each election to raise the temperance cry as a political issue.[112] In the 1860's the Sons of Temperance appeared as a powerful organization which boasted its own newspaper, the *Good Templar*. The *Good Templar* did not attempt to advise its Sons regarding support for particular political parties,[113] but it did assume the work previously conducted by the denominations, of bringing pressure to bear on each successive government. It was no accident that the temperance temples were arranged in districts corresponding exactly with electoral divisions. But two generations of agitation failed to produce any positive legislation on the temperance problem, and it remained to voluntary organizations and religious influences to work what reform they might by moral suasion.

Looking back on the period of the Union, it can be seen that religion played a vital if divisive rôle in the political life of the province. Behind the various conflicts which arose there lay the strong Calvinistic heritage of most Protestant bodies, a heritage which was particularly evident in the popular tendency to judge all public issues on moral grounds rather than by practical expediency. The clash of Protestant and Roman Catholic had its roots in the Old World, and until the great Irish immigration to Canada West the province had largely been spared these acrimonious displays of religious hatred and bigotry.

Between the various Protestant bodies, however, the causes of dissension were mostly indigenous to the province. On the one side were the favoured churches who possessed and believed in distinctive denominational privileges. On the other were the advocates of complete separation of church and state, who held the voluntary principle almost as a dogma of their faith. Their demand for religious equality was part and parcel of the North American way of life, and it found its strongest ally in the concept of the national state. Two basic forces —centrifugal denominationalism and centripetal nationalism—were warring in the bosom of a single country. There were many aspects of this clash, but the major fields of conflict in Canada West were the relations of church and state on the subjects of religious establishments and education.

CHAPTER TWO

THE CLERGY RESERVES, 1839-1849

THE COMPROMISE THAT FAILED

I

THE CLERGY RESERVES controversy was the most practical issue of church and state relations in Upper Canada, both before and after Union. The Reserves amounted to almost 2,400,000 acres, or 3,750 square miles, of the finest land in the New World, approximately equal to the combined areas of Halton, Peel, York, Ontario, Durham, and Northumberland counties. In terms of economics they were a king's ransom. In terms of Upper Canadian politics they were aptly described as "Pandora's Box."[1] On no other topic of the province's history has so much ink and sentiment been expended, yet it remains to this day a subject of conjecture, more talked about than understood. In its broadest aspect the question included not only those reserved lands equal in value and area to the seventh part of the public domain which had been set aside by the Constitutional Act for the benefit of the "Protestant Clergy," but also the endowment of forty-four Rectories with glebe lands.

To whom did this munificent patrimony belong, or more exactly who were the Protestant clergy? No definition of the term was included in the Constitutional Act, and for half a century after the creation of Upper Canada, thanks to the efforts of the Right Reverend John Strachan and the collusion of successive colonial governors, the Church of England retained a monopoly of the Reserves. The struggle of the Church of Scotland to gain recognition as a co-establishment had proved useless, for the favourable decisions of Law Officers and colonial officials in England were not divulged to the colonists.

Of more historical consequence than the efforts of some to share in the proceeds of the Reserves were the efforts of many who refused to accept the principle of state support for religion or of a denominational division of the Reserves, insisting that the whole domain was the collective inheritance of the inhabitants of the province. Those who demanded secularization of the Reserves in the name of complete separation of church and state represented a tradition which had fled the Old World for the New during two preceding centuries. Voluntarism had become the religious hallmark of the new American republic, and advocates of the idea had, paradoxically, found their staunchest ally in the sentiment of strong nationalism. By the opening decades of the nineteenth century Upper Canada was already feeling the strain of its double identity. It was of the British Empire but it was in North America. The form of establishment inherited from the first empire was challenged by the American way of religious life. Would voluntarism or state-churchism triumph in the second empire, or was a compromise possible between these antithetical ideals? That, in essence, was the Clergy Reserves question in Canada West.

The history of Upper Canada was scarred with recurrent battles over that bone of religious contention, the Clergy Reserves. The very success of Strachan's ambitions for his own denomination had made the Church of England appear to be the Church of Ishmael. In twenty years that Church had received £55,600 from the Clergy Reserves,[2] but not a farthing had been given or even offered to the other Protestant bodies, though they outnumbered the Anglicans by more than three to one in 1839. As an economic grievance the Reserves grew more important with each passing year. Their value increased in direct proportion to the improvement of surrounding lands and of the province generally. This of course was the very basis of the Imperial policy of land reservation. But the availability of vast areas of other fertile land necessitated the abandonment of the plan for leasing the Reserves in favour of a plan for selling them. Yet at the very moment when the Reserves were reaching their maximum value, the combined power of responsible government and voluntarism forced a complete reversal on this aspect of Imperial policy.[3] The inheritance of the Protestant clergy in Canada West was seized for the benefit of the nation as a whole. The Imperial land system in Canada was thwarted by its own inconsistencies and the ideology of the American Revolution.

The Union of the two Canadas marked a departure in policy regarding the Clergy Reserves. Monopoly gave way to a compromise with state-church pluralism. But the concessions made did not satisfy either the divisionists or the voluntarists. Within a decade a variety of influences combined to pry open once more the lid of "Pandora's Box," and the final result, while it appeared to be a victory for the force of centripetal nationalism, contained elements which point almost as strongly to a perpetuation of centrifugal denominationalism. At least as far as the Rectories are concerned, the conflicts of a generation resulted in an indisputable draw, and a full study of the Clergy Reserve finances might prove the same conclusion there. To begin an examination of the Clergy Reserves question at the time of Union is to ignore the prologue of the drama, but to see the climax and *dénouement* in closer relation to the greater problem of church and state in Canada West.

II

"The great practical question ... is that of the clergy reserves. The prompt and satisfactory decision of this question is essential to the pacification of Canada. ..."[4] Such was the considered and perspicacious opinion of Lord Durham, yet the policies of smaller statesmen and the course of events merged to frustrate the intention of "Radical Jack" and the majority of Upper Canada that the Reserves should be secularized and the proceeds left to the provincial Parliament for disposal without Imperial interference. It was common sense, not prophetic vision, which moved Durham to add the warning that "Without the adoption of such a course, the most mischievous practical cause of dissension will not be removed."

Successive governors of Upper Canada had inherited a major problem in the form of the Clergy Reserves. For Sir Francis Bond Head and Sir George Arthur there was added a new element of dissension—forty-four Rectories whose establishment, purpose, and confirmation had aroused a storm of protest from all the religiously underprivileged of the province, namely all non-Anglicans. Durham reported that, "In the opinion of many persons, this was the chief pre-disposing cause of the recent insurrection, and it is an abiding and unabated cause of discontent." [5] It was an unenviable state of affairs which faced the policy-makers in the Colonial Office in the wake of the Upper Canadian Rebellion.

Lord Glenelg, the Colonial Secretary, had still been hopeful in December of 1837 that the New South Wales scheme, generally called the semi-voluntary, might be instituted in Upper Canada.[6] Under this scheme the state would grant each denomination a sum equal to that raised by it through voluntary means. Head's failure to gain the consent of the Upper Canadian Assembly for a division of the Reserves probably encouraged Glenelg to urge Arthur to try the semi-voluntary plan. Within a few days of the penning of these Instructions, news of the outbreaks in Canada reached the Colonial Office, and all prospects of settling the religious dispute in the upper province were summarily postponed.

When relative peace had been restored to Upper Canada in the summer of 1838, Arthur promised to introduce a Bill at the next meeting of the Legislature for reinvesting the Reserves in the Crown. His expectation that reinvestment would be carried "by a considerable majority" was wishful thinking, for the "pocket" Parliament which Head had created in 1836 by an appeal to the bread and butter of the Imperial connection showed shocking independence (as they had on other occasions) by rejecting the New South Wales semi-voluntary system.

The response of the Church of England to all and any suggestions of profit-sharing in the Clergy Reserves was an adamant negative. The clergy of the Diocese of Quebec informed the Colonial Office that they, "after a careful and patient investigation of all the arguments which have been advanced on the subject of this reservation, remain not only unchanged but more confirmed in the opinion that the clergy reserves were by that Act [31 Geo. III, c. 31] designed solely and exclusively for the Church of England." [7] As they believed the provincial Parliament incapable of producing any "impartial, equitable and satisfactory adjustment" of the Clergy Reserve question, they demanded "in the name of peace" a judicial decision by judges of the Privy Council of England, or at least reinvestment. Curtly and somewhat testily, Glenelg replied that the Government saw no reason to doubt the validity of the Law Officers' decision in 1819 which had admitted the right of the Church of Scotland, as a co-established church, to a share of state aid.[8]

Despite that statement of the legal equality of the two established churches of Britain, the Church of Scotland in Upper Canada was receiving a disproportionately small share of assistance. By 1839 the Church of England was only twice as large as the Kirk, yet it received five times as much financial aid from the provincial and Imperial exchequers.[9] In addition the Church of England was receiving over £7,000 per annum from the Clergy Reserves, a fruit which the Kirk was still forbidden in practice to taste. The policy of the Church of Scotland was to seek virtual as well as nominal equality with its sister church, a policy opposed and successfully balked by the Church of England at every turn. Yet that very claim of equality preached by the Kirk was as exclusive as the pretensions of the Church of England. It was not the intention of either to do unto dissenters as they would be done by.

As yet only one group of dissenters, the United Synod of the Presbyterian Church, had even requested a share of the Reserves.[10] They, like the British Wesleyans, received £700 sterling and the Roman Catholics £1,500 annually from the government.[11] Glenelg's refusal to consider the Synod's request until after a general settlement of the Clergy Reserves problem was soon to force that body into a union with the Kirk, a fate which it had previously found difficult to accept. The fact that the British Wesleyans received state aid was an embarrassment to their Canadian brethren-in-union, and was a sin which no thorough voluntarist and few Reformers had been willing to ignore since that moment when Egerton Ryerson's letters had supposedly made the Wesleyans a part of Sir Francis Bond Head's baggage train. In 1839 all other Presbyterians and Methodists, all Congregationalists and Baptists, clung stubbornly to the voluntarist principle, receiving additional sanctification in proportion as other angels fell or Rectories and government grants consolidated a hydra-headed establishment.

When the session of 1839 opened Arthur advised the members to seek an early settlement of the Clergy Reserves question, and true to his promise to Glenelg he offered the New South Wales semi-voluntary scheme in connection with a denominational division of the Reserves.[12] But the Parliament, if packed, did not prove pliable, and Glenelg's pet project for religious peace was rejected in the Assembly by a vote of 37 to 6. A chaotic episode ensued, lasting the better part of the session, in which amendments to apply the proceeds of the Reserves to public purposes, to education, or to religious purposes were defeated by widely varying majorities. The net result was a Bill to sell the remaining Reserves and by amendment in the Legislative Council to apply the proceeds to religious purposes. The principle of division was implicitly accepted, by the legislators at least, and the problem of arranging details was passed to the home government. Back in the Assembly the amended Bill was approved by a majority of one, "at a late hour on the night preceding the day of prorogation," as Arthur admitted when he sent the Reserves Bill to Lord Normanby, the new incumbent at the Colonial Office.[13]

Arthur went on to explain that "the Assembly was in fact divided into many small parties," that nothing like "unanimity of sentiment" prevailed therein. Opponents of the Bill wished to maintain the controversy only "for the purpose of agitation," and public meetings of protest could be expected. Only "promptitude of action" and the abandonment of the old exclusive interpretation of "Protestant Clergy" could forestall unrest and satisfy the majority of the people of Upper Canada.

In the Legislative Council only Strachan and John Macaulay had opposed the Bill, Strachan wildly exclaiming that he would rather see the Roman Catholic Church dominant in Upper Canada than submit to the spoliation of his own denomination.[14] The other Anglicans had supported the measure and the Church of Scotland Councillors viewed it as the death blow to the preferred position of the rival Church of England. "We have gained the Victory," James Crooks jubilantly informed William Morris who had been absent from the Council for some days. "The Archdeacon left the House after the vote was taken, completely discomfited. I never saw him so chop fallen, and I think we'll see no more of him. He, however, as was to be expected, died game, using the most shameful trickery to defeat the Bill, by proposing alterations at every Stage. . . ."[15] "As the principal [sic] of a national church has been abandoned," Macaulay wrote his tory mother, "we must only now look to worldly policy. . . ."[16]

Not all Strachan's opponents, however, were satisfied with the Clergy Reserves Bill. The voluntarists shared the Archdeacon's feeling of defeat, though for a different reason. Egerton Ryerson had let certain Councillors know his objections to the provision which would not only divide the Reserves among the denominations, but would assuredly divide his own church.[17] The union of the Canadian and British Wesleyans had been virtually an act of desperation on the part of the colonials, an act which had cost them a measure of self-respect. The divergent attitudes of the two parties towards the relations of church and state had been suppressed but never obliterated. The prospect now for the traditionally voluntarist Canadian Wesleyans was separation or complete submission.

On the same day that Arthur forwarded the controversial Clergy Reserves Bill, he also wrote Normanby in confidence of the impending conflict within the Wesleyan body. The Reverends Robert Alder and Joseph Stinson, leaders of the British element, were "at last" aware of Ryerson's true position and of his voluntarist writings. "Among those who have been hitherto most strenuous in their efforts to prevent the settlement of the Clergy Reserve Question, no person has been more conspicuous than the Editor of the Christian Guardian, who I believe to be in heart an American Episcopalian Methodist." [18] As Arthur had heard that Ryerson intended to go to England to agitate the Clergy Reserves question he felt that the Colonial Office should be forewarned against this disturber.

III

Egerton Ryerson did not go to England in 1839. But Archdeacon Strachan did, partly as a result of the Clergy Reserves Bill but also to receive the mitre which he had coveted so long. Nor were these two reasons for Strachan's voyage unconnected, for the endowment of the new bishopric had been made contingent upon the settlement of the Clergy Reserves question, and this problem of providing for the needs of John Toronto continued to be a source of trouble to the Society for the Propagation of the Gospel and the Colonial Office for several years.

Before his departure Strachan received disconcerting news from the Reverend A. N. Bethune, Archdeacon-to-be.[19] From Cobourg to Kingston the laity of the Church of England were opposed to signing any petitions against the Clergy Reserves Bill. Such a move, it was feared, would invite the revival of the agitation so recently subdued by the solution of reinvestment, and Bethune suggested petitions from the clergy only, petitions which would stress the concessions made by the Church in agreeing to reinvestment and which would be promoted in England by Chief Justice John Beverley Robinson and friendly parties in both houses of the Imperial Parliament. On the Upper Canadian front Bethune advised an approach to the Moderator of the Church of Scotland for a gentlemanly agreement with that body to the mutual advantage of both. Let each one follow the same procedure—that is, no appeal to the laity—and the Reserves might yet be saved for the clergy of the two national churches.

But the discontent reported by Bethune was not the only defection which faced Strachan in his embryo diocese. The futility of ultra-toryism was dawning on John Macaulay, the only man who had supported Strachan in the Legislative Council. Privately he criticized Strachan's apparent stubbornness in defending the Church's exclusive claim to the Reserves. Strachan extolled himself as a misunderstood moderate, and explained to his critic his own plan for achieving religious peace in Upper Canada.[20] An established church was an essential of the constitution, but a subdued establishment receiving not more than three-fifths or less than one-half of the Reserves would be acceptable. "The Scotch &

other Presbyterians" could be satisfied by one-fifth of the Reserves if the aid of such "reasonable" men as Thomas Chalmers, his personal friend, were enlisted in Scotland. As for the British Wesleyans, a "donation" to their missions would suffice, and the remainder of the Reserves could be used by the government for "occasional assistance" to religion. To Strachan the Roman Catholic Church was still the greatest threat to Protestantism, a danger which he forgot conveniently but unaccountably when Roman Catholic political influence could be of assistance to his plans. But for the present he was willing that it should be aided from the Jesuit estates.

Strachan's plan was not the New South Wales scheme but the very system which Arthur had introduced in Van Dieman's Land and which made the voluntary principle merely an auxiliary to state aid. "The difficulties, I anticipate," he confided to Macaulay, "will be neither from Ryerson nor Morris but from the Archbishop, the bishops, the great societies, and Friends of the Church. . . ." Yet there was some hope for success if only Arthur would place his *imprimatur* on this division plan, for Arthur's "high reputation . . . would go far to recommend [it to] the Heads of the Church, and especially the Archbishop, who is well acquainted with His Excellency . . . ."

In England Strachan's efforts came to naught through no fault of his own. The Clergy Reserves Bill had been disallowed on a technicality, the Law Officers of the Crown believing that the provincial Parliament had no right to attach any restrictions to a measure for reinvestment. Strachan was forced to content himself with pressing for the completion of the other thirteen Rectories, a move that seemed feasible since the Law Officers had confirmed the legality of the forty-four patents and the people of Upper Canada had ceased to agitate the issue after one last vain protest.

Meanwhile Lord John Russell had taken over the reins at the Colonial Office from his *locum tenens,* Normanby, and Charles Poulett Thomson, the man with the "magic wand," had arrived in Canada as Governor General, ostensibly to implement Lord Durham's Report. Unfortunately Durham had contented himself with the brief recommendation that the Clergy Reserves provisions be repealed, and the team of Russell and Thomson were left a free hand to tackle the details of the vexed problem. In his Instructions to Thomson, Russell explained the reasons for the disallowance of the Clergy Reserves Bill, and referred the task of settlement once more to the colonial Legislature. "I cannot admit that there exists in this country greater facilities than in Upper Canada for the adjustment of this controversy." [21] Thus the agitation was reopened, not by radicals, republicans, or voluntarists, but by the Imperial government.

IV

Thomson entertained no delusion about the difficulty of finding a solution to the Clergy Reserves question. "I confess I am not sanguine; for there are as many minds almost as men, and they are all dreadfully committed, both in the House and with their constituents, upon this question, for twenty different projects." [22] Nevertheless a settlement must precede the actual union of the provinces as a *sine qua non* for the harmonious operation of the new constitution. Confident that his popularity was at its apogee, and armed with Russell's order to consult the best persons available, Thomson prepared to "try my hand at the clergy reserves." [23]

At the Colonial Office Russell was fully aware that the "prevailing opinion" was opposed to any monopoly of the Reserves funds by the Church of England alone or in conjunction with the Church of Scotland, and also to any extension of benefits to the Roman Catholics. The only alternative that he could see was a division of the loaves and fishes among the various denominations. "Such a course although not in accordance either with the Interpretation given to the Act of 1791, or with any general principle of affording aid to all Religious denominations may however be practically the best and most satisfactory." [24]

When the Parliament of Upper Canada met for the last session in its half-century of existence one of its first moves was to ask the Governor General what action had been taken on the Reserves Bill for reinvestment. Thomson advised them for the first time of its disallowance, and in doing so gave notice that a substitute Bill would probably be introduced soon. [25] Writing to Russell he detailed his hopes and fears for the projected scheme with some measure of prophetic accuracy.

The Clergy Reserves have been, and are, the great overwhelming grievance—the root of all the troubles of the province, the cause of the rebellion—the never-failing watchword at the hustings—the perpetual source of discord, strife, and hatred. Not a man of any party but has told me that the greatest boon which could be conferred on the country would be that they should be swept into the Atlantic, and that nobody should get them.... And when to this never-failing source of excitement here you add the consideration that by the Union, if you left the question unsettled, you would throw the agitation of it into the Lower Province, where, amongst all its ills, the greatest of all, religious dissension, is hitherto unknown, the necessity for a settlement becomes doubly great.[26]

In a tone of resignation John Macaulay informed his mother that he had no doubt that the Governor General would have his own way in the matter of the Clergy Reserves.[27]

During the latter part of December, 1839, Thomson gathered and assessed the opinions of prominent Upper Canadians concerning the Clergy Reserves question and its possible solutions. Among those interviewed were Egerton Ryerson, current editor of the influential *Christian Guardian*; Joseph Stinson, President of the Wesleyan Methodist Conference; and Matthew Richey, sometime Principal of Upper Canada Academy, and now Superintendent of the important Toronto Circuit. These last two, leaders among the British element within the Canadian body, wrote on their own responsibility assuring Thomson that they recognized the Church of England as the true establishment. Presuming that a sectarian division of the Reserves was contemplated, they requested that the Wesleyans' share be given into the control of the British Conference. Here was the very cause of difference between the Canadian and English elements, the New World and the Old, within that denomination, and here too was the seed of disunion within the Conference.

For his own part Ryerson had fallen under the spell of Thomson's persuasive personality and progressive policies, and his knowledge and influence were equally at the Governor General's command. To some extent this respect must have been reciprocated, for Thomson advised the Colonial Office that any share of Reserves allotted to the Wesleyan Methodists should be vested in the Canadian Conference. He also warned Ryerson of the position assumed by Stinson and Richey, which information began the process of disruption when it was imparted to the Conference the following June.[28]

When Parliament reconvened after the Christmas recess, the Governor General outlined the provisions of his Bill for dividing the Reserves. The remaining lands should be sold, and the annual proceeds "distributed according to terms which will be clearly defined, between the Church of England, the Church of Scotland and such other religious persuasions as are recognized by the law of Upper Canada, for the support of religious instruction within the Province, and for the promotion ... [of religion]." [29] "The circumstances of the present time imperiously demand a settlement," Thomson said, and he hoped that his Bill would be "a final and satisfactory adjustment."

Of the Clergy Reserves Fund arising from interest on all sales, rents, and investments, the Church of England was to receive one-quarter of the annual proceeds and the Church of Scotland an equal amount.[30] Until such time as the fund was equal to the stipends already guaranteed by the Crown (including those of the Wesleyans and Roman Catholics), the Casual and Territorial Revenues would supply the deficiency. The remaining half of the total annual revenue was to be apportioned among any denominations who would apply for the same on the semi-voluntary principle.

Thomson's success was immediate, though far from complete. The bulk of the Wesleyan Methodists, led by Ryerson as editor of the Conference's journal, accepted this *via media* solution. The *Christian Guardian* formally recanted the traditional Methodist position: "Up to the present time we have employed our best efforts by every kind of argument, persuasion, and intreaty, to get the proceeds of the Reserves applied simply and solely to educational purposes; but perceiving the absolute impossibility of attaining that object entirely, we cannot deceive our readers by continuing to hold that out to view which is unattainable.... Our only alternative is, to do the best in our power, under present circumstances." [31] That best was to accept the division scheme.

John Strachan, however, was not the man to accept such "spoliation" of his Church supinely. In a circular to the clergy and laity of his diocese he confessed that he had accepted(!) reinvestment because it would remove the source of contention to the Imperial Parliament, the only tribunal which could offer an impartial settlement, a course of which he had expected the whole province would approve.[32] But this new Bill was "as injurious to the Established Church as it is repugnant to the 31st of Geo. 3rd. chap. 31, and the fundamental principles of the British Constitution." By this Bill the national Church would be robbed of nearly three quarters of her patrimony, British birthright would be destroyed, error, schism, and dissent would be promoted by levelling the "clergy" to the status of "dissenting ministers," and the cause of Protestantism would be endangered. Fear not the provincial Legislature, the Bishop exhorted his flock, but lift your eyes unto England from whence alone could come worldly salvation. Above all, the Imperial Parliament must be petitioned in the name of British justice and the true religion against division of the Reserves. John Macaulay echoed Strachan's self-righteous protests but added gloomily, "When such a proposal emanates from the Crown, what can be done?"[33]

At the same time, in the interests of both Christ and of Caesar, William Morris was busily acting as marriage broker for the union of the Church of Scotland and the United Synod. Union of these bodies, which together contained the bulk of Presbyterians, would be advantageous in the matter of settling the Clergy Reserves, and Morris advised Thomson "to recommend to the two Synods the speedy completion of a measure which in a very material degree will simplify the duties of the Provincial Government in making provision for the support of the Ministers of both...."[34] The Reverend William Smart, spokesman for the United Synod, was particularly concerned that he and the other "Fathers of Presbyterianizm" (*sic*) in the province (as he modestly termed his colleagues) should receive a fitting reward for their loyalty to and suffering for the Government. Morris, who had originally belonged to their body, was able to calm Smart's fears with the assurance that the United Synod in union with the Kirk would receive a fourth part of the Clergy Reserves Fund.[35]

Those Reformers who still held out uncompromisingly for devoting the Reserves to education or general purposes (and there were many such idealists, as Thomson admitted [36]) were chagrined but impotent in the face of the combined power of Presbyterianism, Wesleyan Methodism, and the Government. Their only allies were those equally uncompromising members of the Church of England. Still, in a voice which historical hindsight would confidently term prophetic, the Kingston *Herald* of January 14, 1840, warned that though Thomson's Bill might pass, "the question will come up again as freshly as ever," simply because the people believed in using the Reserves for nonsectarian ends. This Bill would merely create a polycephalous establishment; it could not create religious equality.

In the Assembly the division Bill was introduced by Solicitor General William Draper, and passed second reading without opposition. Thomson had offered the legislators a choice between the semi-voluntary scheme, as written into the draft, or a straight per capita denominational division of the second half of the Reserves Fund. They chose the latter. On Colborne's advice Russell had suggested to Thomson that the collection of tithes be legalized, to which the Governor General retorted, "Why, in Upper Canada there are no tithes at all. You might as well try to get the breeches of the Glengarry & Stormont men, who wear none, as to get tithes from them." [37]

At its third reading in the Assembly the Bill met the combined forces of the Opposition. The Tories moved an amendment to revive the reinvestment Bill, while the Reformers demanded the Reserves for general purposes. "The Ultra Tories behaved in the basest way—they turned my Bill out *twice* in Committee by voting with the Radicals to appropriate the *fund for public works*—...," wrote the Governor General.[38] But his "friends" cancelled these votes at the expense of their election pledges, a trivial price in Thomson's eyes so long as the Reserves were retained for religion. "So I got it to the third reading when these ragamuffins, having their names on the Journals, did not dare vote against Religious purposes & then I carried the Bill, as I have said, by 30 [28] to 20. I now only wait for the Council, where I think I am sure." [39] As Thomson had anticipated, the Bill was passed by the Legislative Council "without the change of a word."

But the battle was far from over, and the next round would be fought in the Imperial Parliament under the influence of the Bench of Bishops where the Governor General's "wand" had no chance to perform such magic as turning mice into footmen for the Cinderella-coach of Union. Russell was forewarned of John Toronto's petition against spoliation; "You will remember that it is to Dr. Strachan that we owe this matter being still open—15 years ago he might have settled it, if he would have given any thing to the Church of Scotland...."[40] If necessary the Bill could be re-enacted by the Imperial Parliament, but under no circumstances must it be returned to Canada, "for here it cannot come again without the most disastrous results." "If it is really carried it is the greatest work that ever has been done in this Country, & will be of more solid advantage to it than all the loans & all the troops you can make or send. It is worth ten Unions & was ten times more difficult."[41] "If you will only send me back my Union and the Clergy Reserves," Thomson pleaded with his chief, "I will guarantee you Upper Canada."[42]

V

In closing the last Parliament of Upper Canada, Governor General Thomson appealed for the peaceful acceptance of the Clergy Reserves settlement without further agitation.[43] "It will now be seen," commented the *Christian Guardian* in a provocative tone, "whether public officers throughout the province will pay more regard to the counsels of the Head of the Government by which they are elevated, or to the agitating advice of the Bishop of Toronto."[44] But neither the *Guardian* nor the Governor could intimidate John Toronto, who published forthwith a pamphlet version of his speeches in defense of the Church's exclusive claim to the Clergy Reserves. Characterizing the Bishop's literary efforts as an "anomalous specimen of Episcopal infallibility, justice and charity," the *Guardian* denounced this renewed excitement by "the tolerant Bishop" as "unpatriotic and disloyal ... unwarrantable and suicidal."[45] In Ryerson's opinion the Clergy Reserves Bill would become law despite and because of Strachan's latest effort to salvage the Church's inheritance. "Had the Governor General sent the Church of England to the electors of Upper Canada, instead of interposing his own potent influence and vigorous efforts, in the place of getting lands and £ 10,000 a year, the Church would not [have] been allowed an acre or a farthing."[46]

The handwriting was so plainly inscribed on the wall that only the blindest of Tories or Reformers could refuse to admit that the old order of monopoly in the Clergy Reserves must of necessity yield to Thomson's new order of division. Yet estimates of the benefits accruing to dissenters varied, the Kingston *Herald* of January 28, 1840, predicting that no surplus would be available for at least a generation, and Thomson himself forecasting at least ten or twelve lean years for the underprivileged, second-class denominations.[47] John Macaulay, the chastened Tory, admitted that "A settlement is demanded for the peace of the Country & we cannot contend against the Governor General's proposition."[48] But his flighty and improvident brother, the Reverend William, was still confident that divine intervention would prevent the ratification of the division Bill by the Imperial Parliament. "Our sins have not yet provoked Providence so far."[49]

Under threat of Episcopal opposition Melbourne's shaky Government decided on the advice of its Law Officers to obtain the opinion of the Judges of England upon the legality of Thomson's Clergy Reserves Bill.[50] In all probability Russell hoped to secure a favourable decision to silence the thunder against this spoliation of the colonial Church, which all and sundry expected to emanate from the olympian heights of the Bishops' Bench. In that case, Russell was doomed to disappointment.

Thomson did not share Russell's sanguine hope that the bishops would be powerless to prevent the passage of the Bill in the House of Lords.[51] An editorial of Francis Hincks in the *Examiner* of December 19 condemning the Clergy Reserves settlement as a defeat for the Reformers was causing anxiety on both sides of the Atlantic.[52] Many Reformers, including Baldwin and Ryerson, were embarrassed by this unexpected outburst, and the *Guardian* hastened to defend the Governor General's policy and honesty by classing Hincks as a secret ally of Bishop Strachan.[53] In Britain the *Colonial Gazette* echoed Hincks' charge that Thomson had alienated the affections of all liberals by forcing through the Division Bill.[54] The Governor General intensified his own propaganda campaign with numerous and copious despatches on the Upper Canadian situation, all of which were intended for the instruction of members of Parliament, and in a revealing remark to Russell he commended the *Christian Guardian* as "the only decent paper in both Canadas." [55]

While the Imperial and colonial governments, the colony, and its Governor awaited patiently the outcome of the Judges' deliberations, Strachan pressed on with his petitions to the Imperial Parliament. Despite this discouraging apathy of the laity, he urged his friends in and out of Parliament to exert every effort to nullify a Bill which he was sure pleased no one.[56] Better terms for the Church could have been obtained, he informed the Society for the Propagation of the Gospel, but Thomson was more favourable to the Kirk and "American Methodists" than he was to the national religion. Even the reinvestment Bill, if it could be enacted, would be far better than the proposed settlement. Strachan would accept any "reasonable basis" of settlement in preference to further agitation, providing of course that the established position of his church and clergy was ensured.[57] But on one point at least Strachan agreed whole-heartedly with the Governor General. The Clergy Reserves question must not be sent back to Canada.[58]

When the opinion of the Judges was announced it proved to be more than Russell had bargained for. True, the term "Protestant Clergy" was found to include both the Churches of England and Scotland, and by implication all other legally recognized Protestant bodies.[59] But to the embarrassment of the Imperial Government and all its past policy, the judges decided that the Legislature of Upper Canada had exceeded its authority in passing the Bill because the power conferred by the forty-first section of the Constitutional Act, to vary or repeal provisions relating to the Clergy Reserves, was prospective only and could not apply to allotments already made. Here was the negation of the basic principle on which all colonial legislation on the Clergy Reserves had been founded. Last year reinvestment had been unconstitutional, now colonial legislation was *ultra vires*. Some lawmaker would have to plead lamentable ignorance of the law. The only course now remaining was to enact a settlement of the Canadian Clergy Reserves at Westminster, and the nature of that settlement would rest entirely with the political parties of Great Britain.

The strength of the Tory Opposition in the Lords, particularly among its mitred members, had already been painfully evident to the Government during recent debates on Sydenham's Clergy Reserves Bill. There was no doubt as to who had the whiphand. "After considerable doubt and Hesitation," as Sir Robert Peel explained to Strachan, Russell and the rest of the Cabinet had been forced to accept a modification of their own Clergy Reserves Bill on terms dictated by the Archbishop of Canterbury.[60] The statutory result was 3 & 4 Victoria, c. 78.

The new and certain settlement divided the proceeds of the "old Sales" comprising about one-quarter of the Reserves between the Churches of England and Scotland in the proportion of two to one. The proceeds from "New Sales" in the future would be halved, one part being shared by the same two privileged churches according to the same ratio, and the remainder, being only three-eighths of the whole, would be apportioned among all other Protestant bodies who might apply for the same. Until the Clergy Reserves Fund was sufficient to cover the existing charges, the Casual and Territorial Revenues must supply the deficiency. As for the dissenting Protestants, they would obviously wait for many years before sufficient surplus accrued to allow them to benefit from the Primate's generosity.

Thus the Church of England in Upper Canada, constituting approximately 20 per cent of the population, was given almost 42 per cent of the Reserves, and the Church of Scotland, whose numbers now almost equalled those of the Anglicans, received 21 per cent of the proceeds (a sum almost corresponding to a per capita division), while the other Protestants, one-half of the whole population of the province and including those sworn to voluntarism, would at some future date be offered 38 per cent of the Protestant patrimony.

VI

The deed was done, and though the position of the Church of England had been circumscribed, it was far from disestablished in the opinion of most Upper Canadians. In fact the number of established churches had been multiplied, since all charges for religious purposes were now transferred to the Clergy Reserves Fund. This meant that in addition to the Churches of England and Scotland, the United Synod, the Wesleyan Methodists, and even the Church of Rome were assured of their government grants by Section 3 of the Act and of eventual participation in the Clergy Reserves Fund. Russell's only regret was that the excessive shares given to the two most favoured churches might prejudice the permanency of the settlement.[61]

Strachan, however, would not be reconciled to sharing the Reserves with any dissenters. The Act was "very bad in fact not much better than the one that was carried through the Legislature of this Province by undue influence last winter." [62] Sir Robert Peel and William Gladstone, both of whom the Archbishop had consulted, assured Strachan that these were the best terms available in the opinion of the Peelites.[63] But the Bishop could not forget shame inflicted on the Church by dissenters and papists who had united in unholy alliance "to crush the noblest trophy of the Reformation." [64] The five-twelfths of the Reserves remaining to the Church were "manifestly inadequate" to meet its needs. But however unjust the settlement might seem to Anglican eyes, at least it was final, so Strachan informed his clergy, and the Clergy Reserves question would never "perplex and agitate the United Legislature."

If Strachan was dissatisfied, the Church of Scotland was much more so, and perhaps with better reason. The ratio of division had been based on the census of 1839, the inaccuracies of which were admitted by all. And the chief sufferers from the faulty enumeration had been the Kirk which was credited with only one-half of its real numbers. "Their members are in *fact* almost, if not quite equal to the Church of England," Thomson told Russell.[65] "Your expression that there was 'no superiority' has helped me well with the Scotch who are however furious at having been *jockeyed* out of their fair share."

The Church of Scotland did not contest the principle of division; it objected solely to the basis of division chosen by Russell despite advance warning of errors in the religious returns. The Reverend Robert McGill poured out his sentiments on the Colonial Office to William Morris. "They seems to manage all affairs by 'systematic humbugging.' Plain honest men are not fit to deal with them, they are sure to be cheated."[66] "How Lord John Russell ... could take that census as a basis for the distribution of the proceeds of the Clergy Reserves, I cannot comprehend. I strongly suspect the Puseyism of the House of Lords has mystified him.... This act is worthy to stand side by side with the Ecclesiastical Chart and the Rectory Creation." "It seems to me," added McGill, "that if this be the *finale,* they have acted consistently throughout in their iniquity." [67]

It was high time for Thomson, now elevated to the peerage as Baron Sydenham of Toronto, to use his personal charm once more in the cause of peace, and this he did most successfully in an interview with William Morris. "The Scotch I have in hand," he informed Russell.[68] How well in hand he had these obdurate Scots is shown by Morris's letter to Sydenham after the interview. Although regretting the "blunder in the Returns, and the Consequences thereof," he would "most reluctantly see any attempt to agitate the public mind on the nature of the settlement now made of this tiresome subject...." [69]

The Church of Scotland had been injured, but at least the decision of the twelve judges established its claims in the colony. Morris's only request was consideration of the suggestion by the Moderator, the Reverend Hugh Urquhart, that the United Synod be permanently endowed as compensation for its exclusion from sharing directly in the Clergy Reserves with the Church of Scotland.[70] The fact that the mother church in Scotland had given its blessing to the settlement compromised Morris's position while it strengthened Sydenham's request for peace.[71]

But the Church of Scotland was as tenacious of its rights as Strachan was of the Church of England's. When a *pro re nata* meeting of the Synod was convened in Kingston two weeks after Sydenham's interview with the lay leaders, a memorial protesting the disproportionate share of the Reserves given to the Church of England, the implied inequality of the Church of Scotland, and the unsatisfactory religious census was prepared for the Colonial Office's edification.[72] Sydenham's reply deprecated the tone of the memorial as liable to disturb that harmony and unanimity sought by the Government in settling the Clergy Reserves question. The Imperial Government was equally unwilling to reopen the discussion, and Sydenham inscribed on the margin of Russell's despatch the cryptic note, "defer till Morris and Crooks can be consulted at Kingston." [73]

Like the Churches of England and Scotland, whose grumbling did not cease immediately, the Wesleyan Methodists were also dissatisfied with the settlement of the Clergy Reserves. But their complaint was not so much against the small share which would be theirs as against the partiality shown to two churches at the expense of all other denominations. The new Act seemed to confirm the ideas of semi-establishment, and thereby to vitiate that ideal of religious equality for which they had struggled so long. Small wonder if some Wesleyans were becoming sceptical of the messiahship of Canada's own prince of peace, Charles Poulett Thomson, to whom they had so generously given their political souls and the largest newspaper in the upper province.

The storm which had been brewing since the union of the two Wesleyan bodies in 1834, and which had threatened havoc immediately after the Rebellion, broke at last with its full force at the Conference in the summer of 1840, even while the Imperial Parliament was considering its own Clergy Reserves Bill.[74] Ryerson's political course in the *Christian Guardian* was indicted by his English brethren in the Conference, and though his actions and particularly his attempt to have the government grant transferred to Canadian control were upheld, it was decided to send him with two other delegates to the English Conference, to explain the controversy in Canada. In its broadest aspects the struggle was one for colonial autonomy among the Wesleyan Methodists, but the immediate cause was the Clergy Reserves question.

Before Ryerson left Canada he was warned by Sydenham that the Reverend Robert Alder had written to Russell condemning Ryerson. Unfortunately Ryerson never did procure a copy of this letter, but it is doubtful if evidence of such backstair politics would have changed the attitude of the English Conference. The cold and impolite reception accorded the Canadian delegates was a true portent of what followed. The English Conference summarily dissolved its union with the Canadian body, with results disastrous to both parties. But at least the Canadians would be free to approach the Clergy Reserves settlement from a Canadian viewpoint, without the millstone of respect for establishments to impede their actions.

Sydenham had apparently reported Ryerson's claim to have the government grant transferred to the Canadian Wesleyan Methodist Conference, but Ryerson felt certain that Alder's misrepresentations had prejudiced the mind of the Colonial Secretary. "If you will give Egerton Ryerson what I have asked and what is perfectly just," Sydenham pleaded with Russell, "*I* will keep him quiet when he gets back, but I must have that to do it. I am in the greatest favour with the Upper Canadian Methodists, so a fig for Mr. Alder and the English Conference." [75] But even in Ryerson's absence the difficulties had been multiplied through Lieutenant-Governor Arthur's attempt to ride both horses by giving half of the annual grant to the British Wesleyan Missionaries.

At first Russell decided to leave the adjustment of these financial issues to Sydenham, and the latter sent for Ryerson, "my high Priest," as soon as he returned, to "cool him down upon the Reserves." [76] Once more the Governor General's personal magnetism turned the tables as it had with William Morris, and though the "high Priest" protested "the partial & exclusive provisions" of the Clergy Reserves Act, he generously withheld his own correspondence on the subject and convinced the editor of the *Christian Guardian* not to promote dissention. [77] Thus when that journal announced the passing of the Act, no editorial comment was appended, merely an encomium for the efforts of Egerton Ryerson to obtain a settlement of "this long discussed, important, and absorbing question." [78]

As months passed without a final decision from the Colonial Office as to which of the Wesleyan bodies would receive the annual grant, Ryerson implored Sydenham to consider the needs and rights of the Canadian body. [79] Their union had been dissolved by the English Conference "in consequence of their support which was given ... to Your Excellency's administration." The British Wesleyans in Canada were, he argued, only agents of their Conference, not a denomination, and the Clergy Reserves Act restricted payment to Canadian denominations only. Above all, the original grant had been intended to assist the educational work of the Canadian Wesleyans, the only field of endeavour in which they were willing to infringe the strictest interpretation of voluntarism. Now not a farthing came to the Canadian Wesleyans, although all the other major religious bodies received financial assistance, and to add insult to injury, the London Missionary Committee used grants from Canadian funds "in a hostile crusade against the

Methodist Church in Canada." The solution adopted was to suspend grants to both bodies, pending the reunion of the contestants, or the possible elimination of one of them.[80] The Colonial Office could plead legal technicalities in extenuation of its policy. It was a bitter and empty reward for the denomination which had sacrificed so much, even its unity, for the cause of religious equality, all apparently to no avail.

Thus the settlement of the Clergy Reserves question dictated by the Bench of Bishops in the Imperial Parliament failed to satisfy anyone in Upper Canada. It was an Imperially imposed peace, made only slightly more palatable by the convincing arguments of Sydenham. But it was intended to be a final adjustment of the claims of the Protestant clergy to their own inheritance. Such at least was the belief of its Whig foster-parents, the same politicians who had established "final" parliamentary reform for their own country in 1832. At least the Church of England and the Wesleyans were prepared, however reluctantly, to accept the solution as legislated if only to end agitation of an issue which had contributed to rebellion and bloodshed.

But the Church of Scotland would brook no treatment which carried the stigma of inferiority, nor would the sworn minority of voluntarists, the Baptists, Congregationalists, and other Methodists, be content with anything so far removed from the complete separation of church and state. The Roman Catholics alone stood by as disinterested spectators. The only tangible advantage of the Clergy Reserves Act in the eyes of most Upper Canadians was the cessation of all further reservations for religious purposes. But the advocates of voluntarism would assuredly fight again under the banner of religious equality and behind the shield of non-denominational nationalism.

VII

The larger religious denominations of Canada merely acquiesced in the Clergy Reserves settlement of 1840. The smaller bodies felt equally outraged at the conclusion reached, but suffered in the silence of impotence. The apparent peace which continued for almost a decade after the passing of 3 & 4 Victoria, c. 78, was disturbed periodically by minor incidents, which, if they did not make headline news in their day, and have been ignored and forgotten since, yet upon closer examination are interesting in themselves both as evidence of the weakness of the so-called final settlement, and as partial explanations of the origin of that acrimonious controversy which broke out over the Clergy Reserves in 1850.

To the Wesleyan Methodists the settlement of 1840 made the Clergy Reserves no longer a religious question but a constitutional one, beyond the competence but not the interest of their church. The promise that henceforth the *Christian Guardian* would remain silent on political issues was most carefully observed by all who succeeded Egerton Ryerson in the editorial chair of that influential journal. Hereafter the references by the *Guardian* to the Clergy Reserves can be numbered literally on one's fingers, even including the exciting years of the early fifties. Methodist opposition to the Church of England had concerned the Establishment only, and the temptation to indulge in the traditional Upper Canadian sport of religious controversy was repressed with considerable self-denial, but with only fair success, by the *Guardian's* editors after 1840.

For the Church of Scotland in Canada the settlement of 1840 created at least two unforeseen complications. The appointment of commissioners under Clause

3 of the Act to administer that Church's share of the Clergy Reserves Funds aroused once more that latent but ever menacing internal issue of lay *versus* clerical supremacy in the affairs of the Kirk. The occasional attempts of the Kirk clergy to establish themselves in a sacerdotal position had always been indignantly repulsed, and this incident was no exception. With obvious satisfaction William Morris pointed to the laudable policy of Bishop Strachan who had left the management of diocesan temporal affairs in the competent hands of his Church Society,[81] which included such able laymen as Chief Justice Robinson and P. B. De Blaquière.

The second complication was the disruption of the colonial Church of Scotland in 1844. It proved to have most happy results for the "residual" clergy of that denomination. After the withdrawal of twenty-three ministers from the Synod and the formation of the Free Church, the government decided that the secessionists could not rightfully claim any share of the Reserves funds alloted to the older body. The result, therefore, was a proportional increase per capita for a smaller body, to the great chagrin of the impecunious Free Church and of the Church of England whose fraction of the funds was now proportionately smaller per capita than that of its sister church.

Bishop Strachan's reaction to the spoliation of the Reserves has already been noted, but imbued as he was with an awe of the majesty of the law, he accepted the Church's reduced position and income as legally though not morally right.[82] Henceforth he devoted his energy and ability to preserving and utilizing to the best advantage the decreased patrimony of the Church of England in Canada West. He informed the Society for the Propagation of the Gospel that he wanted the maximum interest and security on all invested funds, and suggested the retention of some of the Reserve lands as inalienable endowments and glebes for his clergy. The restriction provided by Clause 1 of the Clergy Reserves Act which limited the annual sales to 100,000 acres had the full approval of the Bishop. The value of the lands was certain to rise in future, and he suggested further that the King's College plan of demanding twenty shillings per acre be adopted for the Clergy Reserves immediately.

Thus the Clergy Reserves settlement seemed to be off to a relatively auspicious start. But the promulgation in November, 1841, of new sales regulations for the lands opened a new episode in their career. The regulations had been drafted by Sydenham, but were not revealed to the public for some time after his death. The most controversial regulations were the ninth and tenth, which respectively protected lessee's and squatter's rights, and allowed ten years for instalment payments on the purchase price. Obviously the government was more interested in settlement than in a large and quick cash return.[83] Sir R. D. Jackson, *pro tem* Administrator of Canada, was either personally opposed to these terms or apprehensive of their disturbing influence on the province. Stanley, however, refused to interfere with the late Governor General's decision in view of the "very peculiar" circumstances of the Reserves, and similarly informed the vice-regal appointee, Sir Charles Bagot.[84]

Strachan first learned of the new regulations by rumour, and being suspicious of the long silence, he suggested that the Society for the Propagation of the Gospel use its influence to have them referred back to the Church in Canada before their adoption.[85] He felt slighted by being ignored in the formulating of the regulations.[86] When at last he learned the terms through the public press and realized their intention, he understood why the Governor General had not consulted him. The regulations were "most objectionable" and "destructive." At the Bishop's request Chief Justice Robinson drafted a memorial to the Colonial Office outlining the objections to the proposed sales system.[87] But Strachan did not consider it necessary to use the prescribed channels of communication, and Stanley refused to consider the protest until he received Bagot's report on the whole matter.[88]

Bagot entrusted the formulation of a reply to Strachan's remonstrance to R. B. Sullivan, late Commissioner of Crown Lands, who had assisted Sydenham in drawing up the new regulations. Stanley found this report and defence satisfactory and agreed with his previous decision that it would be "unwise and inexpedient" to alter a system so recently established and, in the opinion of all but Strachan, a system so generally satisfying.[89] Two months later, however, Stanley wrote again, this time changing both regulations to the disadvantage of the Clergy Reserves tenants, by demanding one-third of the price as a down payment and allowing only four years more for completion of the purchase. Significantly he enclosed a letter from the Society for the Propagation of the Gospel protesting that the details of the regulations would not obtain the maximum return from leased lands.[90]

In that same month, June, 1842, Stanley forwarded to Bagot another letter from the Society for the Propagation of the Gospel, this one suggesting that the proceeds of the Clergy Reserves sales be reinvested in the purchase of town and city lots which would provide a larger and more enduring endowment and interest.[91] The idea was of course politically impossible as it would have negated the very aim of the recent Act to dispose of the problem of mortmain by liquidating the Reserves lands. It would also have revived the whole agitation of the question which Sydenham had so recently allayed. The architect of the scheme was obviously Bishop Strachan who had convinced the Society for the Propagation of the Gospel of its practicality despite Robinson's advice almost a year before that the proposition would not agree with the terms of the Clergy Reserves Act.[92]

Another year passed quietly before Strachan lifted his pen in connection with the administration of the Clergy Reserves. During that year the Wesleyan Methodists of Canada West, both Canadian and British, again approached the Governor regarding the grant promised them by the Reserves and Union Acts. Victoria College had opened in the autumn of 1842, and the Canadian Wesleyans did not consider that the use of state funds for such a worthy educational project would infringe their form of voluntarism. The British Wesleyans on the other hand held no scruples about accepting government aid, and the Clergy Reserves money owing to the Wesleyan Methodist Church could be used most effectively in the current struggle to dislodge their Canadian brethren from the province. Francis Hincks gave his moral support and advice to the Canadian group, and suggested that a division of the Wesleyan share between the two warring factions might gain government approval.[93] But the claims of both bodies were still denied by the Colonial Office, and only their reunion in 1846 determined the home government to unlock the gate to the garden of forbidden fruit for the benefit of the Wesleyan Methodists.

VIII

The economic and social dislocation which had followed the Rebellion diverted the stream of British capital and emigration away from the Canadian provinces, in addition to sending untold numbers of Canadians into the western United States in search of a more congenial political environment. One result in Canada West was a decline in the sales of the Clergy Reserves, a decline which reached serious proportions in 1843 when only 200 acres were sold in the first six months and only 611 in the whole year. The nadir came in 1844 as total sales dropped to a mere 569 acres.[94] The income of the Clergy Reserves Fund (Canada West), both rentals and investments, dropped by £4,000 or nearly one-third between 1841 and 1843, from £12,830 to £8,815.[95] To Bishop Strachan, guardian of the Church's inheritance, this trend was doubly serious, for the number of Church of England clergy dependent on this income was increasing at the very moment that funds were declining as a result of what seemed to most to be bureaucratic waste and inefficiency. Clearly some new arrangement for managing the Reserves was urgently needed to ensure maximum returns, and the arrangement would have to be something more drastic than his proposal of 1842 for permanent reinvestment in lands if the leak of capital was to be stopped.

The solution proposed was the transfer of control to the Church of England of the portion of the Reserves to which that denomination was entitled. The author of this suggestion is unknown, but Strachan received the popular credit which he did not deny. The plan also had the blessing of Governor General Metcalfe. The first step in the campaign was to have the Church Society of the Diocese of Toronto pass resolutions and the usual petition deploring the present system of mismanaging the Reserves and favouring direct control of the Church's share by the Church Society rather than by the government. The next step was an attempt to enlist the aid of the Church of Scotland. The Reverend Thomas Gale, Moderator of Synod, was informed by Strachan of the Anglican plans, and the suggestion was implicit that the Synod would do well in its own interest to adopt the same course. "Our object," concluded Strachan, "is so just & reasonable that I do not anticipate any serious difficulty in its attainment, more especially as the two Churches feel it so necessary to their extension and well being in the Province."[96] It was ever a fault of Strachan to underestimate the convictions of the enemy.

The next meeting of the Church of Scotland Synod witnessed the disruption of that church, and though the causes of the disruption were in nowise Canadian in origin, at least one incidental result was the exclusion of Strachan's direct control scheme from any official attention or action. The Church Society resolutions were printed in the provincial press but were never seriously discussed by the editors. That the Anglican protest against the high cost of administering the Clergy Reserves (over £14,500 in the four years since the Act was passed) contained a large measure of justice and had considerable support is evidenced by the remarks of the *Christian Guardian* on July 10, 1844. The charges of waste, inefficiency, and speculations were not denied, but ever mindful of past battles in the cause of religious equality, the *Guardian* concluded: "The question is, Shall the Episcopalian Church be followed and assisted in requesting a change in the disposition of the Clergy Reserves? It is time that attention were given to the subject."

The Church Society's resolutions coincided in time with the Metcalfe crisis, but came too late in 1843 to be presented to the provincial Legislature in its current session. Metcalfe forwarded the petition to the Colonial Office early in 1844, but Stanley refused to make any definite reply until Metcalfe should send a report.[97] For the greater part of 1844 Metcalfe was forced to carry on the whole government of Canada with the aid of a three-member executive. Not until the Government could be reconstructed and expanded could the Governor go to the country, and not until Parliament was called would the Clergy Reserves question receive any further consideration. Late in January of 1844, however, Metcalfe addressed the Colonial Office regarding the desirability of improving the administration of the Reserves. His suggested scheme was of course the same one which Strachan had proposed, and which had the vice-regal *nihil obstat* as well as the episcopal *imprimatur*. But at least Metcalfe had doubts as to the universal popularity of the idea in Canada West.[98]

When the new Parliament met in November of that year, Metcalfe's interpretation of responsible government had been sustained by the electors, and the Tories had ridden into power once more on vice-regal coat-tails. Petitions supporting the Church Society's resolutions came flooding into the Assembly, seventy-three of them from the Diocese of Toronto and forty-four from Quebec. By contrast only twenty-eight petitions against the scheme were received, though the very first came from an Anglican, John Wetenhall.[99]

The Assembly appointed two separate and partisan committees to consider each group of petitions, and the expected results were obtained. The first committee, headed by Solicitor General Sherwood, reported in favour of granting the Anglican request for control of their share of the Reserves, of offering a similar arrangement to any other interested communions, and of addressing the Queen to this effect; the second committee entirely rejected the scheme, reporting simply in favour of some less·expensive system of management.[100] Its argument shows once more the inherent centripetal nationalism of the smaller religious bodies from which the Reformers drew so much strength. "According to the present law, the management and disposal of the Lands are in the hands of a Government responsible for the same, and over which the Legislature can exercise an active supervision. Should the proposed distribution take place, they would be placed beyond the control of Parliament, and vested in Ecclesiastical Corporations, responsible to no one, and which would dispose of them to their own advantage, and without reference to the general good." The dying Governor omitted to comment on either report when transmitting them to the Colonial Office.[101]

Thus the issue was deferred for another year, but not forgotten. Ninety-nine petitions, seventy of them from Canada West and bearing, it was said, eight thousand names, were presented on behalf of the Church of England scheme of immediate suspension of all Clergy Reserves sales.[102] Again a committee headed by Sherwood reported favourably. But this time the counter-petitions were more numerous.[103] Among the sixty-six memorials opposing the Anglican request were several headed by the names of dissenting clergymen, including seven Baptists. The report of the committee to which these latter petitions were sent follows the example of its counterpart by repeating almost verbatim the arguments adduced in the preceding session. One noteworthy aspect of all these transactions between 1843 and 1846 is the complete rejection of Strachan's siren song by the Church of Scotland. Not once did its members or its clergy offer support to these latest Anglican pretensions. "They seem to have changed their views," remarked the bishop.[104] Probably the memory of the religious census of 1839 was too vivid in their minds.

The whole issue might once more have been ignored by the Assembly if

Sherwood had not moved an Address to the Queen embodying the report of his committee. In London the Society for the Propagation of the Gospel was already communicating with the Colonial Office as Strachan forwarded the draft of a bill to transfer the Reserves. In the covering letter he expressed doubt of ultimate success, for though the Select Committee had publicly acknowledged the mismanagement of the Reserves it seemed impossible to get an Address through the Legislature as the Colonial Office had wished.

The reason is obvious, the influence of the Church is drowned in the united Legislature—the great majority are her enemies and would desire to see her stripped of every means of support.
It is impossible to get Justice or anything savouring of Justice to the Church of England from the United Legislature in Canada, & this I foretold as my chief ground of objection to the Union. The Roman Catholics can get any thing they want, & the Dissenters much, but the Church can get nothing, that can with any sort of colour [?] be prevented. The property of the Church since the Union has been under the direction of Romanists—the Commissioners appointed to value the reserves were in general low people unqualified, & interested [sic] & in general hostile to the Church in consequence the valuation on an average is little more than ¼. Indeed so much ashamed is the Govt at the valuation, that they have just stopped the sales under the admission that the valuation is too low.[105]

The decision of the Executive Council, taken eleven days before Sherwood's motion, to suspend all sales of Clergy Reserves pending re-evaluation[106] complemented the motion for an Address. The result was a minor crisis and a major debate. The excuse for suspension was a despatch from the newest Colonial Secretary, W. E. Gladstone. The young free-trader had already been numbered among Strachan's correspondents when he was defending the rights of the Church of England in the Clergy Reserves debates·of 1840. Gladstone requested a full report from Lord Cathcart, Administrator of Canada, on the management of the Reserves, as well as Cathcart's opinions for or against Strachan's direct control scheme. The stated purpose of the Executive Council's order was "to prevent a further sacrifice of property, intended for the spiritual advantage of the people." Upon a closer examination of the situation the Executive authorized increases of from 25 to 125 per cent in the selling price of the Reserves.

Cathcart's report must have been as disappointing to Gladstone as it was to the Church of England in Canada West. Currently 40 per cent of expenses of the Crown Lands Department were charged against the Reserves Fund, a charge amounting to some 20 per cent of the Fund's annual income, which, on the advice of the Department itself, Cathcart recommended should be reduced by one-half. Valuation of the lands was admitted by all to be below their intrinsic worth. But as for the general regulations governing sales Cathcart did not share the Executive Council's opinion that alterations were necessary. And he reminded the Imperial bureaucrats that neither of the conflicting reports from the two committees in 1844 had been adopted by the Assembly "and cannot, therefore, be viewed as expressing the views either of that branch of the Legislature, or of the inhabitants of the Province."[107] Indeed during the present session, as during the past one, numerous petitions both for and against the Bishop's control scheme had been presented, and even now a committee report thereon was in the process of preparation.

With this Gladstone had to be satisfied for the moment, and before matters could be further advanced in Canada, Peel's free trade Government had collapsed completely. But one closing remark by Gladstone shows plainly the failure of British Conservatism to plumb the vagaries of colonial opinion, especially in its more radical form of egalitarian frontierism.

Upon a retrospect of what has already occurred, it cannot be said that the transactions with regard to [the Clergy Reserves] since the Act of 1840, have, as a whole, been satisfactory in their character or results, or that justice has been done in all respects to the fund, although it might have been hoped that when the jealousies connected with its former appropriation had been extinguished, by the surrender in 1840 of the exclusive claim of the Church of England, and by the re-distribution consequent on that surrender, there would have been an unanimous disposition on all hands, to unite for the purpose of rendering the fund available for its purposes, generalised, as they were, in the utmost possible degree.[108]

In the Assembly Draper hastened to explain that the suspension of sales was only temporary, being occasioned by the re-evaluation of the lands.[109] Receiver General William Morris announced one month later in the Legislative Council that sales had already been resumed and that the recent suspension was unconnected with the Anglican petitions. But the supporters of John Toronto would not let the controversy die. Solicitor General Sherwood, who had so flagrantly abused Cabinet solidarity during the University debates of the last session, now rose independently to move his Address to the Queen founded on the prayer of the petitions. Sherwood reiterated the claim that the Church of England could manage its share of the Reserves more economically than the government, and offered to divide the actual lands by lot among all interested denominations. This generous proposal was rejected on behalf of the Church of Scotland by John A. Macdonald. James Hervey Price, fated to become the Clergy Reserves' "man of destiny" in a few short years, rose to state that three-quarters of the people believed the settlement of 1840 was an injustice, but had submitted for the sake of peace and prosperity. To vest the Reserves in the clergy would reopen an old wound, and the operation would inevitably result in complete confiscation of the whole endowment. Ogle R. Gowan repeated this warning, and added that the scheme of direct investment would establish a tenant system in Canada West to destroy the backbone of the province, its solid yeomanry.

No one disputed this last remark, for Gowan could speak with first-hand knowledge of the tragedy of his native Ireland. The supporters of the petitions replied that they assumed a limit would be set on the Church's control if granted. It was Baldwin who set the tone of moderation for closing the protracted debate. He deprecated the reopening of the Clergy Reserves question, but he was not so much opposed to the purpose of the petitions as to the possible complications. On this cue Gowan offered an amendment that the Reserves be sold at the smallest expense and as quickly as possible. This amendment was carried 37 to 14, and Sherwood's motion for the Address was lost by 13 to 31, thus ending the Church of England's last hope of managing what it considered to be its own property.

IX

The Government which rejected Strachan's scheme for vesting the Anglican share of the Reserves in the Church Society was the same one which had for two sessions threatened the Anglican hold on King's College. But it was a conservative Government, and the most friendly to the Church of England which was politically possible. The Sherwoods and Boulton were incapable of attracting or holding sufficient power to control the Legislature, split as it was into innumerable, indefinable, and ever changing incohesive groups. With such a chameleon Assembly as that of the second Canadian Parliament, Strachan could not but acknowledge that weak authority of William Draper as preferable to that of

Robert Baldwin. Both were Anglicans, but poor ones in Strachan's estimation, and it was simply a choice of the lesser of two evils. The Bishop now accepted the Government's revision of the administration of the Clergy Reserves, and henceforth kept silent on the subject until time and circumstances forced him to defend the Church's patrimony again in one last glorious but futile battle.

During the remainder of 1846 and all of 1847 hardly a reference was made to the Clergy Reserves question. In 1845 interest on the New Sales under 3 & 4 Victoria c. 78, showed a profit for the first time, but every penny of this £1,524 was already pledged to Anglican stipends.[110] Even when the crucial general election occurred in the last weeks of 1847 candidates neglected the old grievance of Clergy Reserves for what seemed to be a much more exciting and promising issue—John A. Macdonald's University Endowment Division Bill.

Baldwin was one of the few Reformers to mention the Clergy Reserves on the hustings, and this he did only in an off-hand manner. Ridiculing the internal divisions of Draper's Executive, Baldwin reminded his constituents of one striking instance, the Anglican petitions on the Clergy Reserves, where the Administration had "no opinion at all." "Their four Law Officers dividing two and two for and against the investment, and their Inspector-General, Provincial Secretary, Commissioner of Works and Commissioner of Crown Lands, following suit in corresponding couples two for and two against it. And that too on a division of 37 to 14, in a house that gave them as a Ministry, its general support."[111] Thus the election of 1847 passed into history, and the Reformers won a smashing triumph with only scant reference to that staple grievance which had inflamed the whole province exactly one decade before.

Now the Reformers had their first real taste of power since the disastrous day of Sir Francis Bond Head. The brief exodus from the wilderness of opposition which terminated so abruptly in the Metcalfe crisis had embittered rather than discouraged the ideological heirs of Upper Canadian Reformism. Their sense of frustration at the hands of Arthur, Sydenham, and Metcalfe was deeply ingrained, and most of the ills against which Mackenzie, Lount, and Matthews had taken up arms and for which Bidwell still remained in exile were yet to be righted. At last the necessary constitutional power to reform was in their grasp. No muskets would be required to end injustice and establish true responsible government. If such sentiments were not voiced openly, if the feeling of triumph was somewhat anticlimactic, nevertheless the Reformers of Canada West must have looked on the accession of the Great Ministry as the beginning of a reign of righteousness and retribution.

It has been noted that Strachan's hopes between 1844 and 1846, however fruitless they had been in the Legislature, had not been entirely overlooked or forgotten by his political opponents. Hot on the heels of the general elections came the incident which turned the tide in the history of the Clergy Reserves. On January 29, 1848, just five days after the Reformers had swept to victory at the polls, the *Canada Gazette* announced that a surplus of £1,800 from the New Sales, over and above the established charges, had accumulated. All religious denominations were invited to apply for a share thereof. Thus the golden apple of discord was thrown unexpectedly in the path of the Reform racers who had barely entered the course.

The announcement in the *Gazette* stated that each applicant must apply to the Clerk of the Executive Council before July 1 next, and state the number of members in its communion as well as the purpose for which its share of the money would be used. It was a foregone conclusion that such strict voluntarists as the Baptists, Congregationalists, United Presbyterians, and the three smaller Methodist bodies would not yield to the temptation. They would assuredly hold fast to the old faith—Clergy Reserves for education! [112] The Churches of England and Scotland were already in receipt of their shares and could claim no greater portion. The two doubtful cases were the Wesleyan Methodists, whose receipts from state aid were insignificantly small, and the Free Church which had lost its stipends at the disruption.

As the Wesleyan Methodist Conference met in June it was possible for that body to speak collectively. It requested a share of the Reserves money for its educational projects and for "distressed parsonages," a further departure from the voluntarist tradition.[113] The Free Church Synod did not meet until July, but in the interval no less than five congregations, all of them, significantly, in the eastern end of Upper Canada, had petitioned for some of the £1,800. The request of the Brockville Presbytery that Synod take advantage of the Government's offer caused much heart-searching in that body, and a committee finally reported that though the endowments might be legal, their acceptance should be judged by "Christian expediency." [114]

Since the money was offered without reference to truth or error the Synod decided that acceptance would have a divisive effect on the church and "would tend to diminish the usefulness of ministers and the liberality of the people in contributing to the support of the Gospel." The net result of the Synod's deliberations was a resolution forbidding any more congregations to apply for Clergy Reserves money, and the appointment of a commission to visit and dissuade those which had already written to the Government. This victory for voluntarism can be credited to the influence of Peter and George Brown and their *Banner* and *Globe*. The laity of the Free Church had frustrated the desire of its clergy to obtain financial independence.

The Government also received petitions from several other denominations, some of which must have been quite unexpected. In addition to three Lutheran and one Moravian request for money, Vicar General Angus Macdonell requested on behalf of the Roman Catholic Church that its share of the Protestant Clergy Reserves Fund be granted to Regiopolis College.[115] Not all the petitioners, however, were in search of government aid. The United Presbyterian Synod and the Baptist Union both protested officially against the division of the surplus, and reaffirmed their conviction that the Reserves should be used for national education. The Baptist Union went even further. It passed a resolution which voiced the sentiment of all voluntarists, namely,

That the manner in which the funds arising from the sale of that part of the Public Domain, called the Clergy Reserves, are now appropriated, is unsatisfactory to all—that the law upon which that arrangement is based, has always been looked upon in the light of a compromise, —that most, if not all parties, have only been waiting for a suitable time for opening the question afresh, in order to a final adjustment—that such an agitation has been commenced by the Church of England,—and that, in the opinion of this Union, all the said funds ought to be spent in support of Education, to be enjoyed alike by all the people.[116]

How widespread this desire "for opening the question afresh," or for a complete reappraisal of church and state relations in Canada may have been, cannot be accurately known. But the course of subsequent events proves that the desire for drastic action on the Clergy Reserves question was shared by a majority of the lay citizens of Canada West. Even in 1848 as the offer of a division of the spoils was disturbing these various religious bodies, Elgin had prorogued the provincial Parliament less than a month after the session began, his aim being to protect the new ministers from their radical friends. "Besides it is, I think, quite as well," he wrote, "that my reform advisers, who are somewhat recklessly spurred on by a section of their supporters, should have time to look before they leap." [117]

During the latter half of 1848 a number of the smaller religious newspapers began a persistent agitation of the Clergy Reserves issue. The *Record* and the *Globe* combined in an attack on the Wesleyan Methodists for their recent application to the Government. Slowly but inexorably the pressure was mounting for some measure which would close for ever the lid of "Pandora's Box," and dump it and its contents into the sea of public ownership where it could nevermore disturb the religious and political peace of the country. In vain did moderate journals attempt to stem the tide of militant voluntarism. "Would any man but a Demon," demanded one editor, "try to array the people against each other, in a like manner [as in 1837], and under the cloak of religion?" [118] Mistaking the cause for the effect, he warned that the "insidious attempts being made, by self important and giddy pated Editors, to fan the flame of religious discord in the Province ... [will lead] slowly but surely ... to fresh agitation and trouble, and at length to open rebellion."

X

The hopes of the religious reformers ran high as Parliament reconvened in January of 1849. Perhaps at last church and state would be completely separated and the remaining denominational inequalities removed. But these high hopes were doomed to disappointment as Lafontaine pressed the primacy of the Rebellion Losses of Canada East, and in so doing precipitated an Imperial crisis and near civil war. Yet even in the midst of the riots and fire at Montreal, the old grievances of the Clergy Reserves and the endowed Rectories were remembered.

In the Assembly William Notman referred to the existence of the Rectories as a disgrace, and John Wetenhall admitted that the Reserves and Rectories created an odium of his own Church of England. [119] A motion by J. C. Morrison for a committee on Clergy Reserves was supported by Notman and Billa Flint only, but at least it did open a debate on the subject in which the new Ministry were forced to state their position unequivocally. J. H. Price, now Commissioner of Crown Lands, explained that the Executive were not prepared to undertake any measure on either grievance during this session, but these matters would be considered. [120] He also found it necessary to add that the Executive were united on this policy.

The *Globe* approved of the Ministry's explanation. A change must come soon. At present the Church of England contained only two-ninths of the population but received two-fifths of the funds from the Old Sales of Reserves, while the Church of Scotland represented one-fifth of the people and got only one-eleventh of these funds. But the Great Ministry should not be embarrassed by its own supporters during such a crucial period. The issue of church and state relations could be safely postponed until the next session. Nine hundred of Price's constituents in the first riding of York assured him of their continued confidence in his sincere desire to settle the Clergy Reserves question: "Your declaration that no difference of opinion exists between yourself and the other members of the Government upon that or any other Question of general policy assures us, if any assurance were needed, that Reformers have no just cause of Complaint against the present Ministry on these grounds, but your statement that the Clergy Reserve Question would lose nothing by your retirement, is one from which we beg respectfully to dissent." [121]

Obviously the number of Reformers who demanded immediate action on the Clergy Reserves constituted a small minority. But already two sessions of the new Parliament had come and gone. The province would expect action, not words, at the next session, and the Great Ministry would have to bring forward concrete proposals soon if it would retain the loyalty of those Reformers who had hailed it as a politico-religious millenium. The patience of its supporters was only slightly strained, but strain might lead .to exhaustion. The fate of the Government was in its own hands, and the victory of responsible government in 1849 must be justified by practice in 1850. The purposes and power of centripetal nationalism could no longer be denied.

The "final" settlement engineered by Sydenham and circumscribed by the House of Lords had proven unsatisfactory to all but its authors. The creation in 1840 of a pluralistic establishment had seemed a triumph for the centrifugal tendencies of the larger denominations. But even these bodies had merely acquiesced in the settlement, as had the smaller religious bodies, though the reasons and reactions of each had been different. Now a decade later the drastic decline of Clergy Reserves sales, the Anglican attempt to improve the management of the lands, the restored ascendancy of Reformism, and the prospect of a further division of the Reserves funds, all these factors had combined to revive that controversy which had plagued the latter days of the Province of Upper Canada. But the struggle must now be conducted in the United Legislature where new and imponderable forces, unknown before Sydenham's Clergy Reserves settlement, must be faced, utilized, or counteracted, in the defence or destruction of the compromise that had failed.

CHAPTER THREE

THE CLERGY RESERVES, 1849-1857

SECULARIZATION AND COMPENSATION

I

SOMETIME in the latter half of 1849 a decided change in opinion regarding the Clergy Reserves and Rectories occured in Canada West. Religious radicalism became more intimately connected with political radicalism. Hitherto a large part of the population had viewed the settlement of 1840 as a unilateral "agreement" forced on a unwilling but divided province by the home government. A small portion of people comprising the voluntarist denominations had never forsaken the dream of secularizing the Reserves and abolishing the Rectories. Now their appetite had been whetted by Baldwin's University Act which relieved the Church of England of its second dearest temporal possession. But the slowness with which the Reform Government was developing its policies had already drawn the criticism of extremists who expected action on the Reserves and Rectories. The conditions were ready, even conducive, for a union of the forces of political radicalism and militant voluntarism under the newly conceived flag of nationalism. Old and hungry birds of prey were coming home to roost, and to feast on ancient enemies. A complete separation of church and state must soon come. The only question was that of timing.

Perhaps the change began with the great Reform dinner held in Guelph in June, 1849. Responding to the toast "William Notman Esq., and Civil and Religious Liberty," Notman repeated once more that hallowed dictum that all men were created equal. The Clergy Reserves, he declared, were both obnoxious and divisive. For the peace of the province they must go.[1] That same month the Reverend Andrew Ferrier was tried and convicted by the Free Church Synod of advocating voluntarism and disestablishment in his pamphlet, *The Tower of Babel*. The popular reaction to the trial within the Free Church showed that the laity and part of the clergy of that denomination shared Ferrier's convictions.

The continued disturbed condition of the province, the annexation movement, and the British American League, attracted more attention at first than the growing clamour for secularization of the Reserves and Rectories. Elgin seemed quite unaware of this latter development; at least he failed to mention it specifically to Grey until early in 1850.[2] But through the countryside the signs were unmistakable. In September a large public meeting in Darlington Township, attended by Congregationalists, Episcopal Methodists, and other voluntarists, passed resolutions condemning Clergy Reserves, sectarian education, and state aid to religion.[3] Elsewhere Crown Lands Commissioner Price was forced to deny publicly certain press reports that he had left the Ministry because of differences over its Clergy Reserves policy.[4] The Hamilton *Provincialist* and the Guelph *Advertiser* asked why the *Globe*, their acknowledged champion of reform, remained silent on this subject.[5] The *Examiner* too joined the chorus of the dissatisfied and became its strongest voice. The *Globe* replied weakly on November 10 that it favoured reopening the Clergy Reserves question, but "we can see no sense in 'running a muck' about it."[6] George Brown was still confident that Parliament would take all possible steps in the matter at its next session.

Before the end of 1849 the first split had appeared in the Reform party. The Clear Grits had come into being as a separate entity with a popular platform of radical reform and an effective, if small, organization. The nationalization of the Clergy Reserves and Rectories was comprehended in the eleventh plank of their platform—local control of local affairs. Snowball-like the Grits gained followers and newspapers as they moved forward. The Long Point *Advocate* and Dundas *Warder* supported the other Grit journals unequivocally, while the Methodist Episcopal *Canada Christian Advocate* offered its influence to the cause more reservedly.[7] Throughout the winter and early spring of 1850 Grit meetings were held at various points in Canada West, and at each the prescribed resolutions calling for an end to the church-state connection, especially in the form of Reserves, were duly proposed and passed. By the time Parliament met again in May every Reform paper had become involved in the agitation. In addition to the *Globe*, the Bytown *Packet*, the Kingston *Herald*, the Kent *Advertiser*, and the London *Free Press* defended the Government against its impatient critics. But on two points both Grits and Ministerialists were in agreement. The Clergy Reserves belonged not to any particular denominations but to the nation as a whole, and the establishment of perfect religious equality would require the abolition of the Rectories as well.

The first real test of strength between the Grits and the Government came with the by-election for Halton County in March. Caleb Hopkins, radical candidate, spoke in favour of outright repeal of the Clergy Reserves and their devotion to education. John Wetenhall explained the orthodox position that an Imperial Act would be needed so that the Reserves could be disposed of "according to the known wishes of the majority."[8] To the Grits the election brought victory, to the old Reformers defeat, and to Wetenhall insanity and a tragic death.

From this success the Grits went forth to conquer Canada West. Peter Perry, a Reformer tried in the crucible of '37, demanded that the Clergy Reserves be settled in Canada, not at Downing Street.[9] At Markham the "Calebites," as Brown dubbed them, carried resolutions calling for the "abrogation of the fraudulently established Rectories and the appropriation of the Clergy Reserves for purposes of general education."[10] A vote of confidence in the Ministry was lost by a very large majority on this occasion.

Within the Ministry these events were causing consternation and recriminations. Baldwin was making vague promises of action at the forthcoming session, and Price at a testimonial dinner in his honour declared he would never dictate to Britain on the matter of the Reserves.[11] But privately Price and Hincks were pressing their colleagues, particularly Lafontaine, for something more tangible than promises.[12] From the *Examiner* office Charles Lindsey wrote to another Grit editor, Charles Clarke in Elora, of the latest hints dropped by the ministers: "I begin to fear that we shall get no real reforms from the French—there is some truth in the story of 'French domination' depend upon it. What does Hincks mean by saying the French do not feel much interest in settling the Clergy Reserves? Why that they oppose it of course."[13]

In Toronto, where Parliament would soon make its new home, interested parties had stolen a march on the twentieth century by conducting a poll of public opinion on the Clergy Reserves.[14] The results were never announced. A more typically nineteenth-century move was the formation of the Anti-Clergy Reserves Association, one of its purposes being, according to the *Globe,* to pour in petitions from every quarter. Its first meeting was held, significantly, at Knox Church. The speakers of the evening included prominent clergymen of every voluntarist denomination—John Roaf and Adam Lillie, Congregationalists, James Richardson, Methodist Episcopal, James Pyper, Baptist, John Jennings, United Presbyterian, McClure, New Connexion Methodist, and Dr. Willis of the Free Church.[15]

The association was intended to be non-denominational and non-partisan, but the Clear Grits made a concerted drive to capture it for their own purposes. On the usual Reserves resolution Malcolm Cameron, recently converted from Executive Councillor to Grit tub thumper, the difficult Dr. Burns of the Free Church, and James Lesslie, a suspected rebel of '37, all attempted to move an amendment demanding that the Clergy Reserves question be made a ministerial one. This bold attack was repulsed to the tune of much hissing, but by entrenching themselves as executive members of the association, the Grits were able to continue their avocation as thorns in the sides of the moderates.[16]

The silence on the Clergy Reserves of the *Christian Guardian,* the official voice of Wesleyan Methodism in Canada, had been noted and denounced at the meeting in Knox Church. In self-defence the *Guardian* accused the Grits of using the Reserves merely as "a wedge to open the way to other objects of disorganization." Popular opinion as well as the position of the Wesleyan Methodists was so well known that "Denominational agitation is as unnecessary as it is out of place...." As the Reserves did not concern Lower Canada, "It cannot, therefore, be made a *Cabinet* question, even if it were not a matter of legislation now appertaining to the Imperial Parliament. ... We think Lord JOHN RUSSELL has learned some practical lessons on Colonial policy during the last ten years; and that what he obstinately persevered in doing in 1840, he will see the necessity of undoing in 1850."[17]

In April Bishop Strachan departed for England on his vain mission to retrieve King's College for his church. The Reverend Agar Adamson, Church of England, wrote William Morris from Montreal:

I have some notion that the preservation of the Clergy Reserves and of the Rectories will also occupy a portion of his Lordship's attention—of one thing I am quite certain, viz. that it is no light matter which brings him across the Atlantic. ... Mr. Baldwin, I am convinced, will never lend his aid to disturb the present Settlement, but who can tell whether his health will enable him to meet Parliament or if he does, whether he will receive the support of the House of Assembly, and of his Colleagues in resisting the Aggression.[18]

If Strachan did broach the twin subjects of the Reserves and Rectories during the half-year he spent in Britain, there is no hint of it in his correspondence.

From Canada Archdeacon Bethune informed Strachan that the current agitation of the Reserves and Rectories was not serious, but suggested the expediency of a counter-agitation through the Church. "Hints are dropped," he added hopefully, "that the French members (who are far from being pleased with the 'Ministry') will set their faces against any spoliation in that quarter."[19] Such was also the opinion expressed by the Governor General to Lord Grey:

The best friends of the Bishop and the Church. [*sic*] are La Fontaine and his adherents, the very people who have been the objects of their unmeasured abuse. They will vote against any attempt to disturb the Clergy Reserves Settlement—and so long as they do so the U. Canada

Radicals cannot effect their object. This new phase in Canadian politics will I fully expect present itself during the course of next Session and it will be curious to see what consequences it entails—The party pledged to the appropriation of the Reserves to Educational purposes could I rather think carry the majority of the U.C. constituencies. When they find themselves obstructed by their French Canadian allies, they *may* break off from them—in which case the latter will be thrown into the ranks of the Conservatives....[20]

II

As Elgin had anticipated, "this new phase in Canadian politics" did commence with the next session. The absence from the Throne Speech of any reference to the Clergy Reserves and Rectories filled the Grits with righteous glee and the Ministerialists with consternation. The *Globe* expressed regret that the matter was not made a ministerial question, but found some solace in Prince's promise to bring up both subjects as open questions. The Opposition on the right made sport of the Cabinet's lack of progress and the Grits on the left boldly moved a vote of censure.[21]

The *Globe* found itself hard pressed and embarrassed by the Government's silence. Brown accused "the Republican party" (the leading Grit papers, the *Examiner* and the *Provincialist*, now renamed the *North American*) of lacking a sincere desire to settle the Clergy Reserves question.[22] Within the newly founded Anti-Clergy Reserves Association, Lesslie, Dr. Burns, and William McDougall, editor of the *North American*, were the authors of repeated disturbances. But a carefully chosen subcommittee of the association did manage to interview Price and Hincks and to get a statement of policy from these two ministers, for whatever it was worth. In the first session, they explained, the Government was new, in the second it faced the Rebellion Losses agitation. Now it was the intention of their Lower Canadian colleagues to join in an Address to the Queen on the Clergy Reserves, since a Bill would be constitutionally impossible.

These explanations seemed satisfactory to most Reformers and the Legislature moved on quietly to the most momentous episode in the eventful history of the Clergy Reserves—the debate on Price's thirty-one resolutions. The first twenty-seven resolutions contained an historical résumé of the development of the problem. The twenty-eighth asserted that constitutional impediments should have been removed in 1840 to enable the Upper Canadian Legislature to settle the question. The next two declared that no religious denomination had a vested interest in the Reserves, though existing incumbents ought to be treated most liberally, and that the most equitable settlement would be enabling legislation by the Imperial Parliament to provide for continuation of present charges during a limited period, and reinvestment of all future revenues in the provincial Parliament, to be appropriated "as in its wisdom it may think proper."[23] The final resolution called for an address to the Queen, praying for the repeal of 3 & 4 Victoria, c. 78, subject to the conditions enumerated. These resolutions were supported by thirty petitions.

The ensuing debate followed the established pattern, but was conducted, as Elgin reported, "with great calmness. [*sic*]—there has been no excitement either within or without the walls of Parliament."[24] Price, Hincks, and Baldwin begged for moderation. The Clergy Reserves must be secularized, but innocent incumbents must not be made to suffer. The Reserves might well be appropriated to education in Hincks' opinion, if they were reinvested. Henry Sherwood and J. H. Cameron accused the Reformers of hatred of the Church of England, and expressed doubts concerning the good faith of the Government.[25] Why, they demanded to know, should the Church of England be despoiled and thereby destroyed, while the Church of Rome, which was many times as wealthy, was entirely spared? Lafontaine replied confidently that he feared no reprisals on his own denomination.

Each resolution was voted on and passed separately, the majority ranging as high as 63 to 3. But on the twenty-ninth, which denied the existence of any vested rights, the margin in favour was only two votes. Numbered in the yeas were eighteen Upper Canadian members and eighteen Lower, in the nays eighteen Upper and sixteen Lower, including Lafontaine. "Coon" Cameron, who with Caleb Hopkins, had voted with the Tories, now tried in vain to have the issue settled at once by a Bill. On the final vote, for the adoption of the Address, the division was 46 in favour and 23 against, a clear majority of two to one. The essential point, however, was that the resolutions and the Address did not constitute Government policy. They were purely and simply the voice of the Legislative Assembly of the United Canadas.

Elgin was dissatisfied with the course of events regarding the Clergy Reserves and at a loss as to what he should say in his despatch. Privately he told Grey, "I know how very inconvenient it is to repeal the Imperial Act which was intended to be a final settlement of the question—but I must candidly say I very much doubt whether you will be able to preserve this Colony if you retain it on the Statute Book." "I do not hesitate to say," Grey replied, "that in my opinion the Assembly is quite right with regard to what they ask & yet I doubt exceedingly whether any bill for repealing the existing law c^d be carried thro' Parl^t."[26]

After two weeks Elgin summoned his courage and forwarded the Address with a despatch suggesting indirectly, as Grey had requested, the best line for the Imperial Government to take.[27] The Governor General intimated that the present regrettable agitation stemmed largely from the misguided interference of the Imperial Parliament in 1840. The Free Church's jealousy of the share of the Reserves money retained by the Church of Scotland had increased the popular envy of the advantageous position held by the two most favoured denominations. By inference the Imperial legislators were advised that only a Canadian settlement of the Clergy Reserves question could silence "the more violent and unscrupulous" agitators and forestall the defenders of the Reserves from their persistent but short-sighted endeavours to influence English opinion in their favour.

Although Strachan was on the other side of the Atlantic he was kept fully informed of developments in Canada West, and the Church of England opposition to the attack on the Reserves was not silenced by the Bishop's absence.

Your Lordship will ere this have been made painfully aware [wrote Henry Patton, Rural Dean of Cornwall] that our untiring enemies aided by some Judas like Members of our own Communion in the Legislature, have again attempted to disturb the settlement of the Clergy Reserve Question. . . . I am now busy in getting subscribers to a Petition to the Queen, against the iniquitous Scheme of proposing Spoliation. It cannot surely be possible, that the Queen & Home Government will sanction the sacrilegious Act, & yet we have been painfully taught on more than one occasion of late, not to put our faith in Princes.[28]

The Bishop of Montreal had first suggested this counter-attack, and Archdeacons Stuart and Bethune at once called on the clergy of the Diocese of Toronto to defend the existing settlement with petitions.[29] The *Church*, the Cobourg *Star*, and the *Patriot* rallied popular support for this move, the last named paper producing some very Jacobite arguments on behalf of the "National Church."[30]

On the other hand Price's resolutions seemed too moderate for some voluntarists. The *Watchman* objected strenuously to the idea that present incumbents should be assured of their gratuities.[31] But the mild radical storm really centred around the *Christian Guardian* which still maintained its self-imposed silence. At last the *Guardian* was forced to reply to charges that the Wesleyan Methodists had been bribed into silence with a share of the Reserves in 1840. Practically the whole number of May 22, 1850, was devoted to a documentary review of the history of the Clergy Reserves question, and once more the two points of Wesleyan Methodist policy were stated explicitly.[32] Wesleyan Methodism would and did accept Reserves money for education, though not for clerical salaries. It would not join in the agitation of a question which was now entirely a matter for the Imperial Parliament to resolve. Whatever the Wesleyan Methodists thought of the Clergy Reserves, they would abide by the decision of the politicians.

III

With the passing of Price's resolutions the Clergy Reserves question dropped into temporary abeyance for several months. True, the Church of England continued to collect signatures for its petitions against spoliation, but the province seemed to take little notice of this campaign. In fact Elgin could give Grey no information on the subject.[33] Only the most extreme opponents of the Clergy Reserves continued to grumble about the lack of action towards secularization. The year 1850 ended and Grey still had not replied to the Assembly's resolutions. At last, early in March, Elgin issued the text of Grey's reply which had just been received.[34] After full and deliberate consideration, the Imperial Government had decided that, much as the reopening of the Clergy Reserves question was regretted, it was prepared to recommend a Bill to Parliament which would give the provincial Legislature full authority to settle the Reserves as they saw fit, "provided that existing interests are respected."

The *Globe* was overjoyed at the prospect of reinvestment and hailed the decision as irrefutable evidence of the good intentions of the Canadian Government which had been so much maligned by the Clear Grits. The *Christian Guardian* printed Grey's despatch, but its neutrality forbade any editorial declarations thereon.[35] From England came more doleful news for Bishop Strachan. The Society for the Propagation of the Gospel hoped to postpone any Clergy Reserves Bill until the next session of the Imperial Parliament, but it frankly despaired of any ultimate success in warding off the blow.[36] The fate of the Reserves would rest in the final analysis with public opinion in Canada West.

Meanwhile Strachan had found a tardy but useful ally in the Church of Scotland which shared the Church of England's desire to retain the settlement of 1840. William Morris had been commissioned by the Synod to proceed to England to lobby the interests of the Kirk[37] as he had in 1837, but this time he was to defend, not demand, its share of the Reserves. Kingston Presbytery sent a memorial to the Imperial Parliament condemning any diversion of the Reserves from the support of religion to secular education, but Elgin took the precaution of obtaining a scathing memorandum on the memorial from J. H. Price to enlighten the Colonial Office. The memorial from Kingston was immediately followed by a similar plea against dispossession which the commission of the Kirk Synod had prepared, and the colonial committee of the mother church in Scotland asked the Imperial Cabinet directly to reconsider its decision, in favour of maintaining the Establishment in Canada.[38]

Within the Church of England a publicity campaign aimed at public opinion in Great Britain was now under way. The Anglican bishops of Toronto, Quebec, and Montreal had agreed upon an Address to the Queen protesting the spoliation of the "remnant and pittance" of endowment which they still had.[39] Strachan had also prepared a *Letter on the Clergy Reserves Question* addressed to Lord John Russell but intended for popular consumption.[40] Although Chief Justice Robinson had approved the pamphlet the Bishops of Montreal and Quebec objected, as Strachan had anticipated, to his "shortness" with Lord John.[41] The *Letter* was an appeal for protection of the small quantity of Reserves money remaining. The Church of Rome in Canada East had ten times the endowment of the Church of England, but the latter body, which had already been denied its own separate schools and university, was now threatened with the loss of the last vestige of its privileged position. Strachan ignored the fact that most of the Roman Catholic endowment had come from private bequests. Few of its clergy could be classed with the Church of England ministers as civil servants. Strachan's strongest defence of the *status quo* was based on the sacredness of the 1840 compact between Russell and the Bench of Bishops.

From the Society for the Propagation of the Gospel Strachan received intimations that Lord Grey and the bishops favoured self-government for the Church in Canada, presumably in compensation for the possible loss of the Reserves.[42] Even Gladstone, who professed to admire Strachan, was not prepared to oppose the public opinion of the colonists. Hawkins, secretary of the Society for the Propagation of the Gospel, advised Strachan that it was improbable that the Imperial Government could introduce the Clergy Reserves Bill during its current session, but again he warned him, "*Everything depends upon the resolution and perseverance of the Church Party in the Colony.*"[43]

In Canada the situation was complicated for the Church of England by the demand of a score of its clergy that arrears of their salaries dating back to 1833 be paid by the Society for the Propagation of the Gospel, or failing that, by the provincial government. The Reverend Dominic Blake had managed to obtain £900 of back pay, and Strachan could easily foresee the effect of a general move in this direction upon his hopes to save the Reserves.[44] Indeed, he believed that the attitude of these same clergy towards the problem of their meagre salaries in 1848 and 1849 had provided the pretence for the reopening of the Clergy Reserves question.

The attitude of the Roman Catholics in Canada East was a crucial factor in Strachan's plans. Alternately he threatened and cajoled them. Publicly the Bishop warned that the end of the Reserves would encourage attacks on Roman Catholic endowments, while at the same time he invited a *rapprochement* of the two denominations for mutual defence. Privately he accused the Roman Catholics of joining with dissenters and radicals to pass Price's resolutions.[45] In fact he regarded the Roman Catholic votes in the Assembly as a species of revenge on Canada West for Montreal's loss of the seat of government.

The Church of Scotland too was encountering difficulties in its efforts to forestall secularization of the Reserves. "Many of our Church are not sorry at the movement made in reference to the Clergy Reserves," wrote one of its ministers, "as they think it the prelude to the overturning of the whole Roman Catholic Establishment, and look for a religious war...."[46] The publication of

Grey's despatch promising Imperial legislation prepared the Church of Scotland for the necessity of compromise, and the Synod commission on the Reserves advised its envoy, William Morris, of its full confidence in his judgment and authorized him to accept any "proper and reasonable" settlement, provided that it be absolutely final.[47] But at the very moment when Morris was about to sail for Britain an incident occurred which, he said, tempted him to turn back, if it had not been that his passage was already paid.

This incident was the publication of a letter by Captain J. M. Strachan, the Bishop's eldest son, in which he suggested a division of the Reserves among all Protestant denominations on a per capita basis. This proposal seemed to Morris to cut the ground from under the feet of the Church of Scotland. "I cannot fancy that his proposal is made by any authority from the Bishop or authorities of the Church and indeed I am satisfied it is not," Hugh Allan told Morris, although he did believe that division would be acceptable to some Anglicans.[48] The *Globe* noted that such a plan would give the Church of England very little more than its present share, but the Reserves were not the Church's property to dispose of—they belonged to the people.[49] Besides, at least a third of the population of Canada West were voluntarists by the *Globe*'s estimate, and they would never accept public money. Once more the *Globe* asserted that the Reserves must be used for education, or "some general purpose in which all may agree." Such unanimity must have seemed an obvious impossibility, even to the optimistic George Brown.

In England Morris was busy writing W. E. Gladstone and the Duke of Argyll, spokesman for the Church of Scotland, asking them when the dreaded Clergy Reserves Bill would be introduced.[50] The reception of Morris and his mission by officials of the mother church was disappointingly cool. But he was granted an interview with Lord Grey after some delay. Morris explained to the Colonial Secretary that "the members of the Scots church in Canada always looked to their claims on the clergy fund under the two Imperial Statutes as of a nature to render the alienation of it to secular purposes unconstitutional or illegal," to which Grey replied that nothing done by Parliament was illegal.[51]

Receiving no encouragement for the extreme claims of his denomination, Morris offered a compromise, the terms of which are not recorded, but this too was rejected by Lord Grey. In fact, Grey warned Morris that only the salaries of present incumbents would be ensured, and even these would not have been respected by the Assembly but for the efforts of Lafontaine, a Roman Catholic. At least Morris fulfilled one objective of his mission by sending Lord Grey the petitions against the alienation of the Reserves prepared by the Canadian Synod and the Lay Association, as well as the sixty-two petitions from individual congregations.[52] But having failed to dissuade Grey from his avowed Clergy Reserves policy, Morris now turned to the Opposition in the person of Lord Stanley. In a friendly interview Stanley advised against any compromise, and held out the hope that the Clergy Reserves Bill would be postponed in the Imperial Parliament and that a change of government might save the day and the Reserves.[53] This was the same straw at which the Church of England was clutching so frantically, and the Kirk in Canada considered it their best and only chance of stopping secularization.[54]

The announcement that the Bill would in fact be held over until the next session convinced Morris that his petitions might better be saved for a future and fresher submission.[55] It had become increasingly obvious to the Canadian

Kirk that the assistance of its parent Church of Scotland in Britain would be at best of doubtful value, if it were available. As a final step Morris copied Strachan's example and published the arguments of his own denomination, set like a sermon in eleven points.[56] He blamed the long agitation of the Clergy Reserves question on Bishop Strachan, whose exclusive claim to the property had been the cause of the revived interest in 1845 and 1846. Price, not the people, demanded secularization, and the test resolution on that topic had been passed by the narrow margin of two votes. The Legislative Council had been deliberately by-passed when the Address to the Queen was formulated.

Above all, Morris asserted, the prescriptive right of the Protestant clergy to the Reserves had been allowed by the passage of sixty years, and the Roman Catholics should be excluded from sharing in the funds. The Reserves must not be alienated from religious to secular purposes, Morris begged Argyll in a parting letter, to which the Duke replied with the same advice offered Strachan by the Society for the Propagation of the Gospel, "All will ultimately depend on the efforts made in Canada to neutralize the movements against the religious provision of the Reserves."[57]

IV

While William Morris was log-rolling vainly in England, the agitation of the Clergy Reserves question broke out anew in Canada in anticipation of the approaching session of the provincial Legislature. But a most significant change was in process as the result of George Brown's defeat by the returned exile, William Lyon Mackenzie, at the Haldimand by-election held during April of 1851. The famous "Papal Aggression" issue in the *Globe* estranged many Roman Catholics from the Reform cause as represented by George Brown, and this, combined with the lukewarm support offered him by the Ministry, had cost Brown the election. The subsequent policy of Brown and his newspaper towards the Church of Rome and the old Reformers is too well known to need repeating, and though Brown stood apart from both the Clear Grits and the Ministry of the day, the influence of the *Globe* and its editor on the course of the Clergy Reserves question cannot be gainsaid. The reform party gradually lost its most important mouthpiece, and Hincks gained an implacable enemy. The Clear Grits alone rejoiced in the results of the Haldimand election, although some conservatives viewed the "Little Rebel" as a consolation prize— "anybody rather than George Brown."[58]

The spring brought with it a spate of public Clergy Reserves meetings by both parties. At the first of these, held in Toronto's St. Lawrence Hall, the English Revolution was refought verbally with less conclusive results than those of the seventeenth century.[59] But the *Spectator* and the *Statesman* were beginning to revolt against the extremism of the High Church party, whom Brown had dubbed "the Church Union," and criticism also came as expected from the radical press.[60] Strachan at last seemed to realize the potential utility of lay influence and planned to capitalize on it by calling lay representatives to his forthcoming triennial visitation of the clergy. Such a move might offset the continuing unrest among those Anglican clergy who had threatened to address a memorial to the Legislature for their salary arrears last year. That minor struggle was developing as a contest between frontierism and metropolitanism as the backwoods clergy denounced the larger stipends of their urban colleagues. At least one rector said he no longer felt obliged to defend the Reserves, or to work for the return of a member in his country who would be friendly to the Church and its Reserves.[61]

The Anti-Clergy Reserves Association changed its name to the Anti-State Church Association (after the British organization which was supporting secularization in Canada). When a meeting of the association was broken up by a Tory strong-arm squad, this proceeding was lauded by the *Church, Patriot, Colonist,* and the *Mirror.*[62] The fact that the Reverend Benjamin Lett had acted as spiritual adviser to the rioters increased the vehemence of the denunciations voiced by the *Globe, Spectator, Record* and Guelph *Advertiser.*[63] When the adjourned meeting convened two weeks later it was again attacked by rowdies, this time with such violence that the military had to be called out to relieve the besieged Reformers in the St. Lawrence Hall. To Brown's credit it must be said that he was equally critical of the reformers who disturbed a "pro-church-state" meeting in Cobourg.[64]

At Bowmanville where reformism, political and religious, was almost unchallenged, an Anti-State Church Association meeting passed resolutions asserting that the Clergy Reserves Act of 1840 had been submitted to, not acquiesced in, and pledged its members to oppose the election of any legislator not sworn to abolition of the Reserves. The same principles were adopted verbatim at a similar gathering in Brooklin.[65] But the interest shown in these particular meetings was far overshadowed by that shown in the public discussion on the Clergy Reserves and Rectories held at Simcoe under Baptist auspices. Here, for two days running, three ministers of the Church of England and one of the Church of Scotland defended the state endowments of their denominations against the logic and oratory of six Baptists, a United Presbyterian, a Congregationalist, a Wesleyan Methodist, and a Methodist Episcopal, all of whom advocated absolute voluntarism.[66] Among the participating clergy were the troublesome Dr. Burns, John Roaf, James Richardson, and William Ormiston, who, though a Presbyterian, was one of the first graduates of Victoria College, while the Reverend Benjamin Cronyn, future Bishop of Huron, was the outstanding spokesman for the defence. The great discussions solved nothing though they did make clear the differences between the contending forces. But at least, according to all reform accounts, the principles of voluntarism and separation of church and state carried off the palms for polemics.

Added strength for the cause of secularization came in the official pronouncements of two denominations. The Congregationalist Union, whose position had never been in doubt, resolved at its annual meeting that the Clergy Reserves should be appropriated to general education.[67] More important, however, were the resolutions of the Wesleyan Methodist Conference which had hitherto maintained its policy of interested neutrality despite the jibes of absolute voluntarists. The Conference still viewed the settlement of 1840 as "an infringement of the constitutional rights of the people of Upper Canada," and regretted the selfish efforts of the Churches of England and Scotland to perpetuate denominational advantages "at the expense of perpetuating a wrong against their country, and against their brethren of other Protestant churches."[68] On behalf of the Wesleyan Methodists, one-fifth of Upper Canadians, the Conference concurred in the efforts of the Legislature to arrange a truly Canadian settlement based on the voluntarist principle.

By implication the Wesleyan Methodist Church was prepared to forgo its own small vested interest in the Reserves. This policy, explained the *Christian Guardian,* was not dictated by lay pressure, "as between the vast majority, if not all the ministers and people, no diversity of opinion exists on the question of the Clergy Reserves."[69] Despite this disclaimer, the pattern of voluntarism imposed by the laity on a somewhat unwilling clergy seems to parallel the developments which had occurred within the Free Church since the revival of the Clergy Reserves agitation in 1848.

The provincial Parliament which sat at Toronto from late May to the end of August was undisturbed by the violence which raged around it in the temporary capital. Nine petitions mostly from municipal councils were received in favour of devoting all proceeds from the Reserves to education, but sixty-four petitions, including many signed by Church of England clergy and one from Strachan on behalf of the "Episcopal Conference" so recently convened, protested any legislative interference with the clergy's vested rights in the Reserves.[70] Price proposed and carried without serious difficulty an address of thanks to the Queen for the "gracious" reception of the Address of the last session based on his resolutions. The Legislative Council concurred in this by a majority of two to one. The Tories still objected to any disturbance of the existing Reserves settlement and the Grits, only three in number, demanded a secularization Act in anticipation of the Imperial enabling statute.[71] But the whole debate was in Lord Elgin's opinion "not very animated."[72]

Elgin agreed with his Cabinet that the policy of constitutional gradualism must not be surrendered to either party of extremists.[73] The Government had no trouble fending off such amendments but the support which it commanded within the House was not truly representative of its position in the country.[74] The most sanguine Ministerialist could not ignore the fact that radicalism was growing in Canada West, particularly in the Niagara Peninsula, and that the general election, which must come soon, would reflect this popular dissatisfaction with the slow progress towards secularization. But this last session, the "railway Session," of the first Reform Parliament since Sir Francis Bond Head called the "bread and butter" election of 1836, ended on a note of uncertainty and unrest. Robert Baldwin, the man with a single idea, adamantly refused to reconsider his resignation after the desertion of the Upper Canadians on the Court of Chancery question. The leadership devolved automatically on Francis Hincks whose very ability made him suspect among the mediocrity of his fellow reformers. To complete the unsettlement of the Reform party, already split by Clear Grittism and the independence of George Brown and his journal, the Imperial Government announced that its Clergy Reserves Act must of necessity be postponed until its next session. This decision had been long in the making and had Elgin's fullest approval, inasmuch as it had become apparent to Russell and Grey that the Bill had only the slimmest chance of passing the House of Lords.[75]

In Canada this delay was bound to bring hope to the Tories, strength to the Grits, and the confusion of disappointment to the Ministerial Reformers. Strachan confidently inferred that Grey would shelve his Reserves Bill forever "unless goaded on by new applications from this quarter."[76] He spoke wildly of a recourse to violence by even the meekest members of his church if the provincial government attempted to confiscate the remaining Reserves. Price, an inveterate enemy of the Church of England, was responsible for all this trouble, and the desertion of the "National Church" by the home government had encouraged such extremists. Grey's projected measure struck at the very heart of the Imperial connection. "You may rest assured," Strachan told the Society for the Propagation of the Gospel, "that Canada will not continue a British Colony seven years after the confiscation of the Church property." Yet he preferred to believe that his propaganda about religious spoliation was telling on the Roman Catholics. "If we can get them and the Members of the Kirk to join us, on the Reserve question we are safe."

Saner and more realistic clerical heads in the Church of England thought differently from the Bishop, and did not hesitate to tell the facts to the Society for the Propagation of the Gospel. The Reverend Septimus Ramsay considered that repeal of the Imperial Act alone could end the Clergy Reserves agitation, but the effect could be mollified by "clogging" it with limitations ensuring the Churches of England and Scotland of their past grants, dividing the residue among other denominations and ending state interference in the matter "once & forever." [77] "If the Bill be not soon repealed, these Demagogues, the Clear Grits, will make Political Capital of it—and it may, and wd probably be, eventually, much worse for us." Religious tories were beginning to see the light of necessity, and their political counterparts would soon follow suit.

v

The resignation of Robert Baldwin, Attorney General, from the Executive Council was followed by that of Lafontaine and Crown Lands Commissioner Price. Officially the Cabinet reorganization did not occur until near the end of October, but rumours of an impending change were rife even before the close of the session. The Reform press insisted that reunion of the shattered party must be based on the principle of separation of church and state [78] inasmuch as disappointments on the Reserves and Rectories questions had been the cause of schism. The *Globe* openly favoured the retirement of Lafontaine, "our great enemy on the Reserve and Rectory questions," because his principles were not "Liberal." [79]

The fact that Dr. John Rolph, the rebel who had run away in 1837, would now return to fight another day in the revamped provincial Ministry, was common knowledge which did not please many Reformers. Rolph's principles regarding the Reserves and Rectories were in considerable doubt. Was not his brother a rector? Price took occasion to criticize his successor publicly before he himself resigned. [80] The inclusion of Rolph and "Coon" Cameron in the new Executive suggested that the Clear Grits had been bought out by the wily Hincks, while the exclusion of that unimpeachable liberal, John Sandfield Macdonald, was generally resented, most especially by Macdonald himself. [81] The decision of George Brown to contest a seat in the coming election was bound to draw around him many of these dissident elements.

In a series of public letters addressed to Hincks through the medium of the *Globe*, Brown presented a formal indictment of the new Ministry based on its past actions and present professions. Hincks had tried to obstruct Morrison's Rectory Bill of 1851 to suspend the presentation of incumbents, upholding the sacredness of vested rights at the same time that he altered two patents—those of London and Peterborough—by legislation. The Government was pledged to pay all costs of the judicial decision of the Rectories case, and obviously Strachan would fight through every court to save the £200,000 since he was assured of a public expense account for his troubles. The new Ministry promised a satisfactory solution to both Reserves and Rectories questions, but failed to explain how this miracle was going to be achieved.[82] In Brown's opinion religious perfidy was the hallmark of the new Executive, and anti-state church men were warned that Hincks and Rolph asked for their support without pledge or explanation.

Every aspect of the relations of church and state seemed to be on the *tapis* for this general election. At least half of the issues raised by the *Globe* were religious in nature, though the University question was now almost eclipsed by Clergy Reserves, Rectories, separate schools, sectarian money grants, ecclesiastical corporations, and denominational marriage rights.[83] At the hustings the "most outrageous pledges" were being exacted of candidates, so Elgin reported, but the election was described elsewhere as the quietest in a generation.[84] The most significant development was the return of a new group of liberal Conservatives in place of the old Tories, thus adding to the numbers of those of all parties favourable to ending the Clergy Reserves agitation by drastic means, even secularization.[85]

The elections returned the combination of Peelite Reformers and Clear Grits to office, but replaced many old faces with new. Baldwin, Lafontaine, Price, and Notman were gone from the ranks of Reform and John Hillyard Cameron and George Sherwood disappeared from a chastened Tory party. According to the *Globe* of April 13, 1852, nineteen pro-Reserves members had been ousted by anti-state church men. The new Government was as strong an organization as could be created in the new Parliament, in Elgin's estimation stronger than the Great Ministry.[86] But now it faced the opposition of George Brown on the left, and solitary though he might be in the large Assembly, he did control the most powerful newspaper in Canada West, and was the acknowledged champion of absolute religious equality. The Government could not expect or afford any quarter.

For some months the Clergy Reserves agitation in Canada West waned from sheer exhaustion, and public interest in the first half of 1852 turned to the nine-day wonder of railways. No further action could or would be taken on the Clergy Reserves until the Imperial Parliament passed its Act of Reinvestment, and the issue became for the moment one of British policy rather than Canadian politics. Hincks had gone to England early in March as one of the joint delegation on the Intercolonial Railway scheme, and was also empowered to deal with the Imperial authorities in the Clergy Reserves issue.[87] He learned on his arrival that Lord John Russell's Government had resigned and the Tories under the Earl of Derby had taken office at the end of February. All Canada waited some statement of the new Government's policy on the Clergy Reserves and Rectories.

Strachan was overjoyed at the news from London and believed that "the calamity of Earl Grey's threatened repeal of the Clergy Reserve Law of 1840" had been averted.[88] But he stretched truth and his own imagination when he told Hawkins that "the change of Ministry has filled Canada with rejoicing. . . . Were a sound Constitutional Governor to be sent out instead of Lord Elgin things would get right." A sounder governor was not sent out, but the Tory policy announced by Colonial Secretary Pakington was just as effective.[89] No Reserves Bill would be introduced this session in the Imperial Parliament because a general election had occured in Canada since Price's resolutions were passed. The Derby Government was not inclined to consent to any measure which would divert the Reserves from their religious purpose, and the Act of 1840 left no ground "for reasonable jealousy or complaint of undue favour to particular religious denominations. . . ." No "Accidental Majority of the Colonial Legislature, however small," would be permitted to divert the Reserves from their sacred object. "These views . . . cannot but derive additional strength from the numerous petitions, having many thousand signatures . . . praying that the existing Act relating to the Clergy Reserves may continue in force." For the moment at least, it looked as if Strachan's wildest dreams had come true, his long struggle had availed something for the Church of England.

But Francis Hincks was on the spot and was empowered to deal with Pakington in the matter. After a fruitless interview with the Colonial Secretary Hincks advised him in writing that Canada had been led to expect an Imperial enabling Act on the Clergy Reserves, and "no interest will suffer more by delay than those of the Church of England."[90] Pakington refused to do more than provide a copy of his despatch on the subject. Hincks' reply was a lengthy exposition of the past and present history of the Reserves question which left no doubt as to Canadian sentiments thereon. Canadians believed that the Clergy Reserves question, being "one of local interest, should be disposed of by their own Parliament." The Churches of England and Scotland did not represent Canadian opinion, indeed the Church of Scotland spoke only for a minority of the Presbyterians. The Clergy Reserves question, as Strachan had said, did involve the Imperial connection, but for Hincks it had an opposite meaning: "I cannot view without grave apprehension the prospect of collision between Her Majesty's Government and the Parliament of Canada, on a question regarding which such strong feelings prevail among the great mass of the population. Such a difficulty is the more to be regretted, because the question of the Clergy Reserves is the only one, as far as I am aware, at all likely to lead to collision." As for accidental majorities, Hincks asserted that majorities in the Canadian Parliament were no more accidental that those at Westminster. "I am therefore fully convinced that the future action of the Canadian Parliament will   essentially of the same character with that which has been already taken."

Pakington and his colleagues remained deaf to Hincks' arguments. In any case, as Hincks admitted, the current session at Westminster was too far advanced to permit any legislation on the Reserves, and there remained always the slim chance that the Derby Government might reconsider its decision. But at least the Government did allow the amended and reserved Rectories Bill to become law after laying it before Parliament for the prescribed period and Hincks, before leaving England, set the judicial wheels in motion on a Rectories test case. With this sop the Canadians had to be satisfied for the present.[91]

VI

The protest against any alteration of the Clergy Reserves settlement which the three Anglican Bishops had addressed to Her Majesty in 1851 was ultimately received by Pakington, and he in turn directed Elgin to inform the prelates of the Imperial Government's decision not to introduce any Bill on the subject.[92] But when the Church "Union" held its annual meeting in June, 1852, a "wonderful change," as the *Globe* expressed it, had come over that body.[93] A resolution was passed in favour of dividing the Clergy Reserves among all denominations. Of course this scheme of divide and save which Strachan's son had suggested in

1850 was anathema to George Brown, but the resolution led him to comment that little opposition to secularization remained and the provincial Administration therefore had no excuse for procrastination. Slowly but surely Brown was adopting the Clear Grit argument that the Canadian Legislature should pass a Reserves Act with a delaying clause.

The Synod of the Church of Scotland, however, was not prepared to follow even the Church of England's lead. At its annual convention it petitioned the Queen once more not to abandon the principle of establishment.[94] On the other hand the United Presbyterian Synod passed resolutions unanimously favouring complete voluntarism through the separation of church and state.[95] The Wellington Presbytery of that denomination drew up a public manifesto criticizing the Government's slowness in ending state-churchism and calling on all voluntarists to agitate and petition for that end.[96]

The Wesleyan Methodists, who had resumed their silence after Conference had stated its position in 1851, were once more being accused by the *Examiner* of taking government money.[97] The *Christian Guardian*'s answer to its "Ishmaelitish neighbour," that all receipts from the Clergy Reserves Fund went to the Missionary Society in England, evaded the charges by circumlocution. Indirectly the Canadian Wesleyan Methodist Church did benefit by the technicality of having the money applied to its missions, and throughout the Clergy Reserves' agitation that church was ground between the millstones of popular voluntarist sentiment and the Act of 1840 which conferred the embarrassing pittance.

By midsummer of 1852 the policies of the *Globe* and its editor had completed the cycle of change which brought them openly to the position hitherto reserved for Clear Grits. This meant the addition to their election platform of a demand for the immediate passing of a Clergy Reserves Bill and for a legislative enactment to abolish the Rectories.[98] "The State-Church question is now the grand issue of Upper Canada, and all others must bend to it," was the *Globe*'s reply, on July 29, to those who preached patient service through waiting for an Imperial Act.

Within the Conservative party too a change was becoming manifest. The division seemed to parallel that within the greater Reform party as the Conservatives east of Toronto refused to accept the progressive tendencies of their fellows in the western portion of the province. So serious did the division become, particularly as it concerned the party's future policy on the Clergy Reserves, that extra-parliamentary caucuses were held at Dundurn Castle.[99] The Hamilton *Spectator* warned the Tories that they were playing into the hands of the Clear Grits by maintaining their "exclusive stand" on the Reserves question.[100] All the dirty linen came into full view when the *Patriot*, openly seeking an alliance for mutual security with the Roman Catholic *Mirror*, denounced the radicalism of the "Young Tories of the West."[101]

Against the swelling tide of public opinion which demanded action on the Clergy Reserves and which could be heard from the Cornwall *Freeholder* on the east to the Sarnia *Shield* on the west, the Government journals had little defence.[102] Their very interest in the railroads was seen by the secularizationists as a red herring drawn none too skilfully across the Clergy Reserves trail. The Government would be equally helpless in the face of such opposition when the new Parliament met, unless it abandoned its past policy and produced a Clergy Reserves Bill without awaiting Imperial permission. The only hope lay in turning popular dissatisfaction against the obvious scapegoat—the Derby Ministry.

In reply to Brown's questions during the opening debate, the Attorney General stated that the Government intended to proceed with the Rectories' test case, and Rolph repeated the vows made by Malcolm Cameron before the session that the ministers would stand or fall on the Clergy Reserves question.[103] This latter pledge seemed idle as it was highly unlikely that the Derby Government would reverse its stand, but the grand gesture did regain the support of some who had strayed into the no-man's-land of independence between Hincks and Brown. Brown himself could never be seduced by the promise of "shuffling Combinationists" like Hincks and these apostate Grits. He was prepared for a total war, reminiscent of the omnibus grievances agitated by W. L. Mackenzie a score of years before. "Do shoal down petitions about the Reserves, Rectories, Sectarian Schools, Maine Law, and Sabbath desecration," he implored Alexander Mackenzie, stonemason, publisher, and secretary of the reform committee in Sarnia. "The more the merrier." [104]

The statements of Rolph, Hincks, Morin, and Cameron regarding secularization and vested interests were, as the *Globe* said, very vague and contradictory.[105] But the time had come for Hincks' strategic move which would neutralize Brown and regain wavering Reformers. He introduced a series of seven resolutions expressing regret that a Clergy Reserves Bill had not been prepared by the Derby Government and reaffirming the Canadian determination that the Clergy Reserves question must be settled in Canada.[106] Such language in the opinion of the *News of the Week* was tantamount to a threat of rebellion.[107] But the *Globe* and the Guelph *Advertiser* insisted that a Bill should have been introduced to force the hand of the Imperial ministers.[108]

To strengthen his demand for an Address based on the resolutions, Hincks produced Pakington's despatch of April which had refused Imperial legislation. This only proved, said the *Globe*, that Pakington had been well tutored by Strachan to uphold the preferential treatment of the Church of England.[109] But, when the Address was voted on, the Government was able to defeat two Tory amendments by Boulton and two "Grittish" ones by Brown condemning the provincial Cabinet. On every division the ministers were able to produce very large majorities, and carried the Address by a three to two margin, thanks to the solid voting of the Lower Canadians, as the *Daily Colonist* noted, rather than to the success of Hincks' political legerdemain with despatches. "The affair is a fitting conclusion to the Elgin regime, which, thank God, is fast approaching a close." [110] The fact that Elgin gave preference to responsible government over his "pre-conceived opinions" in religious matters could not be known or appreciated by his critics.[111]

The Bishop of Quebec hastened to lay before the Governor General his "solemn remonstrance" against the Assembly's Address, pointing out to Elgin the obvious fact that the Upper Canadian vote in the Assembly on the Address had been carried by a mere 20 to 14.[112] From England, however, Bethune reported to Strachan the gist of an interview with Pakington. "[The Derby Government] are obviously staggered by the large majority against us...." [113]

VII

The policy of the Tory party in England had filled Canadian Reformers of all hues with a deep sense of frustration, but to Strachan and like-minded Anglicans it was at best an occasion for rejoicing, at worst a blessed respite in which to redouble their efforts to save the Reserves from their enemies. In London Archdeacon Bethune had succeeded in getting several articles on the Clergy Reserves published, but he confessed to Strachan that he often felt "baffled & disappointed," a feeling probably shared by his Bishop.[114] The *Christian Guardian* was incensed at Bethune's adept garbling of some of its remarks so as to suggest that the Wesleyan Methodists were favourable to state support for religion. "We stated most distinctly our conviction of the *inexpediency,* at least, of State endowments for the support of churches; and farther, that a large proportion, if not the whole, of the Wesleyan Methodist Church would cordially approve of some other disposition of the Reserves, than for the purposes to which they are now applied."[115]

The Reverend Arthur Palmer, Rector of Guelph, was also in London and he reported most gloomily to Strachan the substance of an interview he had obtained with Pakington.[116] The Colonial Secretary had heard from some Canadian Anglicans that their church would be better off without the Reserves. Palmer came away from the Colonial Office convinced that the Imperial Government would not make the Clergy Reserves an exception to responsible government. But at least it had been intimated that if an Imperial Bill became necessary it would give the Canadian Legislature control of all Roman Catholic endowments as well as the Protestant Reserves. Then the Lower Canadian members would think twice before supporting secularization. Palmer's impression that the Derby Ministry was about to reconsider their Clergy Reserves policy is given an aura of false credibility by two requests from Pakington to Elgin for financial returns of the Clergy Reserves fund since 1840, and the extent and value of the remaining lands. To the last moment of its life the Derby Government remained unrepentant.[117]

The day after these two despatches were written Pakington was engaged in a debate of the Commons on the Government's Clergy Reserves policy. No Bill would be introduced, he stated, because the Act 3 & 4 Victoria, c. 78, was an integral part of the Union arrangement, and the voting on Hincks' resolutions had not shown a clear-cut majority of Canada West in favour of its repeal. These remarks were hailed by the reactionary Barrie *Herald* as "welcome assurance."[118] "Thankful, then we may well be, that the powerful arm of Britain is interposed to ward off the frantic assaults of a 'Clear Grit' government upon sacred and vested rights." But the Reformers' reaction to Pakington's latest statement of policy was one of mingled indignation and surprise. The Guelph *Advertiser* demanded: "Does the noble lord wish to be in power during another rebellion . . . ?"[119]

The Derby Ministry fell that same month, December, 1852, defeated by nineteen votes, eight more than had killed the Russell Ministry, and on an equally distant issue from colonial policy and Clergy Reserves. Numbered among those nineteen were Peel and Gladstone who had been the advocates of the Canadian Church of England in 1840. The Reform press was transported in a delirium of joy at this welcome news. But George Brown and the *Globe* were not numbered among these revellers. Already the Hincksite journals were talking of an Imperial Bill to be prepared by Sir William Molesworth, and of Canadian action on the Reserves in another year. This, the *Globe* commented, was only "the cawing of the whole tribe" at the command of Hincks, the journalistic puppeteer. All the chatter about Molesworth was nothing more than "wile" to divert public attention from the fact that the Clergy Reserves battle must be fought and won in Canada.[120]

Bethune still had confidence that the House of Lords would "throw out any

Bill for our spoliation." [121] His authority was none less than John Colborne, Lord Seaton, founder of the Upper Canadian Rectories. But his optimism would assuredly have waned if he had seen the despatch which the Duke of Newcastle, Colonial Secretary of the new Aberdeen Ministry, was preparing to send to Elgin. The Imperial Government had decided to accede to the Assembly's petition for control of the Clergy Reserves because it was a subject of "strictly domestic interest." [122] The only reservation must be the preservation of "existing interests." Thus the policy of 1791 was deliberately reversed, and the power to settle the Clergy Reserves along with the right to erect a tariff became the twin coping-stones on the structure of responsible government in Canada.

Whether the Clergy Reserves question was a topic for discussion between the outgoing and incoming Cabinets at Westminster is a matter of conjecture. But one interesting footnote to Newcastle's policy is provided by the statement of James FitzGibbon, hero of the Napoleonic Wars and of '37, that Newcastle had called him to Downing Street and asked his opinion of the proposed transfer to the Canadian Parliament of authority over the Clergy Reserves. [123] FitzGibbon recommended that the authority be given, and though by his own account it cost him "the good will of some old Canadian friends," he believed that the final results justified his action and his judgment.

Bethune, who was still stumping England in search of funds for Trinity College, reported to Strachan that considerable popular interest had been awakened there in the Clergy Reserves question, and he was busy composing a pamphlet explaining the Church's claim to the Reserves with the intention of influencing Parliament's action when it reassembled in February. In this brochure he accused the Free Church of reopening the Reserves question out of jealousy of the Church of Scotland, and political free-traders of maintaining the agitation for party ends. The Clergy Reserves were not colonial property but Imperial grants over which the provincial Parliament had no legal authority. [124]

The last general elections, Bethune claimed, "were made to turn almost exclusively upon the Clergy Reserves question," yet despite the misrepresentations and calumny directed against his church the Conservatives had polled a larger vote than their combined opponents, and four avowed "Churchmen" had beaten known secularizationists. If the Church were sacrificed in Canada how long could the same concessions be denied in Ireland or England, or how long would the Roman Catholic endowments in Lower Canada last? Newcastle read these arguments and then informed Bethune personally that the Government would not be deterred or balked in its parliamentary course. Nevertheless, Bethune still had some doubts (or hopes!) as to the pliability of the Lords. [125]

In Canada Rolph permitted the gist of Newcastle's despatch to reach some of the Ministry's more wavering supporters, but he carefully avoided letting George Brown hear this news. "Till Parliament meets," he wrote, "it may be well not to draw off the Globe from its favourite course." [126] In fact Brown was still quite intent on his favourite course, informing a public meeting convened by the Ministerialists at Glenmorris that the Government had violated their party pledges by refusing to proceed by Bill with the Clergy Reserves. [127]

With the next session of the Legislature only days away, the journalistic hue and cry for and against an end to the Reserves was once more under way. The *North American, Canada Christian Advocate*, and Guelph *Advertiser* were grudgingly offering the Government just one more chance to settle the issue, while such Tory journals as the Barrie *Herald* and the Kingston *Daily News* alternately begged and bullied their opponents not to act rashly.[128] During February and March, however, the *Globe* had turned warily to other sins of Hincks such as the Common School Bill, the Three Rivers Cathedral Bill, Roman Catholic endowments and, most important, the infamous £10,000 job.

As soon as Parliament opened the Government lost no time in strengthening its position by unveiling Newcastle's Clergy Reserves despatch. George Thomson described the dramatic scene to his fellow-editor, Charles Clarke:

> Members stood listening with breathless attention and at its conclusion broke out into loud applause, clapping of hands & cries of good, good—. Geo Brown stood the perfect image of Despair, with a face as long as your arm, and broke out in a most insulting manner to Mr White of Halton who had enquired how he (Brown) thought the Glen Morris people would like it.
> The Clear Grits gathered around Dr. Rolph & expressed their congratulations.[129]

Rolph's strategy had succeeded and the *Globe* editorials assumed an obvious air of embarrassment. The *Globe* justified its late opposition with the statement that addresses had been useless in the face of a Tory Government in Britain.[130] It did not try to explain how a colonial Bill on the Reserves could hope to be more effective than the addresses.

Hincks' victory over his bitter enemy from Kent was made complete by the announcement that the Imperial Bill was actually before that Parliament. But there still remained two practical questions of immediate importance: Would the Bill get past the Lords, and if so would it be in time to permit the Canadian Legislature to take appropriate action in its current session? In a final and futile gesture the Society for the Propagation of the Gospel and the Church of England in Canada petitioned against the spoliation of the Clergy Reserves, while Strachan addressed a lengthy letter to the Duke of Newcastle reciting once more all the classic arguments in defence of the Church's endowment.[131] To Hawkins Strachan confessed that he had no confidence in the Aberdeen Administration. "There are in reality no true Friends of the Church in the Cabinet for those, who think themselves Friends, are Theorists the most dangerous of all Politicians for having settled that their Theory is true, they become conscientious destructives." [132]

Apparently Strachan never thought to apply his criticism of theorists to men of religion. He would have been happier had Derby and Pakington been "some what higher Churchmen," but at least they had the interests of the Church at heart. "No prime Minister during the last sixty years has spoken so boldly, and so frankly in favour of Church and State and I must say that I very much regret the change, which has taken place, and that a Presbyterian has succeeded to the head of the Government instead of a good Churchman." [133] For the Church of Scotland it was mortifying that the Earl of Aberdeen and the Duke of Argyll should be members of the Government which introduced the Clergy Reserves Bill, and ironic that Derby and Pakington were the men who presented the petitions left by Morris in anticipation of this very crisis.[134]

Bethune wrote in dismay that Strachan's friends in the Society for the Propagation of the Gospel were really only lukewarm in the Clergy Reserves cause, and that the Bishop of Oxford was openly antagonistic.[135] But Strachan's *Letter to Newcastle* which he had circulated throughout the House of Lords had, he believed, done some good.[136] The Bill was still before that august body when Bethune sailed for home, leaving, as he said, a London alive with the wildest rumours concerning possible alterations in the Clergy Reserves settlement.[137]

On May 12, 1853, the *Globe* carried the electrifying news that the Clergy

Reserves Bill had passed the House of Lords. The reaction of the Reform journals was generally one of satisfaction despite the reservation to protect vested interests. Even some of the moderate Conservative papers hailed the Act as the dawn of a better day for the Church of England.[138] The few Tory die-hards deprecated the enabling measure and withdrew to their last line of defence—the threat of "imminent danger" to Roman Catholic endowments.[139] Looking back on the passing of the Imperial Act, Strachan was inclined to blame everyone but himself for its success. "This statute supported in the House of Commons by Mr. Gladstone & the Peel party & all the Whigs and Radicals was passed by a great Majority but we still had hope in the House of Lords. This hope was disappointed for as Lord Derby wrote me what could we expect when nine Bishops out of nineteen voted for the total confiscation of the Church Property in Canada. . . ."[140]

VIII

At last the Clergy Reserves question had become a purely Canadian matter. The power to settle the old grievance was in the hands of the provincial Legislature, subject only to the reservation in favour of "existing interests." Unfortunately the authority had arrived when the current session of the Legislature was already old, too late indeed for the Government to introduce a Bill and pass it without giving an appearance of inordinate haste. Besides, the issue still had both possibilities and complications, for the measure to enlarge the franchise and parliamentary representation had just been enacted. Should the Government on constitutional grounds appeal to the country for a further mandate to settle the Clergy Reserves, or should it pass a Bill at the next session under the restricted representation? The Government said nothing, and the result was a year of utter political confusion in Canada.

At first even the newspapers supporting the Government disagreed as to the next step to be taken, the *North American* calling for a new election, the *Leader* insisting that no fresh appeal was necessary because the present Parliament was competent to settle the Clergy Reserves.[141] Some journals echoed the disturbing popular suspicion that the question was being held as a reserve *cheval de bataille* for the next tournament of the hustings.[142] The ultra-Tory press was still loudly denouncing the home government's violation of its trust. The Barrie *Herald* vowed that if the secularizationists, whom it had described as itinerant agitators, fortune hunters, and a licentious press, were returned at another election, they must be pledged to sequestrate the Roman Catholic endowments in Canada East.[143]

At this juncture the Gavazzi riots and the resulting "Montreal Massacre" touched off a most violent anti-papal campaign lasting for months, which played into the hands of the Tory defenders of the Reserves. On one hand Protestants generally returned to George Brown's old theme that French Roman Catholic domination was blocking progress; on the other hand Roman Catholics became alarmed at the open threats to their own denomination. The Church of England deftly balanced both sides against each other, warning the former that the Reserves were the last bulwark against the flood of Romanism and the latter that their own munificent endowments would also fall before these radicals who were setting the goddess of reason on the throne of true religion, unless the Anglican claims were supported. Not all the Conservatives accepted this logic. The Bytown *Orange Lily* viewed the Clergy Reserves as the only remaining barrier to a Protestant union, an opinion heartily shared by most secularizationists.[144]

The first intimation of the Government's intentions came in a hint dropped by the *Pilot* that the constitutional issue of representation would delay the Clergy Reserves settlement until the next Parliament, the very suggestion which all the other ministerial journals had previously rejected. The *Pilot's* "trial balloon," as the *Globe* called it,[145] was acceptable to at least one paper, the *Brant Herald,* whose editor was a friend of Crown Lands Commissioner Rolph. The *Herald* believed that a new election would ensure a Canada West majority for secularization.[146] The *Globe,* however, rejected the necessity of the double majority and insisted that any majority would do for secularization, an opinion shared by most Reform papers and Reformers. The Hamilton *Canadian* spoke the collective mind of all except the Hincksites when it said that the Government's excuses for not proceeding immediately with the Clergy Reserves Bill did not deserve the name of "respectable nonsense."[147]

This condemnation of the Government's policy of postponement was not limited to the press. The Anti-State Church committee in Toronto was once more active, this time publishing a manifesto criticizing the delay as "unwarrantable and dangerous, as well as a violation of public faith, and calculated to destroy all confidence in the integrity of the government."[148] The Barrie *Herald* heaped much ridicule on the arguments of the manifesto, referring to its signers as "the Twenty-five Illuminati" and "*Ministers of Peace* who cry 'war to the knife',," but it did not attempt any refutation.[149]

The United Presbyterians and the Methodist Episcopals publicly demanded immediate action on the Reserves and called on their adherents to exert pressure for that end.[150] To the extremists the silence of the Wesleyans was "ominous," and in response to open attacks and veiled imputations the *Christian Guardian* was forced to repeat that the Conference resolutions of 1851 constituted the official stand and final word of that denomination.[151] Its readers needed "neither information nor incitement" to do their duty on the Clergy Reserves question. The Government's inaction on all aspects of the church-state problem was surely and swiftly losing for it the support of those Reformers in Canada West who had hitherto rejected the *Globe's* anti-ministerial course.[152] The provincial press was now clearly divided on the Clergy Reserves question, said the Guelph *Advertiser,* "one portion contending for immediate legislation, another section justifying a dissolution on the 'constitutional' question, whilst a third party denounces the two former as thieves and plunderers."[153] The *Advertiser* placed itself in the first category.

Drastic action by the Cabinet was an obvious necessity. A letter from Rolph, promising a secularization Bill at the next session, to be followed by an immediate dissolution, was artfully allowed to reach the provincial press,[154] and the desired results were to some extent obtained. At least the *Canadian Christian Advocate* swung back into line, raising the old cry against any division of the Reform vote at the polls which might jeopardize the Government's position.[155] Episcopal Methodists were assured that the present Ministry were the men most likely to succeed in carrying secularization.

The good effects of Rolph's letter, however, were largely undone by Malcolm Cameron, the stormy petrel and chameleon of the Reform party, who blamed Elgin for the delay. Elgin, he said, had refused to allow secularization after Imperial permission had been granted, but Hincks had announced only two months before that the Cabinet alone was responsible for the postponement. Obviously, remarked the *Globe* on February 16, 1854, either Cameron or Hincks was lying. Later evidence suggests that Cameron told the truth.

The confusion in the ranks of Reform was further confounded by the revival of Captain Strachan's scheme for a denominational division of the Reserves and their application to sectarian schools. This suggestion, brought forward in apparent good faith by the moderate Conservative *Protestant Guardian* during December, 1853,[156] was vigorously opposed by the committee of the Anti-State Church Association with the vocal support of the *Canada Christian Advocate*.[157] The final disillusionment of the Reformers came when the Roman Catholic Institute of Toronto addressed its fellow institutes in Canada East urging united action against secularization. In the opinion of one Roman Catholic writer, his co-religionists would be "fools ... to fight the battles of the Methodists and Jumpers."[158]

The wild reaction of George Brown to these sentiments was all that Strachan could have desired to convince the Church of Rome of the danger facing both churches. The safeguards given the Roman Catholics in 1760 were "merely temporary," said the *Globe,* and no longer binding on a self-governing people.[159] There was no difference in the eyes of the radicals between the property of the Church of Rome and of the Church of England. Soon the whole discussion of the Clergy Reserves legislation, as the Guelph *Advertiser* noted, dwindled into personal invective, directed largely against Dr. Rolph.[160] Popular opinion would "whirl the Government from power" at the next election, unless the Clergy Reserves question was satisfactorily settled beforehand. The fact remained undeniable that Reformers viewed any further delay by the provincial Government as a breach of trust with the electors. The new Franchise and Representation Acts could not be used as an excuse for inaction.

William McDougall, typical of the Reformers who had hitherto defended the ministers, was now completely disheartened and disgusted by the corruption and jobbery of "Hincks and Company,"[161] Rolph was "politically dead," and the Reform party was disintegrating, he told Charles Clarke. As for the radical leaders, "Hartman keeps dark, White plays fast and loose, and Christie separates himself from the Clear Grits and swallows the Ministerial Reserve policy without so much as a wry face."

All signs indicated that the time was propitious for a combined attack on the Government by the disgruntled radicals and the dogged Tories. Hincks could blame no one else, save perhaps George Brown, for the perilous state of the Reform party, but he himself might have shared the responsibility with Lord Elgin. Despite Hincks' claim that the Cabinet had decided on calling a general election before proceeding with secularization, Elgin's own letters suggest that Malcolm Cameron had been closer to the truth when he charged the Governor General with obstructing reform. To his wife Elgin explained his side of the story months later.

If I had allowed the last Parliament to deal with the Clergy Reserves no doubt they would have secularized them; but they would have done so under circumstances which would have enabled the friends of the endowment to say that the opinion of the province had not been fairly taken on the question, and this allegation would certainly have been very extensively believed in England. In the new Parliament, the fate of the endowment will be the same, but at any rate it will be impossible to say that the country was taken by surprise; and the divisions in the Provincial Parliament will probably show that its preservation was impossible.[162]

IX

The "moment of truth" for the Clergy Reserves approached with the summer of 1854. Parliament had not met since last June. For a full year the province had wallowed in the muck of confusion and vituperation, not the least cause of which was the whole problem of politico-religious strife. As the last session of the "Clergy Reserves" Parliament was called together, the *Globe* complained on May 22 that the Government's programme was still a dark secret, though everyone presumed that a Clergy Reserves Bill would be introduced.

The Speech from the Throne made no mention of the Clergy Reserves.[163] Obviously then the Government intended to use that question at another election, pleading of course the "constitutional question" as its excuse for yet a further delay. But the exasperation of Parliament could no longer be contained. A double-barrelled resolution condemning the Ministry's deception and broken pledges on the Clergy Reserves and Seignorial Tenure issues was passed by a majority of thirteen votes, and after a brief adjournment Provincial Secretary A. N. Morin announced that Parliament would be dissolved without replying to His Excellency's speech or passing the single statute required by precedent at each session.

Nemesis had overtaken a perfidious Ministry at the hands of its "friends" from both halves of the province. The resolution had been offered by Sicotte, "the rising man in Lower Canada," and had been supported by radicals and Tories.[164] Ministerial journals complained that the vote, engineered by Brown and MacNab, was not an honest expression of opinion.[165] The truth was that the old Reform party had been wrecked on the shoal of Clergy Reserves, with assistance from its twin grievance of Canada East, Seignorial Tenure. The aspiration of centripetal nationalism had been flouted too long, and the new Reformers were ready, willing, and seemingly able, to pursue the issue of denominational separatism to the death.

For one fleeting moment some Reformers regretted the Government's defeat and blamed Baldwin's "defection" for the present imbroglio. In Parliament the Reformers met in caucus without the presence of Hincks to discuss policy, and George Brown was one who attended this post-mortem.[166] Then public opinion rallied to complete the destruction at the elections. Upper Canadians could now be divided into three classes on the Clergy Reserves, said the *Globe*.[167] The majority demanded secularization, a minute minority adhered to the settlement of 1840, and a larger minority favoured a new arrangement, namely denominational division. These last, the "new divisionists," were in Brown's view merely unprincipled "old establishment men" holding the "base object of obtaining a sum of money amid a general scramble." If the Conservatives succeeded with this scheme, the four main beneficiary churches, Roman, Wesleyan, English, and Scottish, would receive, instead of trifles, £100,000, £60,000, £150,000, and £37,000 respectively, which, if invested, would return "millions" within a generation.[168]

Such a division was in fact the platform of most Conservative candidates at the elections. The notable exception was their leader, the "gallant Knight," who announced his support for the principle of secularization.[169] Hincks too told his electors that "every shilling of the fund, saving the rights of existing incumbents," would go to the municipal councils on behalf of the nation to whom the Reserves rightfully belonged.[170] No claims other than those existing at the passing of the Imperial Act would be recognized, he stated, and added that Elgin had never opposed this scheme of settlement, although the Roman Catholic bishops of Canada East had.

The secularization was a prominent feature of the election campaign, but it was not the only one. At times it seemed that Brown and his paper were more interested in the defeat of Francis Hincks than in the settlement of the Clergy Reserves question. But among the Reform candidates differences of opinion as to the details of settlement were painfully apparent, some holding for an immediate granting of the funds to the municipalities, others for their devotion to education only. At last when the returns were all in, the *Globe* analysed the Canada West members as twenty-eight independent Reformers, eight pledged secularizationists, fifteen Conservatives, and only thirteen ministerialists.[171] Probably the ministerial supporters of all shades were closer to thirty. Either John Sandfield Macdonald or Sicotte would be acceptable to the *Globe* as Prime Minister because secularization was now an accepted certainty. "Funny," wrote G. B. Thomson, "to see Brown the champion of Protestantism supporting a Catholic like McD." [172]

Even the Conservatives accepted secularization as inevitable now, though it would remain an open question for the sake of party unity.[173] Strachan advised the Society for the Propagation of the Gospel of these unhappy developments in Canada.

The [election] returns leave us upon the Question of the reserves much the same as before. The Legislature meets again on the 5th of Septr. and if the Roman Catholic Members abstain from voting or vote against us secularization will take place, & we shall owe the loss of the Church property to the vote of the nine Bishops, who gave the power to the Colonial Legislature to dispose of it . . . .
Had the Govt at home merely spoken out boldly, that the Church Property Protestant & Roman Catholic must be respected, it would have been sufficient, but the two are separated & the Romanists think, that they may help in sacrificing Ours, & yet retain their own. We shall see.[174]

When the new Parliament met early in September, party lines were so chaotic that the success or failure of the Ministry was quite unpredictable. The Cabinet posts had been shuffled, but the distrust of Hincks was so general that overtures to such independent supporters as A. T. Galt were rejected, and no new blood was added to the old body. The Speech from the Throne this time referred to "a final and conclusive adjustment" of the Clergy Reserves as imminent.[175] The loose fish refused to bite again at this well-known lure. When the dramatic election of Sicotte as Speaker was over, and the Governor General's speech had been heard, the combined Opposition of the Conservatives, Grits, and Rouges, along with Dr. Rolph, Cabinet Minister, defeated the Government on a question of privilege.

The MacNab-Morin coalition of Upper Canadian Conservatives and Lower Canadian moderate Reformers adopted the late Government's programme of reform as a condition of office. They inherited the vineyard just as the crop was ready for harvesting, but the fruit was undoubtedly bitter to many Conservatives. Demands for an end to the Clergy Reserves and Seignorial Tenure and for an elective Legislative Council had been defeated by "old Tory" muskets in 1837. Now they were to be implemented by "new Tory" votes in 1854. Hincks' denial that he had been a party privy to the new political combination, though he approved and supported it, was "too fishy" to be swallowed by most Reformers.[176] "I had [not] the least idea that [Sir Allan MacNab] would consent to the secularization of the Clergy Reserves," he stated, unconvincingly.[177] But his critics were sure he would get his reward.

As for those Conservatives who had recanted the faith of a lifetime by accepting the principle of secularization, they were only making a virtue of necessity, said the Reformers, the reward of such virtue being "a share of the sweets of office."[178] "The promise of the Seignorial Tenure and Clergy Reserves questions being dealt with did not save Hincks and Rolph, can the like promises preserve a combination on no principle and professing none? We trow not," commented the Guelph *Advertiser*.[179]

x

But the new Government meant what it said, regardless of the Reformers' scepticism about political honesty. Addressing his constituents at the by-election following his appointment to the Cabinet, William Cayley announced the Government's intention to give effect to the people's wishes on the Clergy Reserves question.[180] Less than 30 members of the 130 in the Assembly still adhered to the settlement of 1840, he stated. For three weeks that were like the lull before a storm, the province waited for the Coalition Government to introduce the Clergy Reserves Bill. Then the terms of the new settlement were announced.

The proceeds of all sales of the Clergy Reserves were to form the Upper Canada and Lower Canada Municipalities Funds after deducting expenses. All monies in the respective funds would be divided annually among the county and urban municipalities on a per capita basis. The first charge on the funds, however, was to be the existing stipends (as of May, 1853, when the Imperial enabling Act was passed), payable to the incumbents for life. But "to remove all semblance of connexion between Church and State," it was provided that each recipient of a stipend, whether individual or collective, might commute the life claim at the rate of 6 per cent per annum, providing the money was not to be invested in real property. This last provision, for commutation, threatened to reopen the whole question once more, for in it the Reformers saw the antithesis of secularization, "the very injustice, against which we have desired to guard,"[181] namely the permanent endowment of a few privileged denominations.

Bishop Strachan was not content to let well enough alone. He sent to each member of the Assembly a copy of the pamphlet letter which he addressed to the Hon. A. N. Morin, Commissioner of Crown Lands.[182] The letter said nothing new, but it did repeat most forcefully his old threat against Roman Catholic endowments. The Reserves, said Strachan, were necessary to his church's existence, though he had lately claimed that its members in Canada West possessed one-third of the province's wealth. "Is the Bishop's Church founded upon the Rock, or upon the Clergy Reserves?" asked the *Christian Guardian*.[183] "Like a good Christian he will return evil for evil!!" The only effect that the Bishop's letter would have, wrote one observer, would be "to increase the determination of Upper Canadian Reformers (except Brown who wants to defeat the Gov't at once) to sustain the administration until Reserves secularized [sic]."[184]

The Wesleyan Methodists were at some pains to point out to the Bishop and to certain members of the Assembly that their denomination wanted no part of any division scheme which might be concocted as a sop to gain support for maimed exclusivism.[185] Strachan informed Archdeacon Bethune that without commutation there would be no lasting peace for the Clergy Reserves, in which case resistance to oppression, "even unto death," would be justified for the Church of England.[186] He chose to ignore the fact that many of his own denomination disagreed with him as to the function of the Reserves, and as they presumably would not be ready to die for the cause, they would belong with all his opponents whom he called "a disreputable minority." But though Strachan might be willing to accept commutation as the lesser of two evils, voluntarists and Reformers viewed it as a negation of secularization, and prepared to do battle against such subterfuges.

In the Assembly a rash of amendments to the Clergy Reserves Bill was being proposed—J. H. Cameron attempting to send it back to the people in a referendum, Merritt trying to reserve the municipalities' share for common school education, John Langton hoping to exclude mortmain from the commuted funds, and George Brown trying to secure immediate distribution of the balance among the municipalities. The press directed its attacks against commutation particularly. Commutation was not secularization, and commutation with churches would place the individual incumbents at the mercy of ecclesiastical corporations. And by what right did the Church of Rome share in Protestant Reserves? The *Globe* was supported by the *Examiner, Christian Guardian, Canada Christian Advocate*, Montreal *Witness, North American,* and Guelph *Advertiser.* Why, they all asked, should certain preferred churches continue to fatten at the expense of the public purse?

Despite this opposition in and out of Parliament to the details of its Clergy Reserves Bill, the Government pushed the measure ahead relentlessly. Strachan was busy offering George Boulton impractical suggestions for delaying the Bill.[187] The fact that a Seignorial Tenure Act had been demanded and granted for Canada East as a *quid pro quo* for settling the Reserves question spelled doom to Strachan's last hope of alienating the Roman Catholic votes from the Ministry. The Church of England, he complained, had been "regularly sold for office."[188] But the abuse heaped on the Executive by the Tory press was as unavailing as the protests of the voluntarists. The Bill was carried in the Assembly 62 to 39, the minority being mostly radicals, and in the council with only three dissenting votes. The Clergy Reserves Act passed into law in the last days of November, 1854, ending "one of the greatest abuses to which the Province had ever been subjected." [189]

The provincial Parliament recessed in mid-December and for a short time the attacks on the Clergy Reserves Act from left and right abated. Popular interest turned to that colourful spectacle, the Crimean War. But the respite did not last. By the end of January the Church of England had renewed its cries of spoliation, and the voluntarists were busy agitating against the commutation clause. Only the most cynical politicians were willing to call quits to the Clergy Reserves agitation and look elsewhere for a fresh cause. "We must go for *the elective principle*," wrote George B. Thomson, "thats [sic] the trump card now. It will win. The Clergy Reserves is a dead cock in the pit." [190]

The Anti-State Church Association was circulating a petition against the commutation clause, much to the annoyance of the ministerialist *Leader.* The *Globe* estimated that nine out of ten provincial papers were opposed to the clause as "unjust" and "impolitic." [191] The *Canada Christian Advocate* was demanding a reconsideration of the whole Act, remarking that "It seems to have been framed with the view of defeating those just and patriotic ends for which the country has been struggling for more than thirty years."[192]

Strachan was still bitter in his denunciation of the part played by the Roman Catholics in passing the Clergy Reserves Act as he prepared to take advantage of the only loophole he could find in the measure. If his clergy could be persuaded to commute their stipends and leave the management of the funds to the Church of England, the obnoxious Act might yet "be made to yield a considerable residue towards the future permanency of the Church...." He was most anxious to have the thirty-four young clerics appointed since the passing of the Imperial Act included, as their commuted stipends would obviously be very large. In this he was doomed to disappointment. But commenting on the manifesto prepared against commutation, he added, "They have been so long accustomed to make political Capital out of the Clergy Reserves question, that they cannot think of parting with it, so long as the Church retains a single farthing—hence they are preparing for a fresh agitation."[193]

The Church of Scotland was also preparing to take advantage of the offered commutation and had called a special meeting of the Synod committee on Clergy Reserves to arrange details. The Government had decided that it would deal only with the religious corporations, not with individuals, in this matter, and the clergy, especially the Anglican, were therefore put under pressure to accept commutation in the interests of their church. Few refused. The whole process, said the *Globe*, amounted to the establishment of state-churchism, and such was the result of the Clergy Reserves Act, "the fruits of the coalition."[194]

Before Parliament reassembled at Quebec on February 23, several significant events had occurred. First the Lower Canadian part of the Ministry had been reorganized, with Joseph Cauchon replacing Morin as Crown Lands Commissioner, the new Cabinet becoming the MacNab-Taché Government. In the arena of the provincial press the *Globe* had absorbed the *North American*, thereby raising its circulation to more than 14,000.[195] McDougall admitted in his editorial swan song that he was now a "Brownie," because Brown's conduct on the Clergy Reserves Bill "has won the respect and confidence of many who had long doubted his sincerity."[196] On the religious front the committee of the Anti-State Church Association memorialized the Governor General against the commutation clause, complaining that it was not only "subversive of the design of the Imperial Statute, but also of the great object sought by the enactment, viz; the ultimate practical recognition of the civil equality of all religious denominations."[197]

The strong radical-voluntarist opposition to the commutation scheme was brought into Parliament as everyone expected. Petitions of protest bearing more than twenty-five thousand signatures were received,[198] and Brown, now the acknowledged leader of the radicals from Canada West, moved a resolution to exclude commutation from the Clergy Reserves settlement. When the resolution was rejected by 72 to 42, the *Globe* announced, "The deed has been done ... and the Tories and Hincksites are triumphing in their successful villainy."[199] Reformers must now petition against commutation even though they could not change Parliament's decision, so that posterity might have a record of their opposition.

The popular reaction against commutation took on all the aspects of former anti-Clergy Reserves campaigns. Public meetings were held to pass resolutions, petitions were circulated, and Reform editors poured verbal volleys into the ranks of the Coalition Government and its supporters.[200] The "foul treachery of the Coalition" was shown by its refusal to permit individual commutation.[201] The Reformers had been tricked by smooth words and unscrupulous leaders. "A more diabolical act of treachery—a more deeply concocted fraud was never perpetrated upon any community by a Government," wrote one editor.[202] The Methodist Episcopal Conference spoke out officially against commutation as the negation of the very aim of the Clergy Reserves settlement, the perpetuation of the evil of denominational separatism which a generation of Reformers had fought to destroy in the name of religious equality and national interest.[203]

Slowly the furore died away, and after the close of the session at the end of May, 1855, references to the commutation trick appeared only occasionally and with decreasing fervour and frequency. But the Reformers of Canada West would probably have felt their cries of "Treachery!" doubly justified had they seen the letter which Bishop Strachan sent to Francis Hincks, thanking him for his kindness and support in promoting the commutation clause.[204]

XI

What did commutation, the cause of this continued strife, actually amount to? The total paid to the four churches in Canada West on behalf of the incumbents was £381,982, of which the Church of England received 64 per cent (£245,615), the Church of Scotland 28 per cent (£105,665), the Wesleyan Methodists 2.6 per cent (£9,769), and the Church of Rome 5.4 per cent (£20,933). The disparity between the sums given to the last two bodies from the Protestant Reserves is interesting. In addition to the commuted total, £44,441 was invested on account of widows' pensions and a few uncommuted stipends.[205]

From the investment of the commuted stipends the Church of England was required to pay the annual claims of 143 clergy, but there was also the problem of 18 men ordained since the passing of the Imperial Act in 1853 who had no stipends. When commutation actually went into effect Strachan reckoned the interest on the invested fund at £12,244, and the claim at £18,643, leaving an annual deficit of £6,399 to be made up by drawing on the capital sum.[206] The actual history of the use of the funds is a study in itself, and one which has yet to be written, but it is noteworthy that a century after the commutation the Church of England is still drawing a sizable sum on these investments.[207]

The Church of Scotland commuted stipends for seventy-six ministers (three United Synod ministers have been included although they were separated by the Government) and established its share as the Temporalities' Fund. It was converted into a contributory pension scheme, and became the cause of extensive litigation after the union of all Presbyterian Churches in 1875. But even before Confederation difficulties had arisen within the Churches of England and Scotland regarding the administration and appropriation of the funds. The commutation scheme was not a year old when Reverend P. McNaughton withdrew from the Church of Scotland to become a voluntarist and to provide Brown and the Grits with some political talking points, in the form of statistics and accusations of trickery against the Clergy Reserves commissioners of that church.[208] In the Diocese of Huron, noted at its inception for its Low Churchism, similar charges were brought against the Church of England by a voluntarist Anglican cleric who went so far as to write his own experiences into a *History of the Separation of Church and State in Canada* (1887), published at his own expense.

The Wesleyan Methodists left the arrangement of commutation to the Reverend Dr. John Beecham, senior secretary of the London Missionary Committee, who came to Canada specifically to manage its interests in the Clergy Reserves settlement.[209] By his account there was considerable difficulty with the government, and not until the last hour was he sure that an agreement would be reached. It is interesting to note that when the provincial government called on the four commuting churches to account for their investment of the monies received, the Churches of England, Scotland, and Rome replied that their respective shares were now in provincial and bank debentures, because the Clergy Reserves Act prohibited investment in real property. But the Wesleyan Methodists, assuming a more restricted interpretation of "real property," had put their money into mortgages, probably at a higher rate of interest.[210]

When the Clergy Reserves Act was passed some 664,400 acres of the Reserves remained unsold, from which the municipalities of Canada West would eventually benefit through the Municipalities Fund. To the credit of these corporations £297,325 was invested in 1856. In 1855 they received £304,423 on the strength of this credit, and in 1856 another £97,214 were distributed. This was in addition to the adrenalin-like infusion of cheap money made available for hire by the commutation clause, and the pernicious effects of the Municipal Loan Fund, the loans from which, by the beginning of 1858, had reached the staggering heights of £1,823,700.[211] These large sums were pumped into the booming economy of a province containing barely one million souls, to be used for public improvements.

Within two and one-half years after the Clergy Reserves Act the Canadian economy was in the grip of a financial panic of major proportions. The amount of cause and effect involved remains to be determined by economists, but it is evident that there was some direct connection between these two facts. The slump was foreign in origin, but in Canada its impact was heightened by the crisis which had been building up for half a decade in the railway speculation and public works so eagerly undertaken, but so little understood. One result of the depression of 1857 was the defaulting of the Upper Canadian municipal corporations on their debts to the Municipal Loan Fund, the arrears of interest thereon amounting to $3,200,000 by the time of Confederation.[212] Another result, more intimately connected with the Clergy Reserves, was the financial failure of J. H. Cameron, who had been entrusted with the Clergy Reserves fund of the Church of England.[213] Cameron was unable to account for the money, and after turning over his property to his various creditors, he spent the rest of his life in self-imposed poverty and hard work, vainly trying to repay these crushing debts.

Thus the nationalizing of "Pandora's Box" can be said to have brought its share of distress as well as benefits. But the consensus was that the disestablishment was a blessing to the Churches of England and Scotland and to the province as a whole. For the Church of England it meant the beginning of self-government and self-reliance; for the Church of Scotland it made possible the union of all Presbyterian bodies in Canada. And for the Province of Canada the secularization of the Reserves removed the major source of irritation between churches and state, and between denominations. It was truly the end of an era in the history of Upper Canada, and the foundation for the growth of an omnibus Protestant denomination. The last major barrier to Protestant interdenominational co-operation had been removed with the end of the Clergy Reserves, and the way was clear for the evolution of an inclusive denomination based on latitudinarianism and shielded by nationalism. But who was the victor in this contest which had distressed the province for two generations? Not the strongly nationalist forces of voluntarism, for the privileged churches still retained substantial endowments. Nor was it the self-styled national churches, for state and church had been irrevocably separated. The battle of the Clergy Reserves was in fact a draw between centripetal nationalism and centrifugal denominationalism, a typically Canadian compromise of the relations of church and state, an acceptance of the *via media* for the greatest good of the greatest number. In fact the very legal equality of the various denominations permitted the smaller bodies to feel that they were part of a Protestant national church.

The verdict of history on the Clergy Reserves settlement of 1854 may well be that expressed by Governor General Sir Edmund Head in 1857:

I have no doubt that there are many persons who still dispute the propriety of passing such a measure at all. There are others who attack with equal vehemence the moderate form in which it was at length adopted, and who object to the commutation of the incomes of the present incumbents so as practically to supply a permanent endowment on the part, not of the government, but of the Church Society. It is not my business to vindicate the measure itself, though 'perhaps the Vehemence with which it has been assailed by the two extreme parties may be held by some to be the best voucher for its justice and moderation.[214]

CHAPTER FOUR

THE UNIVERSITY QUESTION, 1840-1849

In Search of a System

I

THE UNIVERSITY QUESTION, the "question of questions in Upper Canada" as Ryerson called it,[1] was but one aspect of the staggering problem of nation building, illustrating in its own way the conflict between centripetal nationalism and centrifugal denominationalism. Yet it must be seen against its Old World background to appreciate its complex nature. The intellectual renaissance which swept Scotland during the eighteenth century had its counterpart somewhat later in Germany and in the United States. In England the restricted clientele and curricula of Oxford and Cambridge had resulted in the creation of University College, London, which reflected this crisis in higher education. The new studies such as economics, politics, modern languages, and the physical sciences, the non-residential system adopted from Edinburgh, the absence of religious tests, the emphasis on lectures and single courses, the stock company constitution, and the pervading spirit of democracy at the new metropolitan University were a strange contrast to the older universities. The charge against Oxford and Cambridge was not inefficiency in their chosen fields, but blindness to the signs of a new century and a new age. The declining wealth and position of the agricultural middle classes had turned the Universities into finishing schools for the upper classes only. Religious tests effectively barred all non-Anglicans from their halls, and the Universities' consuming interest in classical studies offered little to attract the youth of the rising mercantile and manufacturing classes whose destinies lay in the non-speculative world of cash books.

Within the basic problem of the nature of a university rest several issues. Shall its curriculum admit the claim of the new studies to share in producing the whole man? What is the relation of the newly discovered scientific truths to those long derived from revealed religion? Shall the affairs of a university be managed entirely by the constituent colleges, thus recognizing the right to autonomy of this microcosm, or shall it bow to external control from business experts of proven ability? Is the lecture system more efficient than the tutorial? And where shall the university be located—in a quiet college-centred town or amid the distracting confusion of a metropolitan area which in itself offers a form of education? Beyond all these queries lies the eternal problem of financing institutions which by their end can never be self-supporting. The attempts to answer these problems in Germany, the United States, and Britain, especially by the bourgeois founders of London University, were in their own turn to influence the course of higher education in Canada.

Nowhere in Canada West did the tutorial system obtain a fair trial, not even in King's College, where Strachan's own educational background nullified the influence of its English prototypes. The assumption that lectures were better suited to the requirements of North American education was never seriously questioned. Nor did the classical disciplines ever have an opportunity to contest the presence of the new studies, however much the latter might be limited in scope by temporary financial stringencies. The revolt of Darwin's disciples against the queen of sciences was still decades away, and few Canadians in the nineteenth century questioned the proposition that education must be based on religion, although the degree of relationship between the fields was given various interpretations by interested parties. In the sparsely populated province of Canada West the problem of location became important when finances were involved. But finances and control were the core of the whole University question.

It was not only the curriculum and internal organization of University College, London, which attracted the attention of Canadian legislators and educationalists. In 1836 that College was joined with its Anglican rival, King's College, to form the University of London. This pluralism of religious and secular foundations within a single unit was further expanded in 1850 by legislation permitting the affiliation of other colleges regardless of their religious or non-religious bases. The University of London thus became an examining and degree-granting body which attempted to establish common standards for its component colleges. This example proved very attractive in Canada, where, after 1850, a number of denominational institutions co-existed with the secularized state institution. Unfortunately most parties in Canada overlooked one vital fact which prejudiced such an establishment in this province. Unlike the University of King's College, Toronto, London University lacked any endowment to excite the cupidity of penurious member colleges.

II

Historians have yet to do justice to the liberality and breadth of Strachan's views in higher education. The charter obtained by Strachan for King's College in 1827 is remarkably liberal, considering the absolute proscription of all dissenters and Roman Catholics from higher education which then existed in England. The emendations made by Strachan in that original charter of King's College, despite the objections of his English friends,[2] are undeniable evidence of his conscious attempt to reduce clerical influence, particularly Anglican, that the University might better claim the widest possible support from the religiously heterogeneous population of the province. The tests which did restrict the council and faculty to members of the Church of England were not of Strachan's wishing. The subscription to the Thirty-nine Articles required of them was considered by Strachan himself as injudicious.[3] But more basic and lasting was the antagonism created by the munificent endowment of the University amounting to more than 225,000 acres from the national patrimony.[4] The endowment had been intended for grammar schools and "other seminaries of higher learning," a stipulation which seems to have been ignored by all parties until 1847. The amendments made to the charter in 1837[5] to eliminate Anglican influence failed to reconcile the opposition to even the remaining limited privileges. Except for the educational voluntarist minority, no one would question the benevolence of Imperial policy in utilizing waste lands for education. In reality the majority were protesting the extravagance of the grant to a single denomination which constituted only a fraction of the population. The issue was not one of land reservation, for these same opponents favoured applying the Clergy Reserves to educational purposes. The issue was civil and religious equality, the right of all to share in a national endowment.

The greater part of the endowment was still intact when King's College, after sixteen years of paper existence, came into operation at last in June, 1843. Expenses of administration and financial irregularities committed by council members, even including the Right Reverend John Toronto, had consumed over half of the interest of the endowment,[6] but the most serious drain on the capital grant had resulted from the legislative adoption of Colborne's parasitic progeny, Upper Canada College. "The very name of King's College has become a by-word throughout the Province to represent the worst kind of jobbing," stated Francis Hincks.[7] Meanwhile two rivals had appeared to challenge King's College's prospective monopoly of higher education and the University endowment. Queen's College (the name chosen as a deliberate counterpoise),[8] had been operating at Kingston since March, 1842, on a scale so modest as to discourage its Church of Scotland founders and its would-be historians. A charter more exclusive than any Strachan had ever suggested imposed the Westminster Confession on all professors, divinity students, and on the fifteen laymen who constituted a slight majority of the Board of Trustees. In other respects Queen's was intended to be a copy of Scottish universities. Its charter had been obtained only at the price of disallowance of the provincial Act of Incorporation.[9] The Act had promised to Queen's a cash settlement in lieu of the Church of Scotland's claim through co-establishment to an endowed chair of theology in King's College. As a result of this disallowance a long protracted controversy between the Honourable William Morris and the Honourable R. B. Sullivan regarding the annual value of the chair was terminated, and that endowment lost for all time. Queen's found itself even at this early date faced with financial difficulties occasioned by traditional Celtic parsimony and deafness to repeated appeals for funds, aggravated in Scotland by the disturbed state of the national church.[10]

Stimulated by the efforts of the Church of Scotland to fill the void in higher education with a denominational college, the Wesleyan Methodists had procured in 1841 through the good offices of Lord Sydenham an Act of Incorporation extending the privileges of their preparatory school, Upper Canada Academy, at Cobourg, to match those possessed by Queen's.[11] The original charter of the Academy had been literally unrestricted in its provisions. Its College Board, comprising the trustees and visitors, was dominated by the large majority of lay members. No test of any kind was imposed on staff, students, or board, though ultimate control of appointment still lay with the annual Conference of the Wesleyan Methodist Church. Unlike Queen's in another respect, Victoria College, as the collegiate department of the Academy was named, was primarily intended to be a literary institution, offering general education based on Christian principles. The financial problems of Victoria dated from the depression and political disturbances of Upper Canada's last years, and had by the time of incorporation become so desperate that Sydenham engineered a provincial grant of £500 which later became annual.[12]

Yet another institution must be mentioned although the rôle it played in the University question was always of minor importance. Regiopolis had been established at Kingston by Bishop Macdonell, and its clerical Board was empowered in 1837 to hold land but not to grant degrees.[13] Its pecuniary problems were always disproportionately large considering its small enrolment, and as late as 1845 its buildings were still unfinished.[14] Regiopolis soon sank back to the status of a preparatory school when faced by competition from Ottawa and St. Michael's Colleges, two institutions which exemplified growing interdiocesan rivalry in the Roman Catholic Church.

Such, then, was the state of higher education in Canada West when the question of University reform and union came before the public early in 1843. Two denominational colleges established as a result of the long incubation of King's were now facing the crucial test of insufficient financial support. The third, Regiopolis, showed little evidence of fulfilling its founder's pious intentions of serving the educational needs of the Roman Catholics. But King's College, so amply endowed with public lands, continued to excite opposition and envy, even of some Anglicans, as long as the Bishop of Toronto and a section of his co-religionists managed its affairs and appointments in such a way as to nullify the amendments made to the charter in 1837. The liturgy at chapel services and the existence of a chair of theology for the Church of England betokened to the popular mind at least a *de facto* control of the University by that church.

III

The first suggestion for amalgamation came from the Honourable John Hamilton and F. A. Harper, financial agent of Queen's, as early as May, 1842. Writing to William Morris on the twenty-fifth of that month, Harper pointed out that the serious financial position of the College showed no prospects of improving. Only £163 remained for the salary of a third professor. The problem in Canada was simply too many colleges and not enough students to fill them for several years. Why not a "united University" with King's College teaching arts and the Churches of England and Scotland having separate chairs of divinity? Besides the economy gained, such a union "would present a strong point against the encroachments of the Romans & others." Harper suggested that Morris "broach the subject confidentially to H.[is] E.[xcellency] Sir Charles, who might refer the matter to the heads of the two Colleges for consideration as a suggestion of his own,"[15] thereby relieving both parties of the embarrassment of approaching the other. The equivalent for the lost divinity chair would make an effective big stick to wield for this end, especially as there was some opposition in the Kirk to having the chair physically separated from Queen's. Lastly, he remarked, the success of such a union would be an example to the Christians in general, and Scotland in particular.

Morris apparently got his interview within a month but found Bagot unwilling to take the initiative in opening negotiations. William Draper informed Strachan that Morris had something afoot regarding King's College but both assumed that Morris was simply reviving the claim for a chair of divinity.[16] The urgency of Queen's' predicament was accentuated late in the summer by unwelcome news from the Colonial Office—no funds were available for assistance to Queen's.[17] Evidence suggests that, henceforth, Morris played only a secondary rôle in the events preceding Baldwin's University Bill of 1843. Whatever the reason, Morris yielded the first place to Queen's' newly appointed principal, the Reverend Thomas Liddell. No estimate of Liddell's influence on education during his brief sojourn of four years in Canada has ever been attempted, but certainly few individuals ever arrived in this country who recognized so quickly and correctly its needs, shortcomings, and possibilities.

Before returning to Scotland for his family in the summer of 1842, Liddell sent Morris a lengthy and comprehensive account of his personal opinions on the

University question,[18] an account which deserves particular attention because it outlines so exactly the policies which were adopted, probably through Liddell's influence, by the Church of Scotland during this first phase of the search for a comprehensive system of higher education in Canada West. Since his arrival, Liddell states, his conviction has increased that amalgamation would benefit not only the Church of Scotland but the province at large. While the funds of Queen's had proved inadequate to support both a literary and theological establishment, the large endowment of King's would soon ensure to the latter institution a success which Queen's could never expect. King's College, being, as it ought, a provincial institution, should provide arts training for all denominations, and Queen's should be restricted to divinity. The education of the youth of all religions together would allay more than anything else the sectarian animosity "which has been, & threatens still to be, the bane of this country."

The amendments to the King's College charter in 1837 had made that institution theoretically liberal. Liddell now offered two plans to make it liberal in practice. The first, his own preference, is similar to Harper's plan. Make both colleges into divinity schools, and let a new institution assume the arts teaching. As an alternative, it would be better for Queen's to surrender her degree-granting powers and leave King's intact, than that the two colleges continue to the disadvantage of each. But an endowment is a *sine qua non,* and no amount would be too large, even for the theological professorship. Liddell confided to Morris that five of the staff and trustees in Kingston had discussed amalgamation favourably, and that two leading ministers of Synod had come to the same decision independently. "I need not add that they all feel the importance of keeping the matter perfectly secret at present."

Here the matter rested until the autumn of the year when the Board of Trustees, presumably after considerable discussion, took definite and official action in the form of three resolutions reviewing the relative positions of King's and Queen's. They were willing to accept any legislation which would recreate Queen's as a theological college in Toronto, provided that Queen's was secured in her privileges and fair share of influence in the administration of King's College. The very phraseology was that of Liddell's letter. A fourth resolution appointed commissioners to communicate with the Governor General and "to take such other action ... as they may see fit." A letter from the Honourable John Hamilton, another of the commissioners, informed Morris late in October that Liddell would go to Toronto to sound out the members of King's College Council on the proposed union, using of course, "caution and skill."[19]

When next the board met on March 1, 1843, the commissioners could only report that a majority of the King's College Council were unfavourable to the idea of union, but that Strachan had not yet replied to their request that the case be laid formally before the council.[20] This the Bishop later refused to do. Two months later they reported more hopefully that the same documents had been presented to the new Governor General and that he and the Executive Council approved the scheme of union, but believed that the co-operation of the Methodists would be essential to its success. The immediate resolve of the board to seek the support of the Wesleyan Methodists changed the complexion of the agitation by introducing for the first time into the University question a religious body which possessed not only a natural interest in its solution, but sufficient influence and numbers to constitute a balance of power between the Churches of England and Scotland.

Previous to any overtures to the Methodists from the board of Queen's, Liddell had been corresponding with Ryerson at Victoria, outlining the plans for union. His first letter proves that in prior conversations (presumably even before the trustees' resolutions of September 5, 1842) the subject had been often examined, and Liddell believed Ryerson was ready to support any move for University reform. Liddell's next letter, dated May 16, was an official communication, for such correspondence was now sanctioned by the board's resolution to seek Methodist support. It reveals by implication the substance of Ryerson's reply to the previous overture and the major objection raised by the Principal of Victoria, namely the heavy investment made in the Cobourg buildings.

Liddell's solution to Ryerson's question regarding disposition of the Victoria staff and buildings indicates a close liaison between Queen's and the government of the day, more probably through the agency of Hamilton than that of Morris. A subsequent reference to a plan of Francis Hincks, for vesting financial management of the University in an external board representing various interests in the province, raises an unanswerable query regarding Hincks' relation to Baldwin's first University Bill. Liddell's suggestion of some direct representation to the annual Wesleyan Methodist Conference in June was rejected by Ryerson in favour of independent action by the two churches. As a result the Conference failed to take any recorded action. Thus it was left to the Synod of the Church of Scotland at its meeting the following month to make the first formal approach to the Legislature in the form of a petition to the three branches of Parliament, setting forth the reasons for Queen's establishment, the educational advantages of the scheme of union, and the popular stake in the endowment of King's, as premises for consideration.

The lists were now fairly drawn for any and all journalistic combatants who might wish to defend or oppose the scheme. The *Patriot,* organ of King's College Council, supported the *Church* in its rather weak defence of the *status quo* of King's and condemned the movement as a crusade against the Church of England.[21] On the other side the *Banner* and the *British Colonist* gave their fullest support to the cause of University reform, while subscribers of Queen's were circularized by the trustees.[22] The letters of "Veritas" in the *Colonist* denouncing the mismanagement of King's College and the endowment were answered in kind by the *Patriot*.[23] The editor of the latter was characterized by "A Canadian Catholic" as patriotic in name only.[24] The Reverend Robert Fyfe, writing above the *nom de plume* of "A", in the Baptist *Register,* accused the high Presbyterians of wanting only to share King's College endowment with the Church of England.[25] He excluded from this class the *Banner* and its supporters, but deprecated the "Knoxian narrowness" which had become too apparent in the Church of Scotland of late. Earlier the *Register* had demanded that the provincial legislators "rescue the University from the grasping hand of Prelate STRACHAN."[26]

Numerous meetings were held throughout the province, all in favour of University reform, the most important being one held in the Wesleyan Methodist Newgate Street Chapel in Toronto.[27] Here lay and clerical representatives of the Church of Scotland, the Congregationalists, and the Wesleyan Methodists formulated a petition to Parliament against the sectarian character of King's which they entrusted to known supporters and local members, including William Henry Draper. Members of the Church of England participated in other meetings. As yet the *Christian Guardian* confined itself to news coverage of these various events and avoided any editorial reference to the movement. But as Scobie stated in the *Colonist* on October 3, the ball was indeed rolling, the contagious inspiration of the union of the two Canadas was spreading to regions Sydenham had never known.

IV

Baldwin's University Bill, which Hincks considered the most important measure presented to the first Parliament,[28] made its *début* in the Assembly on October 12, 1843. Its terms[29] reflected the influence exerted by the Church of Scotland during the preceding months, with some parts patently reflecting some aspects of University College, London. Above all it exemplified the mind of Baldwin himself—doctrinaire, verbose, and legalistic. The Bill would have constituted King's as a non-sectarian arts college in the "University of Toronto." Queen's, Victoria, and Regiopolis would become satellite institutions at Toronto with some vague status, perhaps as divinity halls, by exchanging their degree-granting powers for an annual sum of £500 assured for four years. Control of the University would rest with an external board representing, as Hincks had suggested, the variegated interests and groups in the province. One clause, however, which met with almost universal disapprobation would have eliminated all religious tests for staff and students in arts. Subscription to the doctrine of the Trinity and the inspiration of the Scriptures was one provision of the amended charter of 1837 which met with almost universal approval.

Of the twenty petitions presented to the Assembly calling for the liberalizing of King's College,[30] the majority came from the Church of Scotland and Baptist congregations. One from Professors Croft and Gwynne, both Low Church Anglicans in King's College, protesting undue clerical influence in the institution, was the dissent of a bold minority from the petition of their colleagues. Significantly no petitions came from the Wesleyan Methodists. The trustees of Queen's who had been favoured with an advance draft of the Bill passed resolutions at their meeting in October and petitioned the Legislative Council against the absence of any religious test for professors, the small endowment demanded of any colleges affiliating in future, and the insufficiency of the grant offered to Queen's in exchange for independence.[31] Liddell echoed these sentiments in his last two letters to Ryerson, but explained that though he had urged these points "as strongly as possible" to various members of the Government, Baldwin himself was so busy he could not be seen. Need, not greed, was indeed the determining factor in Queen's policy.

Although the *Christian Guardian* had reported events and quoted contemporaries concerning the agitation of the University question, no official action was taken by the Methodists until the last week in October when the Victoria College board defined its position in a series of resolutions on Baldwin's Bill.[32] Like the trustees of Queen's, the board objected to the absence of any religious test, the insufficiency of the endowment required of future affiliates, and the injustice of the financial arrangement to its own institution. In this last connection the board noted that the three other denominations mentioned by the Bill were in receipt of substantial shares of Clergy Reserves funds. Further, the debt-encumbered buildings at Cobourg were a liability which the other participants in union would not sustain, and for which "arrangements" were demanded. Finally the very terms of subscription for Victoria asserted that unlike the other colleges Victoria was primarily intended to be a literary institution. Thus the board, while expressing "cordial approval" of the Bill and thanks to the Government, reserved judgment on union as outlined by Baldwin, from a conviction that the sacrifices demanded would not equal the benefits conferred. Ryerson added an unofficial explanation of the Board's moderation in a letter to the *Guardian*.

As a Body, we gain nothing by the "University Bill." . . . Our omission therefore from the Bill would be preferable. . . . But such an omission would destroy the very character and objects of the Bill. As a provincial measure, it cannot fail to confer lasting honour upon the Government and unspeakable benefits upon the country. Viewing the measure in this light, the Board of Victoria College have consented to resign certain of their rights and privileges for the accomplishment of general objects so comprehensive and important.[33]

In his capacity as President of King's College Strachan made his defence of the Anglican control of the University in a memorial to both houses of the provincial Parliament,[34] a step delayed until November by his absence from Toronto. His reaction to the Bill was violent, as he described it as an irreligious and revolutionary attempt to proscribe the Church of England and to destroy the sacred charter and endowment of King's—an attempt, encouraged by "senseless and unjust clamours" against the institution, which would degrade the Crown, disgrace the province, jeopardize property, and "place all forms of error upon an equality with truth." The endowment itself, he stated in a tone which was to be heard again during the Clergy Reserves controversy a decade later, was equally as sacred as Roman Catholic endowments. In Canada East the endowments of Roman Catholic institutions were ten times as large as that of the University. Confiscation of the latter would lead inevitably to similar action against Roman Catholic property. To the *Christian Guardian* such rabid language from Strachan was simply proof "that the Bill is not very far from being just what Canada wants. . . ." "The University of King's College, at Toronto, in its present illegal and illiberal management, is A GRAND 'ERROR!' THE HON. MR. BALDWIN'S BILL IS A GRAND CORRECTOR!"[35]

In an equally strong letter to the Governor General Strachan presumed that His Excellency's approval of the "withering provisions" of the Bill resulted from ignorance.[36] But one chord which the Bishop struck—the Bill's restraining effect on the royal prerogative—must have caused a sympathetic response in Metcalfe, for Liddell had warned Ryerson in his last letter that the gubernatorial mind held certain reservations regarding the competency of the Legislature to interfere with the royal charter of King's. The importance of this letter from Strachan on the course of subsequent events, especially the resignation of Baldwin's "Cabinet," may have been decisive.

Liddell did not get the opportunity to "pound and expound" the Bishop's petition, but Ryerson, who was probably the abler controversialist, at least the more profuse, did use Draper's defence of King's College's charter at the bar of the Assembly as the text and occasion for an exhaustive examination into the legal status of said charter.[37] The choice of "Sweet William," the most accomplished of the conservatives, was a happy one for the council and perhaps also for Draper's party. It was a confident Government which permitted such liberties to its most dangerous opponent. For over two hours Draper skilfully urged two points—the Legislature cannot erect universities without usurping the Crown's prerogative, nor can it by the same principle interfere by right or reason with any powers granted to a corporation by the Crown.[38] Three days later Metcalfe accepted the resignation of all but one member of an Executive Council which seemed bent on usurping the royal prerogative.

Ryerson's rebuttal was explicitly directed at Draper, "the Advocate of others," not at his friend Draper "the Statesman," who as events proved did not believe the very opinions he expressed. After demolishing the constitutional precedents cited by Draper in defence of the sanctity of royal charters, Ryerson declared that Baldwin's Bill did not create a university *de novo* but simply altered the existing charter so that all Canadians might share in a national legacy unjustly monopolized by the Church of England. If Ryerson was not, as he said, prepared to argue for any particular University Bill, he did for the time range himself unequivocally on the side of such advocates of a national university as John Macara, the *Colonist* and the Kingston *Chronicle and Gazette*.[39]

The fears expressed in Macara's pamphlet that the High Church party would bribe the leading denominations into silence, and the *Colonist*'s prophesy that University reform would be the leading question at the next election, failed to materialize as the issue of party patronage absorbed the interest of the province. But Wakefield's charge that the Ministry had resigned to avoid inevitable defeat on the University Bill[40] deserves at least a passing comment. Hincks cited part of Viger's pamphlet to disprove the accusation, and both Scobie and Buchanan admitted that the moderates were in complete agreement with the ex-ministers on this point.[41] The ministerial Reformers were prompt to point out the disparity between Wakefield's statements and those of other supporters of Metcalfe.[42] On three occasions Ryerson denied that the Governor General was opposed to the University Bill or that the University question had any connection with responsible Government, but Metcalfe himself went no further than to deny responsibility for the Bill's introduction.[43] The *Colonist* confessed that the principle of Baldwin's Bill was generally accepted, though "the public were no means wedded to all its details."[44] The Governor, the late ministers, Reformers of all hues, and even a number of moderate Tories—in short the majority of the populace—favoured the abortive scheme of University reform. The only dissenters were High Churchmen.

v

In the midst of the political furore of 1844 several events occurred which decisively affected the future of the University question. The disruption of the Church of Scotland in Canada reduced the number of students at Queen's from thirty to eleven,[45] just one more than at its inception, and the influential group of Presbyterians who formed the Free Church soon established Knox College as an appendage to King's. The appointment of Ryerson as Superintendent of Education for Canada West and his fifteen months' absence from Canada not only removed one of the prime figures in the University controversy but inaugurated an era of decay for Victoria College which seriously diminished the influence of that institution in every sphere.

King's College had been saved for Strachan by the events of the preceding winter, but the Bishop was fully aware that this was only a temporary respite from attack. A positive defence for the College must replace the negative stand taken against Baldwin's Bill, and by midsummer Strachan had stated privately to Archdeacon Bethune two alternate schemes for reform.[46] These were the only solutions acceptable to him, and as long as he was President of King's, they were the bases of all future action and negotiations by the College Council and the Church of England. These proposals came before the public through a letter of

"Amicus" in the *Church* of February 28.[47] The Bishop's preferred scheme of reform would have restored King's to its original footing of 1827 and provided a liberal endowment for other colleges, perhaps from 900,000 acres still remaining in the Clergy Reserves. As a *pis aller*, however, he would submit "with great reluctance, and as it were, under compulsion," to the division of the original endowment of King's on the same principles as the Clergy Reserves Settlement of 1840. Whatever the Bishop's motives, such magnanimity was bound to be misinterpreted by his opponents as a monstrous attempt to extend the spoliation of public lands for denominational ends.

Despite the failure of the *Globe* and the *Banner* to turn the University question into an election issue, it was generally assumed that the new Government would bring in some measure for reform. The rumour that William Morris was preparing such a Bill was current during the last weeks of 1844, and Strachan hastened to warn his spokesmen in the Assembly, W. B. Robinson, W. H. Boulton, and Solicitor General Sherwood, that such authorship would render any Bill unacceptable to true sons of the Church.[48] Although his party might not be pledged on the University question by its pyrrhic victory in the late elections, Draper committed himself when he gained the representation of London in the Assembly by assuring his constituents that a University Bill was soon to be introduced.[49] Morris had in fact prepared at least the draft of such a measure and, having shown it in Kirk circles, received excellent advice from his co-religionists. Scobie and Buchanan both warned that postponement or failure would ruin the Government, and Scobie forecast correctly the form which opposition to the Bill would take.

The Church of England would oppose any interference with the University, as it now stands, and Dissenting bodies, who do not wish to go to the trouble or expense of obtaining Royal Charters for their Colleges, would denounce your Bill, as being the height of illiberality, and pass resolutions and public Speeches, in favor of Mr. Baldwin's Bill, & if they do not succeed in obtaining that, they would support the Church of England, in favor of no change, with the hope of getting Mr. Baldwin and his friends, back to power again which, indeed, appears to be the chief object of their desire.[50]

That Morris's Bill would evince strong Presbyterian influence was generally assumed and deprecated. The *Christian Guardian* erroneously pre-judged the Bill in that respect and repeatedly accused its authors of favouring the Churches of Scotland and England to the exclusion of popular rights, and of attempting solely a measure of expediency. "Mr. Baldwin's Bill named FOUR Upper Canada Colleges, but this honours by name only TWO.... How hard it seems for public men to divest themselves of the prejudice, that some British subjects are SUPERIOR and others INFERIOR on account of religious worship!"[51] Two weeks later the *Guardian* even expressed opposition to the amalgamation principle and preference for Strachan's proposals for separate universities instead of a provincial institution.

Such random criticism ended and denominational lines of interest hardened when the real terms of Draper's University Bill and its two supplements received first reading on March 4. Like Baldwin's Bill this one provided for the amalgamation of Queen's and Victoria at Toronto with some undefined relation to the University,[52] and future affiliation by other denominations on the same basis. Significantly, it was not thought necessary to mention Regiopolis. King's was similarly reduced by a supplemental Bill but returned by implication to Anglican control. In other respects the departure from Baldwin's example was quite marked. Most important was the erection of the "University of Upper Canada" (an attractive title) replete with the endowment of King's as the teaching and examining body in arts and sciences. The sliding scale of payments to the affiliated colleges was more generous, and control of the University was vested entirely in academicians representing the groups within it. The requirement that all students belong to the college of their faith was recognition of the religious basis of education. Thus the Bill attempted a happy compromise between national and sectarian interests by combining at one time and in one place the advantages of the residential college and centralized university, teaching secular education in a religious *milieu* with state endowments for religious purposes.

Such a settlement might well have proven, as Draper hoped, a final solution to the University question but for the separatist interests of extremists. The support of the Kirk was of course assured but this would be automatically offset to a large degree by the Free Church influence. The Wesleyan Methodist paper belatedly supported Draper after its earlier excursion into sectarian polemics. The Wesleyans were, however, facing a lay revolt on the important Toronto Circuit, commenced as a protest against Ryerson's intervention in the recent Metcalfe crisis. For several months the dissident element even published a monthly paper, the *Toronto Periodical Journal,* which in April accused the Conference and its journal of preferring Strachan's "equal justice" division schemes to the ministerial measure, and of using their position as a lever to drive a hard bargain at the expense of other denominations and the good of the country.[53]

Opposition to Draper's Bill came, as Scobie had warned, from a combination of the Free Church, Baptists, Congregationalists, and the minor Methodist bodies on the left, and the Anglican defenders of King's College on the right. The *Canada Christian Advocate* spoke for the New Connexion and Primitive Methodists when it opposed Strachan's division schemes and criticized the Bill as too illiberal to give general satisfaction or do justice to the people of the province.[54] Similarly, the *Globe* and *Banner* voiced the moderate opposition of the Free Kirk to "this mass of High Churchism."[55] The fact that Draper's plan resembled in some measure that of Baldwin moderated the tone of their opposition but did not silence them. Individually they were minority groups and in the case of the Free Church practically unorganized as yet; hence the relative weakness of their position.

The response of the Church of England on the other hand manifested an earnestness and urgency which betrayed its awareness of the critical nature of the events. The *Church* regularly stigmatized all agitation of the University question as political in its purpose.[56] Strachan realized as well as the Kirkites that the Imperial government would be unwilling to interfere with such a settlement, especially since it came from a nominally conservative ministry. He dispatched letters to William Henry Draper, William Boulton, and Inspector General W. B. Robinson denouncing the amalgamation Bill as subversive of public morality and good order, warning them against treason to their church (or was it to their diocesan?).[57] Strachan also wrote directly to Draper. This Bill, he protested, was worse than Baldwin's. The only acceptable solution must be one of his division schemes. "No amalgamation" would be the oriflamme of the Church in defence of its sacred rights.

Strachan and the other authorities of King's College were prepared to use every available means to stop the course of these Bills which were the more dangerous because Draper stood much higher in the counsel and esteem of the Church of England than did Baldwin. A petition from the visitors of King's

College stressed the illegality and inexpediency of interfering with the royal charter, and J. H. Cameron, speaking at the bar of the Assembly as counsel for the College, took the identical ground which Draper had so ably expounded in the previous Parliament against Baldwin's Bill.[58] As on that occasion, the *Patriot* and its echo the *Church* denounced any division or spoliation of the endowment as sacrilege.[59] Cameron's speech occupied fourteen columns, half of the four-page issue, of the Toronto *Herald* of March 31. But the Kingston *Chronicle and Gazette* readily reduced it to one simple proposition: the Crown cannot withdraw a charter except for neglect or gross abuse of its terms.[60]

In the face of the threatened resignation of Solicitor General Sherwood and Inspector General Robinson, Draper rose on March 18 to move the second reading of his University Bill. It was another of his oratorical *tours de force* lasting for hours, yet lucid and convincing in its exposition of the principles of the measure. The House was startled by his revelation of two despatches of 1828 and 1831 which had been suppressed by Colborne. The earlier stated the desire of the Imperial government to grant no charter contrary to the wishes of the colonists, the second was a fruitless demand for the surrender of King's College charter by the council.[61] But the amended charter could not now be surrendered, said Draper, and as no voice had been raised against the amendments in 1837, it should have been accepted and implemented. The voice of the people had been heard in favour of reforming King's that it might be a national institution. Draper believed his Bill would effect this by providing a common education in the University for students of all faiths while preserving and safeguarding the central principle of the necessary connection between religion and learning. Far from creating an infidel university these arrangements would destroy sectarian intolerance.

Draper dealt at some length with two of the several pamphlets which had appeared on both sides of the question. He used McCaul's dry repetitious brochure against amalgamation to prove his own contention that reform was needed. In reply to Strachan's two proposals Draper insisted that the endowment was not intended solely for the Church of England, nor was division feasible on the basis propounded by the Bishop. Any return to the *status quo* of 1827 would simply revive all the original difficulties. Baldwin in his turn claimed that the Bill would multiply denominational colleges but not abolish Anglican control of the Caput. More pertinent was his reminder that a large portion of the country viewed public endowment for denominational purposes of any kind with extreme distaste. William Hamilton Merritt's suggestion that provision for grammar schools should precede any action on the University question was a point well taken, for the whole educational structure was indeed being approached on a questionable premise.

When W. H. Boulton, Strachan's spokesman in the Assembly, moved that consideration of the Bill be postponed until the next session to take the sense of the country again, Draper rose to state his willingness to accept the postponement requested by a majority of his supporters, but only if the Bill passed its second reading. Never would he hold office on Boulton's terms. Boulton's resolution was defeated, and the Ministry stayed on, but seriously reduced in power and without the University measure on which they had promised to stand or fall.

Sherwood, the perennial intriguer, recanted his threatened resignation and received the merited castigation of the *Globe* for his inconsistency.[62] Robinson, however, left the Executive Council with the full approval of his constituents, announcing publicly that far from being pledged to the University Bill, he had consistently opposed its introduction and believed that making the question an open one would be a negation of responsible government.[63] The editor of the Toronto *Herald* agreed with other Reformers that Draper's Ministry were playing a double game.[64] Nor could Robinson be seduced by later overtures to resume his seat at the Council table on Metcalfe's promise that the University question would not be made a Government one, but would be left open in the House.[65] Robinson's acceptance of the implications of responsible government won for him the approval of the Reform press as "the only *honest* politician in the Ministry."[66] His former colleagues were in turn accused by the same journals of using the University Bill as a "plaything" to catch votes, of making responsible government a "humbug," and of gross hypocrisy in their promise to stand or fall collectively on this measure.[67]

The net result of Draper's attempt to settle the question was to hasten the disintegration of a tottering Executive and a divided party, to degrade the vaunted ideal of ministerial responsibility, to confound the confused state of higher education, and to encourage popular scepticism regarding the true intentions of provincial politicians. The moderate minority had lost their only opportunity to resolve the differences of educational nationalists and separatists, and the extremists on both sides were soon to have the field to themselves.

VI

The failure of both political parties to achieve university amalgamation encouraged speculation on the question of questions. Strachan's division schemes, or variations thereof, received considerable attention, and later were the basis of J. A. Macdonald's attempted settlement. The indecision of the *Christian Guardian* on the University question evident during the winter months of 1845 became a complete *volte face* after the shelving of Draper's Bill. The Wesleyan Methodist paper now confessed its lack of faith in the amalgamation principle and gave unequivocal support to the decentralized London University system. Its editor envisaged the creation of a provincial university to control curricula and examinations only, with a division of King's College endowment among the other colleges in their present locations. Canada was not ready for such an "Owenite" scheme as Draper's or Baldwin's.

Denominational education for colleges is the order of the day in England, and in the United States. It is the order of the day in Canada, only wanting greater efficiency and a less exclusive government patronage; and yet some persons,—from, we fear, very selfish and sectarian motives, —wish to break up the established order of things, and to substitute some new and untried theory, under the cover of liberality and unsectarianism. . . . The amalgamating, irreligious college would soon become more unpopular than the present one is. Finally, it would become merely a richly endowed school for the people of Toronto.[68]

Apparently the leaven of Strachan's division schemes was working in other denominations than his own.

The appointment of William Cayley in Robinson's stead served to maintain public interest in the University question. The truth of the *Globe's* assertion[69] that Cayley had accepted office on the same conditions as his predecessor —unpledged on the University question—was shown later in the University debates of 1846. The anticipated collapse of this reorganized Ministry and the departure of Metcalfe raised Reformers' hopes that their political Canaan was near, and the widely advertised University meeting held at Toronto during the first week of February was but one of several intended to publicize Reform opinions and unity on the particular issues.[70] The resolutions passed in the Reverend John Roaf's Congregational Chapel opposed any division or sectarian application of the endowment of King's College, and demanded the end of all religious tests and theological teaching there. To ensure further the University's non-sectarian character it was resolved that financial control should be vested in an external body directly responsible to the Legislature.

These opinions were expressed by leading clerics of the Baptist, Congregational, and Free Churches, none of which yet possessed their own colleges. The Churches of England and Scotland and the Wesleyan Methodists were represented by prominent lay members of each. The *Christian Guardian* accused the four Wesleyans who attended the meeting of forming "a party" (a horrible word!) and named Dr. Burns, firebrand of the Free Church, as "the root and spring" of the meeting.[71] The *Canada Christian Advocate* intimated that "the party" was more widespread on the troublesome Toronto Circuit than the *Guardian* would dare to admit.[72] The *Advocate* added its *nihil obstat* of the resolutions to that of the *Banner* and the secular Reform journals.[73]

Similar letters from Governor General Lord Cathcart to the heads of the four incorporated Colleges inviting them to give opinions on reform brought replies which testified to a general change of attitude.[74] King's College Council suggested minor changes in the University charter, but insisted that rival colleges be endowed from the Clergy Reserves, not from a division of the University funds. Privately Strachan informed the Governor General that no settlement of the University question could possibly please everyone. Ryerson as nominal Principal of Victoria replied that while the College board was not disposed to dictate any settlement to the Government, it now favoured a division of King's endowment among the separate institutions, or failing this, a sufficient and permanent endowment from other sources for Victoria at its present location. Regiopolis similarly expressed preference for a four-way division of King's College endowment or a separate endowment, but rejected the principle of amalgamation in elementary or higher education *in toto*. Queen's alone still plumped for a centralized university with surrounding theological halls, and lauded the incalculable advantages of Draper's Bill in the highest terms.

In view of these clearly expressed opinions from the largest denominations and the resurgence of Reform strength shown by such events as the Toronto University reform meeting, it is difficult to account for the reappearance of Draper's Bills during the session of 1846. Draper was fully aware of the changed attitude at Victoria and expected that the division cry would soon be raised at Queen's. "If this is so," he confided to Ryerson, "I may look on the fate of my bills as sealed—and I shall be driven to abandon all hope of being the party by whom the University Question is settled. . . . Some one else must undertake the task if division is the principle."[75] Ryerson reassured Draper that the University question was "the only serious obstacle" to his "continued & increased success," holding out at the same time the hope that the Victoria College board might be swayed from their stated purpose.[76] But at the same instant a letter over the well-known pseudonym "A U.E. Loyalist" appeared in the *Christian Guardian* on March 25 advocating the London University system. The only newspaper still supporting Draper's scheme of amalgamation plus sectarianism seems to have been the Kingston *Argus*.[77]

Why then did the Honourable George Barker Hall, independent member for Northumberland (South), where Victoria College was located, reintroduce Draper's Upper Canada University Bill? The debate as recorded by the *Mirror of Parliament* suggests that Hall's move came as a complete surprise to the Attorney General West, and that Draper's subsequent revival of the two supplementary Bills was an attempt to make the best of a bad beginning.[78] No mention of the controversial issue had been made in the Throne Speech, and the University question as such had not been discussed previously during the session. In the eyes of the Reformers Hall's gesture was an insult, a bad joke, a result of vexation caused by the Government's evasive tactics. In any case the familiar pattern of petitions, King's College counsel at the bar, mutual recriminations among the Ministry and its so-called supporters was repeated again. The debate covered precisely the same ground as that on the same Bills on the previous session, with confused references to the Robinson episode. The only incident of importance was the defection of several members who opposed the measure now because it was a private Bill, and the action of Inspector General Cayley who defied his leader by advocating division of the endowment.[79] Draper had no choice this time regarding postponement of the Bill. Boulton's amendment on the second reading hoisted the Bill into limbo by a majority of 40 to 20. With the Bill went the amalgamation principle, to be revived in an attenuated form two generations later as the basis of the present system at Toronto.

VII

Popular interest in the question seemed to wane during the winter of 1846-7. The two strongest advocates of the limited amalgamation scheme retired from the combat. Liddell returned to Scotland with a deep sense of frustration arising from the apparent apathy of the Board of Trustees of Queen's towards their own resolutions of September, 1842, and more convinced than ever that Canada was not yet ready for a university.[80] Draper, weary and disgusted with the pettiness of provincial politics, finally obtained Hagerman's seat on the Bench just after the session opened in 1847. The appointment of Sherwood as Attorney General West to succeed the rival who had forced him out of the Cabinet short months ago seemed to presage a restoration of High Church ascendancy. But Elgin, the newest Governor General, made no more reference to education in his Speech from the Throne than had Cathcart at the preceding session. It must therefore have come as a surprise when the same Ministry which had delayed the calling of Parliament out of fear of its opposition dared to introduce a University Bill which was a radical departure from either of its ill-fated predecessors.

John A. Macdonald, the unknown "third rate lawyer" and "*moderate Conservative Anticompact*" Draperite,[81] had insisted on attempting to settle the University question virtually as a condition of his joining the Sherwood-Daly Government. "Many questions of more real importance may arise, but none which operates so strongly on the principles or rather prejudices of the public, and if the Conservatives hope to retain power they *must* settle it before the General Elections."[82] The failure to effect that settlement did indeed contribute to the party's defeat, but Macdonald had counted on Draper's continuing in the Ministry. Nevertheless a Presbyterian came closer to success than had two Anglicans, since he at least got the support of the President of King's College for his plan of dividing the endowment. Perhaps it took a Scot to convince a Scot.

The two Bills introduced by Macdonald on July 9 were the essence of simplicity when contrasted to Baldwin's lumbering 108-clause effort. The first repealed the amendments to the charter of King's College made in 1837 and restored the institution to absolute control by the Church of England. The second transferred the University endowment to a board composed of one government nominee and one representative each from King's, Queen's, Victoria, and Regiopolis, which was to superintend the investment and distribution of the funds among the colleges. Queen's, Victoria, and Regiopolis were promised £1,500 each per annum, but King's as a token of vested rights was to have £3,000. Another £2,500 would be divided among the district grammar schools, and any surplus remaining was to be invested for the benefit of any colleges incorporated thereafter.

These proposals recognized the inherent relation of religion and education, and established the principle of collegiate establishments under denominational control for which the High Churchmen and Roman Catholics had consistently contended. At the same time it provided an assured income to colleges for whom finances were the prime consideration. Macdonald envisaged nothing more, or less, than a galaxy of independent denominational colleges scattered across the province, each receiving a modest income from the state. He defended this plan as "the only manner in which the question could be settled with a proper regard for justice," and sanguinely hoped that it would "meet the assent of all parties." [83]

The reaction of the various interested groups was immediate and unmistakable. Over sixty Baptist congregations petitioned the Assembly through their Union against the Bills as "unjust . . . and injurious to the interest of education." [84] The division of the endowment was opposed on the grounds that the Church of England would receive a disproportionate share, that the endowment of only four denominations ignored the rights of nearly half the population and prejudiced the work of other unaided institutions, that the proportions allowed to the four colleges named would not be sufficient even for their needs. Above all, the province required at least one institution which would be open to all, which would be unblighted by sectarian influences. Petitions to the same effect were received from the Congregationalists, from the inhabitants of Toronto, Hamilton, Cobourg, Kingston, Beamsville, Russell, Chinguacousy, Johnstown District, and even several from Canada East. Macdonald's remark that these petitions were not numerous could not have been made had the session lasted longer.

The journals of the Free Church, Episcopal Methodists, and New Connexion Methodists loudly protested the spoliation of a property which belonged not to any sect but to the people of Canada. [85] The income of the endowment was not yet sufficient to support one good college; its division would be robbery. The *Globe* called on its readers for a "flood" of petitions to protest this bribery offered to three particular denominations. "Insist that all denominations shall have an equal claim to manage and enjoy the benefits of this great institution, and that not one copper of the funds shall be alienated from its original purpose." The approval of the University Bill by the *Colonist* and *Christian Guardian* "is enough to stamp the measure as utterly base and worthless." [86]

The debate in the Assembly took place on the first reading, an evidence of the intense interest which the question held for legislators. The strongest denunciation came from Baldwin, spokesman of the secularists, who damned the measure roundly. "Settling the question indeed, by sweeping the University from off the face of the earth, and giving the Country, in its stead, a few paltry

Institutions, in none of which could there be any possible pretention to those attributes which it was the highest behest to a University to a possess."[87] The division of the endowment was nothing more than "well understood" political *ad captandum*. But the support of such Tories as Cameron, Boulton, and Sherwood was encouraging to Macdonald in view of their stand on Draper's Bills.[88] In addition he had the full backing of the *Christian Guardian* and the Wesleyan Methodist authorities, now reunited with their more conservative British brethren. The *Guardian* gave three sufficient reasons for supporting Macdonald's plan—its "comparative equality and liberality," its practical provision "for a Christian in contradistinction to a secular or infidel education," and its recognition of "*denominational* colleges." The editor noted the shift from amalgamation to secularization which had occured in Reform policy on the question. "There is a wide difference between the Provincial University talked of in 1844 and that which is now advocated by the opponents of present measure. The same phraseology is used, but a very different thing is meant; and thus a gross sophism is played off upon the public."[89]

Although no official statement of policy by Queen's appeared while the Bills were before the House, Macdonald's close connection with that institution assured him of the Kirk's support. And Scobie now reversed his stand on Draper's Bill to bring the weight of the *Colonist* to the Receiver General's aid.[90] Similarly it can be assumed that the trustees of Regiopolis favoured the measure which would bring the financial succour for which they had been importuning Parliament. But the rank and file of Irish Roman Catholics were still wedded to the Reform cause. In the case of King's College a statement of policy was forthcoming. In reply to J. H. Cameron's plea to McCaul for a favourable expression on the "*vexata questio*" the College council refused "to assent to any alienation of the property committed to their charge."[91] To reinforce its position the council stated specifically its objections to the plan, including the financial control by an external "mixed Board," and the inadequacy of a mere £3,000 per annum. It is noteworthy, however, that only five councillors signed this document, and Strachan had already ceased to attend their meetings, probably because of his differences with McCaul over the principle of dividing the endowment.[92]

Macdonald's decision not to proceed even to the second reading of the Bill was undoubtedly prompted by the growing opposition both in and out of the House. Open defiance by two Conservatives and the opposition of two pledged Methodists and all the Roman Catholic members, the obvious internal divisions of his party—all this was sufficiently disheartening without the added affliction of impending domestic tragedy.[93] As for the tradition created by Macdonald himself that Strachan withdrew at the last moment from their gentlemen's agreement, the weight of evidence seems to point as much to a plot among Macdonald's colleagues as to duplicity on the part of the Bishop. One author without citing authorities insists that McCaul was responsible for convincing Strachan of his error.[94] Yet the estrangement between these two did not end then, and also as late as July 19, just seven days before the Bill's demise, Strachan wrote to Solicitor General Cameron assuming that if the bills had not yet passed, certain changes might be considered.[95] No letter to Boulton has ever been found, but it seems equally strange that a trained lawyer should accept such circumstantial evidence as the word of political associates whom he had every reason to distrust. Neither version of the incident is satisfactory.[96]

One small event which has apparently received no notice lends weight to the suggestion that Macdonald's story was an apocryphal attempt to explain to posterity the failure of his first legislation as a Minister of the Crown, that the real reasons were those given in the Assembly on July 26, 1847. A postponement of the Bills had already been mooted in the Cabinet in response to petitions and the request of party supporters. "Under these circumstances," Macdonald stated, "and as the Administration were convinced that the more the Government Measures were known, the better they would be liked, they had come to the conclusion not to press the Bills through the House during the present Session." That same morning before he rose in his place to make this statement, a petition against his Bills had been read from his own constituency, where two of the four colleges involved were located.[97]

VIII

Every interested body, and this seems to have embraced the entire population of the western half of the province, took advantage of the postponement of Macdonald's Bills to air its views. Church authorities passed resolutions and formulated petitions; meetings under lay auspices copied this clerical example. The decision late in the year by a hesitant Ministry to risk a dissolution and face the country merely elevated the University question one step further to the level of an election issue. But it was an issue of such consequence that it almost submerged that other burning issue of the 1840's, responsible government.

Wesleyan Methodist support for Macdonald's division scheme continued undiminished, and Ryerson so far forgot his official position as to publish a long encomium on the scheme, repeating the same reasons that the *Guardian* had already given on November 17, and the same strictures on Baldwin's plan. The special committee of Conference went further and embodied these sentiments in a petition to the Assembly urging adoption of the Bills which it requested all members and friends of the denomination to sign.[98] Such tactics the *Globe* considered to be "disgusting blasphemy," a priestly attempt to seduce the people from their genuine interests, a "new manœuvre" bearing the stamp of Ryerson's influence, to rescue Victoria from impending ruin.[99] All this the *Christian Guardian* denied on November 24, disclaiming all interest in party fortunes and reiterating naively the argument that the University question was not a political one. "Had we even the power to do so, we would never for a moment think of committing the Church on a political question to a political party." Despite these disclaimers the *Guardian* was never more completely a partisan journal than during the election months of 1847.

The Church of Scotland Synod still clung tenaciously to its conviction that the paucity of students suggested the efficacy of centralization.[100] But as the principle of division now seemed to be generally accepted, the Synod was "content to acquiesce" in such a settlement. Perhaps the Synod held its fire too long for it did not issue its petitions until the elections were under way. Macdonald was getting scant support from his own church whom he had sought to benefit and whose college stood in his constituency. Nor was the response from the other college in Kingston encouraging. The lengthy address on education from the Roman Church to its adherents condemned the religious indifference of King's College as a menace to Catholic students, and called on its adherents to pledge their candidates to obtaining an endowment for Regiopolis—an endowment, however, from the Jesuit Estates rather than from any partition of the funds of King's College.[101] In the fate of this latter institution Roman Catholics were told they could have no interest.

On the hustings of Canada West the University question was generally conceded to be the most important issue. Baldwin's address to the electors of the fourth riding of York sounded the keynote of the Reform campaign. He expressed his conviction that King's College should be "relieved of that character of exclusiveness which now attaches to it," and its success ensured by preserving the integrity of its endowment. Macdonald's Bill was nothing more than a "delusion and a snare," its financial terms intended "to catch some breath of popular favour."[102] Other candidates echoed Baldwin's denunciation of any division of the national endowment for sectarian purposes. Behind the Reform party was thrown the weight of Baptist, Congregationalist, Free Church, Methodist Episcopal, and New Connexion influence.[103] The *Record's* strictures on the University Bills were later supplemented by Dr. Burns' letters to the Governor General printed in the *Banner*.[104] The Reverend Robert Fyfe explained the voluntarist position of the Baptists through the medium of the *Globe*.[105] Even a group of Wesleyan Methodists revolted against the "political intermeddling" of the *Christian Guardian* and the Conference special committee, and countered the Church's official pronouncements by proclaiming that any division of King's College funds "which belong equally to all the Inhabitants of Canada" would by a violation of the Golden Rule.[106]

The most representative document to emanate from Reform sources was, however, the "Address to the People of Canada from the Central Committee at Toronto for promoting University Reform." The Administration's "spoliation plan" was characterized as grandiloquent demagoguery, as a bribe to gain the support of certain denominations.

Fellow Countrymen! That Administration has not scrupled to ask your consent to your degradation. You have been asked to barter your dearest rights and the noble inheritance of your children for delusive promises, which can never be fulfilled. You have been asked to sacrifice the most magnificent Educational Endowment . . . to a few Sectarian Colleges already languishing, because of the exclusive principles on which they are founded. You have been asked to squander this noble endowment, legally secured to you without distinction of party, or creed, among the Leaders of a few Religious Denominations, whose cupidity has made them the willing prey of a needy Administration.[107]

King's College must be purged of every trace of denominationalism, its endowment carefully husbanded, and its theological chair liquidated. "We do not deprecate Theological Learning, but we think that it may well be taught by the several sects out of their own funds." The numerous signers of this polemical item were drawn from no less than nine denominations. Only the Church of Scotland and the Wesleyan Methodists were unrepresented.

Conservative candidates seemed generally prepared to state their approval of the University Bills or at worst to be non-committal. The Kingston *Chronicle and News* of December 22 noted that they were more definite than the Reformers. If pledges were not demanded at least the electors were advised to know their candidate's opinion on the University question before giving their votes.[108] To the electors of Kingston Macdonald explained his University Bills in detail and successfully used the University issue as his main plank for re-election. He described how he had obtained the approval of the four religious bodies who possessed colleges by direct consultation (a stratagem which both Baldwin and

Draper had ignored). In his opinion the country had rejected the amalgamation principle three times and he was now convinced that any permanent settlement would require a new vision and a new man.[109]

Macdonald stressed the religious nature of his proposals as contrasted to Baldwin's "Godless University" scheme, and emphatically denied the Reformers' accusation that his measure excluded other denominations than those named from obtaining the benefits intended for sectarian colleges. Proportionate assistance was ensured for all chartered colleges which might be established in future. Macdonald explained that the distinction between his University Bill and all its predecessors was that whereas the latter uniformly envisaged one great institution at Toronto, "inaccessible to the great body of the people," he aimed at placing the advantages of a university education within their reach by means of a decentralized system of sectarian colleges fed by scholarship students from district schools. His *argumentum ad ecclesiam,* the promise of more accessible education through denominational colleges, is misleading simply because the colleges would *not* be centrally located in the province.

If the election results are judged by the standard of popular approval of Macdonald's University scheme, the returns from Canada West were indecisive, for the total victory of the Reformers in the western peninsula was balanced by the Conservative successes along the Ontario Strand. The failure which Macdonald had foreseen for his party and his University Bills turned finally on the Canada East votes irretrievably lost in the disastrous attempt to win French-Canadian support through the agency of R. E. Caron.

IX

The first session of the Parliament was held in 1848, lasted only one month and is notable in Canadian history for nothing. If the Reform supporters expected some attempt at University legislation they were disappointed. But the Administration were not allowed to forget entirely the issue which in the western extremities of the province had been so largely responsible for their success at the polls. Dr. Burns continued the agitation for a single provincial institution possessed of the undivided endowment in his series of open letters to the Governor General published in the *Banner.*[110] The Synod of his Church passed a declaratory resolution reaffirming their desire to see King's College "freed from its present sectarian management, so as to deserve the confidence of the community at large," and appointed a committee chaired by Burns to watch over any University Bill which might be introduced into the Legislature.[111] Except for this action by the Free Church, the country seemed to show little immediate interest in agitating the University question.

Late in the year, however, the *Globe* announced with obvious satisfaction that a new University Bill was being prepared that would be generally approved of by the community.[112] The University would be henceforth conducted on Christian principles without any invidious religious tests or sectarian distinctions. Secularization was clearly foreshadowed but religious influence would be protected by the presence of a board of management of one representative from each theological college. Having seen a draft of the proposed Bill in the *Globe,* the *Canada Christian Advocate* declared that the Methodist Episcopals would certainly support such a plan.[113] Some secular journals were of a different opinion. The Perth *Constitutional* defined the issue as "Religion *vs* Radicalism" and accused the Reformers of preferring their party to Christ's cause.[114] The Cobourg *Star* also stressed the anti-religious nature of such a Bill. "If our University is to be a hot-bed of infidelity, away with it; scatter it to the four winds of Heaven. Let not such a deadly *Upas* take root in this virgin soil."[115]

The speech delivered from the Throne when Parliament reassembled on January 18, 1849, gave ample notice of impending legislation on the University question.[116] The *Christian Guardian* of January 24 wilfully misunderstood the warning, preferring to believe that no "final settlement" would be essayed during the session, especially not along the unpopular lines which had recently been suggested by journalistic contemporaries. For ten weeks no move was made by the Government towards introducing a University Bill. While the *Globe* prodded the Administration with no visible results, the Conservatives became hopeful that no action would be taken. But Baldwin's delay was not the effect of timidity or heart-searching. The Government, he explained, were awaiting some report from the commission appointed by King's College Council to investigate the charges of carelessness and mismanagement in the University's affairs.[117] John Wetenhall, member for Halton and one of the commissioners, could supply the House with no official statement, and intimated that no report would be forthcoming for some time.

Soon the petitions demanding reform of King's College ceased to be presented to the Assembly, and the matter of University legislation seemed forgotten in the rising tide of sentiment on the Rebellion Losses Bill, Navigation Laws, and annexation. In the midst of these distracting matters Baldwin suddenly introduced his University Bill. Its terms were, as the secularizationists had promised, more extreme than those of the Bill of 1843.[118]

First and foremost, every vestige of denominationalism was obliterated from the University. Not only were all religious tests abolished and Beaven's divinity chair overturned, but no ecclesiastic was eligible as Chancellor or President. The incorporated colleges would upon affiliation be reduced to divinity halls as had been planned in 1843, but this time they would receive nothing from the endowment. Their representation in the Senate by one member would be considered a sufficient safeguard for the Christian basis of the University. The whole endowment was preserved, as the Reformers had demanded, for the benefit of the new University of Toronto. A further departure from the Bill of 1843 was the explicit repudiation of the collegiate system in favour of the professorial. Henceforth the University would teach and examine in all subjects except divinity. In one respect only did this second Bill by Baldwin approach the schemes suggested by the Conservative Bills—in place of an external board of control, the Government would nominate the members of the Senate, an insignificant number in such a large body. But here the sting was in the tail, for the University finances became the preserve of a three-man Endowment Board, the chairman of which would be the Crown-appointed business manager of the University. The intention of the whole Bill was obviously to create one centralized provincial university and to reduce by starvation the other two chartered colleges that Baldwin's creature might monopolize higher education in the province.

The positions that the religious bodies held on Macdonald's Bill were now completely reversed. The secularizationists—Baptists, Free Church, Congregationalists, the minor Methodist groups, and some dissatisfied Wesleyans and Anglicans, the same who were demanding an end to the Clergy Reserves—gave unstinting support to the University Bill.[119] With them too stood the Council of King's College except for its new President, McCaul.[120] The Roman Catholics again offered the tacit support of neutrals who sought thereby to advance their own peculiar interests.[121] In opposition this time were the supporters, both lay and clerical, of Victoria and Queen's, and the few Tory Anglicans who stubbornly refused to relinquish control of King's. This last group included W. B. Robinson and W. Boulton who stood in a minority of two on the five amendments which they offered during the second reading,[122] and of course Bishop Strachan who refused to desert the cause of religion in his educational offspring, even though he had retired from its presidency more than a year before.

Strachan's petition to the Assembly against the University Bill repeated many of the same arguments he had directed against Baldwin's first measure. The Bill was an interference with corporate privileges and vested rights; the scheme it embodied was without precedent in the world, "and must, in practice, create jealousies and distrust, and destroy everything like harmony in the working of the Institution."[123] Above all the Bill showed "striking opposition to Religious truth" and "particular enmity" to the Church of England, which for its part could have no connection with an institution where its religion was proscribed. The proposed scheme could never settle the University question, for only a fraction of the population, "noisy from ignorance," would benefit while the four largest denominations at least would ostracize such an infidel university. Was it fair that the "National Church" should be despoiled of its university charter while Queen's and Victoria retained theirs?

The petition from the trustees of Queen's stressed the unnatural separation of religion from education and the dire effects of such a centralized monopoly which would destroy "generous rivalry" between the colleges.[124] The trustees now definitely rejected amalgamation, recalling that the original endowment was intended for "seminaries," and refused to surrender the university powers of Queen's. The Wesleyan Methodists as a church took no official action on Baldwin's Bill, but the *Christian Guardian* devoted two lengthy editorials on April 18 and 25 to denouncing the leading principles of the scheme, "Infidelity" and "Centralization." The fate of France was cited as an admonition against irreligion. The editor repeated Macdonald's and his own arguments against central amalgamation, and for the London University system.

Can any sane man suppose that an equal amount of good can be accomplished by one Giant University in an extensive Province, as can be accomplished by a dozen University Colleges scattered over the whole? . . .
The whole basis of the bill is bad. It is founded upon principles subversive to the best interests of the Country,—principles alike repugnant to the religious feelings of the great majority of the Canadian public, and to their sense of justice and good faith.

Like the board of Victoria College the authorities of Regiopolis had recently been petitioning the Assembly for an endowment for their college, and now considered silence on the University Bill the best policy. During the session the Roman Catholics did obtain an Act incorporating the College of Bytown, on the same basis as Regiopolis, that is without an endowment or degree-granting powers.[125] But this was effected by the French-dominated diocese of Ottawa, the ambitious young rival of Kingston. In any case no new institution would be permitted to impair the monopoly which Baldwin's system intended to bestow on the University of Toronto.

The *Church* viewed the University Bill as the anti-religious counterpart of the disloyal Rebellion Losses Act. "Our Rebel-paying Coryphoei at Montreal, after the outrage which they have just consummated upon the *political* predilections of every decent man in the country, are going to carry out . . . their projected insult to the religious feelings . . . by passing their impious University Bill."[126] The "turpitude" of this latter infidel bill "immeasurably surpassed" that of the Rebellion Losses payments. The *Guardian* gloomily predicted that the Ministry would have no trouble such as Draper and Macdonald had encountered. "With their present majority they could carry a Bill, even more objectionable. . . ."[127]

Nevertheless the Reformers did have the support of a number of journals both secular and religious. The *Globe* and the *Canadian Free Press* approved the principle of the Bill as "national, not sectarian," and particularly the proposed reduction of Victoria and Queen's to the status of divinity halls.[128] The *Record* referred to the literary department of Queen's as "a great mistake" which the Free Church Synod decided to avoid by limiting Knox College permanently to divinity, thereby leaving the arts subjects entirely to King's.[129] The *Canadian Christian Advocate* claimed for the Bill the support of a majority of the people, not a fraction as Strachan and Ryerson asserted, and the Baptists viewed it as a victory for voluntarism. "The People will neither suffer *John* or *Egerton* to deprive them any longer of their just rights." Certainly the *Advocate* spoke for all Methodists outside the Wesleyan body, and some within, when it said that the *Guardian's* opposition was motivated by cupidity, not religion. "*It is simply because the Government has not given the Wesleyans one-fourth of the College Funds,* and because the great Dr. will never be allowed to hold the office of Chancellor or President."[130]

x

Baldwin's University Bill passed into law as everyone expected it would. In vain did Strachan seek its disallowance through the influence of Sir Robert Peel.[131] Personal remonstrances to Baldwin were of no avail.[132] An attempt to circumvent the Governor General earned the Bishop a sharp reprimand from the Colonial Office.[133] The home government refused to interfere with the workings of responsible government. The first phase of the University question in Canada West, the search for a system of higher education, was closed. The triumph of the centripetal forces of nationalism and secularism over denominational separatism seemed complete. One "godless" institution now appropriated the former Anglican monopoly of the national educational endowment, and its chartered rivals at Cobourg and Kingston were left out to die of financial malnutrition.

Throughout this decade the attempts at settling the University question had ranged from the compromise of centralized amalgamation with denominational participation suggested in 1843 and 1845, to the extremes of complete denominational control in 1847 and the final secular monopoly in 1849. One large but heterogeneous group had consistently upheld the claims of secular nationalism in the field of higher education. This comprised voluntarists—Baptists, Congregationalists, Free Church Presbyterians, Primitive, New Connexion, and Episcopal Methodists, Bible Christians, and a sprinkling of Anglicans and Wesleyan Methodists—the same religious interests which demanded the secularization of the Clergy Reserves. In constant defence of separate denominational education stood the bulk of the Church of England. The Wesleyan Methodists, only lukewarm towards centralization at the outset, changed in mid-conflict to the side of the Anglican separatists. The Church of Scotland, which first brought the issue of amalgamation into the arena of politics, sought a compromise solution as long as there was any reasonable hope of obtaining peace with honour. But as in the conflict over separate elementary schools the deciding vote lay with the Roman Catholics. In the University question that large and influential body supported the cause of nationalized university education for political rather than religious reasons. Strong political ties with the Reform side more than offset the weak leadership offered during this decade by the clerical authorities of the Church of Rome.

The question of questions in 1850 was now whether the remaining denominational colleges would be absorbed into the unilateral system, or whether the vagaries of politics might not reverse this trend of higher education in Canada West.

CHAPTER FIVE

THE UNIVERSITY QUESTION, 1850-1867

A Pattern Established

I

THE PURPOSE of Baldwin's University Act of 1849 was unmistakable. The University of Toronto was to be the provincial University, the only institution in possession of the endowment which had been given for the "seminaries," and the only one with degree-granting powers. Provision for the affiliation of Queen's and Victoria with the provincial University on surrender of their charters had been made, but no financial encouragement had been offered them. In view of this latter circumstance and of the widespread objection to the "irreligious" atmosphere of the University, it was highly improbable that these other universities would commit suicide by reducing themselves to divinity halls. Victoria in fact was not intended as a theological seminary, and did not introduce such studies for another generation. But Baldwin's whole scheme of a unified system of higher education postulated an absolute monopoly for the Toronto institution, and the success or failure of the scheme would be determined by the fate of these two rivals.

The opposition to the new University intensified after the crises of the Rebellion Losses Bill and annexation had passed. The aging Bishop Strachan had undertaken a twofold attack on the University Act by petitioning for its disallowance, and by starting a movement for the creation of an exclusively Anglican university. The Synod of the Church of Scotland copied the Anglican example of petitioning the Throne for amendment, but the Colonial Office, true to the principle of responsible government, refused to interfere in the matter.[1] Any remedial action must come from the provincial government. Both Queen's and Victoria had refused to join the infidel University and even the Free Church had expressed disappointment at its irreligious tendency.[2] The *Christian Guardian* of February 27, 1850, was able to list at least nine newspapers which opposed Baldwin's University settlement.

As Lord Elgin foresaw, Strachan and the Orange Order were preparing a crusade against the University, and the Tories were using the question of questions as a political "stalking horse" in the provincial Parliament.[3] The defence of the new institution undertaken by the *Record* and the *Watchman* against the *Christian Guardian* and High Church journals was not very effective.[4] Both sides claimed the support of the Roman Catholics, but later events placed that body definitely on the side of the denominational colleges. The *Christian Guardian* maintained that the Methodist Episcopals and many Presbyterians as well as the Roman Catholics now opposed the Act. Even the *Examiner* had changed sides. "At the very lowest we may safely say that three-fourths of the country are opposed to the Bill, and that proportion is daily increasing."[5]

Prodded by public opinion and the Governor General, Baldwin finally brought forward a declaratory Act to "Remove Certain Doubts respecting the Intention of the Act of the Last Session." Its preamble acknowledged that "notwithstanding the distinct avowal of the principles on which the said Act was based, doubts have been raised as to the Christian character of the said Institution." But it denied explicitly that the non-sectarian provisions had originated in anything more than "a sincere desire for the advancement of True Religion, and a tender regard for the conscientious scruples of all classes of professing Christians." In effect, however, the only change was some nebulous permission for denominations to impose religious training or tests on their own students.

Innocuous as the Act might be, it did influence the Wesleyan Methodist policy for Victoria College. An enabling Act was obtained by that body to authorize the transfer of Victoria to Toronto.[6] Thus a breach in the opposition seemed to be made, and the Government was prepared to follow it up by using financial coercion on the recalcitrant Queen's College.[7] The stoppage of the annual grants to these rivals was intended to hasten their submission to the new order in university education.

Despite the *Guardian*'s injunction on March 13 that Victoria must not be given up, the Wesleyan Conference considered the future possibilities for Victoria—removal to Toronto or remaining at Cobourg.[8] A minority were prepared to jettison the whole establishment. The sudden desertion of Principal Alexander McNab to the Church of England and other disruptive incidents left the College completely demoralized. In the end the decision to remain at Cobourg until some satisfactory disposition of the buildings could be made was announced to the "brethren and friends." The four students who appeared in hopeful anticipation of Victoria's reopening in September, 1850, were detained almost literally by their coat-tails by Samuel S. Nelles, the new acting Principal and for the moment the sole staff member *in situ*. For Queen's the prospects of 1850-1 looked brighter, and the Synod approved the decision of the trustees to carry on the College work, confidently expecting that the measure of 1849 would prove a failure because of its irreligious character.[9] The policy for Queen's had changed permanently from supporting centralization to support for the ideal of a decentralized university. Among the reasons given were the increase in population and the threat of Romish influence.

While Baldwin was engaged with Elgin's blessing in trying to bring Queen's and Victoria to heel, his provincial institution was threatened by Strachan's scheme for establishing a "Church University." A mere divinity college would of course be in accord with the one-university system, but such a school of Anglican theology already existed at Cobourg. If Strachan established an arts college it would impair the monopoly of the University at Toronto, and if *per fas et nefas*, the Bishop ever obtained a charter with degree-granting powers for his church university, the system for which Baldwin had laboured would be ruined. Such an example would undoubtedly encourage Victoria and Queen's to continue separately. In place of one university there would then be four or more, and the denominational institutions would share the work of higher education with the provincial institution. Such a pluralistic system was in fact the basis of the pattern established between 1850 and Confederation. But for the moment Strachan and Baldwin bent every effort to thwart the educational dreams of each other.

II

Strachan's campaign for a church university opened in February, 1850, with a pastoral letter to the clergy and laity of the diocese.[10] The Bishop noted that hopes for the disallowance of the pernicious University Act had not materialized; the destruction of King's College as a Christian institution was now an accomplishment. "Deprived of her University, what is the Church to do? She has now no Seminary, at which to give a liberal education to her youth. What is enjoyed by all the other large Denominations in the Province is denied to her." Once more the Church of England should petition its temporal Head for redress from the wicked, infidel, disloyal, unpopular Act by restoration of *her* University. Should these just claims not be admitted, a church university must be established, for which the Bishop asked his flock to contribute an endowment of 80,000 acres. Already some £17,000 was available for the project, Strachan stated encouragingly. Large subscriptions by the Church in Canada would prove the earnestness of their intentions to the brethren in Britain where Strachan would soon go in search of financial aid, and perhaps a charter.

The *Globe* saw evidence in this pastoral letter of "back stairs influence," and warned Strachan that conditions and opinions in Britain had changed since 1827.[11] The University had not lost its Christianity, only its Puseyism, in the *Globe*'s estimation. Queen's and Victoria were self-supporting except for the annual £500 grant which the editor hoped would soon be withdrawn. If the Church of England wanted its own college let it be supported by voluntary aid. Ignoring the *Globe*'s criticism, Archdeacon Bethune announced exuberantly to the Society for the Propagation of the Gospel that his mentor's pastoral was "much admired by foes as well as friends, & is kindling quite an enthusiasm amongst Churchmen."[12] Strachan also reported its "wonderful effect" in obtaining subscriptions.[13] Elgin, however, thought differently, and informed Grey of widespread and not-so-silent opposition to Strachan and his plan among the Anglican clergy and laity.[14] Elgin might also have mentioned that the townsfolk of Niagara had censured the pastoral at a public meeting as "unfounded, and only calculated to promote a ceaseless agitation on religious matters."[15]

Upon his arrival in England Strachan immediately communicated with the Church societies and formed a committee to assist in raising funds.[16] With this assistance and by personal appeals from pulpit and press his errand was tolerably well received and he collected some £16,000 in a few months.[17] His reception by the prelates was, he wrote Chief Justice Robinson, all that he could desire.[18] His reception by politicians and government officials, however, was rather different. Wellington and Peel he found sympathetic but powerless; Lord Carlisle was non-committal. After being snubbed three times at the doors of the Colonial Office, Strachan at last reached Grey, the real focus of his efforts, only to find him virtually unco-operative despite his outward civility. Strachan expressed his willingness not to present petitions about King's College to Parliament if he obtained aid in establishing his university.[19] Specifically he asked for a royal charter similar to that of Bishop's College, a Queen's letter for collections in English churches, and a royal donation to head the list of public subscriptions.

Grey rejected both requests for financial aid, and refused to consider granting a charter until the matter had been referred to the provincial government in conformity with the usages of responsible government. This was the last thing

Strachan wanted and he replied that such a reference would be vetoed in Canada because of the avowed intention of the promoters of the new infidel University to brook no rival institutions. Strachan could see no reason in Grey's adherence to the practice of governing through a colonial "Cabinet." The facts of the University controversy were sufficiently well known, and reference back to Canada was "tantamount to a refusal." To Strachan Grey's attitude appeared "a cruel mockery," and to Chief Justice Robinson it was "Scarcely credible." [20]

The draft charter which Strachan submitted to the Colonial Office was unexceptionable, being based on those of King's and Queen's Colleges. [21] But his refusal to publish it after his return to Canada aroused more than speculation. Peter Boyle De Blaquière, an Anglican and in Elgin's estimate a Tory, had recently been installed as first Chancellor of the University of Toronto. Having learned the true intent of his Bishop's efforts in England, De Blaquière brought the matter before the Senate of the University. In a draft memorial to the Governor General he claimed, erroneously, that Victoria had closed and Queen's would follow suit soon. [22] As the revival of the exclusive privileges of King's would excite religious asperities and interfere with the University of Toronto, the Chancellor prayed that no charter be granted to Strachan unless it was for a theological college affiliated with the University.

When De Blaquière tried to get a copy of the proposed charter, Strachan indignantly refused it, unless the Chancellor would first give him copies of the "slanderous document" presented to the Senate and of "the violent and abusive speech with which you were pleased to introduce it." [23] The slander, De Blaquière retorted, had been made by Strachan in England; the Bishop had, he charged, no intention of publishing the terms of the charter until it was granted. The futile exchange of letters ended in gross personal vilification on both sides. At De Blaquière's request, the *Globe* published all this correspondence with obvious relish, and took up the hue and cry against Strachan by accusing him of trying to obtain sole control over the proposed institution. [24] The *Courier*, the Hamilton *Spectator*, and even the *Patriot* joined in the chorus against the "one-man-Charter," and Edward Ermatinger, former M.P. for Middlesex, another Tory Anglican, accused the Bishop of trying to prepetuate a dominant church. [25] There was in fact a large measure of truth in the *Globe*'s assertion that most members of the Church of England were against Strachan and his university scheme.

Grey and Elgin agreed that justice should be done to the Church of England in this matter of a charter. "On the whole I agree with you in thinking that it is better that we should put no difficulty *here* in the way of the Bishop's getting a charter," wrote Elgin. [26] At the same time he reminded Grey that the Government's policy was to set up a single provincial university. Victoria was on the point of affiliating, and Queen's must die of inanition if the annual grants were stopped. "Baldwin feels strongly that if just at this moment we are parties to setting up a Church of England College with a power to grant . . . all degrees, we shall be acting inconsistently and doing what we can to defeat our own policy." Ryerson gave Elgin his backing and advice on this point. [27]

It was then practically a foregone conclusion that the provincial Executive, on considering Grey's reference of the charter matter, would not approve Strachan's scheme. The Bishop in his turn rejected the Administration's offer to charter a theological college affiliated to the provincial University. [28] He would accept nothing less than the same privileges which the Church of Scotland and the Wesleyans possessed. Elgin now offered him a modicum of hope by admitting that he would consider it the lesser evil to multiply colleges rather than submit his own church to injustice. Nevertheless Elgin still hoped that all denominational colleges would join with the University of Toronto, and he knew this to be the sentiment of many Anglicans. Grey seconded the refusal of a charter as long as negotiations with the two other colleges were still in progress.[29]

Though no royal charter might be forthcoming in the foreseeable future, Strachan pressed on with his preparations for the church university, and the cornerstone of the building was laid in April of 1851, just nine years and one week after the same service had been performed for the ill-starred King's College. Meanwhile the Great Ministry neared its end as the Clear Grits revolted against the conservatism of Baldwin. Both of the other major religio-cultural problems —the Clergy Reserves and separate schools—were engaging the country's attention to such an extent that the University question was relegated to a secondary position. Strachan, at Chief Justice Robinson's suggestion, sought and obtained without difficulty the Act of Incorporation that was a legal necessity until more auspicious circumstances for obtaining a charter existed.[30] "I really believe," he informed Ernest Hawkins, his confidant in the Society for the Propagation of the Gospel and his chosen successor as Bishop, "that Lord Elgin is at heart favourable but is prevented from acting by that miserable faction around him."[31]

Before the next session of Parliament met in May, 1851, Henry Sherwood had publicized, through the columns of the *Colonist*, another scheme for settling the University question.[32] He proposed to copy the system of London University as the best adapted to the needs of Canada. The University of Toronto would become an examining board for denominational colleges, and would apportion the University funds among the affiliated institutions according to the number of graduating students. Such a plan had been suggested by Strachan on his return from England, as the best system, if affiliation must be the principle of any settlement, and Sherwood's explanatory letter to the public was a literal echo of the Bishop's words. Both the *Church* and the *Christian Guardian* added their blessings on Sherwood's scheme; other journals ignored the whole episode.[33]

The Press and public were so preoccupied during 1851 with the Clergy Reserves agitation that the University question was all but forgotten. In the Assembly Sherwood's Bill received scant attention, and after repeated post-ponements was withdrawn before the second reading. In its place William Boulton, Sherwood's colleague from tory Toronto, was offering a modification of the London University system which contained some novel concepts of higher education.[34]

Like Sherwood's plan, Boulton's was intended to establish a university to examine candidates and maintain uniform standards among the affiliated colleges. But no financial provision was made for these colleges; instead a new institution, University College, was to retain all the endowment and the teaching functions of the present University. A grant of £500 taken annually from the endowment must cover the University's expenses until these were assumed by the govern-ment. The most striking feature of the Bill was its suggestion of educational imperialism. Not only might any degree-granting college in Canada affiliate with the University but also those "in any other part of Her Majesty's Dominions" and all institutions "in connexion with the University of London." Here was a vision to catch the fancy of old or new imperialists.

Boulton's Bill is of particular interest as many of its proposals were embodied in Hincks's University Act of 1853 and in other developments during the fifties.

This Bill followed the course of Sherwood's—it never came up for a second reading.[35] The whole affair of these two Bills is shrouded in mystery, made the deeper by the total absence of any letters between the interested parties, since Parliament was currently sitting at Toronto. As Elgin said, the settlement of 1849 was threatened, but there was never any suggestion that these tory proposals were apples of discord to be cast before the quarreling Reform racers. The sincerity of their authors was sufficiently proven when Hincks's University Bill, based on the same decentralized affiliation principle, was before Parliament in 1852–3. The London University system had been brought to public attention by Ryerson in his exposition and defence of Macdonald's Bill of 1847, and its success in England was now receiving the serious consideration of Canadians.

III

During the summer and autumn of 1851 several developments, some entirely unrelated to the University question, changed the whole course of higher education in Canada West. The trend towards centralized secular university education which had been initiated and fostered by Robert Baldwin and the Reformers had now reached its apogee. The granting of a charter to Trinity College reversed this trend in favour of an educational pluralism which recognized denominational colleges as an essential component of the system, legally if not practically the equals of the state institution.

The defeat of Baldwin in the Assembly on the Chancery Court issue devolved the leadership of the "old Reformers" in Canada West on Francis Hincks, whose approach to educational matters promised to be more progressive and less doctrinaire than that of Baldwin. The elections in the closing days of 1851 were marked by a distinct shift to the left which removed Baldwin finally and completely from the political arena. But if the composition of the new Assembly and of the new Administration was more progressive, its interest was centred on other problems than the University question which had scarcely been noticed at the hustings.

For reasons unknown the offer of Victoria College to dispose of its buildings to the Government for £6,000 had not been taken up, and by midsummer of 1851 it seems to have been settled that Victoria would conduct business as usual.[36] There is little record of the protracted and abortive negotiations of Victoria for affiliation, and none whatever of Queen's. The number of students at Victoria had increased to forty-five, and the college authorities announced that in view of all these changed circumstances, an intensive fund-raising campaign was now to be launched.[37] Queen's and Trinity were also engaged in fund-raising drives during the autumn and winter of 1851–2.[38] It was thus sufficiently evident to all legislators who would look away from railways and Reserves even momentarily, that Queen's and Victoria had nailed their charters to the mast, and that the "Fighting Bishop" was still intent on having his church university, with or without benefit of charter.

Strachan recognized fully the implications of these various developments and as soon as his new College was opened in 1852 he drew the Governor General's attention to the fact that, Queen's and Victoria having declined affiliation with the University of Toronto, "there remains no fair ground for desiring to oppose the extreme willingness of Her Majesty's Government, to deal as justly with the Members of the Church of England as with others."[39] Elgin signified his agreement to the granting of a charter with university powers, and another draft, the third to be submitted by Strachan, was forwarded to Sir John Pakington, Colonial Secretary of the new Conservative Administration.[40]

The erection of Trinity, Strachan's "Church University," was an ironic vindication of the principle of voluntarism. Hawkins flattered Strachan with the suggestion that his success in obtaining the charter resulted from the very popularity of the College,[41] and the old Bishop's elation at this happy culmination of a lifelong effort was understandable even to his opponents. It was left to George Whitaker, the first Provost of the new College, to show the Church's traditional exclusiveness even in the moment of victory. "It cannot but be a matter of regret," he told Hawkins, "that we shall share the privilege of conferring degrees with three other independent or hostile bodies in the province. . . ."[42]

IV

The grant of a royal charter to Trinity University destroyed the basis of Baldwin's plan for a single provincial university. Instead of one degree-granting body, there were now four in Canada West. It was also becoming increasingly obvious that the Act of 1849 had failed in other respects as well. The University of Toronto was not meeting with the public support which its creator had anticipated. Its income was increasing annually but fewer students benefited each session.[43] While Queen's and Victoria were making definite progress despite their financial predicament, Trinity was fulfilling Strachan's ambitions for the Church of England and at the same time drawing off students from its older rival in Toronto.[44] Public sentiment seemed more favourable than ever to the cause of denominational colleges. The experiment in secularization at Toronto had failed and now constituted an embarrassment to the political party that had instigated it.

In the distracting concurrent agitation of both the Clergy Reserves and separate school questions, Hincks deemed it advisable to face some facts by dealing with the third religio-cultural issue, the University question, it being the least contentious at the moment and therefore the most probable source of much-needed political capital. Yet considering that the antagonism of the Clear Grits to his Administration was being daily augmented and abetted by George Brown and the *Globe*, Hincks took a courageous step which invited further opposition when he dared to lay hands on the University settlement of his former chieftain.

At Hincks's request Ryerson offered his suggestions for reform of the University in an elaborately detailed letter and a sketchy draft Bill.[45] His indictment of the University of Toronto foreshadowed some of the charges which were to be levelled at the same institution just seven years later. Waste and inefficiency were the cause of the University's present unsatisfactory condition. But the real error had been its separation from religion by the Acts of 1849 and 1850 which had antagonized so many groups that the University was practically friendless. Nor was there the least prospect that the University would regain public confidence under its present management. To secure the greatest benefit to the people at large demanded recognition of the essential relation of religion and education. But the case for religious instruction at college was different than in the system of elementary education, for the older students were almost invariably far away from the parental influences. This was a point which Ryerson had frequently to defend against both the extremes represented by George Brown and Bishop de Charbonnel.

The changes proposed by Ryerson were similar to those schemes presented by Sherwood and Boulton the preceding year when the Superintendent of Education had been in Europe. The decentralized affiliation system of London University should be introduced. Aid granted to denominational colleges under such a scheme was not aid to sectarianism because no tests would be demanded of the students. A clear division between arts and science on one hand and theology on the other could be easily established. Nor need such a system multiply the number of denominational colleges, in Ryerson's opinion. He assumed, erroneously as time proved, that all varieties of Methodists would gladly patronize Victoria College. For those, however, who wished no religious influence, the collegiate department of the University of Toronto should be continued with an endowment on the same scale as that proposed by Macdonald's Bill, that is, twice as large as the grant to each denominational college.

The provincial University would be maintained in Ryerson's scheme, but its endowment would be transferred to the trusteeship of the Crown. Apparently Ryerson agreed with Baldwin that teachers should confine themselves to teaching, and meddle not with business affairs. One interesting suggestion he made has since become a part of the present University confederation. The University should have a small number of professors besides those belonging to the various colleges. One other suggestion—that the teaching of medicine and law be relegated entirely to incorporated bodies outside the University—was in fact adopted despite strong public protests, and John Rolph in his dual rôle as Commissioner of Crown Lands and Principal of the Toronto School of Medicine generally received the blame for Ryerson's reactionary innovation.[46]

Hincks replied to Ryerson that he felt the latter's scheme would give general satisfaction, and, "if brought forward boldly by the present Ministry, it might be carried."[47] He agreed that the Government should control the endowment, that the University should be modelled on the London plan, and that some division of professional labours could be made by instituting University lectureships. He was also agreeable to the idea of a University College purged of law and medicine. The one point on which Hincks required further instruction was the system of affiliation, which Ryerson had entirely ignored. Hincks was particularly concerned about the attitude of Trinity towards affiliation, but Chief Justice Robinson, as Chancellor of that institution, rejected the offer of any government grants which might encourage governmental interference.[48] Ryerson in his turn was requested to sound the Congregationalists, the Free Church, and the United Presbyterians, in hopes that they too, being "sick of the present system," might support the new affiliation scheme.[49]

A week after receiving another draft Bill from Ryerson, Hincks advised him that the absence of all tests except for divinity students and professors was a political *sine qua non* for passing the measure.[50] The Bill in its final form was presumably the work of Attorney General Richards, and Ryerson did not confer with Hincks personally after it had been introduced in the Assembly.[51] The *Christian Guardian* hailed the Bill as an admission of the signal failure of centralization and monopoly.[52] "We need scarcely here repeat the expression of our approval of the principles upon which the Bill is based, as the only ones which are capable of being applied . . ." in Canada West. "The University funds could be more effectively employed in the education of the youth of our country, by affording aid to separate colleges than by sinking the whole amount in the dead sea of one great university . . ."[53] The *Examiner*, currently absorbed in the

Clergy Reserves agitation, belatedly gave the Bill a similar recommendation.[54]

The *Globe* complained that Baldwin's plan had not been given a fair trial, that Francis Hincks, the apostate Reformer, was filling Strachan's old demand for sectarian and sectional education by reviving Macdonald's scheme of 1847.[55] The "little trumpery institutions" should not be allowed to fatten on the public purse. "It is only another conspiracy of Dr. Strachan, Dr. McCaul, Dr. Ryerson and the other political priests, to get the money of the country into their hands. . . ." The *Record* also came to the defence of the integrity of the University endowment, and the Guelph *Advertiser* wished for this renegade Reform Administration the same retribution which had overtaken the Conservatives in the elections of 1847 for their attempt to despoil the people of their patrimony.[56]

The *Globe* continued to fulminate in each and every issue against what it insisted was the endowment of sectarian theology in "a dozen different half-fledged colleges, with half-bred clergymen for professors."[57] Sneeringly the editor remarked that the only journalistic support for the Reform Ministry's University Bill came from such small Conservative papers as the Cobourg *Star*.[58] To renew faded memories of a vanished idol in the hearts of a backsliding party, the *Globe* of November 11, 1852, reprinted Baldwin's speech against Macdonald's University Bill. When the second reading of Hincks' Bill was postponed until the next session, the same newspaper credited the Government's move to shame at its own perfidy and alarm at the opposition raised by the measure.[59] Privately Brown must have hoped that this postponed Bill, like Draper's or Macdonald's, would never see the light of Assembly.

Despite the wishful thinking of Brown and the Clear Grits the Bill was introduced again on February 25, 1853, when the Parliament reassembled.[60] Few petitions against it were presented and these concerned themselves with protesting against the abolition of the Faculties of Medicine and Law.[61] The division on the second reading when only two votes were recorded under "noes" was indicative of the smooth course which the Bill had in Parliament. One observer described the event thus: "The Govt had quite a triumph last Friday evening upon the 2nd reading of the University Bill. There were only *two votes against* it, Brown & Cauchon, which some factious member termed a 'Brown pig'. I should think the Professors of the University would all die of mortification to think none of their *Tory allies* voted in support of their salaries."[62] A. N. Buell congratulated his nephew Attorney General Richards who was conducting the Bill through the Assembly at "the progress recently making in liberal measures in placing the Provincial University in a more favourable aspect before the Public of Upper Canada. . . . The University Bill seems also to acquire favor with the Public since its provision for granting aid to Sectarian Colleges is to be struck out."[63]

Amendments were indeed being made, apparently to appease the secularism of the Grits. The clause which would have given a stipulated sum to affiliated colleges was eliminated in favour of an ambiguous authorization that any surplus of the University fund might be "from time to time, appropriated by Parliament for Academical Education in Upper Canada."[64] This was to be the rock on which the ship of University reform later foundered, but at the moment no objection was raised against the change. On the contrary the Ministry and its measure were under attack by the *Globe* from the other direction. Week after week its editorials repeated the story of the University's destruction by a "liberal Government!"[65]

During the debates on the second reading of the Bill, Brown was cheered by the Conservatives when he called the measure a triumph for the Opposition.[66] He now occupied the same ground that Baldwin had held in 1847. Brown charged once more that the Wesleyan Methodists sought public money to educate their clergy, an accusation which the *Guardian* vehemently denied.[67] The *Patriot* and its new Tory Anglican companion, the *United Empire*, showed little interest in the current phase of the University question.[68] How could it be otherwise, asked the *Patriot*, since King's College had been deprived of its religious character. On the final reading Brown and Adam Fergusson respectively moved and seconded no less than seven amendments, with their minority ranging from two to thirteen.[69] But all such delaying tactics were in vain. The final vote, 57 to 3, was quite representative of the general attitude of the House, and probably of its electors. The subsequent failure of this University settlement would seem all the more surprising in view of the unanimity which existed in 1853.

The terms of the Act as passed did not differ substantially from the scheme outlined by Ryerson and developed by Hincks and Richards, except for the vague financial advantages offered to affiliating institutions and the elimination of University lectureships.[70] The title of the Act, "to Amend the Laws relating to the University of Toronto by Separating its Functions as a University from those Assigned to it as a College, and for making better provisions for the Management of the Property thereof," tells the major changes effected in Baldwin's settlement. The separation of the teaching college from the examining university proved to be a utilitarian improvement for University College.

The secularization of 1849 was not undone, but the Act of 1853 was an admission that centralization and secularism had failed to gain popular support. Henceforth the pattern of higher education in Canada West acknowledged the coexistence (if not the equality) of the denominational colleges and the national college. The first step towards a satisfactory compromise of the two tendencies, centripetal nationalism and centrifugal denominationalism, had been made in the field of higher education in Canada West.

v

For six years following the passing of Hincks' University Act of 1853 the University question lay dormant. This is not to say, however, that higher education in Canada West stood still during that time. That Act was but the legislative acknowledgment of the alteration made in Baldwin's one-university scheme by the granting of a royal charter to Trinity University. Four universities existed in fact where the Reformers of 1849 had intended only one. Hincks' Act attempted to compromise practice with theory by affiliating the three denominational universities to the state University, and thereby to retain the fiction of a single university in Canada West. But the state University, through no fault of its own, did not fulfil its end in the scheme of affiliation. University College still held the bulk of the endowment intact *de jure*, and the total *de facto*. The sin of Adam decreed that there should never be a surplus of the fund to divide among the affiliated colleges. The problem of affiliation will be considered later, but first one immediate result of Hincks' policy must be discussed.

The pattern of higher education in Canada West now displayed three denominational universities and one non-denominational super-university, with an affiliated non-denominational state college. This arrangement, by acknowledging the existence if not the equality of these denominational institutions in the system, implied that every religious body had a right to share in the work of higher education by creating its own distinctive institution. The result was that multiplication of denominational colleges which the Reformers had so long deprecated and sought to prevent by legal enactment. The 1850's saw the establishment of the principle of denominational education both elementary and superior as a component part and an ever enlarging influence in the pattern of education. Writing a generation later Hodgins said: "Except in freeing King's College from sectarian control the Acts of 1849-1853 accomplished nothing in the desired direction of University consolidation. Indeed they had the opposite effect, for the Bishop on one hand rallied his friends and established Trinity College, and the Methodists and Presbyterians on the other hand, finding the affiliation clauses of the Act delusive, soon withdrew all connection . . . [from the University of Toronto]."[71] The disappointment, isolation, and straitened circumstances of the outlying colleges culminated in the struggle of 1860-2 which for the bitterness and ill-will engendered exceeded all former contests on this question.

Of the ten colleges, besides Trinity, established or incorporated during the decade of the fifties, half belonged to the Roman Catholic Church, one each to the Methodist Episcopal, Congregational, Baptist, and Free Churches, and only one was non-denominational. This last institution, Hamilton College, was incorporated in 1855, but seems never to have gone into operation. The Free Church finally incorporated Knox College which had been in existence almost since the disruption. It is noteworthy that the development of the six other institutions paralleled that of Victoria College, in-as-much as they each commenced as classical academies. The preoccupation of Ryerson with his system of common schools, and of politicians with the University question had left the grammar schools of the province so weak and inefficient that a preparatory school was accepted as a necessary adjunct of each chartered college.[72] No doubt it was the intention of the founders of these newest institutions to avail themselves of the affiliation provisions of the University Act, but it was also possible if necessary to copy the example of Upper Canada Academy by superimposing university functions on the original preparatory schools.

The creation of Bytown College by the ecclesiastical authorities of that Roman Catholic diocese has already been mentioned. The oldest Roman Catholic institution, Regiopolis, had still failed to rise above the level of a classical school. Two more colleges connected with that church were now erected through the efforts of the Irish Basilians whom Bishop de Charbonnel had brought back with him to Canada because they spoke English. St. Michael's College in Toronto opened in 1852, and three years later was incorporated and affiliated with the University of Toronto. Assumption College at Windsor had also come under Basilian influence two years after its commencement in 1855, although De Charbonnel jealously opposed this latest extension of their interest. St. Jerome's College in Kitchener, intended specifically for the education of German-speaking Roman Catholics, was not in operation until 1865-6 (after erection of the Diocese of Hamilton) although De Charbonnel had suggested such an institution in 1855, and St. Ignatius College at Guelph was incorporated in the same diocese in 1862.[73]

Without exception these Roman Catholic colleges were conceived and operated as diocesan colleges, and they suffered and benefited proportionately from interdiocesan rivalry. While the "Papal Aggression" controversy and George Brown's anti-Catholic crusade were at their height in the fifties it was natural that these schools should receive some attention from their Protestant adversaries. St. Michael's College for instance was referred to as the Canadian Maynooth because it received government grants which Protestants believed were used to educate priests.[74]

Two other colleges begun in this period and belonging to the Methodist Episcopals and the Baptists had strikingly similar histories. The very differences between the Wesleyan and Episcopal Methodists were such as to discourage the latter body from sending students to Victoria, Ryerson's hopes notwithstanding. The Episcopals clung tenaciously to the ideal of voluntarism and avoided all who accepted state aid until practical experience taught them the necessity of compromise. A denominational college for the Methodist Episcopals had been mooted in the *Canada Christian Advocate* in the early fifties.[75] During 1853 collections were begun and £4,000, half of the objective, was subscribed that year.[76] It was 1857, however, before the college was incorporated and opened.[77] Another three years passed before the Belleville College, later Albert College, was affiliated with the University of Toronto.[78]

The Baptists were cursed by a long tradition of educational apathy, and many opposed an educated ministry, that is, man-made ministers in contradistinction to God-ordained.[79] Despite three failures to establish theological halls in Canada, the Baptists were persuaded by the Reverend Robert Fyfe to commence a college which would include a coeducational literary department as well as a theological department.[80] Not the least of their motives was the inferior state of the grammar schools. The building of the Canadian Literary Institute, or Woodstock College as it became later, began in 1857 and after three years it was opened under the principalship of Fyfe. The interests of the Institute and of this man were more closely connected than even those of Trinity College and Bishop Strachan.

The financial depression of 1857-8 seriously affected the work of all the denominational colleges, and soon led to the reopening of the University question. But the newly established Baptist and Methodist Episcopal institutions were the most materially damaged. Fortunately for the Canadian Literary Institute it had a generous patron in William McMaster, millionaire captain of industry, who not only contributed munificently to its erection but, when fire destroyed it one year after opening, gave $4,000 for rebuilding. On the occasion of this catastrophe the trustees of the Institute, true to their avowed voluntarism, refused to permit the Woodstock Town Council to raise relief funds by taxation. The Belleville College suffered no similar disaster, but faced with the consequences of the depression it was forced to relinquish its voluntarism for lack of a McMaster. Considerable moral courage must have been needed by its trustees to recant their earlier rejection of £750 of government aid and to accept the proffered *pourboire* of $800 in 1858.[81] The Congregational College at Toronto was not incorporated until 1864 when it was moved to Montreal as an adjunct of McGill.[82] It made no mark on the educational history of Canada West.

The larger educational institutions were also feeling the effects of the commercial depression—all except University College in Toronto. Since the passing of Hincks' University Act in 1853 no surplus funds had been permitted to accumulate for division among the affiliated colleges as authorized by Section 54 of the Act. The College council needed no encouragement from John A. Macdonald to create at Toronto that solid anchorage which even Methodists could not steal.[83] University College continued to monopolize the University endowment as successfully as had King's College, but it too paid the price in the form of continued governmental meddling, abuse, and nepotism.[84] These facts were hidden from the eyes of all except John Langton, Provincial Auditor and Vice-Chancellor of the University. But knowledge of these conditions would hardly have forestalled the rankling sense of injustice growing among the affiliated institutions at what appeared to be the deliberate flouting of the Act of 1853.

Unfortunately the actual relation of the affiliates to the University was and is obscure. The vague terms of Sections 17 and 18 of Hincks' Act were never explained and authorities differ widely as to which institutions were actually affiliated. The *ex officio* members added to the University Senate included representatives of Queen's, Victoria, Regiopolis, Knox, Bytown, and Upper Canada Colleges. Trinity alone refused to participate, and Provost Whitaker was never seated in the Senate.

In view of Trinity's action it must be presumed that the other colleges accepted affiliation since their representatives were received as members of the Senate. Yet there is no record of any college utilizing the advantages offered of sending up students for examination, or of any student outside of University College receiving one of the numerous scholarships offered.[85] The three denominational universities continued to grant their own degrees; Regiopolis sent its students to Laval; the others had no hooded alumni. Were the parties who revived the University question in 1859 acting as affiliates of the University or as independent groups in their attempt to implement the Act of 1853? The most definite statement that can be made is that affiliation was to all intents and purposes practically inoperative.

VI

Rumblings of discontent at the way in which University College was being managed to the detriment of its fellow colleges had been heard distantly and intermittently for about three necessitous years before the Wesleyan Methodist Church opened a new chapter in the University question with eight resolutions thereon at its Conference in June of 1859.[86] The resolutions protested that a majority of Canadians believed that higher education required a religious *milieu.* Hence the policy of applying the University endowment exclusively to a secularized institution "is grossly illiberal, partial, unjust and unpatriotic, and merits the severest reprobation of every liberal and right-minded man of every Religious Persuasion and party in the Country." In consideration of its work "Victoria College is justly entitled to share in the Legislative provision for Superior Education, according to the number of [its] Students. . . ." Therefore it was resolved that Wesleyan Methodists should use their influence to elect public men favourable to these views.

Those strong resolutions were placed before the laity at the quarterly meeting of each circuit and also published in the *Christian Guardian* on June 22. The immediate result was the opening of a newspaper war, with the Brockville *Recorder,* Hamilton *Spectator,* and Quebec *Chronicle* joining the *Guardian* in its support of denominational colleges, the *Globe, Leader,* and *Montreal Witness* raising the cry of sectarian bigotry against the Conference.[87] The burden of these latter journals' defence of the "Toronto College" had a familiar ring. The Wesleyans were charged with enmity toward the University College, with seeking public funds to educate their clergy, with inconsistency for opposing separate elementary schools. The *Globe* blamed the agitation on "the reverend chiseller,"

Dr. Ryerson, who secretly wished to destroy the University, who favoured state aid for the sectarian principle—a man obviously unfit for his office.[88]

Both Nelles and Ryerson replied on behalf of Victoria.[89] No one, they averred, sought to deprive University College of its just share of the University endowment, but the expenditure of £16,000 per annum on management, scholarships, and buildings was extravagance in the extreme. "The financial features of the law have marred the whole affair" of affiliation. The preamble of the Act of 1853 recognized the rôle of religion in university education and the right of "other seminaries" to share in the endowment. The endowment of irreligion was worse than a state church. Christ's cause was being served by denominational colleges, and it was a damning indictment of the Toronto system that even such strong voluntarists as the Episcopal Methodists and the Baptists found it necessary to establish their own colleges. The affiliated colleges received students of every religious persuasion, but University College seemed more an adjunct of the Free Church than a national institution.

The Conference president, Joseph Stinson, supplied the Wesleyan Methodist clergy with the correct answers to any queries regarding Victoria's policy and reminded them incidentally that the University question was neither sectarian nor party political in Wesleyan Methodist eyes.[90] Public meetings under Wesleyan auspices and Conference inspiration were held at various places across the province, at each of which resolutions were passed in favour of a fair division of the University endowment among denominational colleges.[91] As both the Synod of the Church of Scotland and the trustees of Queen's had met previous to the Wesleyan Conference no official statement was made by these bodies. Stinson and Nelles, however, personally interviewed Dr. Cook, Principal of Queen's, and John Paton, secretary of the Board of Trustees, to obtain the support of Queen's for their endeavours. Their reception was most encouraging. "I am glad to learn," Nelles informed Paton, "that there is with your people a favorable feeling toward the present movement and I trust that mutual effort may succeed in putting university matters on a more equitable basis." [92] The partnership for University reform thus formed by the two most interested bodies worked harmoniously for over three years, but their "mutual effort" was not fated to be successful.

The next move came from the Wesleyan Conference's Special Committee, and it projected the whole issue into the political arena of Parliament. A memorial was prepared late in 1859 and presented to the Assembly when it convened in March of the next year. The memorial reviewed the developments which had frustrated the intentions of Hincks' University Act. "A Provincial University should be what its name imports," but "it is unjust to propose, as it is unreasonable to expect, the affiliation of several colleges in one University, except on equal terms." University College should be continued, and its primacy recognized by a double share of the endowment; but to create an effective provincial university, other colleges must be "placed on an equal footing according to their works." The Wesleyans demanded the same rights for others as for themselves, but as limited voluntarists, rejected any and all support for theological teaching. The memorialists prayed for an investigation of the recent management of the University, and an Act to establish all colleges "upon equal footing in regard to public aid, either as so many co-ordinate University Colleges, or, (which we think the best system), as so many Colleges of one University." The memorial was supported by over 120 petitions from Wesleyan groups, and by the publication by Ryerson of eight lengthy "Proofs" of the Conference memorial.[93]

Against such a deluge of petitions no government could afford to remain indifferent, least of all the present Cartier-Macdonald Administration. Parliament reassembled in the afterglow of the Great Reform Convention, as the machinery of the Union was grinding ever more slowly, towards deadlock. No issue of the day could hope to be debated and resolved on its own merits. The great Upper Canadian questions of elementary and higher education were even more adversely affected than the Clergy Reserves had been by all the malignant aspects of the Union. The Wesleyan memorial was supported at the last moment by a petition from the trustees of Queen's College which repeated the same points as the memorial in more concise terms.[94]

VII

This attack on the "Toronto College" was not allowed to go unchallenged. The Free Church defended the institution which provided gratuitous literary education to its sons.[95] Knox College prayed "that all attempts to impair the efficiency of the University College, Toronto, may be resisted," and private individuals petitioned against any grants to denominational institutions.[96] Nor were the managers of the University of Toronto and University College willing to permit their opponents to score by default, however weak the reply might be. The petition which De Blaquière and Langton presented in the name of the Senate denied that standards had deteriorated or that building expenses had been excessive.[97] The central issue, the right of denominational colleges to share in the endowment, was ignored. Only one telling point was made by this counter-petition—that the non-sectarian principle on which the University was established was also the basis of the system of provincial elementary education. By implication the impairment of the one department would invite the destruction of the whole.

The petitions of the Wesleyan Methodist Conference and of Queen's University and later petitions of other interested bodies and individuals were referred by the Assembly to a nine-man Select Committee composed of such divergent elements as Malcolm "Coon" Cameron, John A. Macdonald, George Brown, Cayley, and Michael Foley.[98] During its sittings, which lasted a full month, almost every conceivable aspect of higher education came under discussion. The better part of Volume XV of Hodgins' *Documentary History* is devoted to these proceedings. Most of these aspects had been debated in Britain a generation before, but from the mass of information elicited by the Select Committee, the issue of dividing the University endowment stands out as the basic consideration of the University question in Canada West. Too often it was presented as the *only* consideration and the true motives of the parties were intentionally ignored. The genuine desire for a comprehensive and national system of higher education was deliberately lost sight of, and the University question made to assume the appearance of a mere struggle for loaves and fishes.

The discussion before the committee of the rôle of options in higher education marked the spokesmen for the denominational colleges as defenders of the classic disciplines, those for University College as progressive educationalists. History has decided in favour of the latter. As for the charge that academic standards had been lowered at Toronto, Professor Daniel Wilson and Langton pleaded with some justification that the educational conditions in Canada, particularly in the grammar schools, necessitated the reduction of entrance requirements.[99] On this point they were supported by the testimony of Whitaker and Ambery, the representatives of Trinity College.[100] The accusation that the University and University College had become synonymous was admitted by Langton, but this too was an unfortunate necessity, he contended.[101] The other colleges had neglected their responsibilities in the Senate, and this lack had had to be filled by the addition of University College professors. As for examinations, it was considered by all undesirable that teachers should judge their own students, but Canada lacked sufficient competent individuals for the task. Langton's statements were undoubtedly the most able of all those submitted.

When the advocates of denominational colleges ventured to accuse the University of religious indifferentism, they were on less firm ground. Wilson refused to acknowledge the distinction they tried to make between sectarian and denominational education.[102] "The Religious argument"—that the churches had a vested interest in education—would then be equally valid as an indictment of the system of national elementary schools. Time and time again the agitators were hoisted ungraciously on their own petards by their opponents' judicious use of documentary evidence implicating the former, particularly Ryerson, in the very transactions or developments which they were now denouncing.

The cross-examinations by Brown were marked by personal antagonism, and Wilson's counter-charges against Ryerson soon degraded the proceeding into a campaign of derogation directed against the Superintendent of Education and his whole Department. Personalities were dragged into the discussion of wholly extraneous topics, but it must be confessed that Ryerson's remarks about Family Compact influence in Toronto and his rather emotional and personal mode of delivery provided a welcome opportunity for George Brown and others to air their old grievances.[103] The *Globe* charged that Ryerson hated the University because he could not control it as he did the rest of the educational system, and proclaimed in the most violent language that Ryerson had been "well punished" by Brown for meddling with University reform.[104] The very presence of Ryerson may well have defeated the purpose of the committee.

The discussion of the prime issue of finances showed the ability of both parties to juggle statistics for their own ends. In answer to the charges of extravagance, the defenders of the University cited their parliamentary authorization for the expenditure of nearly $300,000 on the new buildings, the comparative equality of scholarships in other universities, and the legitimate financial requirements of a provincial university.[105] On these several points the University's attackers again came out second best.

The most equivocal aspect of the financial question was the interpretation of Clause 54 of the University Act of 1853. What was the true intent of the framers of this ambiguous passage? Were their original purposes, as Ryerson asserted, to grant specific amounts to the other colleges from the endowment, to ensure to denominational institutions an equitable share of the public support, or as Langton contended, merely to affiliate the other colleges, for academic purposes, without any commitment to aid them financially? "That Section, the only one in the Act which refers to Surplus Income, is significantly silent with regard to Denominational Colleges, and simply enacts that any Surplus Income which may be left, after the general purposes of the Act have been fulfilled, shall be set apart to form a fund to be at the disposal of the Legislature for educational purposes." [106] Langton's argument as deduced from the statutes has a most plausible sound and its correctness was subsequently verified by the author of the Act himself. "I cannot believe it possible that it was ever contemplated by the Act of 1853 to depart from the principle of Mr. Baldwin's Act, beyond separating the University from University College, so as to permit the affiliation of other colleges in the mode adopted by the University of London." [107] Unfortunately Hincks was not available for consultation in 1860, but the net result was the same.

The London University system naturally was referred to frequently during the proceedings. Wilson pointed to his opponents' idealization of the Oxford-Cambridge curricula, and reminded them that "the very Act under which our University and College exist, specifies London University... as our model,—London University, established in the Nineteenth Century, with a view to meeting all the advanced requirements of this age. . . ." [108] Stinson had charged that the London scheme envisaged by the Act of 1853 had been frustrated by the policy of building up one college and thereby crushing all others, to which Wilson replied that the scheme had been frustrated by the refusal of the denominational colleges to co-operate to that end. [109] It remained for the *Globe* to point out the essential and important difference between the situations of the Universities of Toronto and London. The affiliates of the latter University were self-supporting. There simply was no general endowment there to be divided or fought over. Therefore, if London was the model as the statutes said, it remained for the affiliating denominational colleges in the University of Toronto to provide for their own necessities. [110]

The proceedings of the committee did little more than crystallize the differences between the extremes represented by the two parties, each of which was more convinced than ever of the justice of its own position. The complete unanimity of the authorities of Queen's and Victoria during this whole episode in the University question contrasts noticeably with their mutual suspicions of the 1840's. Cook suggested a plan to unify the standard of the various colleges and divide the endowment by legislation. [111] Ryerson had made these suggestions in 1852, but the Act of 1853 had failed to secure them. Ryerson himself repeated to Macdonald his opinions of that year without change and drew up another draft University Bill similar to that which he had submitted to Hincks, but defining the terms of affiliation and grants in unmistakable terms. [112]

Neither of the two reports prepared by members of the committee (and representing the two opposing groups) was submitted to the Assembly. The report drafted by the chairman, Malçolm Cameron, favoured the cause of the memorialists. It proposed limiting the share of the endowment given to the University of Toronto and University College to £7,000, and dividing the balance among the other colleges providing they held their university powers in abeyance and received no further legislative aid. "The happiest results," it said, "may be expected from an equitable affiliation of the several Colleges in one Provincial University, under one common Senate. . . ." The draft written by Cayley, with Langton's aid, recapitulated the various charges and refutations heard by the committee, and while denying the legal right of the denominational institutions to share the endowment, magnanimously upheld the claim of Queen's and Victoria to some public aid, which, if it came from a division of the endowment surplus, should also be extended to Trinity College. [113]

The Church of England and Trinity College still held aloof from the agitation. The attacks on the "unsafe" theology of Trinity which had been made by the

Low Church element headed by the Bishop of Huron were a sufficient distraction for that church.[114] The United Presbyterians, the Congregationalists, and the Free Church (all of which had theological halls in close proximity to University College) voiced their opposition to this latest spoliation attempt through the *Globe* and the *Leader*.[115] The *Christian Guardian* was filled week after week from May to July, 1860, with editorials and articles denouncing the "Toronto monopoly." It claimed that clergy and laity were united in sentiment on the University question despite the *Leader*'s contrary assertions, but soon admitted that at least some members of the Wesleyan Methodist Church were "quite scandalized" by this clerical interference with political issues.[116] A voluminous pamphlet war conducted largely by the Wesleyans on one side and Messrs. Wilson and Langton on the other started as soon as the Select Committee rose, and augured a protracted struggle. "It is possible," Dr. Cook wrote to Professor Williamson, John A. Macdonald's brother-in-law, "nothing may be done this Session. But a foundation is laid for extensive and effective agitation, and we will succeed ultimately. Government is certain to be neutral."[117]

The Government was indeed neutral, neutral to the point of pusillanimity in the face of an issue which could as easily wreck it as it had another administration in which John A. Macdonald had been an apprentice minister. Despite Macdonald's apparent encouragement to Ryerson, it is doubtful whether he intended to disturb the uneasy sleep of that contentious mastiff, the University question, either at this point or even after the elections of 1861. In any case he could during the remainder of 1860 plead preoccupation with princely chaperoning as an excuse for inaction. But the departure of the Imperial heir apparent was a signal for the Wesleyan Methodists to renew their agitation. The *Christian Guardian* gave fair warning to all politicians of the purpose of nine more conventions about to be held. "The object of the Conventions this year, and the prayer of their memorials, is not Parliamentary inquiry, but *Parliamentary legislation*."[118]

VIII

During the summer of 1860 the Wesleyan Methodist Conference had repeated its statement of policy on the University question as adopted at the preceding Conference.[119] A special public meeting held at the same time in Kingston, where the Conference sat, heard Victoria's position explained by its representatives who had testified before the Select Committee, particularly Ryerson.[120] The Synod of the Church of Scotland approved a petition to the Legislature drafted by the Reverend Dr. Williamson, demanding for Queen's the share of University endowment which was rightly hers by virtue of the royal grant to "seminaries."[121] New strength was acquired at this time by Queen's in the person of the Reverend William Leitch, a worthy successor to Liddell as Principal.

The most important of these many public meetings was that called by the Mayor of Kingston on March 6, 1861, just ten days before Parliament reassembled. The speakers, who included Leitch, Nelles, and Ryerson, declaimed for more than four hours.[122] Leitch drew on Old World examples to prove that a truly national system of university education required a single university with a number of colleges enjoying equal rights in affiliation and endowment. Nelles supported Leitch's remarks with the assertion that the people of Canada West had proven their preference for denominational colleges. Of the seven resolutions passed the two moved by these Principals respectively called for division of the endowment among the decentralized denominational colleges and the establishment of an efficient university to maintain uniform standards among the affiliated institutions.

The defenders of the University and of the "Toronto College" in their turn organized a less successful counter-meeting at Woodstock under Fyfe's leadership.[123] The *Globe* and the *Canadian Baptist* both represented any and all support for Queen's and Victoria as nothing less than an Erastian connection of church and state, while the *Record* reminded its Free Church readers to petition against division of the endowment at once while Parliament was still in session.[124] The Congregationalists also petitioned both Houses against "sectarian distribution of the University Endowment."[125] The case of the Clergy Reserves was cited as a demonstration of the "innumerable evils" which resulted from the violation of the non-sectarian principle. But numerically the petitions from Wesleyan and Church of Scotland congregations in support of the resolutions of Conference and Queen's overshadowed those of their opponents.[126]

With a general election planned to take advantage of the absence of George Brown, Macdonald advised Ryerson that no action on his or any other plan of University reform was likely for the present. The Attorney General's definition of the real election issue as "limited Constitutional Monarchy or a Yankee democracy" smacks of a bid for a "U.E. Loyalist's" support in return for University legislation which was politically inexpedient at the moment. "No time must be lost in calling on the W.M.'s in every constituency," Macdonald advised Ryerson. "The cry is 'Union,' 'No looking to Washington' and University Reform."[127] This order of precedence speaks for itself.

Williamson, who occasionally acted as his brother-in-law's self-appointed adviser in such matters, again warned Macdonald against procrastination. "If the University question is not ripe for adjustment this sitting of Parliament it must come up & with tenfold more urgency the next time. In the mean time, do the just thing by giving each of the three chartered Colleges not less than £2,000 this session. You will thus secure the gratitude & support of four of the leading denominations in Upper Canada. But we ask it for the public benefit above all, and on the principle of equal justice to all."[128]

Perhaps Williamson's counsel did bear fruit, for Macdonald wrote to Ryerson next month offering two inducements in avowed anticipation of gaining Wesleyan votes.[129] A University Commission was proposed, its personnel to be subject to Ryerson's manipulation. Next came an Order-in-Council for aiding the denominational colleges from the surplus income (if any) of the University and its College.[130] The publicizing of this latter inducement was left to the discretion of Ryerson and the Wesleyan Conference. Macdonald's action gave "entire satisfaction" to all the Wesleyans consulted, and Conference duly issued an official appeal that the "dear Brethren and Friends" support "only those men of any party in the pending elections, according as we believe they will support or oppose University Reform and equal rights to all Colleges."[131]

Such bare-faced political manœuvring by their pastors was too much for some flocks, and a few daring sheep bleated a public denunciation of Conference's meddling with the things of Caesar. The *Guardian* regretted this disagreement but repeated the time-honoured cliché that the University question was not a party political one, and Conference was claiming no authority over its adherents by advising this course of action.[132]

Scarcely a week passed without some editorial on University reform occupying the columns of the *Christian Guardian*. The *Norfolk Messenger* of June 20 praised the *Guardian*'s stand and the policy of the Conference, and quoted Macdonald's promise to the electors of a University Commission to investigate the "crying evil" of extravagance at the University of Toronto. The editor of the *British Herald* was in favour of division of the endowment surplus, with or without affiliation.[133] However, the Congregational minister who conducted the Bowmanville *Statesman*, the *Globe*'s lusty echo, had characterized the *Guardian* as "the Ryersonian Organ Grinder." [134] The neighbouring Oshawa *Vindicator* claimed the appeal had been railroaded through Conference and copies distributed by thousands in "those constituencies wherein they could reasonably be expected to accomplish their wretched purpose—that of elevating the petty Question of University Reform above every other principle. . . in the selection of members of Parliament." [135] "Spartacus," a correspondent of the *York Herald*, accused the Wesleyan clergy of rigging public meetings to obtain the desired resolutions.[136] "We hope," added its editor, ". . . that *no man is elected who is not determined to guard the University from the interference of Dr. Ryerson and his abettors.*" The Bradford *Chronicle* copied the editorial remarks of the Montreal *Witness* which deplored the Conference's policy of ignoring the major election issues "in their eager chase after an endowment for their College." [137] It seemed that the Wesleyan Methodist appeal had raised as much opposition as support for University reform and once more that church was threatened with division on the problem of church-state relations. For once, however, the *Globe* did not join in the general *mêlée*, being more interested for the moment in "Rep. by Pop." and the American Civil War.

As in 1847 the election of 1861 found the Wesleyan Methodist Church and the Church of Scotland allied in opposition to "monopoly" at Toronto. The Roman Catholic Church was neutral as ever, while on the other side the Congregationalists, the Free Church (now joined to the United Presbyterians), the Episcopal, and the other small Methodist bodies defended non-sectarian university education against the denominational separatists who would despoil the national seat of learning. Only the Church of England had altered its position. Despite the efforts of the Reverend Dr. T. B. Fuller to commit the Toronto Diocesan Synod to the cause of division, Strachan's policy of wait and watch triumphed.[138] The independence of Trinity from that political interference which had cursed King's College would not be bartered at any price.

IX

The election victory of the Liberal-Conservatives proved within eight months to be more apparent than real, but Macdonald proceeded to announce the appointment of the promised University Commission soon after the election.[139] The members of the commission were chosen to represent the major interests involved—Dr. Beatty for Victoria, John Paton for Queen's, and James Patton for the University of Toronto, of which he had been elected Vice-Chancellor in the preceding year to succeed Langton. There is no evidence to support the claim that Patton had been elected through the influence of Queen's and Victoria to further their own cause, although it was known that he was friendly to reform of some sort. Nevertheless Macdonald feared that the commissioners' recommendations might be too extreme. "I hope they will be moderate," he told Ryerson. "If they recommend the use of the Knife too freely, the House won't stand it." [140]

After investigating the University's finances the commission reported that expenditures had by the most liberal interpretation been disproportionately large and inexpedient, and suggested a number of means for retrenchment.[141] Next the commission turned to the problem of affiliation and obtained the opinions of all the colleges through replies to a series of questions. The principals of Queen's, Victoria, and Regiopolis, speaking for those institutions, were in agreement on the necessity for a system of affiliation, with a provincial university acting as examiner and guardian of standards, and the colleges receiving fixed and equal shares of public aid in return for leaving their university powers in abeyance.[142] Provost Whitaker was opposed to any affiliation which would impair Trinity's university powers. The best he could suggest was a co-operative commonwealth of universities. The real surprise came in the answers of the University of Toronto. The Senate agreed unanimously with the propositions of Queen's, Victoria, and Regiopolis for effective affiliation with a truly provincial university. It preferred, however, Whitaker's suggestion that the colleges should grant degrees, and insisted on preserving the integrity of University College's endowment. The report of the University Commission adopted every principle suggested by the University Senate, advocating a University of Upper Canada with affiliated colleges retaining degree-granting powers and receiving equal aid except for a reconstituted King's College which would receive a larger share. A settlement of the question acceptable to all at last seemed a real possibility.

Leitch, however, was striving valiantly to add the Church of England to the cause of reform and had communicated with Strachan and Whitaker to this end.[143] The terms which Strachan proposed as the only acceptable basis for affiliation by Trinity were precisely those proposed by the University Commission, and Leitch informed Ryerson of this unanimity existing between the three major Protestant bodies. Anxiously, he sought to capitalize on Strachan's altered attitude by pressing the Government to introduce an amended version of the Bill drafted by Ryerson in 1860. "The Government," he told Ryerson, "will be very glad if we let them be for some time yet, but we all feel that it is a favourable conjunction that may never return." The prophecy came true sooner than any might have anticipated. Within a month the tide of politics had sealed the fate of University reform.

Exactly one week before the report of the commission was submitted, the Liberal-Conservative Government resigned on the defeat of its Militia Bill. Macdonald could not have legislated on the University question while the commission was still sitting, and the educational policy of the new Ministry was ominously undisclosed. In any case the Civil War raging to the south and particularly the crisis of the Trent affair held the attention of legislators and public. The few references to the University question in the press of the day were limited to a desultory discussion of its relation to a national system of education. The secularizationists persisted in identifying denominational colleges with the issues of separate schools, which had now replaced Clergy Reserves as the principal grievance of the Reformers. Nationalism was gaining new strength under the stimulus of the political crises created by Union in Canada and fratricide in the United States. The unhappy conclusion of the University question agitation in 1863 reflected the changed attitude not only of the University of Toronto Senate but of the people as a whole.

During the remainder of 1862 the only action on the University question was that of religious bodies. The Wesleyan Conference addressed Viscount Monck, the new Governor General, on the question, and the trustees of Queen's commissioned Principal Leitch to prepare a statement of their position.[144] The Synod of the Free Church resolved to petition Parliament against any financial aid to denominational colleges as destructive of the "unsectarian System of Education" in Canada West.[145] The Conference of the Primitive Methodist Church sent a memorial to Parliament to the same effect.[146] But the most interesting and important development occurred in the Synod of the Diocese of Toronto where Strachan effectively blocked the efforts of Fuller's University committee to align the Church of England with the advocates of denominational colleges and division of the endowment. Strachan denied any intention of surrendering the sacred trust of Trinity's university charter for any consideration.[147] James Patton accused certain members of the Synod of misrepresenting the scheme of affiliation which had been approved by all but Trinity. A majority, however, refused to sanction the report of the committee, lest the independence of Trinity might be thereby compromised, and the withdrawal of the report undid the work and hopes of Fuller and Leitch that the proposed plan for a truly provincial and inclusive pattern of higher education would include the Church of England.

x

The publication of the report of the University commissioners early in January of 1863 set the scene for the last chapter of the University question prior to Confederation.[148] The report was greeted with concerted opposition from the Reform press, with the *Globe* of January 20 denouncing its authors as "the most impudent men the Province contains." The proposal to divide the endowment again raised the cry of spoliation of the nation's patrimony, but the mild criticism of the University's financial management was interpreted as justifying the *status quo ante* investigation. The commissioners were characterized as "one of the most sectarian, one-sided cliques that ever pretended to investigate . . . the claims of an institution they were pledged to subvert. . . ."[149] The council of the united counties of York and Peel joined many editors in lumping denominational colleges and separate schools under the same heading—centrifugal sectarianism.[150]

The indignation meeting held at Toronto early in March to protest the recommendations of the University Commission got considerable publicity from the most powerful provincial newspapers, the *Globe* and the *Leader*, and even the *Guardian* seemed to protest too loudly when it belittled at considerable length an affair which it termed merely an outburst of student spirits.[151] In truth several of those who moved or seconded resolutions in defence of the integrity of the University endowment were members of the University Senate—Adam Crooks, the Reverend Dr. Lillie, T. A. Maclean, Edward Blake, and James Morris. The last two of these gentlemen along with three others, including Dr. Fyfe, had been appointed to the Senate since the publication of the report,[152] and this seemed to be the Government's answer to University reform.

Adam Crooks gave notice to the Senate that he would introduce resolutions to reverse the answers sent by that body to the commissioners in the preceding March. He contended that the commissioners' letters had exceeded their powers, and that the Senate had therefore erred in replying. But most important, Crooks asserted that the report was opposed to the real opinions and interests of the Senate. Yet those answers had been approved by the Senate just a year ago, apparently *nem. con.* Crooks' action was the more surprising as he had seconded

Commissioner Patton's re-election as Vice-Chancellor in December, just three months before. Ryerson, Nelles, Leitch, and Patton strove vainly to stall or quash these resolutions. Ryerson, who was detained at Quebec by the crucial separate school legislation, obtained J. S. Macdonald's opinion that Crooks' resolutions would be out of order, that the report was the business of the Government, not of the Senate. A postponement until May was agreed to by Crooks, but a further respite in May on the death of Chancellor Connor did not materialize. The Senate defenders of the *status quo* pushed the resolutions through the largest Senate meeting ever held up to that time.[153]

Vainly Ryerson, Leitch, and Nelles (all of whom had just returned from some mysterious discussion in Quebec) offered amendments that no business could be legally transacted, that the question of the commission's authority pertained solely to the Government and that the Senate's opinions of the previous year could not be altered. The Senate was unmoved by appeals to legality or consistency. Patton's rulings on procedure were overridden on appeal. The advocates of decentralization and denominationalism through University affiliation were defeated on every vote by a majority of two to one.

XI

After this sudden and unexpected *volte face* by the Senate of the University of Toronto the agitation against monopoly and in favour of division of the endowment died quickly. The work of the University Commission was as fruitless as that of the Select Committee which it was intended to complete. The representatives of the denominational universities no longer deigned to attend the Senate meetings. The Reform Government of the day and its coalition successor were respectively too indifferent and too preoccupied with Confederation to bother with the University question. Henceforth, only the most occasional references to the long-agitated issue appeared in the provincial journals. In the closing phase of the Union, the influence of denominationalism in higher education was confirmed by the incorporation of several denominational colleges as universities. Another generation was to arise before the present settlement was achieved.

Since the Great Ministry had secularized King's College in 1849 and Strachan had obtained a royal charter for Trinity University, the centrifugal and centripetal forces in higher education had stood in equipoise. The secularists had failed to annihilate the denominational rivals of the national University; but the separatists had equally failed to gain recognition as partners with the provincial institution. Indeed, the Churches of Rome and England had consistently stood aloof from the efforts of Victoria and Queen's to gain University reform and a share of the University endowment, and these two colleges had together faced the phalanx of smaller denominations (invariably voluntarists) and other defenders of nonsectarian education. There was more involved than a mere struggle for loaves and fishes, but this remained the occasion and focus of the question, regardless of the educational principles. The pattern of higher education established in Canada West between 1850 and 1867 was a patchwork of sectarian colleges, denominational universities, and in solitary splendour, the nationalized, secularized University at Toronto, monopolizing the rich legacy bequeathed to the nation for the maintenance of "other seminaries."

CHAPTER SIX

RELIGION AND ELEMENTARY EDUCATION, 1841-1851

PROTECTION FROM INSULT

I

UNLIKE the other two religio-cultural problems which have already been examined, the problem of religion and elementary education remains to this day a very live issue in this province. The related problems of separate schools and religious teaching in the public schools have been topics of discussion in recent years, and the strong reactions to the Hope Commission's recommendations are indicative of that underlying but none the less fervent religious intensity which has been inherited from the troublous times of a pioneer era. That present-day opinions are often dictated more by sentiment and prejudice than by reason and fact does not diminish their genuineness. Developments in this century suggest that a satisfactory compromise between the forces of unifying nationalism and religious separatism in this field may not yet have been achieved. Instead the resurgence of the latter force threatens to upset the educational dualism, reached in 1863, and enforced as it were by arbitration at the time of Confederation.

It is of course impossible within the limited scope of such a study to attempt an evaluation of all the various elements which have influenced the development of the present system of elementary education in Ontario. Most of these aspects can be at best merely hinted at, while the attention is directed particularly to factors which created before 1867 the dualistic system of non-denominational public schools and separate Roman Catholic schools which continues almost unaltered to this day. How far this system was the unhappy by-product of the forced marriage of two religiously distinct populations and how far it was simply protection of minority rights cannot be resolved by debate. But on either assumption the historian is reminded painfully of the complexity of human motives and events. The relation of religion to elementary education in Canada West is a prime example of faith transcending reason in political affairs.

II

The picture of primary education presented by Canada at the moment of Union is deceptively simple. In the lower province the control of every phase of education by the Roman Catholic Church was complete and unquestioned. Only one statute graced the legislative annals. Otherwise the educational policies and institutions of the *Ancien Régime* were still intact. South of the Ottawa River successive attempts at legislation had failed to provide satisfactory school facilities.[1] Far more important than political differences in retarding educational progress in the upper province was the inability of the inhabitants at large to agree on the nature of an educational system, though all and sundry piously deplored its lack.

The enquiries of a Commission on Education in 1839 at least proved the existence of this negative unanimity by its condemnation of the existing insufficiency and inefficiency of schools, teachers, and system (if such it may be called) in Upper Canada. But the latest Common School Bill introduced had been vetoed by the Legislative Council because the proposed taxation would bear too heavily on a depressed economy already burdened with new rates for gaols, courthouses, and macadamized roads.[2] It would be unfair to presume that the passing of any Bill in 1839 would have prevented the educational difficulties experienced during the Union. No first Act struck off by colonial legislators could hope to be finality itself. The subject would have been raised soon in the United Parliament, probably with the same political necessity of involving Lower Canadian votes in an Upper Canadian problem. Lord Sydenham's attempt to settle for ever the Clergy Reserves antecedent to Union did not succeed, and the course of educational legislation for the upper province would probably have been identical even had the Common School Bill of 1839 become law.

The most important fact which appears from the educational history of Upper Canada is the total absence of controversy regarding the place of religion in elementary education. Reformers criticized what they considered to be a monopoly by the Church of England of educational offices, and Bishop Macdonell did establish Roman Catholic schools in very limited numbers with the aid of public funds. But at no time before 1841 or in the decade after were separate denominational schools demanded as an abstract right.

The severely circumscribed connection of church and state permitted by the Union was generally considered to be a vestigial remain to be tolerated until its disappearance from attrition, but certainly not to be resuscitated or encouraged under any circumstances. It was popularly expected that under the stimulus of Union education would be systematized on a national scale. The details of the educational scheme would be worked out pragmatically on the basis of civil and religious equality, and for a decade this policy progressed without serious challenge from the advocates of special denominational privileges.

III

When Lord Sydenham delivered his Speech from the Throne to the first session of the first Parliament of the new Province of Canada he reminded the members that one of the first duties of the state was "a due provision for the Education of the People."[3] His forecast of the educational legislation of the session held a touch of prophecy. "The establishment of an efficient system," he warned, "is a work of difficulty." "If it should be found impossible to reconcile conflicting opinions, so as to obtain a measure which may meet the approbation of all, I trust that, at least, steps may be taken, by which an advance to a more perfect system may be made; and the difficulty under which the people of this Province now labour may be greatly diminished, subject to such improvements hereafter as time and experience may point out."

Before a Common School Bill was actually introduced a petition concerning religion in the schools arrived, the first of a series which directly affected the form and fate of that Bill. A Church of England congregation in the Eastern Townships prayed that the Bible "as a whole" be prescribed as a textbook for Protestant schools and seminaries.[4] This was followed by a number of petitions to the same effect from the Synod of the Church of Scotland and its congregations, but extending the prescription to "all the Schools of the Province admitted to a participation of any grant of public money." After futile attempts to have the petitions referred to a Select Committee of the Assembly, they were finally presented for consideration by the Committee of the Whole on the Common School Bill.

There is no record of the Assembly's opinions on the request, but in the Legislative Council a statement by William Morris caught the deepest import of this pressure: "... if the use, by Protestants, of the Holy Scriptures in their Schools, is so objectionable to our fellow-subjects of that other faith, the children of both religious persuasions must be educated apart; for Protestants never can yield to that point, and, therefore, if it is insisted upon that the Scriptures shall not be a Class-book in Schools, we must part in peace, and conduct the education of the respective Bodies according to our sense of what is right."[5]

In introducing this Common School Bill to the Assembly, Solicitor General Day noted that "the present measure was but one part of the great general system of National Education."[6] It is noteworthy that the Bill originally contained no mention of religion or provision for separate schools of any description. Clearly the intention was simply to take a first step towards a unified national system of secular elementary education. But this very silence occasioned three petitions which altered the course of the Bill and all future legislation on the subject.

The first of these three petitions came from Bishop Strachan and his clergy, who prayed that the Church of England be entrusted with the education of its own children, aided by an annual grant from the local taxes.[7] Three weeks later at his first episcopal visitation Strachan advised his clergy that a day school "in which religion shall form the basis of all instruction" should be attached to every congregation.[8] The teaching of the Church's distinctive principles would check the spread of dissent. Since the Church of England alone possessed true Christianity, its children could be trusted only to Anglican teachers. The Bishop's opponents were the same "spurious" liberals who had excluded clerical control from the Common Schools Bill and who would banish the Bible from Her Majesty's colony. As will be seen, Strachan did not soon relinquish his campaign for Anglican schools, but his arguments and phraseology were adopted by Roman Catholics a decade later with considerably more success.

In the Legislative Council (composed exclusively of equal numbers of members of the Churches of England, Scotland, and Rome), Strachan's petition was presented by Peter Boyle De Blaquière. A scant decade later, as first Chancellor of the new University of Toronto, De Blaquière was the strong defender of Baldwin's scheme of secularized and centralized higher education against the attempts of his diocesan to establish a Church of England university. De Blaquière agreed with William Morris that in view of the controversy over the use of the Bible, "it was quite hopeless that Protestants and Roman Catholics could be educated together." But, he added hopefully, it was not impossible that the Protestant denominations who formed the majority of the upper province's population could unite in a system possessing "the essential religious basis upon which all education should rest."[9]

The other petitions came from the Roman Catholic Bishops of Kingston and Quebec. Together they opposed the principles of the Bill and requested a delay until Roman Catholic and other denominational opinions were known. The result of this twofold attack by the Churches of England and Rome was the appointment of a mixed committee to deal with the government measure.

Of the forty-two petitions presented in connection with Day's Common School Bill, thirty-nine had asked that the Bible be used in the schools.[10] The effect of this issue of prescription or proscription of Holy Writ was evident in the compromise offered by the committee on Day's Bill. Perhaps the composition of that committee—fifteen members from Lower Canada to eight from Upper Canada—gave a sufficient indication of the probable outcome of its deliberation. Their amendments,[11] which were adopted apparently without much opposition, established the principle of separate denominational schools within the framework of the common school system. Clause 11 authorized such dissentient schools "whenever any number of the Inhabitants of any Township, or Parish, professing a Religious Faith different from that of the majority" so desired. Clause 16 established municipal boards of examiners, each with separate but numerically equal Protestant and Roman Catholic departments.

The purpose of the Act was to create a single system of elementary education for the United Province, recognizing, however, the rôle played by the Roman Catholic Church in Lower Canada. Since dissentient schools for Protestants existed there it seemed only just that equal opportunities be provided for any dissentients in the upper province. The amendments added by the committee were undoubtedly a response to the petitions from the bishops of the Anglican and Roman churches. The biographer of the Archbishop Lynch, however, says that separate schools were embodied in the act of 1841 "chiefly because the Protestants of Lower Canada objected to sending their children to the Common Schools, as these schools would of course be composed mainly of Catholic children, and presided over by Catholic teachers."[12] But the amendments were equally applicable to any religious minority dissatisfied with the common schools.

The cases for separate schools in the two parts of Canada constituted the obverse and reverse of the same coin, rather than parallel situations as Roman Catholics have generally assumed in their arguments for extended educational privileges. The common schools of the lower province were and are denominational, those of the upper province were non-denominational. In Canada East the transgression of the doctrine of the educational sovereignty of the nation stemmed primarily from the historical pattern inherited from New France, and perpetuated by the Union Act. But it is only fair to note that the similar claim of the Church of England might quite as easily have achieved the same result had Strachan commanded sufficient voting power to establish the educational system of old England in Upper Canada. The actual influence of the Anglican position in assisting the designs of the Roman Catholics cannot be measured, but if the former denomination had joined with other Protestants in accepting the national system of schools and thereby presented a united front to the separatist pressure of the Roman Catholic Church, the course of educational development in this province would assuredly have been different. The changed attitude within the Church of England which came in the 1850's as a result of "Papal Aggression" and Puseyism occured belatedly and incompletely, and the earlier agitation by Strachan must be judged to some extent responsible for the success of Roman Catholics in obtaining separate schools. But for better or worse, depending on the religious point of view, the principle of separate schools was established by Day's Common School Act of 1841.

IV

Day's Common School Act aroused no particular journalistic interest. The *Christian Guardian* of November 24, 1841, called the move "very satisfactory" and discussed the Act's provisions with special reference to the teaching profession. "The Masters now employed are, in many instances deficient in numbers and abilities," their moral qualifications occasionally very objectionable, and some being "still more objectionable by the views on religious topics entertained. ..." The editor of the *British Colonist* admitted that many readers had written denouncing the third part of Clause 7 which permitted the Order of Christian Brothers to teach even if they were not British subjects.[13] The only question in his mind was whether this constituted the extension of a privilege or merely the confirmation of an existing right. He expressed himself as opposed to any extension of privilege to the Roman Catholics which was not also given to the rest of the community. About this time, the *Catholic* quoted with approval Daniel O'Connell's defence of the Irish national educational system against the objections of, ironically, the Wesleyan Methodists.[14]

The Act, however, in practice proved unsuitable for the educational requirements of both parts of the United Province and was repealed only two years later. The objections raised in Upper Canada were not directed against its irreligious provisions but against its cumbersome and impracticable administrative machinery.[15] But it was obvious that the sections establishing separate schools were too sweeping and generalized. The mere dissent from "the regulations, arrangements, or proceedings, of the Common School Commissioners"[16] required to effect a separation was the ultimate in educational free trade, and placed a premium on the capricious whim of local inhabitants. The whole arrangement was too conducive of discord to be permitted to continue, even if no public objections had yet been raised against its implementations. In fact the whole Act showed the unskilled, if not unskilful, hand of an author who had relied on the advice of pure theoreticians.

No action was taken on the matter of elementary education in the second session of the first Parliament, but by the time the third session assembled in the autumn of 1843, some change in educational legislation had become a crying necessity. Unfortunately common schools played a weak second fiddle to the King's College controversy in the Assembly. Nevertheless the legislation on elementary education was of prime importance because of the principles it established.

The first Bill on the subject was brought in by A. N. Morin. It repealed the whole of the Act of 1841 and adjusted certain financial arrangements by an indemnity. The next Bill, that of Francis Hincks, established a new system of elementary schools for Upper Canada alone. The attempt to obtain a uniform system in both parts of Canada was abandoned, and the embryonic federation within the Union was thus tacitly endorsed for the field of elementary education.

At the second reading of his Bill Hincks explained "That the objections to the late Bill of 1841 were, on account of its details, and not as to its principle."[17] "No man is more sensible than I am of the defects of the late School Law," he told guests at the public dinner honouring Metcalfe's ex-ministers, "so great, indeed, were they, that it has been found impossible to work it. That ... School Law was not framed by any Ministry, responsible or otherwise; it was hastily put together in a Select Committee of the House of Assembly, consisting of [twenty-three] members; without that deliberation and care which such a measure ought to have received."[18] But not one word did Hincks or any other member say at any time during the Bill's passage through Parliament regarding the separate school provisions in Day's Act or in this new Bill.

Hincks' Bill provided that ten or more freeholders, Protestant or Roman Catholic, might establish a separate school only if the teacher of the common school belonged to the other major body of Christians. This was a radical departure from the limitless provisions for denominational schools of any church backed by any number of dissentients, however small, which had been allowed by the former Act. Separate schools were entitled to share the government grant in proportion to the children in attendance, not the number of freeholders supporting it. A safeguard, however, was provided for the religious scruples of Roman Catholic children or others attending the common school. The Bill ensured that no child need read any religious book or join in any devotional exercises objected to by the parents. Thus Hincks' Bill drastically curtailed the provisions for separate schools by restricting them to either Roman Catholic or Protestant ones, backed up by a numerically substantial group differing in religion from the teacher of the common school.

It is noteworthy that only three of the seventy-one clauses of the Bill dealt with the religious question. Their restrictive nature marks a new and reactionary policy on this issue, but a policy which met with general approval for several years. Hincks and the Reformers were well aware of the implications. They had not, according to Hincks' own statement, legislated in the hasty or irresponsible manner of 1841.[19] Baldwin, by his political creed, was prepared to stand behind the Act, and this is particularly significant in view of the considerable and undeniable dependence of his party on Irish and French Catholic votes. Nor was there any protest against the terms of Hincks' Bill from any member of the Roman Catholic Church. In fact the sole protest from all the branches of Christianity represented in the province was entered by Bishop Strachan, who prayed vainly of the Assembly that "the monies appropriated for Common School purposes be placed at the disposal of the several Denominations of Christians, in proportion to their numbers."[20]

The implicit assumption of the Act was that the number of separate schools in Upper Canada, whether Roman Catholic or Protestant, would be insignificant, that provision for their establishment was ample protection for the minority rights of either group and a sufficient protection against insult or the tyranny of the majority. Separate schools, wherever and whenever necessary, would remain an integral part of the general system of education in the western portion of Canada. Every factor surrounding the passing of Hincks' Common School Act of 1843 confirms this interpretation.

v

The appointment of the Reverend Egerton Ryerson as Superintendent of Education for Upper Canada in 1844 was probably the most important single event in the educational history of the province. Under his direction the common school system received that form and substance which it retains with slight alterations to this day. His appointment to the post had been mooted by Sydenham shortly before the latter's tragic death, but when the Reform party gained control of the government, the Reverend Robert Murray of the Church of Scotland was appointed instead. Murray's incompetence soon became apparent and the coincidence of the Reform Government's retirement and a vacancy in the staff of King's College provided the opportunity for a change. Metcalfe referred to Murray's transfer as a "benefit to the public interest," but time showed that it was not entirely a benefit to King's College.[21]

Metcalfe had invited Ryerson to an interview to discuss the University question early in 1844, but the discussion turned to the subject of education in its widest aspects. Impressed with Ryerson's ability and grasp of the subject, the Governor General renewed Sydenham's invitation that he assume the superintendence of the schools of Upper Canada. After some delay Ryerson accepted, despite his awareness that the job would prove short-lived if the Reformers won their contest with Metcalfe over the interpretation of responsible government. To George Brown must go the credit of immortalizing the fiction that the appointment was Ryerson's price as a political pamphleteer defending the Governor General. Years later Ryerson stated the true sequence of events in personal vindication of his political independence,[22] and apparently Baldwin at least was satisfied to retain him after the return of the Reformers in 1848, when the party cried for vengeance against the individual whom they blamed for their defeat in 1844. Nevertheless, Ryerson's appointment was an honour bestowed on the Wesleyan Methodists, a body who had until then been sedulously excluded from all emoluments by the Reformers.

Ryerson's success was bound to incite jealousy and opposition among old and new political opponents. Within his own denomination a considerable stir and some antagonism was created.[23] Outside it, the attack came from the chagrined Reformers on the left and the Church of England on the right. This latter body, through its journal, accused him of desiring to control the elementary educational system as well as the University. The job, Ryerson commented, would afford him "an opportunity to establish throughout Canada other than a sectarian system of education. . . . But this is not *Puseyism*—it is 'schismatic' Methodism—& therefore *The Church protests*."[24]

The educational Grand Tour of Europe which Ryerson took to fit himself for his new responsibilities lasted from October, 1844, to December, 1846. In all his correspondence and in his exhaustive report of the trip Ryerson makes no reference to separate schools. But he did on numerous occasions state his hopes and ambitions for a national system of education in Upper Canada, and these expressions as they bear on the religious question deserve serious consideration since they show the basis of his future policy concerning this troublesome subject.

The most explicit statement of his ideals was made by Ryerson in a retrospective view of his career when he left the Department of Education in 1876. Writing to John George Hodgins, his *alter ego*, Ryerson said, "We have laboured . . . to promote the best interests of our country, irrespective of religious sect or political party—to devise, develop, and mature a system of instruction which embraces and provides for every child in the land a good education. . . ."[25] Prospectively he wrote:

If it be intended that the system of Public Instruction be Provincial, or National, it must be one throughout the Province. There cannot be a distinct system, or no system, as it may happen, in every County, Township, or School District. . . . In order that a system of Instruction may be Provincial, the machinery of it must be so. . . .

I assume, also, that Christianity—the Christianity of the Bible—regardless of the peculiarities of Sects, or Parties is to be the basis of our System of Public Instruction, as it is of our Civil Constitution. . . .[26]

In his Report of a "System of Public Elementary Education for Upper Canada," Ryerson felt it necessary "to adduce the testimony of the most competent authorities, who, without distinction of Sect, or Country, or form of Government, assert the absolute necessity of making Christianity, the basis and cement of all the structure of Public Education." [27] "I propose to show also how the principles of Christianity have been, and may be carried into effect, without any compromise of principle in any party concerned, or any essential deficiency in any subject taught." Education must be universal and practical, and therefore established on "Religion and Morality." "By Religion and Morality I do not mean sectarianism in any form, but the general system of truth and morals taught in the Holy Scriptures. Sectarianism it not morality. . . . Such sectarian teaching may, as it has done, raise up an army of pugilists and persecutors, but it is not the way to create a community of Christians."

His summary for the case of non-denominational but Christian education in Canada leaves no doubt as to Ryerson's position in this issue.

> The inhabitants of the Province at large, professing Christianity, and being fully represented in the Government by Members of a Responsible Council—Christianity, therefore, upon the most popular principles of Government, should be the basis of a Provincial System of Education. But that general principle admits of considerable variety in its application. . . . Such may, and should be, the case in Canada. . . . The Law provides against interfering with the religious scruples of each class [Roman Catholic and Protestant], in respect both to religious books and the means of establishing Separate Schools.
>
> In School Districts where the whole population is either Protestant or Roman Catholic, and where, consequently, the Schools come under the character of "Separate" there the principle of Religious Instruction can be carried out into as minute detail as may accord with the views and wishes of either class of the population; though I am persuaded all that is essential to the moral interests of youth may be taught in what are termed Mixed Schools.[28]

Clearly Ryerson conceived of separate schools as the exceptional means of protecting minority rights within the unitary whole of the provincial system. Nor had he any reason to think the system would develop on other lines than those he had laid out, if one discounted the impracticable designs of Bishop Strachan. Yet he was as limited in the system which he could create as had been the Demiurge of Plato's *Timaeus*. Conditions as they already existed must be accepted with little hope of undoing the work of others.

VI

To implement his recommendations for the founding of a provincial system of public education, Ryerson drafted a Common School Bill which recited verbatim the three clauses concerning separate schools and religion in the Act of 1843. No objection to this procedure was raised in the Legislature, but the Assembly did oppose an amendment suggested by the Legislative Council to permit children outside a given school section to attend a separate school within it. The division of school monies on a basis of attendance would of course have borne unfairly on the residents of that school section without financial assistance from those surrounding sections whose children were being educated there. After a conference of representatives of both Houses, the justice of the Assembly's position was admitted by the Council, and the Bill became law without any change in the separate school provision of the Hincks' Act.

The only reference to separate schools made during the debates came from William Henry Boulton in the Assembly, who requested that the Church of

England be given the same rights as the Roman Catholics, and "trusted that the Members of the Church of England would insist on this being passed, or the clauses erased." [29] Otherwise the Assembly accepted Ogle R. Gowan's invitation to consider the Bill as a national measure rather than a party one.

In his charge at the visitation of the Anglican clergy in 1844, Bishop Strachan had again demanded the right to establish separate Church of England schools.[30] Clause 55 of Hincks' Act provided only for Protestant or Roman Catholic schools, the Bishop complained, "thus compounding the Church of England with the myriad of Protestant denominations, and depriving her of any benefit which might derive from this Enactment, while such benefit remains to the Roman Catholics." Further, throughout the whole Act "there is no reference to Christianity." On behalf of the Church of England Strachan and other Anglican clergymen petitioned the Assembly in 1845 that elementary education be left to the exertions, voluntary or otherwise, of the various denominations. Petitions to the same effect also came before the Assembly in 1846. It was probably as a result of this pressure that all clergymen were made visitors of the common schools in the Act of 1846.

In conformity with Clause 3 of the Common Schools Act, Ryerson and Draper undertook the formation of a Board of Education to assist Ryerson in his departmental work. Ryerson would have preferred a board composed of clergy representing the major denominations, because such men had the advantages of better qualifications and more free time than the average layman.[31] Draper, however, doubted the "propriety" of making the board entirely clerical.[32] Ryerson admitted that "there would be a cry that it was a *clerical* Board, etc. etc." unless some lay representatives were included.[33] This decision permitted him to exclude Mr. Burns, the fire-brand of the Free Church "a *wasp*—an insulter of all who differed from him, & a perfectly impracticable man to act with." Besides, he added, "the newspaper organs and legislators of [the ecclesiastical radicals] object to *priestly* representation or control. It will therefore be more in accordance with *their* professed sentiments to be represented by *laymen*."

When Ryerson approached Strachan regarding his participation on the board, Strachan refused because his presence "Could rather hinder than help on the work," since "the opposition would then say everything was concocted & done" by Ryerson and himself. Instead he suggested the name of the Reverend Henry Grasett. Ryerson reported with satisfaction that "His Lordship highly approved of the appointment of the Roman Catholic Bishop Power." Indeed this was one name on which all were agreed. The Board as finally constituted was a nice balance between the claims of the various denominations and between lay and clerical representation. Its members, besides Ryerson, were Grasett and the Honourable S. B. Harrison from the Church of England, J. C. Morrison of the Free Church, J. S. Howard, Congregationalist, Hugh Scobie of the Church of of Scotland, and Bishop Power.

At the first meeting of the board, Bishop Power was elected chairman, a position which he filled most efficiently until his lamentable death on October 1, 1847, from emigrant fever. During that time all evidence attests that the Roman Catholic Bishop of Toronto acted with the other members of the board in the friendliest and most harmonious manner. There is no suggestion of that antagonism towards the common school system which was later imputed to Power by his co-religionists.[34] On the contrary Hodgins who was present as secretary to the board at every meeting asserts that the Bishop's actions were always most co-operative. At a later date Ryerson penned the following high tribute to his memory: "Bishop Power, virtually a Canadian, being born in Nova Scotia, had a particular desire to elevate the Roman Catholic population of the Country and believed that it would be best effected by their children being educated with the children of other classes, wherever party feeling did not oppose insurmountable obstacles to it."[35]

Ryerson was "astonished and deeply affected" by the death of Bishop Power.[36] The *Globe* also expressed the public regret at the Bishop's demise. There can be no doubt that this tragic loss of an enlightened educationalist injuriously affected the future course of elementary education in the province. In fact, Bishop Power's co-operation with Ryerson in the scheme of national education seems to have been an embarrassment to the extreme advocates of Roman Catholic separate schools ever since. Power viewed the existence of separate schools in the same light as Ryerson did—as an unfortunate necessity, not as an essential principle—and for more than a year his successor, De Charbonnel, also termed them a "protection from insult."[37]

VII

One of the first subjects to come under consideration by the new Board of Education was the establishment of a mixed normal school. This project was an essential part of the plan for improving and standardizing the provincial system of elementary education, and it is noteworthy that Bishop Power gave it his full support.[38] Another subject resolved was the delicate matter of religious exercises and instruction in the common schools. Ryerson drafted regulations which permitted trustees to devote as much as a whole day of the school week to instruction of the pupils by their respective ministers. Of course the statute had provided that no pupil must attend at any religious exercises in the school to which the parents objected.

Bishop Power stated that he had no objection to these *Forms and Regulations* "as Roman Catholics were fully protected in their rights and views, and as he did not wish to interfere with Protestants in the fullest exercise of their rights and views."[39] Bishop Strachan, however, had told Ryerson that the Act of 1846 had no Christianity in it.[40] His approval of these regulations, and his promise to write his clergy requesting their support and aid for the common schools,[41] was therefore a victory for Ryerson and his non-denominational system of elementary instruction. Draper was more than pleased with the success of his Chief Superintendent. "You, (to whom I expressed myself about three years ago on the subject of the importance of not dividing religious from Secular instruction) will readily understand the pleasure I feel that in Common Schools at least the principle & proposed application of it—for mixed schools—has been approved by the Bishop of my own Church and by the Roman Catholic Prelate."[42]

In his report for 1847 Ryerson could say with justification and pride, "I am not aware of a single complaint on this subject [of religious exercises and instruction]." "Thus, without kindling the flames of religious contention on this subject, and yet maintaining inviolately the principles of Christianity, as the basis of our Educational System, each School Municipality, or Section, is authorized to provide, according to its own judgment, the nature and extent of the Religious Exercises and Instruction that shall be observed and given in the School."[43] He could also report that the Bible was used in almost two-thirds of the common schools. "This fact is the best answer to the objections of those who have represented our Common Schools as 'Godless', and as excluding Christianity from these Schools. . . ."[44]

Nevertheless the results of the Act of 1846 were not all sweetness and light. Administrative difficulties had appeared at almost every level and soon they cried aloud for redress. Ryerson blamed this failure on the amendments which had been made by the Legislature.[45] The district councils seemed divided in opinion on the efficacy of the whole educational policy and machinery. The arguments adduced were similar to those which had persistently frustrated the educational efforts of the Legislature of Upper Canada, and might well be called one skirmish in the battle between classic and progressive educationalists.

The remedial legislation passed in 1847 to correct the deficiencies of the Act of the preceding year contained a new provision regarding urban separate schools which in effect extended the restrictive policy inaugurated by the Act of 1843. The Board of Trustees of any town or city were now empowered "To determine the Number, Sites and Description of Schools, which shall be Established and Maintained in Such City and Town aforesaid, and whether such School, or Schools shall be Denominational, or Mixed."[46] Hodgins attributes this further reactionary change to Ryerson's desire "to modify the Separate School provisions of the former Acts, and to give them a less positive form."[47] Yet it does not appear that this policy was directed against the Church of Rome. On the contrary the evidence suggests that it was intended to forestall the demands of Strachan for separate publicly supported Anglican schools. The Act became law a full two months before Power's death, yet he offered no protest and continued to fill the post of chairman of the Board of Education. Indeed M. T. O'Brien, a prominent lay spokesman of Toronto's Roman Catholic population, who had in 1845 petitioned for a more equitable division of the legislative grant between the common and separate schools of that city [48] (the *only* protest of any kind from Roman Catholics against the educational system), was now petitioning Parliament against Macdonald's University Bill. He and others demanded that King's College endowment be kept intact "for the Education of all Classes and Denominations of the people . . . and [not] to divert it to sectarian objects."[49]

Ryerson himself had drafted the amending Bill of 1847 and the engrossed Act was almost a literal transcript of the draft. In a letter to the Honourable Dominick Daly, Provincial Secretary, Ryerson explained fully the purpose of this Bill. He favoured vesting control of urban schools in the municipalities, rather than in district councils. The density of population in cities and towns justified the centralizing of educational powers in municipal hands rather than leaving it entirely in control of each ward or school district authority. Thus he explained the new powers of the urban Board of Trustees, without any reference to the separate schools. But two days after submitting the draft Bill, Ryerson advised Draper that Strachan was still insisting that the Church of England had a right to separate schools and a share of the school fund.[50] Ryerson had reminded the Bishop that the first Upper Canada School Bill, which Strachan had prepared, had postulated mixed schools. The Bishop expressed his opposition to the Irish national school system; "he preferred *separate* Schools, if they could get them." Perhaps Strachan was influenced by the fact that the Low Church group, whose opposition to his personal plans was increasing, was largely the Irish element within the Church of England.

In any case Ryerson warned Draper that if Strachan were to receive a share of the school funds, it "would create as much if not more religious party feeling than did ... the Clergy Reserves question." It is important to note that the claims and aims of the Anglican Bishop were the same as those put forward by his Roman Catholic counterpart beginning five years later. The granting of a share of public monies to denominational schools simply as such, without the justification of protecting minority rights from insult, would make a public institution "subservient to the purpose of religious party."

From all this it seems that the new control exercised by the municipal Boards of Trustees had merely a utilitarian purpose, or if there were any ulterior designs they were directed against the Church of England, not the Church of Rome. Some critics suggested that this provision would encourage the multiplication of separate schools, and Ryerson felt it necessary to refute the charge in his annual report. The separate school provisions in the other three Acts passed since Union were "much more objectionable," and in Ryerson's opinion unnecessary in view of the safeguards provided for conscientious objectors to the accepted forms of religious exercises in the mixed school.[51] In fact the number of separate schools had actually declined within twelve months as a result of the new provisions. As to the claim that every denomination had an equal right to separate schools, such arrangements were permitted by the Act of 1847. "Therefore, the Autho-rities of no Religious Persuasion have opposed, or petitioned against it, as some of them did against the previous School Act." But the decision to establish any denominational school rested with the authorities "who are responsible for all the Schools in each City, or Town, and for the means necessary to support them," not with the religious bodies.

This, then, was Ryerson's answer to Reform critics, as it was to the advocates of denominational schools. It was fated to satisfy neither group. At the moment, however, all eyes were directed to Macdonald's controversial University Bill, and to the general election which everyone knew must come soon. The silence of Bishop Power can only be proof of his assent to this new arrangement. But Strachan favoured the suggestion of Lord John Russell that the government match any amount raised by a religious body for its own school, without, however, any government interference.[52] The present Act was in Strachan's opinion modelled on the "democratic" system of the State of New York, which constituted an educational despotism by placing the state *in loco parentis*. Such was indeed the philosophy of Ryerson, who declared publicly his faith in the government as the "collective parent" of all children.

Strachan made no public comment on this new legislation, but this silence, especially when he addressed the second visitation of his clergy while the remedial Act was before the Assembly, is not conclusive. There is a tantalizing lacuna surrounding the Act of 1847, similar to that in the contemporary incident of Strachan's actions on Macdonald's University Bill. Any correspondence which could have shed light on both these episodes is gone, presumably for all time.

VIII

For two years the remedial Common School Act of 1847 functioned more or less successfully. Finances and teacher-trustee relations were the major problems arising out of the Act, but all objections seem to have been against details not principles, and to have been of minor importance. Ryerson reported in 1848: "There are four classes, or coteries, of persons who always have been, and who, in all probability, will be opposed to the provisions of any and every general School Law, and who, though not numerous, make up in occasional dogmatism and vehemence what they want in numbers."[53] One of these coteries he defined as those persons "who are opposed to any other than Denominational Schools." The educational system of Canada West must, he insisted, be general and homogeneous. "To... yield to any one class of these objectors, is out of the question...." Those classes constituted only a "small and insignificant portion of the community," and their opposition to the school law had "diminished and disappeared just in proportion as it has become understood...."

Some minor adjustments in the school system were obviously desirable, but a more extensive revision of the statute was practically necessitated by the passing of Baldwin's Municipal Corporations Act. Ryerson had already submitted two draft Bills, and from these and the Acts currently in force, the Honourable Malcolm Cameron undertook the compilation of "An Act for the better Establishment and Maintenance of Public Schools in Upper Canada, and for repealing the recent School Act." The Bill was introduced late in the memorable session of 1849, amid the tensions of Rebellion Losses and annexation. It came up for second reading only five days before prorogation. Despite the complaint of W. H. Boulton against the introduction of such an important measure so late in the session, the Bill received a perfunctory second and third reading all in one day. In Cameron's words the purpose of the Act was to introduce "a systematic code" of common school legislation.[54] But its implication and innovations were revolutionary, and the Act became the occasion of an episode unique in Canadian parliamentary history.

Cameron had taken the School Bill in hand as early as January of 1849, but Ryerson was not informed of its provisions until late in April.[55] The Chief Superintendent was, not unreasonably, suspicious of this delay, especially since the new Ministry contained enemies sworn to his destruction for the part which he had taken in defeating the Reform party at the elections of 1844. He had been warned during the Metcalfe crisis of the probable result should the Reformers regain power. Yet for more than a year Baldwin had held the reins of power, and Ryerson was still Chief Superintendent of Education for Canada West despite the pressure of vengeful Reformers to obtain his dismissal. The reluctance of Baldwin to cashier a civil servant who had blighted the hopes of the party was just one more reason for the growing revolt of the radical element against their conservative leader which led to the separation of the Clear Grits from the amorphous political conglomeration which supported the Great Ministry.

It was only when Cameron's Bill received its first reading that Ryerson became aware of its true intent—the destruction of his whole scheme for a provincial system of elementary education. Hastening to Montreal to protest in person, Ryerson arrived there the day after the burning of the Parliament Buildings, when the Legislature could hardly be expected to give its attention to the School Bill. Inspector General Hincks gave Ryerson a warm welcome, "but Mr. Cameron looked very sour."[56] It was obvious that Cameron was entirely responsible for the obnoxious Bill, and Ryerson left the capital with the understanding that the measure would either be dropped or amended to conform with his suggestions of the previous autumn.

When, to Ryerson's surprise, the original Bill was enacted, despite his recent complaints, he interviewed Baldwin, and submitted his resignation together with a lengthy exposition of his objections.[57] The upshot of these events set a precedent for constitutional historians to ponder. Ryerson was invited to continue to administer the Department of Education as though Cameron's Act had never passed, with the promise that his own suggested legislative changes of the school system would be undertaken at the next session. As the School Act was not to become operative until January, 1850, Ryerson allowed the Cabinet to resolve the problem during the autumn. By the end of the year Ryerson could write to his assistant, J. G. Hodgins, that "the scandalous School Bill" had been "upset."[58] "The members of the Govt. (even the Governor General personally) have examined my long paper of July last, & have come entirely into my views. Malcolm Cameron is also out of office...." Such were the surprising results of an Act which had been intended among other things to oust Ryerson from his important position.

Cameron's abortive School Act bore directly on the question of religion and elementary education at two vital points. The Chief Superintendent protested against the first which was the exclusion of the clergy as visitors to the common schools.[59] He did not protest, however, against the second—the lack of any reference to separate schools. There can be only one possible interpretation of the latter omission by the Act and by Ryerson. The number of separate schools of all types, Roman Catholic, Protestant, and coloured, was declining. There was every reasonable expectation that the trend would continue. In the two draft Bills prepared by Ryerson for Baldwin's Government there had been no provision for separate schools. Therefore, the omission in Cameron's Act conformed to Ryerson's own intention of allowing the separate schools to disappear by the natural process of attrition.

The passage of Cameron's Act had received as little attention outside Parliament as it did within. Although the Bill was before the Houses for six weeks, not one petition against it was presented. This, of course, resulted in part from preoccupation with the University Act and distraction by the catastrophic events occuring in Montreal. It is noteworthy that the Roman Catholic Church authorities confined themselves during the session to obtaining an Act of Incorporation for Bytown College, and in pushing the claim of Regiopolis College for some public financial support. In this latter connection they stressed the need for religious supervision of college students, in the same terms used by the defenders of Victoria and Queen's. They did not refer to any such religious need of children attending elementary schools, close to their homes and churches, where sufficient means and safeguards for religious instruction already existed. It is therefore a fair assumption that at this time Ryerson was not the only individual who felt it "no contradiction to support a common elementary education but a denominational system of higher education...."[60]

IX

When the provincial Parliament reconvened in May, 1850, all three major religio-political problems—Clergy Reserves, University, and separate schools—came up for consideration. The Bill which Ryerson had been promised as part of the price for withdrawing his resignation was carried through the Assembly by his very co-operative acquaintance, Inspector General Francis Hincks. Before this Bill which Ryerson had drafted was introduced, a number of petitions were presented to the Assembly, petitions which were political storm warnings pointing in two directions. The old order was rapidly approaching its end, and the new era was soon to be marked by religious controversies of an intensity and violence hitherto unknown in the western portion of the Province of Canada.

Numerous demands were again being heard in Parliament that the Clergy Reserves and Rectories funds be appropriated to the purpose of general education. This important subject has, however, already been considered in connection with the general question of the Clergy Reserves. More pertinent to elementary education were the petitions from Roman Catholics praying for the re-establishment of separate schools. These, three in number, came from the town of Picton and from Kitley Township. Feeble as their voice might be, these petitions were symptomatic of a growing sentiment.

The real test of the session came later on the separate school provisions of the new Common School Bill. Hincks adroitly guided forty-eight of the forty-nine clauses of the Bill through the House without substantial amendment, but not without considerable debate on various aspects. On the nineteenth clause alone, that providing for separate schools, was Hincks forced to accept, with Ryerson's concurrence, an effective amendment. The original clause had vested the power to establish separate schools in the municipal authority of each township subject to its discretion. Both the Roman Catholics and the Anglicans were dissatisfied with the circumscription of rural separate schools which paralleled the provisions for urban separate schools in the Act of 1847. The Roman Catholic Vicar General at Kingston and the Administrator of the Toronto diocese petitioned for amendment of the disputed clause "to enable the Catholics of Canada West to establish separate schools, wherever they may deem it expedient."[61]

Here was an opportunity in the eyes of the High Anglicans to obtain their desired end of establishing Anglican schools through a co-operation with the Church of Rome without infringing their exclusive principles. An agreement for joint action on the nineteenth clause was reached by members of the Assembly from each of these churches. The Ministry learned of the plot, and turned the occasion to the best advantage by offering the Roman Catholics a compromise which met their requests. The former arrangement of permitting Roman Catholic separate schools wherever the common school teacher was Protestant and *vice versa* was inserted into the nineteenth clause, and the original wording amended to make it *"the duty of the Municipal Council of any Township, and of the Board of School Trustees of any City, Town, or Incorporated Village, on the application, in writing, of twelve, or more, resident heads of families,* to authorize the establishment of one, or more, Separate Schools for Protestants, Roman Catholics, or Coloured People."[62]

The Church of England groups who were demanding separate schools "boasted that they would have a majority of fourteen, or twenty, votes against the Government, on the 19th Section of the Bill."[63] When the division was called they found themselves in a very small minority as the Roman Catholic members voted with the Ministry. Their bewilderment at this turn of events brought derisive laughter from the rest of the House. The Roman Catholics had for the moment been satisfied by these concessions, and certainly had no wish to upset their traditional alliance with the Reform party led by Lafontaine.

Hincks confessed to the House that he preferred the original terms of the nineteenth clause, but had accepted the compromise in deference to the "strong feeling" of his colleagues.[64] But for the first time the public press voiced its opposition to the educational privileges granted to Roman Catholics. To voluntarists the concessions were too reminiscent of the Anglican influence in King's College which had so recently been abrogated. In all other areas the relations of church and state seemed on the point of that complete separation for which most of Upper Canada had so long aspired. The *Watchman*, unofficial journal of the New Connexion Church, felt that the peculiar privileges granted the Roman Catholics in the New School Act were "of questionable character."[65] The *Globe* of July 9 expressed mild regret that Hincks had given way by permitting Roman Catholic separate schools. "The principle thus admitted strikes at the root of our whole system of national education." If one denomination were entitled to such preferential treatment, then all were. This privilege was the thin edge of the wedge, the *Globe* warned. George Brown seemed ignorant of the historical antecedents of the nineteenth clause, but his editorial has still the ring of prophecy. Ryerson's policy of discouraging the expansion of separate schools was indeed approaching the crisis which resulted in a retreat to at least partial defeat.

In a circular letter to the town reeves, Ryerson candidly explained the reasons for the alteration of the nineteenth clause in favour of separate schools. As no complaints had been made against the separate schools provisions of the City and Town School Act of 1847 (which left the matter to the discretion of the municipalities), it had been the intention to apply the same principle in rural areas. But objections from both Protestant and Roman Catholic members of the Legislature had resulted in the re-enactment of the original provisions with the additional requirement of a petition from twelve heads of families. Although this general arrangement had existed since 1843, the number of separate schools in Canada West had declined from fifty-one in 1849 to forty-six in 1850, and of these more than half were Protestant. In Ryerson's opinion there existed "no probability that Separate Schools will be more injurious in time to come than they have been in time past."[66]

Supporters of separate schools still could claim no exemption from local school rates, and could obtain no government aid beyond the share of the school grant provided for the teacher's salary on the basis of enrolment in the separate school. The schoolhouse and all its appurtenances must be supplied entirely by those who used it. The law provided adequate safeguards for religious minorities, within the mixed schools. Those who insisted on separate schools could not expect the community to tax itself for sectarian or sectional interests. With the exception of the slight concession made by Hincks' Common School Act of 1850, the policy towards separate schools since 1841 had been increasingly restrictive. Yet the only protest of consequence had come from the Church of England.

x

During the latter half of 1850 Pius IX re-established the papal hierarchy in Great Britain. He also invested a French count, Armand François Marie de Charbonnel, as second Roman Catholic Bishop of Toronto, succeeding the lamented Bishop Power. The two events were pregnant with a fire not celestial, which was soon to fall upon Canada with unforeseen and cataclysmic effects. Many "Dissenters" like Egerton Ryerson at first viewed the so-called papal aggression with a measure of approval, as a merited rebuke to Anglican claims of apostolic succession.[67] This tone soon disappeared as the plans of the Roman Church Militant unfolded. When George Brown accepted Taché's challenge to publish the relevant documents on papal aggression in the *Globe*, he took up a fiery cross which ultimately divided the province into two hostile armed camps, Roman Catholic *versus* Protestant. A century has passed but the heather is still burning, or at least smouldering.

Bishop de Charbonnel brought to his see an ultramontanism born in part from the disturbed condition of his native land. The same trends toward infidelity and indifferentism which he saw in France had, in Italy, destroyed the liberal proclivities of the new incumbent of Peter's chair. But in Canada, where he had already laboured for several years, De Charbonnel was looked upon without suspicion. He was appointed to the Council of Public Instruction (successor of the Board of Education) in Power's stead, and there was no expectation that his policy there would be less co-operative and helpful than that of his predecessor.

Ryerson was absent in Europe on a trip, prolonged to eight months by his participation in the Clergy Reserves question, when the issue of separate schools again arose late in 1850. The Toronto Board of School Trustees rejected the application of certain Roman Catholics for the establishment of another separate school. The request was not unreasonable in view of the size of the city, but as the latest School Act had constituted the whole city as a single school section, it was not legally permissible. On appeal to the Queen's Bench, that court upheld Attorney General Baldwin's interpretation by deciding that the Board's refusal was justified by the letter of the law, "whatever might have been the intention of the Legislature." [68]

Writing to Hodgins from Paris, Ryerson recorded his approval of the Court's decision.

The Roman Catholics have commenced to use the 19th clause of the School Act in a very different way from what was intended and from what they professed to me to desire [it]. I suppose the late proceedings of the Pope & Bishops in regard to Separate Education in Ireland have promoted this change. The decision of the Judges, while it affords them due protection, will prevent them from making an undue use of this clause in Cities & Towns. In country places they cannot do so. [69]

Hincks resisted the pressure of Roman Catholic supporters of the Ministry for remedial action by Parliament until Ryerson could be consulted. Here the matter stood for some months, as the Chief Superintendent did not return to the province until June, 1851.

In this interval Strachan had reopened his campaign for Church of England schools, undeterred by the fiasco which had greeted his efforts in the last session. His first step was to inject the controversy into his "Letter to Lord John Russell" which had primarily been intended as a defence of his church's share of the Clergy Reserves. The Bishop complained of the injustice of permitting Roman Catholic separate schools while denying them to Anglicans. The votes of Romanists, he charged, had balked his efforts to provide that Christian education which the provincial school system ignored. [70] In the reply which Elgin had requested to Strachan's pamphlet, Ryerson noted the double game which the Bishop was playing with the Roman Catholics in Canada and anti-papal aggression in England. Once more the Chief Superintendent denied that his schools were infidel, and as for separate Anglican schools, they were, he insisted, legally permissible, *if* the people of Canada could be convinced by the Bishop of their necessity. [71]

When the Bishop convened his clergy and laity synodically in May, he again drew their attention to the "intolerable degradation" of the educational system which was turning Anglican children into "infidels."[72] "We must demand what the Roman Catholics already have obtained,—Separate Schools; and I honour them for insisting on this concession." In one breath he chided the Roman Catholics for ignoring Anglican rights while seeking their own benefit, and warned that Protestants should "Perish" rather than give their children a Romish or infidel education. Strachan described the two extremes in public education as complete state control and laissez-faire. "In this Province the system adopted cannot with accuracy be said to come under either of these two." Although it was certainly not his intention, Strachan was actually paying a tribute to the Canadian compromise between denominational and state education established by Ryerson's instrumentality, a system which then seemed to be an unqualified success.

Shortly after Ryerson's return from Europe the cornerstone of the new normal school was laid. During the ceremonies on this momentous occasion Ryerson adverted to the Christian principles on which the institution was to be based. In replying to Ryerson's address the Governor General went even further by referring as pointedly as the Chief Superintendent could have desired to "the firm rock of our common Christianity" which was the foundation of the common school system. "We invite the Ministers of Religion, of all Denominations,—the *de facto* spiritual guides of the people of the Country,—to take their stand along with us."[73] If this invitation was directed to John, Bishop of Toronto, it went unheard because that personage was conspicuous by his absence; if directed to Armandus, Bishop of Toronto, it was not heeded in later years. At the moment, however, Elgin believed he had succeeded.[74]

The petitions for separate Anglican schools which Strachan had requested of his flock were duly presented to both Houses of the provincial Parliament when its session opened in the summer of 1851. Roman Catholic petitions from Brockville and Belleville also came in, "praying for the Amendment of the Nineteenth Section of the Common School Act of 1850, so as to provide more effectually for Separate Schools in certain cases."[75] But these voices of denominationalism did not pass unchallenged. The municipal council of the County of York deprecated the provisions for separate schools as "injurious and baneful in the extreme to the otherwise progessively harmonizing effects of generally diffused Education." The logical sequence of such concessions to Roman Catholics must mean schools for every denomination. The ultimate result would be the "prostration of the Education of the people at the shrine of Religious sectarianism," with every evil attendant thereon. Similar expressions of opinion also came from the municipal councils of Peel, Wentworth, and Halton.[76]

George Brown was still smarting from his April defeat in the Haldimand by-election, to which his anti-Romanist editorials in the *Globe* had contributed. To these latest overtures from the Churches of England and Rome Brown gave a stinging reply. He agreed with the York county council that the Church of England should have the same rights as the Church of Rome, *if* separate schools were allowed to continue. The Bishop's petitions could not be justly denied as long as Clause 19 remained on the statute books. Yet the hue and cry of "religion in danger" was in his opinion just a priestly scheme to gain control of the means of education for sectarian and sacerdotal ends. "Can no member of Parliament be found who will bring in a bill for the repeal of the 19th clause of the Common School Act?"[77]

There was indeed such a member, and, ironically, it was none other than

Brown's successful rival from Haldimand, William Lyon Mackenzie. Ryerson had rejected the draft of a remedial Bill prepared by Bishop de Charbonnel and Vicar General Macdonell as inadmissible, but stated his intention of seeing separate school rights lost by the Act of 1850 restored to the Roman Catholics on the same basis as in the Act of 1846. The Roman Catholic prelates agreed that the right to have a separate school in every city ward would be satisfactory and Ryerson immediately produced a Bill incorporating the necessary changes.[78]

He took the precaution of explaining his action to John Ross and Hincks, who were to introduce the Bill in the upper and lower Houses respectively. He conceded the justice of the Roman Catholic position, and warned that refusal would ally that body with the High Church party on the separate school issue, and on the University and Clergy Reserves questions.[79] De Charbonnel and Macdonell having expressed their satisfaction with his Bill, Ryerson met most of the Assembly and explained the problem and his solution. When Hincks moved the second reading of the Bill, the little rebel rose to strike a blow for secularism.

Mackenzie's amendment took the form of a Bill which he had in fact already introduced two weeks before.[80] Its terms were simple in the extreme—to repeal the nineteenth clause of the School Act of 1850. It was the natural postlude to Malcolm Cameron's Bill of 1849. Its preamble embodied the educational ideals of the Clear Grits, though its author was a fellow traveller rather than a member of that group. The existence of sectarian schools was characterized as "a dangerous interference with the Common School System of Upper Canada." It would be just as reasonable to have denominational grammar schools and colleges. Protestants should not be taxed to support the teaching of Roman Catholic doctrines, or *vice versa*. Sectarian elementary schools were nothing more than "nurseries of strife and dissension." The solution was obvious—to all political and ecclesiastical radicals. Expunge the nineteenth clause of the Common School Act of 1850, and expunge therewith all separate schools.

Only four members supported Mackenzie on his amendment and Hincks carried the original Bill by a vote of 25 to 7. Bishop de Charbonnel expressed his pleasure at this act of redress and his hopes that Roman Catholic education would continue to improve.[81] Thus the problem of extending separate school facilities in urban areas seemed to have been solved to the satisfaction of all parties except those extremes of left and right, the Grits and the High Church Anglicans. The provisions for separate schools were now precisely those which had existed five years before when Ryerson presented his first report and draft Bill for the establishment of a common school system in Canada West. A *via media* between the conflicting claims of state and church seemed to have been achieved in the field of elementary education.

XI

Mackenzie's action in introducing his anti-separate school Bill had been motivated partly by convictions and partly by factious animosity towards the Ministry. But taken along with Cameron's Bill and the decision of the Queen's Bench on the appeal of the Roman Catholics of Toronto, it could not fail to arouse a feeling of insecurity and uneasiness among advocates of separate Roman Catholic schools. Add to this the known attitude of the Clear Grits and the anti-French-Canadian, anti-Romanist expressions of George Brown and the *Globe*, and the situation became one which invited attention and action by Roman Catholics.

In at least one county the issue of separate Roman Catholic schools became a rallying cry for party politicians during the general elections of December, 1851. The Guelph *Advertiser,* a radical Reform journal, unequivocally stated on November 6, 1851, its opposition on principle to all denominational schools. The local candidates immediately took up the question, each accusing the other of hostility to the Roman Catholic schools. But one voter, describing himself as "Irish Catholic," charged the Tory nominee with desiring to invoke Irish conditions in Canada.[82]

In his "Open Letter No. VI" to Hincks, George Brown asserted that Hincks had conceded separate schools to save his party from a revolt of the Lower Canadian members.[83] The nineteenth clause of the Act of 1850 was a shame to a "Reform" ministry. In the midst of the election campaign the *Globe* accused Hincks of desecrating the name of reform by making his supporters jettison their principles and accept separate schools.[84] The Roman Catholic clergy would next ask for a share of Clergy Reserves for separate schools as a saw-off for supporting secularization, the editor warned.

On the other hand a new Roman Catholic policy was also taking form. The "Papal Aggression" controversy had aroused bitter disagreement in Canada as well as in the mother country. The ultramontanism of De Charbonnel reinforced a latent tendency in that direction possessed by Irish and French Romanists in Canada. Further, the number of Roman Catholics had increased in less than a decade by more than 100,000, from 65,203 in 1842 to 167,695 in 1851, or by 157 per cent. Much of this growth resulted from the potato famine in Ireland, and the destitute immigrants who arrived in the province brought with them not only the plague which killed so many, including Bishop Power, but also memories of injustice and persecution suffered in the cause of their religion. The majority of these new Canadians settled in the urban centres of Montreal and Toronto, where their depressed condition produced such social wens as Montreal's Griffintown and Toronto's Cabbagetown, hotbeds of poverty, disease, and social strife. Some thirty-four thousand came to Toronto in 1847 alone.[85] Here was a voting power to be conjured with, to be wooed and perhaps seduced by politicians; here was a host of children lacking that education which under existing regulations and financial conditions could not be supplied through separate schools unless some drastic changes occurred.

The Great Ministry had ended, and with it passed the era of good feelings in the field of elementary education. Adequate provision and safeguards for religious instruction had been established, and about two-thirds of the common schools now used the Bible either as a text or devotional aid. No objections had been raised against these practices during the forties. The protection against insult provided by separate schools had been tested and found satisfactory by the Church of Rome whenever necessary. The Church of England had demanded the same privilege in vain. But by and large the issue of religion in elementary education had aroused little denominational interest, and had seldom impinged on party politics between 1841 and 1851. As Ryerson recorded, "Until 1850, the leading Men and Newspaper Press of all parties acquiesced in the Separate School provisions of the Law. I do not recollect there was even a discussion on the subject, either in, or out, of Parliament, or any objection to it from any quarter ... until 1852 Separate Schools were never advocated as a theory, much less as a doctrine, and still less as an article of faith." [86]

As the decade closed, however, a new spirit was evident on both sides. The era of the fiery fifties was at hand, and the storm over the separate schools broke quickly and furiously. The compromise of the forties was washed away, and in its place a political controversy protracted for more than another decade disrupted social harmony and political alignments. The result was a stalemate solidified by the British North America Act into a *mariage de convenance* which left both contracting parties unsatisfied and unpacified.

CHAPTER SEVEN

RELIGION AND ELEMENTARY EDUCATION, 1852-1867

THE WAR OF TOTAL SEPARATION

I

STORM WARNINGS of a clash between denominational and national interests in elementary education had appeared for a short time before the events of 1852 opened a conflict over separate schools. That conflict bedeviled the remaining days of the Union and left a legacy of distrust and antagonism to the Province of Ontario. Ryerson professed to be surprised by the sudden change of Roman Catholic policy and indeed even the modern historian must look beyond the confines of Canada to discover the more obvious premonitory trends which shaped this revolution in education. Like some recurrent pestilence the acrimonious controversy broke out periodically, upsetting the delicately balanced structure of politics and society in the United Province. The compromise on separate schools reached and completed by Confederation was not an Upper Canadian solution, indeed even less so than the settlement of the Clergy Reserves question. The Act of Union predestined that the pattern of elementary education in Canada West would be formed by forces and sentiments in every respect foreign to the will of the majority of the inhabitants.

Three specific cases occurred early in 1852 which brought Ryerson and Bishop de Charbonnel into conflict. The first, involving the separate school at Chatham, was mooted by the Bishop himself,[1] when the trustees of that school complained of receiving treatment inferior to that accorded to coloured people in the matter of sharing the provincial grant. Ryerson defended the letter of the School Act as justifying this financial disparity. De Charbonnel next charged that an anti-Catholic book was used in the Chatham common school, and denounced the educational system as "a regular disguised persecution."[2] The Chief Superintendent pointed out that no child was forced to read any objectionable book, that adequate religious safeguards were provided in the system of mixed schools, and that many Roman Catholic children attended common schools in areas where separate schools existed. This soft answer failed to turn away episcopal wrath, and De Charbonnel added a new accusation, that mixed schools were "the ruin of religion, and a persecution for our Church."[3] "We must have, and we will have the full management of our Schools, as well as Protestants in Lower Canada. . . ."

To this latest and unequivocal demand, a demand which dominates the issue for the remainder of the Union, Ryerson replied that it originated in the "new class of ideas and feelings" which De Charbonnel had introduced from Europe. He contrasted the opposite policy which Bishop Power had always pursued. The province had already voiced its opposition to the very principle of separate schools.

The provision of the law for Separate Schools was never asked or advocated until since 1850 as a *theory*, but merely as a *protection* in circumstances arising from the peculiar social state of neighbourhoods or Municipalities. I always thought the introduction of any provision for Separate Schools . . . was to be regretted and inexpedient; but finding such a provision in existence, and that parties concerned attached great importance to it, I have advocated its continuance, leaving Separate Schools to die out, not by force of Legislative enactment, but under the influence of increasingly enlightened and enlarged views of Christian relations. . . .⁴

Ryerson believed that he had always rendered justice to Roman Catholics, and, indeed, only one complaint had been heard in seven years against the system. That complaint, urged in the same month that he wrote, concerned the patent infringement of the religious liberty of certain Romanists at Georgetown by common school trustees overzealous for student discipline. The Georgetown case had been settled quickly and justly by the Chief Superintendent, but with a verbal rebuke to the plaintiffs who had preferred to air their grievance in the columns of the *Mirror*, before seeking redress through the proper departmental channels.

As for the claim of Chatham separate schools to a share of the local assessment in excess of the proportion equal to the government grant, there was no legal foundation for such novel ideas. The disposition of all funds except the statutory provision for separate schools rested entirely with the local authorities. "But if . . . a Municipality must be compelled to tax themselves to provide Separate School houses for religious persuasions, in addition to Public School Houses, there may be a high degree of 'civil liberty' secured to certain religious persuasions, but a melancholy slavery imposed upon the municipalities."⁵

The third case, similar to that at Chatham, had arisen in Belleville. Here the same answer was given by Ryerson—Roman Catholics had received their lawful due, however inequitable the arrangements might seem to separate school supporters. But De Charbonnel was not content to let the matter die, and again he returned to his claim for complete educational separation for Roman Catholic children. He cited the statement of the bishops of the Provincial Council of Baltimore, that teachers and texts in mixed schools endangered the souls of the faithful, and he theatened to invoke the sacramental authority of his church if necessary to remove Roman Catholics from mixed schools.

Ryerson reminded the Bishop that no state in the neighbouring union had aided the establishment of sectarian schools, and in Canada West the school texts were the very ones used in the Irish school system which De Charbonnel professed to admire. Neither the province nor its schools were sectarian or anti-Catholic, but Ryerson would reject the theory of papal supremacy as completely as had Henry VIII.

I can appeal to the history of the past in proof of my acting towards the Roman Catholic Church in the same spirit as towards any other church, but I must be unfaithful to all my past precedents, as well as to the trust reposed in me, and the almost unanimous feelings of the Country, if I should not do all in my power to resist—come from what quarter it may—every invasion of "the blessed principles of religious liberty and equal rights", among all classes of the people of Upper Canada.⁶

De Charbonnel terminated the controversy abruptly but ominously. "The conclusion of our Correspondence must be that our opinions on Separate Schools are quite different. . . . But I hope that by making use of all constitutional means, in order to obtain our right, I will not upset the Government of Canada nor its institutions."⁷ He had been worsted in the exchange. His impassioned but ill-informed arguments could not withstand the cold facts and logic employed by

Ryerson. But a corner had been turned in the development of separate schools in Canada West, and the ideological bases as well as the concrete aims of each side had been clearly stated. Henceforth there could be no doubt as to ends sought by the supporters of separate schools. For De Charbonnel and many, if not all, Roman Catholics, separate schools were no longer a means of protection from insult—they were an inalienable and sacred right which must be obtained to satisfy the conscientious convictions of their religious belief. The appeal was to an authority higher than that possessed by man-made governments or institutions.

Undoubtedly this policy in Canada was simply an extension of the aggressive tactics currently being employed in Europe and Great Britain by the Church of Rome in its revival of the Counter Reformation. De Charbonnel had dropped hints that his action was motivated at least in part by pressure from parties more extreme than himself. The allusion is veiled, but the criticism which he had received may not have been from his ecclesiastical superiors alone. In Toronto two neophytes had assumed the $56,000 debt on the new cathedral, and one of these men, Colonel John Elmsley, became the most vocal lay advocate of Roman Catholic separate schools within the next few years.

For Ryerson these new claims of religious superiority posed a threat, not merely to his hard-won educational system, but also to that civil and religious equality for which he had fought in past years. This latest danger came from a foe more powerful and sinister because it wielded a spiritual authority which even Strachan would never have claimed. The demand for special educational privileges, if granted, would undo the sentiment of national unity which the school system sought to foster. Both Roman Catholics and Protestants would be the losers from such a course. Ryerson viewed De Charbonnel's demand for control of his own denominational schools as a declaration of "war of total separation," the success of which would create a nation within a nation. It remained to be seen what means the Bishop would consider constitutional and justifiable to obtain that end—"the full management of our Schools, as well as Protestants in Lower Canada."

II

As in the University question, so with separate schools; finances were but the occasion of controversy, while the real principles involved were often confused or obscured by these outward appearances. Such was the case with the Belleville and Chatham separate schools during the winter of 1852, and another similar incident arose in Toronto even as Ryerson and De Charbonnel were engaged in their exchange of letters. Here the separate school trustees enquired of the Public School Board what proportion of the school funds they might expect for the coming year. A committee of the board advised that the separate schools were not entitled to any part of the local assessment in excess of the government grant, the same point that had arisen at Chatham.

At the same time the committee proclaimed its faith in the complete separation of church and state and its repudiation of the very principle of separate schools of any kind. To reinforce their position, the board requested a definition of the Common School Fund from the Attorney General. Richards, however, did not consider it "compatible with his official duties" to give an opinion which might be reversed by the courts in some test case.[8] Such instances of evasion and procrastination were soon to become the hallmark of Hincks' administration in other spheres than education.

It was not only the Church of Rome which was currently advocating denominational schools. Bishop Strachan had not given up his dream of separate Anglican schools either. Indeed, as late as Confederation he and a number of High Church clerics continued to press for equal privileges for the Church of England. Another petition was prepared in 1852 for the edification of Parliament, a petition which repeated the charges of irreligion and injustice in the common school system, and demanded an equal footing with Roman Catholics in Canada and with fellow-Anglicans in the "Fatherland." [9]

Even before the first session of the fourth Parliament assembled in August, 1852, the Hincks-Morin Government had been made painfully aware of the Roman Catholic pressure for extended separate school rights. It was agreed that Ryerson should prepare a draft of a supplementary Common School Act which would, in addition to correcting some weaknesses in the system, meet Roman Catholic demands with the minimum of concessions. Certainly Ryerson would be unwilling to make any change in the latter direction. He had stated his personal opinion thereon often enough, and always unmistakably. Now, however, the two pillars, Baldwin and Lafontaine, had been removed from the porch of the temple of responsible government and the substitute supports, Hincks and Morin, were less sure of their control over the Reform party, particularly the Irish and French Roman Catholic portion. Compromise in their eyes was a political necessity in 1852, but compromise on separate schools was just one more blow on the wedge which was splitting Brown, Mackenzie, and the Clear Grits away from the slow-moving conservative Reformers.

Ryerson's concession to the separate school agitation was considerable, though grudgingly given. He outlined a practicable solution of the school tax problem to Hincks. "The most simple and perhaps the most satisfactory mode of silencing clamour on the part of parties demanding these Schools, (if they are permitted to continue at all,) is ... to relieve the parents and guardians sending children to these Schools from paying any School Tax whatever, and then allowing them to share in the School Fund with the other Schools, according to average attendance in the same municipality in the Legislative School Grant alone...." [10] Such a plan would end all the disturbances about public taxation for denominational purposes, and about equitable division of funds. Ryerson warned against any attempt to make the municipality the tax collector for separate schools. "The very mention of a separate column on the Tax Roll for a Separate School, excites an hostility and feeling which you can hardly conceive." [11] Like the nineteenth clause of the Act of 1850 this arrangement would still leave the individual free to choose which school he would support.

Behind the scenes the Roman Catholic hierarchy were busy marshalling their forces for the coming struggle. Archbishop Turgeon of Quebec assured De Charbonnel that Morin had voluntarily pledged himself and his colleagues "to give the Catholics of Upper Canada the same advantages which the Protestants in our part of the Province enjoy." [12] Morin had already expressed his surprise that his co-religionists of Canada West were "satisfied with so little." [13] Attorney General Richards also informed the bishops that he sought "to give the Separate Schools in Upper Canada the same rights and powers that the dissentient schools in Lower Canada have." [14] In the light of these promises and subsequent government correspondence with the Department of Education, Ryerson would have been as justified as De Charbonnel in accusing the Ministry of duplicity. Perhaps the habit of dissembling with which posterity has charged John A. Macdonald was a congenital disease transmitted by Hincks and Morin to their successors in the Executive Council.

In the Assembly the forces of secularization were busy presenting petitions in favour of abolishing Rectories, devoting Clergy Reserves to education, and repealing the provision for separate schools.[15] Brown introduced a Bill to prevent the application of public money to sectarian schools, with no hope of passing it, but with the certain result of disturbing the Roman Catholics. Strachan's petition for Anglican schools was read and ignored. Several weeks passed thus but still the Government made no move to introduce the Bill which Ryerson had drafted.

Petitions had come from the Roman Catholic Bishop of Kingston and from London, C.W., praying for amendment of the Common School Act of 1850, but it was not until mid-October when another arrived from the Archbishop of Quebec demanding rights equal to those of the Lower Canadian Protestants that the Government was forced to move in the matter. A Bill drafted by some Roman Catholic members, which Hincks had mentioned to Ryerson,[16] came at last to the Attorney General, and Richards hastened to get Ryerson's opinion upon its separate school provisions. The Chief Superintendent saw its enactment as the destruction of the public school system, and he left immediately for the seat of government to forestall the impending catastrophe.

The compromise Government Bill as drafted by Ryerson was introduced while he was in Quebec, but too many ministerial cooks had made such hash of the measure that it was returned to Ryerson for further revision during the winter prorogation. As Parliament was about to reconvene in February, 1853, Richards returned the revised draft to Ryerson in the form which he hoped to submit to the House. His letter indicated that the Ministry had had the foresight to obtain advance approval from Roman Catholic members for the separate school clause. But for several weeks the House busied itself with Hincks' controversial University Bill, and it was May 3 before the Supplementary Common School Bill came up for second reading, and yet another full month before it was debated in Committee of the Whole.

Outside of Parliament the *Globe* had for some time been proclaiming the approaching destruction of the national educational system, if the separate school clauses of the Bill passed. "We might have expected differently from a truly Reform Government, but not from a coalition of French Tories and unprincipled Clear Grits," the *Globe* remarked on March 31.[17] The *Examiner*, the Sarnia *Shield*, and the Guelph *Advertiser* shared the *Globe*'s fears, but the *North American*, the Government's only journalistic voice in Toronto, wrote unconvincingly of the intolerance of refusing equal rights to Upper Canadian Roman Catholics. If petitions presented in the Assembly are any indication, then Canada West was almost unanimously in favour of the total abolition of separate schools. Significantly the only petitions demanding separate Roman Catholic schools in Canada West came from Canada East, particularly Quebec city where the perambulating Parliament was currently sitting.

In committee, Brown and Mackenzie moved to expunge "all recognition of any portion of the community in a sectarian capacity."[18] Later these two combined in an equally futile attempt to give the Bill the six months' hoist. But like the amendments on other sections of the Bill, they were defeated here by Government majorities which depended on Lower Canadian votes. During the debate Hincks accused Brown of making "a crusade" against separate schools where no public excitement had previously existed. "And I will admit that he has succeeded in producing a very pretty little agitation in Upper Canada upon it." [19] Reminiscing thirty years later, Hincks was more disposed to forgive and justify the action of those Reformers who differed with him on the separate school question.[20]

Thus De Charbonnel's agitation had borne its first fruits, with the aid of some ecclesiatical influence and many votes from Lower Canada. For Roman Catholics the fourth clause of the Act meant a measure of personal pecuniary relief, and sustenance for their separate schools. It did not change the conditions for the establishment of such schools. The conditions regarding the religion of the teacher, the number of petitioners, and the division of the legislative grant continued the same as heretofore. But to "broad Protestants" like George Brown, and even Ryerson, the fourth clause was one of those "priestly encroachments" which threatened the very destiny of the nation.[21]

III

Ryerson hoped, confidently, that "the happiest results" would follow the implementation of the Supplementary School Act. Thus he stated publicly,

> If Separate Schools have not hitherto endangered our School System, there is still less danger of their being able to do so under the Supplementary School Act of this year, the provisions of which put it out of the power of any opposers to shake the foundations of that System, or get up a plausible pretext of agitation against it, on the plea of Religion, or justice. The withdrawment of a few persons, here and there, from the support of the Public Schools, will scarcely be felt by the people at large, even in a pecuniary sense. . . .[22]

In his report for 1852 the Chief Superintendent defended the existence of separate schools as a vested right established by Day's Act of 1841, and also on utilitarian grounds. "This provision . . . while it is practicallly harmless to the School System, prevents opposition and combinations which would otherwise be formed against it." [23] He believed that practical experience with separate schools would convince Roman Catholics of their disadvantages and inexpediency. He could not foresee that every successive report would show a further increase in the number of separate schools, or that future Lower Canadian interference would materially alter the pattern of Upper Canadian education. But his position was seriously weakened by his admission that "Religious minorities in Upper Canada, whether Protestant, or Roman Catholic, cannot be fairly denied that relative protection, or right, which, under the same Legislature, they enjoy in Lower Canada." [24] In closing Ryerson rebuked the advocates of separate schools for their treatment of himself. In their newspapers they had called for his dismissal, but refused to print his part of the correspondence with De Charbonnel. Above all he deprecated "The invoking of Lower Canada interference in an exclusively Upper Canada question,—getting up discussions and petitions in Lower Canada, for Legislation in the school matters of Upper Canada." [25]

Many parties remained unconvinced by the Chief Superintendent's logic. At least four county councils protested against the preferential treatment accorded to one denomination and against the principle of separate schools. On the other side Bishop Strachan reiterated his demand for Anglican schools at his triennial visitation to the clergy. A debate ensued in which Ryerson and his "irreligious system" were personally attacked,[26] and the assembled clergy once more resolved to petition the Legislature in the same terms as during the past three years. For mixed motives various newspapers joined in this vendetta against the Chief Superintendent, while others, notably the *Christian Guardian,* replied in his defence that Strachan's remarks were merely cant intended to "conceal the designs of a bigoted sectarianism."[27]

The real test of the new Act's popularity, however, would be its reception by the prime movers of the recent agitation, the Roman Catholic hierarchy. Would De Charbonnel be satisfied with these latest concessions? His first reaction was one of jubilation, and he issued a pastoral letter commending the Act.[28] But his tone soon changed. By the beginning of August the Bishop was complaining to Hincks that common school trustees in Toronto were hiring Roman Catholic teachers, thus depriving his church of the legal right to maintain separate schools in that city. The surprising fact is that this loop-hole in the law had not been discovered and exploited before.

Hincks expressed his regret at these obstructionist tactics and promised to investigate the matter. The close liaison between the various Roman Catholic dioceses is shown by Vicar General Cazeau's letter to De Charbonnel informing him that Hincks would write "strongly" to "Mr. — — — — [Ryerson] to make him interpret the law in such a way as to do justice to Catholics."[29] Apparently Hincks also committed himself to introducing a new Bill if the existing provisions proved unsatisfactory, a promise of which Ryerson was left in ignorance. At times it must have seemed to Ryerson that his only ally in stemming the Roman legions was George Brown, who did more to aggravate than pacify the enemies of the common school system.

While the *Globe's* inflammatory remarks on the Gavazzi riots sustained the anti-Romanist feeling created throughout the province by the papal aggression controversy, the Toronto Board of Common School Trustees continued its unco-operative policy towards the metropolitan separate schools.[30] Almost thirty disputes concerning separate schools were referred to Ryerson during the year following the passing of the Supplementary School Act.[31] Roman Catholics blamed Ryerson for the difficulties encountered, although the causes were almost invariably local. There was no appeal from the power of municipalities to govern the number and kind of schools established, unless of course the existing laws were amended, a fact which the Churches of Rome and England seemed slow to grasp.

As the next session of the Legislature approached in the spring 1854, the intensity of the Roman Catholic campaign for further revision of the separate school laws increased. With the founding of the Toronto *Catholic Citizen* De Charbonnel had yet another journalistic sounding-board, and one which soon took on the appearance, if not the name, of his official publication. In an address to the Catholic Institute of Toronto the Bishop complained of the Government's treachery in the Supplementary School Act, and read letters from various politicians who had promised equal educational rights for the Roman Catholics of Upper Canada. He admonished his listeners to promote the cause of separate schools by every physical effort and constitutional means. Commenting on this episcopal tocsin-beating, the editor of the *Catholic Citizen* on May 4 praised Hincks and Rolph for their past efforts on behalf of separate schools, but warned the Government that "if they do not prepare and carry through such a Bill as may meet the just requirements of Catholics, some independent member will, and ... they may then assuredly reckon on the hearty co-operation of every Catholic, in carrying out to the full extent the spirit of the resolution passed at the meeting of the Catholic Institute, viz., to oppose and unseat any ministry who refuse to grant to the Catholic body what as citizens they have a just right to demand." The opportunity to make good these threats came sooner than anyone expected.

The following day the *Citizen*'s more vociferous colleague, the *Mirror*, hinted openly at "invoking the sympathy and assistance of ... fellow Catholics in Eastern Canada" to obtain educational justice in Canada West. To this the *Christian Guardian* replied, "The School Law, as it now stands, gives to Romanists all the rights to which they are entitled as subjects of the State, even in view of their religious creed, and we trust that this threat ... will be met by the firm resistance of every friend of equal rights and privileges in the entire province."[32] By maintaining these unjust and unreasonable demands for government aid without government supervision, Bishop de Charbonnel was in effect teaching "Church above State."[33] Thus the Wesleyan Methodists' anti-Romanism found its voice on a very concrete issue.

One week before the session commenced seven Roman Catholic bishops asked for the "aid and protection" of the Governor General, "to enable them to obtain a just and equitable law in favour of Separate Schools."[34] "They claim no exclusive privileges, their sole prayer being that the law which governs the Separate Schools in favour of the Protestants of Lower Canada, may be put in force in favour of the Catholics of Upper Canada. This is a right which we feel assured they will not invoke in vain from Your Excellency." Before this petition could be forwarded to Parliament, the Hincks-Morin Government had been defeated by a double-barrelled no confidence motion on Seignorial Tenure and Clergy Reserves. The Ministry's sudden and unexpected appeal to the country left the Opposition chagrined and confused, but gave the forces of educational separation in Canada West a chance to turn their voting power to account in the cause of separate schools.

IV

Despite the efforts of De Charbonnel to use Roman Catholic ballots as a lever, separate schools did not become a major election issue in the summer of 1854. Clergy Reserves and £10,000 "jobs" occupied the attention of most Upper Canadians. Ultimately most Roman Catholics seem to have supported the "corrupt administration" of the co-operative Inspector General Hincks, but the Reform party lost ground in Canada West none the less, and the Clear Grits and Conservatives gained a combined majority in the upper half of the province.

Bishop de Charbonnel had been busy organizing his supporters, but he did find time to write numerous members of Parliament requesting new separate school legislation, either in prospect or in consequence of Roman Catholic support at the hustings.[35] He now required three alterations in the law, and Hincks, who had received several written reminders from the Bishop, asked Ryerson to go as far as possible to meet the Bishop's wishes.[36] Roman Catholics sought exemption from paying to the separate school an amount equal to the common school rate, power to unite municipal separate school corporations into a single Board of Trustees, and payment of school money directly by the Chief Superintendent to avoid the partial and vexing arrangements sometimes imposed by local authorities. However much he himself was opposed to any further concessions, Ryerson was loath to embarrass a Government which had helped him and which was headed by a personal friend. He steeled himself to compromise in deference to Hincks' urgent request.[37]

First Ryerson told De Charbonnel that the law requiring Roman Catholics to pay their separate school an amount equal to the common school rate was really a benefit to their school, but he would not insist on retaining this provision if Roman Catholics viewed it as coercion.[38] On the second complaint Ryerson replied that he too was in favour of union boards for municipal separate schools, and had already advised these trustees that such action was permissible without any legislative change. The third complaint he considered "frivolous" and merely a veiled attempt to place him in a position that would permit continued agitation. Nevertheless, as Hincks could see no possibility of such complications, Ryerson was willing to concede this alteration too.

Before he submitted a draft of these changes to Hincks, however, the Chief Superintendent sent De Charbonnel a sharp reply to the latter's recent personal attacks. Twice he had been charged with "falsehoods" when he defended the Upper Canadian separate school laws as essentially the same as those of Lower Canada. "I am quite aware that these attacks upon me ... were designed to influence the recent Elections; and for that very reason I thought it proper not to notice them until after the Elections—so that your Lordship might have every possible benefit of them, and that I might not give the slightest pretence for a charge that I interfered in these Elections."[39] At considerable length Ryerson dealt with and refuted thirteen points of alleged inequality between the separate school laws of the two parts of the province. As in 1852, the Bishop's ignorance of the facts was unmercifully exposed in the Chief Superintendent's carefully documented reply. The Bishop, he asserted, was seeking to inculcate a spirit of religious intolerance completely at variance with the liberty and harmony that characterized Canada West.

Nor can the fact fail to be noticed, nor its legitimate inference be overlooked, that these disputes between Separate and other School Trustees, are, so far as I know, confined to the City of Toronto; and as the noise about the School Law has been commenced and perpetuated by an ecclesiastico-political Institute, of which your Lordship is the animating spirit, there must be some other cause than anything unjust and oppressive in the provisions of the School Law in regard to any party.[40]

At the beginning of September Ryerson sent Hincks a short Bill incorporating the three changes which De Charbonnel had demanded—the exemption of separate school supporters from all school taxes upon annual notification to the municipal clerk, union of separate school trustees in cities or towns, and division of legislative grants by the Chief Superintendent. Separate schools would of course still receive a share of the government grant proportional to the school attendance but the assessment and collection of all other monies was the responsibility of the separate school trustees. Ryerson was confident that these provisions would, "without undermining our General School system, provide for all that even the ultra advocates of Separate Schools have professed to demand, and all that I think that the Country can be induced to give."[41]

Hincks was advised by Ryerson that the policy of conciliation had now reached its extreme limits, beyond which neither he nor the majority of Upper Canadians would go. Protestants held "conscientious convictions" as strong as those of Roman Catholics.

I think our next step must be, if further legislation be called for, to take the sound ground of the United States of not providing, or recognizing, Separate Schools at all. In this we should have the cordial support of nine-tenths of the People of Upper Canada; while, in the course now pursued, the more you concede, the more you contravene the prevalent sentiment of the Country, and the greater injury you are inflicting upon the great body of the parties for whom Separate Schools are professedly demanded, and who have not, as far as I am aware, any safe and adequate means of speaking for themselves, or of even forming a judgment.[42]

Ryerson arrived in Quebec en route to New Brunswick on September 9 to find that the Hincks-Morin Government had fallen and that Sir Allan MacNab was trying to form a coalition with the Lower Canadian members of the late Ministry. He was given to understand that the Gallant Knight, who had good prospects of success, would adopt Hincks' programme for the session without alteration, and would in return receive the support of Hincks "and Company."[43] Returning from the Maritimes six weeks later, Ryerson again went to the capital to expedite the passage of the new short Bill. John A. Macdonald assumed responsibility for the measure, and Morin expressed his satisfaction with its terms.[44]

While this legislation was pending the Church of Rome extended its educational plans yet another step. No less than eight petitions were presented demanding a share of the Protestant Clergy Reserves for separate schools. The petition of eight Roman Catholic bishops to Lord Elgin was also read for the edification of the Protestant legislators, as was the annual prayer of the Anglican Diocese of Toronto soliciting separate schools for that denomination too.

The Reverend C. F. Cazeau, the vicarious eyes and ears of De Charbonnel at Quebec, informed the Upper Canadian bishops during the session that MacNab and Macdonald, as titular and actual heads of the Upper Canadian Conservatives, had both promised satisfaction and justice to the separate schools. But with a sense born of worldly experience Cazeau expressed his anxiety for deeds, not words, from the new Administration. Encouraged by these reiterated promises, but irritated by the continued inaction, the bishops used the recess to apply more pressure to the Executive. This session would be the last at Quebec for two years, and it was easier to get results from an agitation on separate schools while Parliament sat in that city. Interestingly enough, the bishops of Lower Canada left negotiations entirely to their Upper Canadian peers during the rest of the episode. Apprehensive that the Attorney General's delay signified some treachery concocted by him and the Chief Superintendent, the bishops submitted a "protestation" and draft Bill of their own.[45]

As De Charbonnel had presented these two documents in person to John A. Macdonald, Ryerson was hastily summoned to the capital for consultation. To Macdonald and Morin, Ryerson demonstrated that the bishops' Bill was inadmissible and that the protestation which compared the separate school laws of Canada East and West was very inaccurate. The Chief Superintendent offered De Charbonnel the three clauses he had prepared for Hincks last summer. Beyond these, he told the Bishop privately, he would not go; "but, after hours of discussion, we were where we began."[46]

Ryerson returned to Toronto, convinced that he had satisfied the two Attornies General and with "the firm belief that no Separate School legislation would take place that Session."[47] In a lengthy letter to Macdonald he resumed his analysis and rebuttal of the arguments contained in the protestation and Bill of De Charbonnel.[48] The protestation was no more than the statement which the Bishop had made to the Toronto Catholic Institute the previous summer and which Ryerson had answered after the election. As for the draft Bill, he outlined six major objections, some of which seem at this distance of time to have been occasioned by faulty logic rather than by destructive intent aimed at the "System."

The Bill proposed to appoint a special superintendent of separate schools, to whom alone the trustees would be responsible. Trustees would have the control of all separate school property, the power to tax all property, and to employ the municipality as its tax collector. Roman Catholics would hereafter have no choice but to send their children to separate schools. Finally, public school trustees must provide separate schools with an equivalent for any improvement made to the public school.

These "monstrous propositions" would be as repugnant to most Roman Catholics as to Protestants, in Ryerson's opinion. Such satisfaction demanded in the name of conscientious convictions would infringe the rights of Roman Catholics, Protestants, and municipal authorities alike. In defence of his past policy of conciliating Bishop de Charbonnel, the Chief Superintendent complained to Macdonald that whatever the Bishop "professed to be well satisfied with at one time, he complained of at another; and that he has made every new concession the starting point of a fresh agitation for further concessions. It may also now be submitted, whether I have not rather erred on the side of concession than otherwise." [49] With this statement Ryerson virtually closed his remarks and left the matter entirely in Macdonald's hands, anticipating the same close co-operation that he had received from previous governments.

Six weeks passed, and Ryerson could presume that *quieta noli movere*. In this interval Morin retired to the Bench because of poor health. It was not until May 18 that Ryerson was informed by a private member, J. W. Gamble, by telegram, that Taché had introduced a Government measure on separate schools in the Legislative Council one week before.[50] The Chief Superintendent immediately informed Macdonald that the Bill would benefit Strachan's High Church supporters only, at the same time destroying the school system by permitting individuals to avoid all taxes simply by subscribing a nominal sum to any private institution. The solution which he suggested to this dilemma, and which Macdonald adopted, was to restrict the Bill to Roman Catholics.

The session was old when the Bill came before the Assembly. Gamble, Langton, Robinson, Hartman, and Mackenzie were numbered with Brown in the minority of seventeen who opposed the first reading. Thus the voting cut across both party and religious lines. The *Globe* announced on May 22 a crisis in the rule of Canada—"Romish Priests" *versus* enlightened principles. What had Taché to do with the common schools of Canada West? The editor accused certain miserable traitors of sacrificing Upper Canada to gain French votes, a trick they would not have dared if Parliament were sitting in Toronto. Important restrictive amendments were added in committee, but the Bill was passed by a majority composed almost exclusively of Lower Canadians in a House reduced to one-third. The next day Parliament adjourned.

In the Assembly the whole transaction had taken only seven days. Thus the first Separate School Act for Canada West had been railroaded through a near-empty Legislature by French votes, against the known sentiment of most Upper Canadians. A new era in education had opened for Canada West, and Ryerson found himself in a new relationship to the school system and to his governmental superiors. De Charbonnel and Brown had destroyed the age of good feeling between denominations; Macdonald had now destroyed the age of co-operation between the Administration and the Department of Education.

v

In its final form the first Separate School Act permitted five Roman Catholic heads of families to establish a separate school simply by informing the local authorities of their intention. No longer was it necessary that the common school teacher be a Protestant. Separate school supporters were exempted from all common school rates upon giving annual notice of their decision. Separate schools would still get a share of the legislative grant proportional to the average attendance, but an amendment carefully excluded them from any claim to any other common school monies. Roman Catholics still legally had a choice as to which system they would support, though this might be negatived by the sacramental authority of their church.

The Church of England was deliberately excluded from the benefits of the Act. While it did secure a number of advantages to the Church of Rome, the new statute was far from meeting the extreme demands which had been made by De Charbonnel and his colleagues. In later years when the "restoration" of certain separate school rights was being pressed, Ryerson could with considerable satisfaction remind the hierarchy that their grievances were in fact of their own making, since they had drafted Taché's Act.[51]

Immediate opposition to the Taché Act was surprisingly limited. The *Globe* had stated its views, but the only papers to voice similar opinions were the "Gritty" Guelph *Advertiser*[52] and the Low Church Anglican *Echo* which called the Government's policy "truckling to Popery."[53] On the other hand the *Mirror* of June 8 hailed the Act as "a complete triumph," the "Magna Charta" of educational freedom. Bishop de Charbonnel had given his approval to the "harmless" Bill and thanked the Government for this measure of justice to his church.[54] The Bishop had scarcely arrived back in Toronto from the part-time capital when he discovered that he had been duped again. His aims had been frustrated by the amendments made in Committee of the Whole after his departure. "He has got a new light," Macdonald warned the Chief Superintendent, "and now he says the Bill won't do." Ryerson was advised to play the role of peace-maker at every opportunity by stressing the Act's innocuous effects on the common school system, ("this for the people at large"), and its beneficence for Roman Catholics, "this to keep them in good humour." But even Macdonald, the manager of men, questioned the probable success of his manipulations. "If the Bishop makes the Roman Catholics believe that the Bill is of no use to them, there will be a renewal of an unwholesome agitation, which I thought we had allayed."

The "unwholesome agitation" did not materialize at once, although De Charbonnel resigned from the Council of Public Instruction in protest against the Government's duplicity. Vicar General Cazeau apparently did not share De Charbonnel's dissatisfaction with the new "contaminated" Act.[55] Both the Bishop and Ryerson left during the summer for extended visits in Europe, probably nursing similar feelings towards Attorney General Macdonald. In a circular letter to separate school trustees explaining the new law Ryerson disclaimed all personal responsibility for it and defended the liberality of the common school system.[56] The last word on the separate school controversy during 1855 came, however, from the *Mirror*.[57] It was an explicit denial that the Roman Catholic bishops of Canada West had wielded an "undue ecclesiastical influence" in the recent events. Bishops never interfere in secular matters. Separate schools, however, involved the Faith.

When the unwholesome agitation did come with the new year, 1856, it originated not with the exponents of separate schools, but with an outraged Protestantism. The horrible death of Robert Corrigan had shocked the majority of Upper Canadians; the Government's apathetic search for the culprits irritated them; the action of Judge Duval and the papist jury in exonerating the murderers infuriated them. Few newspapers in the upper province could view this travesty of British justice with even a semblance of dispassion. Tory and Grit were united in the cry for vengeance, and the repeal of all provisions for separate schools would pay in part the debt demanded by Corrigan's blood.

This unrest in Protestant minds was further increased by De Charbonnel's pronouncement in his Lenten pastoral message that Roman Catholics who did not employ their franchise to further the cause of separate schools were guilty of mortal sin. Even political moderates were alarmed at this open declaration of war. The *News of the Week* which consistently upheld the *status quo* of separate schools—no more, but no less—gave a reply on February 2 typical of the Upper Canadian attitude. "We join in no crusade with the *Globe* and its allies against the Roman Catholics as a body; but we do raise our voice against a despotism that would crush liberty of conscience and freedom of thought, a despotism unknown to members of Protestant communions."[58] The Ministry could expect no quarter from the offended half of the province when Parliament met on February 15.

When the legislators assembled in Toronto they were greeted by a flood of petitions from Upper Canada demanding outright repeal of all separate school legislation. Sixty-five such petitions were received by the Assembly alone and only one came in defence of separate schools. No less than twelve county and twenty-four township councils were among the petitioners. A writer to the *News of the Week* expressed pleasure at the number of repeal petitions, and pointed to Corrigan's murder as evidence of the poisonous fruits of popish education.[59] The Guelph *Advertiser* of March 8 copied the following *Globe* comment with approval. "The School Bill of last Session is the most notable ... of many instances in which Lower Canadian ideas and principles have been crammed down our throats against the recorded votes of a majority of our representatives."

This unmistakable display of Upper Canadian opinion against separate schools through mass meetings and petitions did not deter certain Roman Catholics from attempting to extract further concessions in the name of conscientious convictions. The Upper Canadian bishops applied to the Government for an amendment to their "iniquitous" Separate School Act, but Macdonald and his colleagues were well aware of the temper of the Grits, the Orangemen, and Canada West. If any Bill were introduced it would not be a Government measure.

Within two weeks of Parliament's opening John G. Bowes, Conservative member for Toronto, introduced a private Bill to exempt separate school supporters from paying common school rates simply by producing a receipt for taxes paid to the separate school. This was less than the bishops had hoped for, but it was an advance. But the Bill never reached second reading. After several postponements, it was withdrawn when Ryerson, fresh from Europe, met Bowes and somehow convinced him that the proposed amendment would destroy the common school system.[60] In the interval petitions for repeal continued to come before the Assembly, at least one of them objecting to the new Bill too. Indeed, the Bill seemed to stimulate the petition-signing mania, for sixty-one of the sixty-five petitions postdated the appearance of Bowes' Bill.

Strachan's interest in denominational schools was suddenly revived by the sight of this latest Roman Catholic effort. "Surely our claim is as good as that of the Roman Catholics," he wrote John Hillyard Cameron.[61] Not all Anglicans, however, were sympathetic to their Bishop's dream. The editor of the *Echo* believed that the tone of De Charbonnel's Lenten pastoral required all Protestants to forgo denominational interests in favour of mixed schools which would include Roman Catholics.[62] Exciting meetings which condemned separate schools and the Executive's "vacillating" policy received wide publicity in the provincial press, and at least one gathering ended in an affray reminiscent of a certain celebrated Hibernian fair.

Despite the withdrawal of Bowes' Bill, the separate school question did reappear in the Assembly. Brown opened the festering sore with a resolution based on the numerous petitions which had been received, that is, to repeal all separate school legislation by placing "all the National Schools under one uniform system of Superintendence and Instruction," while safeguarding religious conviction from insult.[63] Immediately W. L. Felton, an Anglican, moved the amendment beloved by De Charbonnel, that Roman Catholic separate schools in Canada West be placed on the same basis as dissentient schools in Canada East. It was now time for the Rouges to record their educational ideals, so Joseph Papin moved an amendment demanding a uniform and national system of free non-sectarian schools. Papin's resolution was easily defeated by a large majority, and the Government then offered its own amendment favourable to maintaining the educational *status quo.*

Twelve fruitless divisions later, after a night-long debate on the separate school question, the weary House adjourned the debate for five weeks. Again the Administration was saved only by the strength of its Lower Canadian supporters, the Upper Canadians voting 20 to 15 against the motion. The *Globe* complained bitterly on May 7 that educational reform was being denied to Upper Canada by French members. The Government was, in the editor's opinion, caught tightly in the grasp of the "priest party." But to the editor of the *News of the Week* the attack on separate schools was simply that retribution which he had prophesied one year ago would overtake Roman Catholic abettors of secularization of the Clergy Reserves.[64]

When the adjourned debate was resumed on June 12, Felton's amendment was defeated by 46 to 40. A Grit amendment proposed by L. H. Holton was also rejected, but by a much larger majority, 73 to 22. Finally, Brown's original motion was voted down 64 to 31. Of all the divisions it was that on Felton's amendments for equating the Upper Canadian system to the Lower Canadian which produced the loudest repercussions. The *Mirror* admitted that Bowes' Bill was lost for the present but printed each of the division lists of the recent debate that Roman Catholics might know the "traitors" to the separate school principle.[65] Donlevy, editor of that journal, expressed the hope that Felton would take up the Bill abandoned by Bowes at the next session. Then it would be sure to pass through "this thoroughly demoralized" Assembly.

The Roman Catholic hierarchy viewed the Government's inaction and its votes against Felton's amendment as practical dereliction of its pledge. Bishop de Charbonnel circularized all Roman Catholic members who had opposed Felton warning them against any repetition if and when Felton introduced Bowes' Bill. The erring Cabinet ministers, however, did not escape the episcopal wrath so easily. A letter was read from every pulpit in the Toronto diocese denouncing Cauchon, Cartier, Lemieux, and Drummond for their perfidy to the "higher law."[66]

Protestants were more disturbed by the Bishop's political fulminations than Roman Catholics seemed to be. The *Echo* of July 25 warned half-hearted Protestants that such interference was the effect of popish ascendancy.[67] The *Christian Guardian* copied, with approving comments, an editorial from the *Colonist* which upheld the right of private judgment and the responsibility of Parliament to the country rather than to any pressure bloc.[68] The *News of the Week* accused the hierarchy of dictatorship.[69] De Charbonnel's action amounted to "filtering British liberty through the will and pleasure of the Roman Catholic Church," which should be a lesson to all Protestants that their constitution and liberty were in danger. The Markham *Economist* noted that the separate school controversy was cutting across party lines, as some Tories were joining the Reformers in opposition to this religious separatism.[70] Even the Orangemen were torn by the question between their religious and constitutional traditions and their political allegiance to the Conservative party.

For the first time Protestant churches other than the Church of England spoke out officially on the question of denominational schools. The Free Church Synod expressed its entire disapproval of all separate schools, and the Wesleyan Methodist Conference unanimously adopted a resolution praising the common school system.[71] But within the Church of England the issue caused an open rupture. At his visitation in May Strachan had again attacked the common school system, describing it as "rotten to the core, and... its tendency is to produce unbelief."[72] The Bishop wanted Anglican schools in town and cities, and in rural areas as soon as population warranted. The battle which ensued between High and Low Church elements was so furious that Strachan at length requested that the matter be dropped.

The combined influence of Taché's Separate School Act, Corrigan's murder, and Bowes' abortive amending Bill had at last aroused the Protestants of Canada West to an energetic and vocal defence of their national system of mixed schools. Admittedly, the separatist tendencies of the Anglican High Church party were undiminished, but now an opposition within that church was gathering strength rapidly. A distinctly belligerent feeling had developed in the upper province, reinforced by the "broad Protestant principles" which George Brown and the *Globe* had proclaimed for several years.

With the Clergy Reserves gone, the interdenominational feuds of Protestant bodies were giving place to an almost united Protestant front which opposed any and all evidences, real or imaginary, of popish aggression. The tide was running unmistakably against separate schools, and like the 'Prentice boys of Derry, the motto of the majority henceforth would be "No Surrender." If the provision for separate schools were not repealed, at least the conscientious convictions of the Church of Rome would receive no further concessions from the hands of Upper Canadian Protestants. It would be a courageous Administration which would hereafter dare to invoke Lower Canadian votes to subvert the Upper Canadian way of life.

VI

For more than six years after Bowes' Bill touched off the memorable debates in the Legislative Assembly, the separate school question provided a recurrent theme for editors to expound; but despite many administrative incidents and journalistic tilts by interested parties, no alterations were made in the existing law and no serious threat to the common school system occured. The line of battle shifted into a series of attacks on Ryerson and his system, attacks which came from all sides, but uniformly impugned the Chief Superintendent's honesty and ability and the efficiency and morality of the public school system.

Bishop de Charbonnel retired first from public affairs, and then, after finding a coadjutor in John Joseph Lynch, he retired from Canada and this sinful world to the tranquillity of a French monastery. His polemical duties and interest in the separate school question were assumed by J. M. Bruyere, Rector of St. Michael's Cathedral. During the winter of 1856-7 Bruyere, with the approval of De Charbonnel and the assistance of Bishop Pinsonnault of London, carried on a war of words with Ryerson through the newspapers.

Ryerson's suggestion that the municipal share of the Clergy Reserves be used for special educational purposes was made the occasion for renewal of the Roman Catholic demand to share in these funds.[73] Bruyere incidentally accused the Chief Superintendent of bigotry, and reiterated the time-worn charge that his system was infidel. In his typically logical reply, Ryerson showed that the rector had no better command of facts that did the rector's diocesan. Before the controversy had run its course it had begun to acquire some contemporary American political terminology, as the Roman Catholic clerics and the editor of the *Catholic Citizen* countered Ryerson's allusion to "foreign ecclesiastics" with accusations of "nativism."[74]

In point of fact, these various effusions in ink did little to affect the educational set-up of Canada West. Nor was Ryerson unduly alarmed. His position was consolidated, and most Upper Canadians were well satisfied with the progress made during the past decade under his supervision. Even Attorney General Macdonald, though he would have liked to dispense with Ryerson's services, frankly confessed lack of courage to take the step.[75] Personally Ryerson was not averse to Strachan's proposal to establish denominational schools in cities and towns, although such a plan would be impracticable in rural areas.[76] He did not, however, voice this opinion openly in Canada. Instead the Council of Public Instruction went part way in 1857 to meeting the demand for extended religious exercises by setting aside one-half day per week for religious instruction in the public schools, a compromise suggested by J. H. Cameron during the separate school debates of the previous session. Strachan considered this "a very considerable advance in the right way,"[77] but reaffirmed his conviction that the Synod of his diocese was duty-bound to continue their agitation for state-supported Anglican schools.

The session of 1857 passed with little reference being made to separate schools. Only seven petitions on behalf of repeal were presented, one of which, as in 1856, came from the Synod of the Free Church. The new monthly journal of this church, the *Canadian Presbyter,* devoted three articles, in January, February, and March, to a defence of the non-sectarian religion of the common schools, accusing Roman Catholic priests of forcing Roman Catholic children to attend separate schools. A few secular journals also spoke out in support of the public schools but the latter half of 1857 was, like that part of 1856, almost devoid of any references to the subject.

In the general elections held during December, 1857, the issue of separate schools played a very insignificant rôle. Reformers and Clear Grits had made their position known long ago. Candidates of these parties stated their convictions but no attempt was made to pledge individuals on the question. It was generally understood that Conservatives were at least in favour of retaining the educational *status quo,* but no secular newspaper of that political hue ventured to suggest that the separate school principle ought to be extended,[78] regardless of the Opposition's statements that John A. Macdonald would give De Charbonnel all he asked if the Ministry had its own way.[79] Within the fold of the Roman Catholic Church D'Arcy McGee and his journal, the *New Era,* were disturbing Upper Canadian Roman Catholics by suggesting that the separate school law was of no value whatever. The *Mirror* insisted that repeal would ruin Roman Catholic schools, and expressed fears that the advocate of "More power to the Pope" might turn traitor by voting with the Grits on this question.[80] With some pride the *Mirror* informed its readers that eleven Ministerialists who had voted against Felton's motion were not returned to Parliament.[81]

Probably the most notable statement on separate schools during 1858 came from the Chief Superintendent as a result of the new Governor General's request for enlightenment on this controversial subject.[82] Ryerson explained that a comparison of the separate school legislation of Lower and Upper Canada proved that the advantage was with the latter. While most Protestants objected to the very existence of separate schools as threatening the national system, Roman Catholics made vague general complaints and demanded equal rights with Lower Canada. Three Separate School Acts had been passed since 1850, each of which was at first approved, but later rejected, by Roman Catholic authorities. But Lower Canada's public schools were denominational, and therein lay the essential difference. Separate schools of Upper Canada existed within a single system, but Roman Catholics had demanded such a complete separation in Bowes' Bill as would destroy any semblance to national education. Above all, Ryerson warned that the sentiment of Upper Canada would justifiably prevent municipal authorities being used as tax collectors for denominational purposes.

After replying to Sir Edmund Head, Ryerson decided to supply members of the Legislature with a similar authoritative statement, even though Macdonald refused to take any responsibility for this report.[83] In this special report to the Legislature[84] Ryerson recalled that "until 1850, the leading Men and Newspaper Press of all parties acquiesced in the Separate School provision of the Law." "Until 1852, Separate Schools were never advocated as a theory, much less as a doctrine, and less still as an article of faith." Now, however, the Church of Rome was attacking the "hellbegotten" national school system with the intention of destroying its reputation, while demanding at the same time separate schools which would be agencies of that church, though supported by public funds. Despite the violent language which had been used by Roman Catholic papers (and Ryerson quoted the most apt portions), the Chief Superintendent was no more favourable to repeal than to extension of separate school privileges. His comparison of these "corporate rights" to university charters must have evoked bitter memories in many hearts, and suggested too a parallel in the recent secularization of the Clergy Reserves. It was not a happy choice of phrase, and opponents of Ryerson and his system made the most advantage of it later.

Ryerson had accepted the compromise of national and separatist educational interests which had been reached in 1855. His position was essentially that of the Conservative party, and from this time dates his growing friendship with John A. Macdonald. Ryerson's aim henceforth was to maintain this limited educational dualism against the secularists who cried for total repeal and ecclesiastics who demanded the extension of the separate school provisions. Before the session of 1858 had commenced, he had warned Hodgins that the Romanist bishops of Canada West were "moving heaven and earth to get a Separate School bill." [85] Thus Ryerson's action in presenting the report and allied correspondence to the Legislature was not madness. But the Bill for repeal which T. R. Ferguson vainly offered to the Assembly in 1858 and again in 1859 must have proved an embarrassment to the moderates. It could not hope for success, yet it was certain to excite Roman Catholic apprehensions. The Government's promise of new legislation to the Romanist bishops, if a promise was actually given, was deliberately forgotten with that facility peculiar to politicians. [86]

One further incident in 1858 involved separate schools indirectly and provided ammunition for another war of words in the provincial journals. This time Ryerson's opponent was no Roman cleric but George Brown. The short-lived Brown-Dorion Ministry had undoubtedly agreed to accept McGee's proposition to introduce the Irish school system in exchange for the traditionally Reform votes of the Irish Roman Catholics which McGee expected to attract. [87] It is doubtful if any of the Executive, including McGee, knew what was implied by this substitute plank in their platform. Though McGee had defended the right of separate schools in his speech on Ferguson's Repeal Bill, [88] Mowat, his erstwhile associate, returned to his electors in August reaffirming his opposition to separate schools, [89] and the Grit journals denied with fervency the "corruptionist" charge that Brown had "sold" the public schools of Upper Canada for union with Dorion. [90] Of such heterogeneous elements was the four-day Ministry and its supporters.

Ryerson denounced Brown's subservience to McGee in educational matters as a complete lack of statesmanship. "I believe you knew no more than a child what you were doing, when you agreed to the Irish importation." [91] But the Irish system was only one of the myriad subjects discussed by Brown and Ryerson in their two-month exchange of letters. Besides personalities and popery, they dealt with the principles and development of separate schools. Here Ryerson's history of the various Acts provides many details unrecorded elsewhere. Brown's "literary forgeries" from Ryerson's reports received the same crushing repudiation as had the assertions of De Charbonnel and Bruyere. The Chief Superintendent stated that his aim had been to make the school system non-partisan, while Brown, on the contrary, had been responsible for making it "a party question and a subject of party negotiation." [92] Compromise in education as in government was the only alternative to tyranny or anarchy.

This row with Ryerson, which entertained if it did not edify the newspaper readers of Canada West during the first months of 1859, may have salved Brown's wounded pride after his ministerial failure, but it could only weaken public respect for the school system. The confidence of public school supporters in the system and its chief would be shaken, and the advocates of denominational education would be encouraged by this rift between their opponents. The three years since the passing of Taché's Act had been relatively quiet, and even Brown admitted that the Roman Catholics had not been the agitators of the separate school question during 1856 and 1857.[93] The next four, however, were marked by persistent pressure from the Churches of England and Rome for further concessions to denominational education, a pressure culminating in a measure of victory for the latter church alone in Scott's Separate School Act of 1863.

VII

The action of the Wesleyan Methodist Conference Committee in reopening the smouldering University question during the summer of 1859 had important repercussions on the separate school controversy. George Brown and many others had long contended that denominational colleges had no more right to state aid than separate elementary schools. Against the logic of this position (which most Reformers held) Ryerson had contended rather unsuccessfully on numerous occasions. Thus the reopening of the University question invited attention to the related issue of public support or recognition of sectarian elementary institutions, and both controversies became inseparably linked, to their mutual disadvantage.

The Hamilton *Spectator* was one of those papers which gave mild support to the principle of separate schools for denominations[94]—a principle which was implied, in the editor's opinion, by the Wesleyan memorial on University financing. The *True Witness* heralded this apparent shift of opinions as presaging a time propitious for the liquidation of the common school system,[95] a suggestion which the Bowmanville *Statesman* denied with considerable heat. The national school system had the support of many outside the ranks of the Clear Grits, the latter's editor insisted, and though "Jesuitical Ryerson" and a few of his "dupes" might favour sectarian schools, the majority of the Wesleyan Methodists were as strongly opposed to such a change as other Protestant bodies.[96] "The coming struggle will not be carried on from the same standpoints as has been the wont of the combatants. It will be 'Protestantism vs. Roman Catholicism'; and may the former be triumphant."

Seven years had passed since Ryerson had made his first educational Grand Tour of Canada West to explain the school system. Many changes had occurred during this time, and Ryerson, feeling that a repeat performance was desirable, if not overdue, toured the province again in the first months of 1860. At none of the meetings was the issue of separate schools raised, a point to which the Chief Superintendent drew Macdonald's attention when he went to Quebec in March to supervise certain needed alterations in the common school law. He found the Government reluctant to undertake the requested legislation. But within hours of his arrival at the capital, a new episode in the troubled story of separate schools had been opened by the introduction of a Separate School Bill by a private member, R. W. Scott, member for the city of Ottawa.

Scott's Bill provided for the establishment of separate schools in incorporated villages and towns, one detail omitted through oversight in the hastily drafted Taché Act. It also would have relieved separate school supporters from the necessity of giving annual notice to that effect, this being in fact an unjustifiable inconvenience to all concerned.[97] Bishop Horan of Kingston had given the measure his approval "in the fullest manner," [98] and Bishop Farrell in Hamilton had expressed himself as "quite satisfied" with it.[99] On May 16, two months after the Bill's introduction, Scott tried vainly to have it read a second time. Three days later the *Globe* attributed the Bill's immediate demise to Brown's threat to speak against it. Ministerial influence probably exercised a greater deterrent effect, as Ryerson had been sternly upbraiding the hard-pressed Macdonald out of fear that common school legislation might provoke another political crisis, if separate school supporters in the Assembly tried to make the Bills concomitant.[100]

But the Grits were likewise being taunted for their silence on the separate school question in the House, and at the recent Clear Grit Convention when the subject was "ingeniously tabooed" so that Roman Catholic delegates could not voice their opinions.[101] The Great Convention had, in fact, caused much heart-searching among Roman Catholics and an open rift between the *True Witness*, which urged them to attend the Convention "to *force* the School Question," and the *Canadian Freeman*, which refused to make itself "ridiculous" by copying the fanatical tactics of the Bowmanville *Statesman* "in order to satisfy the dictates of Ministerialists in disguise."[102] Roman Catholic votes would go to the highest bidder, but the bidder must offer more than simply separate schools.

Although Macdonald freely admitted that his policy towards the separate and common school Bills was governed by political expediency,[103] he was prepared to state unequivocally the basic educational principles which tempered his policy. In the face of recent demands for the abolition of separate schools the Attorney General West told guests at a testimonial dinner that Baldwin and the old Reformers were responsible for the creation of separate schools. Conservatives, however, would honour the agreement as if made by themselves.[104] As a Protestant, Macdonald would ensure that his children attended the public schools. Nevertheless, he could appreciate the position taken by Roman Catholics, and he personally favoured the existing system which gave to each of the two Christian groups a controlling voice in the education of its youth. Privately, Ryerson expressed his admiration of Macdonald's efforts to preserve the *via media* against the separatist demands of sectaries.[105]

Roman Catholics were not satisfied with Macdonald's stand and accused him of hedging.[106] Their aim was still assimilation of the Upper Canadian separate school law to that of the lower province. Their only opponents, they believed, were Scotch Presbyterians, their supporters a majority of the Anglicans and a large proportion of the Wesleyans. In this they deceived themselves. With the Presbyterians were the Baptists, the Congregationalists, all of the small Methodist bodies, and most of the Wesleyans as well as the Low Church Anglicans. As for the supposed support of Strachan and his High Church party, this too was self-deception, for these were bitter rivals from the Canterbury Road, not fellow travellers on the Appian Way.

Roman Catholic newspapers in Canada West still gave lukewarm support to the Conservatives, despite broken promises, simply because it was popularly believed that the Grits would abolish separate schools at the first opportunity. Individually, many adherents of the Roman Catholic Church supported the Reformers, particularly in predominantly Scottish districts, and a few daring souls followed the Clear Grit banner despite the "No Popery" cry raised by George Brown prior to the fiasco of the four-day Ministry. The *Canadian Freeman* had gradually replaced the *Mirror* as the voice of Roman Catholicism in Canada West, but its moderation was under constant attack from the *True Witness,* the self-appointed mentor of McGee and other Irish papists. In the estimate of the latter's editor, his Upper Canadian co-religionists did not deserve a better separate school settlement because they supported Clear Grits. The *Freeman* of December 27 denied that Roman Catholics had given their approval to the Reform Convention, and appealed most piteously against judging the majority by the acts or opinions of a few.

Undeterred by his failure in 1860, Scott brought a new Bill before the Assembly in 1861.[107] This contained three additional clauses, one of which, like Elmsley's draft, provided that separate schools would share in all public educational grants. The Bill created no interest in or out of Parliament, and like its predecessor, never reached a second reading, although Scott, Ryerson and Bishop Lynch had discussed amendments to the existing law and Macdonald had indicated that the Ministry was favourably disposed towards Scott's efforts.[108] The general elections of that summer were similarly conducted with little or no reference to the controversial separate school issue. Later, in its issue of July 18, the *Canadian Freeman* boasted that Roman Catholics had voted "almost unanimously" for certain successful Conservative candidates, but education was only one of several reasons given for this support of men, who, ironically, also owed their return to Orange votes. Thus the year 1861 passed almost untroubled by the separate school question, as the nation turned its attention to defence, the Northwest, and "Rep. by Pop."

Ryerson and the Government of John A. Macdonald may well have congratulated themselves on the present state and future prospects of the school system of Canada West. The number and quality of common schools showed constant improvement, and though separate schools were increasing, at least three times as many Roman Catholic children were attending the former as the latter.[109] Ryerson's references to separate schools in his annual reports had become perfunctory and purely statistical. Bishop Lynch, De Charbonnel's personally picked successor, showed no desire to meddle with the politics of his adopted country. As the year 1861 closed, the cloud of future trouble on the horizon appeared no bigger, and probably smaller, than Scott's hand.

VIII

It was the *Canadian Freeman* which served notice on January 24, 1862, that the drive to obtain revision of the Separate School Act was about to be intensified. With another session of Parliament near at hand, now was the time for the Ministry to redeem pledges regarding separate schools, which, the *Freeman* asserted, had been given in exchange for Roman Catholic votes at the late elections. "If the Ministry take an early opportunity of rendering us justice on this vital matter, they will afford us, proof that our votes and confidence were not thrown away in the last election, and they will, further, establish for themselves a claim to our future support." The clergy would be the best judges of what changes were required in the existing law. The editor closed with a brief warning which hinted at Fenianism—the Government might soon encounter crises when Roman Catholic support would be needed.

Ryerson was willing, perhaps anxious, "to meet the reasonable objections which had been urged against the Taché Separate School Act," although the Act had been entirely of Roman Catholic making.[110] Early in March he sent the Government a draft Bill which would have removed a number of minor but legitimate grievances, such as annual notices of tax exemption from separate school supporters, the impossibility of having separate schools in incorporated villages, and the restrictions on forming separate school union sections. "No new principle is introduced into this Draft of a Bill," Ryerson wrote, "nor does it contain any provision . . . which was not embraced in the Common School Acts of 1850 and 1853." Hence the title "An Act to Restore Certain Rights to the Parties therein mentioned in respect to Separate Schools." Substantially Ryerson was offering precisely the objectives of Scott's Bill of 1860.

Ryerson's action was the outcome of two conversations with Bishop Lynch, at one of which Vicar General Macdonell was also present. Ryerson believed their views were practically identical, but Bishop Horan of Kingston, after some correspondence, decided that the suggested amendments were "not sufficient."[111] "If there is to be any legislation on this matter . . . it should be of a kind to set this long-vexed question at rest. . . ." Horan offered new terms which he assured the Chief Superintendent were certain to give "very general satisfaction." These were merely elaborations of Ryerson's proposals, and some at least found their way into Scott's newest Separate School Bill.

The Throne Speech on March 20 made no reference to education, but within three weeks Scott had presented another amendment of the separate school law. So far the pattern of events followed closely that of the previous two years. But here the similarity ended, for Scott's latest draft was a radical departure from its two still-born precursors. It provided for separate schools in incorporated villages, which Ryerson had already conceded, and for unlimited union of school section trustees, which Ryerson would only accept in an attenuated form. Ryerson would also be opposed to the exemption of all Roman Catholic property from education taxes. But the three most threatening clauses smacked unmistakably of the rankest ultramontanism. Priests were established as *ex officio* trustees, the Church was to control all rules and curricula in the separate schools, and the schools themselves were to be exempt from the observance of all common school holidays or vacations and free to set their own instead. These clauses like most of the Bill were a verbatim copy of one drafted in 1857 by Colonel John Elmsley, a convert from Anglicanism to Romanism. The Bill received official sanction among some Roman Catholic clergy, yet Bishop Horan, convinced that political prospects had improved, found the Bill unsatisfactory and wished to demand more extreme amendments.[112]

When the Bill appeared for second reading Scott informed the House that it had Ryerson's approval.[113] Ryerson, however, was temporarily *hors de combat*, suffering acutely from some illness which incapacitated him for all work and rendered his presence in the lists at Quebec impossible.[114] In fact he had not yet seen a copy of the Bill, as Scott had just forwarded the document, expressing the hope that it would have Ryerson's approbation and the wish that the Bill might prove itself "a finality."[115]

Macdonald also wrote, inviting the Chief Superintendent's opinions. Having seen the Bill at last, Ryerson replied that it was "most objectionable and injurious."[116] "It ought by all means to be rejected." To the author his answer had been given in an open letter to the *Leader*. Some of the Bill's provisions were unobjectionable, some impracticable, but some were "inconsistent with rights of Municipalities and citizens, and such as, I think, no Member of the Legislature can constitutionally consent to. If Mr. Scott's Bill be pressed, I hope, for the honour and character of Upper Canada, it will be rejected by the united vote of both parties of Upper Canadian Representatives." [117]

Ryerson's protests to the Government and to individual members came too late. Scott's Bill was debated for the best part of two days, and at two o'clock in the morning[118] the six months' hoist was defeated by 93 to 13, thanks to the Government's intervention. Macdonald felt obliged to explain this policy to Ryerson. "Dick Scott who is a very *good* fellow although no Solon, introduced the present Bill without showing it to me. Notwithstanding that I thought it well to support the principle of his Bill on an understanding that it should be sent to Special Committee and made to suit me." [119] William Ryerson, M.L.A., advised his brother that Macdonald had promised to send Egerton a copy of the Bill when it was introduced one month before. At the same time William chastised Egerton for his negative criticism which had failed to impress any of the members. "You have not stated one point, or one clause, of the Bill to which you object, nor have you given your reasons for objecting to the Bill itself. You merely condemn the Bill *in toto* and call upon the House to throw it out."

As yet the press had shown little interest in the Bill. Being ignorant of the behind-the-scenes machinations they did not know whether the play would be a tragedy or just another farce. On April 29 the *Globe* charged that Bishop Lynch had extracted a Government promise of any separate school legislation desired (despite De Charbonnel's unhappy experiences with politicians), in return for "effectual aid" at the late elections. "We have to offer our congratulations to Dr. Lynch and his faithful followers on the immense results that have attended their extra ordinary exertions of the past year. They preached and they prayed, they rode and they ran, and they have as their recompense—a broken promise of Mr. John A. Macdonald. They ought to put it in a glass case, and send it down to posterity as a relic." Lynch, it was stated, had been sold by John A. Macdonald like many others, for the Government would not dare to pass another Upper Canada School Bill with French votes.

During May, however, a number of journals spoke out in opposition to any proposed extension of separate schools. The Whitby *Chronicle* of May 15 accepted them only as *fait accompli* which gave no benefits, and hoped that this "staple grievance of political declaimers" would soon be finally settled. One week earlier the *North Ontario Advocate* had called Scott's Bill "exceedingly objectionable";[120] no preferential treatment should be given to these "separatists" who were fomenting religious dissensions. The Stratford *Examiner* and the *Christian Guardian* shared this opinion, the latter adding, "It is really only a *minority* of the Catholic people that sympathize in the agitation for separate schools." [121] But the *York Herald,* nominally Conservative, parrotted the traditional charges of Brown and the *Globe,* that Ryerson was to blame for separate schools, and that he traitorously sought to destroy the common school system.[122]

A prime reason for the charge of "traitor" levelled at Ryerson was his recent advocacy of denominational ragged schools.[123] The High Church Anglicans espoused his plan in hopes of obtaining at last their own separate schools. A committee recommendation to the Toronto Synod in 1862 for a petition to Parliament in favour of equal separate school rights for the Church of England was debated at considerable length and accepted by a vote of 74 to 21 with a majority of both clerical and lay delegates. By the same majority an amendment by Hodgins stating that the diocese wished no "exclusive privileges" was defeated. Widespread popular interest in the Synod's proceedings caused Hodgins to explain his stand through the medium of the press, and a number of journals, secular and religious, voiced their opinions too, all of them denouncing the Anglican position, most blaming Ryerson for encouraging this separatist attitude.[124] On July 2 the *Christian Guardian* again denied that the Chief Superintendent had instituted separate schools, but the *Canadian Independent*, fearful that the High Church party's action would aid the Roman Catholic demands, asked pertinently. "Has the Diocese of Huron absorbed the liberal element [of the Church]? Or has Trinity College filled the parishes with sectarian zealots?"[125]

The subject of separate Anglican schools was brought up at each Toronto Synod meeting for the next three years, but no petitions were even suggested on these occasions. It was not until 1866 that the Synod could agree on the wording of a petition regarding vagrant or ragged schools.

IX

Before Scott's Bill came back from the Select Committee, the Macdonald-Cartier Government had fallen on its Militia Bill, and the John S. Macdonald-Sicotte Ministry had assumed power. Its internal division of opinion on the separate school question, between the new Attorney General, a confirmed opponent of denominational interests despite his religion, and McGee, Scott's most vocal supporter, had the whole province wondering what its policy on this subject would be. The *Canadian Freeman* called for a fair trial of the new Ministry and offered Roman Catholic support in return for "liberal dealing," a bargain which would "entirely depend upon the manner in which they and their followers will dispose of the School question. On that point there shall be no compromise, no half measures."[126] But the St. Catharines *Journal* of June 25 considered the Conservatives' fall a lucky stroke which would save the common school system from its worst enemy—Egerton Ryerson.

The Select Committee, composed of Scott, John A. Macdonald, Michael Foley, and four lesser personages, had purged the Bill of the clause making priests into trustees, and had limited property exemption to land within the municipal confines.[127] This was all that John A. Macdonald required, but the ailing Ryerson now arrived on the scene in defence of his system (the remarks of the *Globe* notwithstanding), to demand and obtain more drastic amendments. Property exemption was restricted to the school section, the committee's interpolated clause creating separate school teachers' examining boards was deleted, and the ultramontane clauses regarding separate school holidays, rules, and curricula were dropped.

These last sections Ryerson had objected to as being "unsanctioned by the example of Lower Canada in regard to the Dissentient Schools, and as unparalleled in any Country in respect to Schools to which legislative aid is given. I wished that the Separate Schools in Upper Canada should be subject to public authority and oversight, the same as are Dissentient Schools in Lower Canada."[128] Finally, Ryerson insisted that the Bill must have the Government's approval and be accepted by all parties as a final settlement. Vicars General Macdonell and Cazeau signified their acceptance of his draft and terms on behalf of the Church of Rome, and this agreement was offered to the Cabinet for further action which never came.

The Bill was withdrawn ostensibly because of the opposition of T. R. Ferguson, of Repeal Bill fame, and of others in the House at the second reading. It is interesting to note that in a colony which delighted in addresses and memorials, and which had so often voiced opposition or approval of similar Bills through petitions to Parliament, only two petitions against this Bill were received, and none in its defence. It is therefore suggested, although no proof can be offered, that Scott and the prelates agreed to withdraw the Bill at the request of a divided and disorganized Cabinet, presumably with promises of better things to come next session.[129] In any case Ferguson, son-in-law of Ogle R. Gowan, was praised publicly by the Orangemen of Simcoe County as the saviour of the common school system, which he did not deny, and the *Globe et al.* wounded three birds with one stone by connecting the separate school and University questions to the detriment of Ryerson's public character.[130] Prospects for peace in 1863 were not encouraging, and the *York Herald* of November 28 warned that supporters of separate schools could be counted on to make "a violent effort" to destroy the educational system in the next session of Parliament.

The Bill which Scott introduced at the session of 1863 was the same one agreed to by its author, Ryerson, the Government, and the Roman clergy one year before, but the popular excitement which it created surpassed any caused by earlier agitations. An attempt by Leonidas Burwell to invoke the six months' hoist at the second reading failed by a vote of 22 to 80, 21 of the yeas being from Upper Canada. Alexander Mackenzie explained the reasons for this opposition to the Bill—that the Bill would injure the common school system and also encourage other denominations to demand similar concessions. A general cry was raised by journalistic opponents of separate schools against Ryerson, as the "coadjutor" of Scott, and the Chief Superintendent, now in Quebec at the Government's request, was referred to as the "subtle ecclesiastic" who was using his great influence improperly to promote Roman Catholic sectarian schools.[131]

Before the third reading a series of Opposition amendments was defeated by majorities which depended on the Lower Canadian votes. On the final vote only two Upper Canadian Reformers supported the Bill, and the Upper Canadian vote stood 31 to 21 against the measure. This defection by Government supporters occasioned a major Cabinet crisis, with J. S. Macdonald threatening to resign if the Clear Grits and their fellow-travellers did not bow the knee in repentance for their disobedience.[132] A party caucus settled the matter to the Cabinet's satisfaction, but the principle of the double majority, which Macdonald had so long championed, had been killed in its first battle. The Conservatives had the satisfaction of twitting the Reformers with inconstancy to their former professions of opposition to separate schools, while confusion reigned in Government ranks with McGee claiming the Act was a ministerial measure giving final satisfaction to the conscientious convictions and Scott admitting that the Cabinet had not been consulted before its introduction at this session or the last.[133]

Popular feeling against the Act ran high in Upper Canada and few could be found who would defend it. The "iniquitous measure"[134] was worse than anything John A. Macdonald had ever done.[135] "The people of Upper Canada have been tampered with," exclaimed the Bowmanville *Statesman*,[136] and those members who voted for it were afflicted with either "culpable blindness" or "paralyzed cowardice." The *Watchman* and others insisted that such traitors must never get an opportunity to repeat their disgraceful performance.[137] The *Globe* devoted space to the Separate School Bill almost daily for several weeks. Few editors would accept Ryerson's public explanation that the Act contained "not the slightest extension of the principle of Separate Schools, but a mere correction of the anomalies and inequalities of the existing Separate School Act," it being favourable, rather than detrimental, to the common school system, and accepted by the Roman Catholic Church as a sufficient protection from insult and a final settlement.[138] Several weeks later Scott received a telegram from Bishop Lynch assuring him of the "perpetual gratitude of Catholics of Canada." [139]

The assertion of finality the *Globe* denied. The *Canadian Freeman* had warned before that the concessions were but an instalment.[140] Assembly members who believed McGee's promise of finality were ignoring the fact that McGee spoke for no one but himself.[141] Bishop Lynch's statement that he believed his fellow bishops and co-religionists were generally "quite satisfied" was denounced as a "transparent humbug." The Romish hierarchy could not be bound by one bishop to cease the agitation.[142] The *Canadian Freeman* itself confirmed the *Globe's* contention. "We regard the slight concession contained in Mr. Scott's bill only in the light of an instalment of our legitimate demands. Sooner or later the whole debt must be acknowledged and paid." [143]

Such opposition to the new Separate School Act did not end after its passage by Parliament. The controversy which had split both the Reform party and the Orange Order into two factions continued to disturb the social peace of the province. Numerous anti-separate school meetings were held throughout Canada West. When a meeting in Toronto's St. Lawrence Hall was broken up by Irish rowdies, it reassembled later in Queen's Park under police guard where the concourse of thousands passed resolutions defending free speech and condemning rowdyism, separate schools, and all members of Parliament who had voted for Scott's Bill.[144] During the general elections later in 1863 the separate school question and "No Popery" were made into touchstones for candidates, and affected the results, in a dozen or more constituencies.[145] Numbered among the defeated was Scott, whose fall according to the *Canadian Freeman* of July 2 was the corrupt work of J. S. Macdonald and the Scottish Roman Catholics. "The ministerialists have endeavoured to get up a Protestant cry with a view to exciting Religious animosity against me," Scott reported to John A. Macdonald.[146] A two-hour visit by Macdonald might have held the constituency, lamented the defeated candidate. "I don't think I got *twenty Protestant votes*, what do you think of that intollerance [*sic*] towards me?" [147]

x

The year 1864 brought a respite from the separate school question as all agitation ended and the nation turned its interest to Confederation, the panacea for that deadlock of which Scott's Separate School Bill had been the first fruits. The number of separate schools continued its annual increase but Ryerson reported with satisfaction that more than 75 per cent of Roman Catholic school children attended common schools.[148] This was more probably caused by the preference of parents than by the necessity created by restrictions on establishing separate schools as some Roman Catholics stated. But the movement towards Confederation was itself the occasion for yet another sally by the separate school advocates against the national school system.

The Quebec Conference had vested educational matters in the local legislature, but had also accepted McGee's rider to protect the minority rights of the separatists in both Canadas by freezing the separate school systems in each of these sub-provinces "at the time when the Union of the Provinces goes into operation." [149] This last clause gave the supporters of denominational education only one more opportunity to do or die in their attempt to assimilate the school systems of Upper and Lower Canada.

The authorities of the Church of Rome were neither slow nor reluctant to reopen the agitation of the disturbing issues. With Parliament called to meet on January 19, 1865, the *Canadian Freeman* sounded the clarion call to agitation two weeks in advance. The editor hoped that his readers would not find fault with him for resuming "the agitation for a more just and liberal Separate School Law." [150] Now was the time for "a grand and final struggle" to obtain the same privileges as Lower Canadian Protestants. "We make the demand ... not in the name of our Prelates and Clergy, but in the name of the whole Catholic population ..." and it behoved the laity to bear the burden of the campaign and thus disprove their opponents' claim that they were indifferent to their educational rights.

Apparently the laity still required some prodding or guidance, for more than half of the thirty-three petitions sent to the Assembly demanding equal rights with Lower Canadian dissentient schools were forwarded from clerics. Probably the numerous public meetings held by Roman Catholics, at which "Resolutions of a more sweeping character than usual passed unanimously," were similarly inspired by the clergy. The excuse for the renewed agitation, according to the *Canadian Freeman*, was the effort being made by the *Watchman* and certain Montreal Protestants to obtain a dissentient school system in Lower Canada which would be completely separate from the provincial schools. [151]

Ryerson did not hesitate to use his pen again in defence of the school system against these attacks from several journals and various quarters. He would not blame Upper Canadian Roman Catholics for seeking the same privileges granted to Lower Canadian Protestants, "but that is a very different thing from a crusade agitation against the Separate School Act of 1863." [152] In letters to various newspapers and in a pamphlet treating the new agitation exhaustively he sought to meet and defeat all the arguments of his opponents and detractors. He did admit that certain new concessions had been made in the Act of 1863 regarding the establishment of separate schools, which he claimed were as practical as possible. He insisted that a property tax supporting the common schools was a patriotic duty, that exemptions could not be extended, nor should the state collect taxes for religious purposes if separation of church and state was to have any meaning. The latest demands were for a Roman Catholic Superintendent of Education, Council of Public Instruction, and normal school. But Bishop Lynch was already a member of the existing Council, and if Lower Canada had three normal schools, the language difficulty which necessitated that arrangement did not exist in Upper Canada. Here twice as many Roman Catholics were employed in teaching in common schools as in separate schools. [153]

The more general charge that the Act of 1863 was a "cruel hoax," "a transparent deception," and "a sham and a fraud," [154] raised the question of the finality of the Act. This charge was an imputation "upon the Roman Catholic Prime Minister and his Colleagues," and upon "the discernment, if not the honesty, of the venerable ecclesiastical personages, who, as Representatives of the Authorities of the Roman Catholic Church," had not only aided in formulating the

Act, but had accepted it "as a satisfactory and final settlement of the Separate School question," and "an honourable compact between all parties concerned."[155] Separate schools were inexpedient for both state and church, and Ryerson was prepared to advocate, if any change in the existing laws was really contemplated, that separate school laws be abolished altogether.

The import of Macdonell's and Cazeau's presence and concurrence at the 1862 conclave in the Parliamentary Library was debated by both sides, Ryerson claiming that the agreement reached then was final for separate school legislation, the *Freeman* and those clerics involved denying the same proposition with the ability of sophists and the acumen of politicians. Fortunately and fortuitously, Ryerson had previously stated his version of the incident in response to the attack by George Brown when the latter charged him with being too helpful to separate schools in 1862. Now Ryerson marshalled the facts once more to prove the intention of all parties that the Act of 1863 should be final, not just one payment on the separate school instalment plan. Ryerson's concluding remarks could well serve as a summary of this chapter, if not of the study itself.

The tendency of the public mind and of the institutions of Upper Canada is to confederation, and not to isolation,—to united effort, and not to divisions and hostile effort—in what all have a common interest. The efforts to establish and extend Separate Schools, although often energetic and made at great sacrifice, are a struggle against the instincts of Canadian society, against the necessities of a sparsely populated Country, against the social and political present and future interests of the parents and youth separated from their fellow citizens.[156]

While the river of ink was being spilled into the provincial press the separate school question was also before Parliament where the debate on the Quebec Resolutions was laying the constitutional foundations of Confederation. The compromise accepted the previous October, to leave education under the local legislatures, but safeguarding existing minority rights, won the approval of the Assembly and a relatively small amount of time was actually devoted to discussion of the educational resolution. But the admission that the compromise had been adopted with the understanding that the Lower Canadian law of dissentient schools would be revised[157] (as the *Watchman* and company had demanded), aroused twofold opposition and let loose birds which came home to roost only a year later.

McGee led the discussion by asserting that, though he had accepted the Act of 1863 as final, he would insist that any privileges granted to the dissentient schools of the lower province must also be extended to the Roman Catholics of the upper province.[158] In this demand he was joined by other members, including J. S. Macdonald, who warned the Administration that concessions to the former group would be used as a lever by his co-religionists in Canada West. Further unrest was excited by the Ministry's refusal to explain the details of the proposed legislation, or to say when the Bill or Bills would be submitted. Eventually it was announced that the final educational settlement must await Imperial approval, thus postponing indefinitely its presentation to the provincial Parliament. J. S. Macdonald moved an amendment that local majorities should not be hampered by any provisions in seeking separately for educational settlements, while a Lower Canadian member solicitously tried to make equal concessions for Upper Canadian separate schools a written commitment of the constitution. But the Government successfully resisted both of these flank attacks, and the principle of the compromise was sustained and retained in the

Address to the Queen, to become in turn Clause 93 of the British North America Act.

XI

Confederation was almost a *fait accompli* as the last session of the United Parliament met in June, 1866. A political era was closing and so was an era in the educational history of Canada West. The province had accepted Scott's Separate School Act of 1863 for better or for worse as the last instalment due to the Roman Catholics. The temper of their reaction to the recent attempt to upset this settlement had shown a solidarity of sentiment against any further tampering with the educational system. Therefore the course of the last desperate attempt in this closing session to extend the powers of separate schools was predestined to failure, a fact which must have been as evident then as it is now.

The dissentient school Bill which the Ministry had promised during the Confederation debates was introduced into the Assembly by Finance Minister Galt, the acknowledged, though somewhat reluctant, spokesman for the Protestant minority of Lower Canada. The *Canadian Freeman* of June 28 gave the Bill its approval, providing parallel legislation was passed for Canada West. It echoed McGee's speech of the last session in which he had demanded equal rights. "This is our ultimatum—equal rights for all, privileges for none." Readers were reminded that although Lower Canadian Protestants had no less than fourteen representatives in the Assembly, Upper Canadian Roman Catholics had none. "It is, therefore, absolutely necessary that our readers should, without the loss of a single day, by letter or by personally going to Ottawa, bring their influence to bear on the members for whom they have voted, to secure for the western minority the passage of the same Bill, *mutatis mutandis,* which Mr. Galt proposes to bring in."

How effective the *Freeman*'s exhortation may have proved cannot be judged. But not one petition from the Roman Catholic laity was received by the Assembly, and it was left to their bishops, nine in number, to pray the Legislature for equal rights and privileges. Three days before this petition was presented to the Assembly, Robert Bell, the second member for Russell County, introduced a Separate School Bill for Upper Canada as an undisguised *quid pro quo* for Galt's measure.

Bell's Bill contained most of the arrangements for a completely separate Roman Catholic educational system which had been purged from Scott's Bill under Ryerson's critical eye. This latest piece of ultramontanism would establish a Roman Catholic Deputy Superintendent of Education, normal school, and Council of Public Instruction. The municipalities would become tax-gatherers for separate schools which would also share proportionately in corporation taxes.[159] Property of non-residents could also be assessed for separate school purposes, and finally, Roman Catholic educational institutions of every description would share all legislative grants for education. Small wonder that Ryerson protested against this "outrageous Bill" to Provincial Secretary McDougall,[160] who sat for the same county as Bell. Ryerson called the whole measure an insult to Upper Canada, and it behoved the Government, in his opinion, to prevent any private member from subverting the system which had been established and which had been accepted by the Roman Catholics as a finality.

When the Bill was withdrawn on the first reading, Upper Canadian newspapers hailed its demise with such captions as "THE BISHOPS FOILED,"[161] or "THE LATEST PAPAL IMPERTINENCE."[162] "A separate School Bill," exclaimed the Markham *Economist,* "is solicited for the purpose of entrammeling the mind and suppressing the independence. . . . We have been called upon for inch after inch of exclusiveness in the Educational Institutions of Canada, which being granted, however reluctantly, the *long Ell* is now demanded with a barefacedness of the most impertinent nature."[163] Other editors spoke of the Bill as "glaring injustice," and "a breach of faith," and asserted that at least nine-tenths of the population considered separate schools as "inimical to the best interests of Upper Canada."[164] "If Separate Schools are entirely swept out of existence, those who favour such institutions will only have their own bishops to blame."[165]

The only *Defensor Fidei* among journalists was, of course, the *Canadian Freeman,* which stigmatized the remarks of Protestant legislators during these debates as "gross and disgusting bigotry," the like of which the editor had never seen.[166] "The way in which that Bill was opposed must have shown Lower Canadians, what their brethren in the West have to expect, when at the mercy and under the control of a local legislature." The Imperial government would be justified in "direct interference" at the Westminster Conference with the Canadian Legislature's educational arrangements. Otherwise the Roman Catholics of the new Province of Ontario would be at the not-so-tender mercies of the Protestant majority, with every likelihood of having all separate schools abolished.

The only result of Bell's Bill was the resignation of Galt, a step which he himself proposed, to prevent "a total disruption of the Government."[167] The onus for this development was laid by Upper Canadians on the Roman Catholic bishops, though one journal noted that this ironically was the same fate which Galt had so recently imposed on Brown.[168] But if nemesis had overtaken the Minister of Finance it had equally caught up with the prime movers of the two Bills which were both in limbo now.

Thus the contest was a draw with neither of the suppliants able to obtain concessions, yet each being able to frustrate the ambitions of the other. No one had profited by this last and latest episode, and the compromise of 1863 had become Ontario's educational legacy from the United Province of Canada. But it was a legacy embittered and jeopardized for the heirs by the memory of harsh words, fanatical opinions, and shattered dreams, dreams both of unity and of separation.

XII

"Perhaps no issue in Ontario during the past hundred-odd years has been debated so continually as that of separate schools."[169] A century ago the separate school controversy was more exciting because the principles involved were more novel. Today the existence of separate schools is an accepted fact, although opinions for and against the exclusive principle are held with no less conviction.

Not until the early years of the "fiery fifties" did the problem of religion in the elementary educational system become a political issue in Canada West. For this unhappy development George Brown and Bishop de Charbonnel must share the burden of responsibility. Yet they in their turn were responding to a considerable extent to influences which arose beyond the narrow confines of the United Province. But as a Canadian problem the issue of separate schools often cut across party lines, adding fuel to an eternal fire of religious controversy, and so persistently disturbing the province that succeeding generations have assumed its existence to be part of a way of life.

Considered as one aspect in the process of creating a nation from the raw material of a pioneer colony, the conflict of the centrifugal force of denominational elementary schools *versus* the centripetal influence of a national educational system evidences the same basic pattern which we have seen in the realms of higher education and religious establishments. On the one side ranged the Church of Rome, the High Church party of Anglicanism, and perhaps some Wesleyan Methodists of immediate English extraction, each claiming an exclusive position in Christendom and special privileges from the state. On the other side stood all those religious bodies which believed in voluntarism and the separation of church and state, supporting nationalism on principle and as a defence of their individual positions as minorities.

Scott's Separate School Act of 1863 established a pattern for elementary education which remains to this day practically unaltered. The Act can be viewed variously as a victory for the conscientious convictions of Roman Catholics or as a compromise between the contending forces of separatism and centralism. At the moment of passing it seemed to be a victory for the Roman Catholics alone— a defeat for nationalism. But in the longer view it was a compromise which, though satisfying neither party, has been virtually sanctified by time, as each succeeding conflict resulted in a draw between balanced forces. Yet the school system established in the 1850's and 1860's was also a victory for the principle of unity, if only because separate schools remained within a single modified system and under one general control, rather than becoming a complete educational dualism.

Granting the previous existence of separate schools, the concessions permitted or exacted, thanks to Lower Canadian interference, were not unreasonable. If centripetalism in education was fighting a losing battle to 1863, at least the lines were stabilized then by a compromise which has been relatively successful and permanent. The conscientious convictions of Roman Catholics have not, and may never, be fully met by the Protestant majority of the province, but the very legal existence of separate schools still maintains their original purpose in certain areas by protecting Protestant minorities from insult.

RETROSPECT

LOOKING BACK on that colourful and tumultuous quarter-century of nation-building which preceded Confederation, the solution of the complex problem of relations between church and state in Canada West shows a distinct tendency towards compromise between the claims of centrifugal denominationalism and centripetal nationalism. The Old World concept of an established church had been discarded long before Confederation. The New World ideal of complete separation had seemingly triumphed. But the commutation money given to the four largest churches and the legal perpetuation of the forty-four Rectories left a vestigial remains of establishment which for a time irked voluntarists.

The failure of Reformers to reduce the denominational universities after the nationalization of King's College and its endowment left the problem of religion in higher education unresolved. The state institution at Toronto continued to monopolize that ample endowment, to the chagrin of its rivals, but the latter in their turn continued to receive government grants, to the chagrin of the extreme voluntarists.

In the field of elementary education the era of good feeling ended soon after the arrival of Bishop de Charbonnel in Canada West. This was in part merely a coincidence in time, for the temper of the whole Church of Rome was changing to one of aggressive militancy. De Charbonnel was as much a reflection of his age as he was the innovator of a war against non-sectarian education. Throughout the fifties and sixties the Roman Catholics struggled towards the goal of their conscientious convictions—a separate system of denominational schools. The settlement written into the constitution of the Dominion was in fact another compromise, inasmuch as the state retained ultimate control of the educational system while admitting the rôle of religion in the training of youth.

The high-water mark for all these changes in the relationship of church and state occurred during the Great Ministry. The first phase of reconstruction after the Rebellion closed with the triumph of responsible government. Yet this first victory for the cause of nationalism was followed immediately in Upper Canada by a tendency to modify its extreme implications by compromising with the older, established forces. The immediate reaction of true Reformers was disappointment in the conservative leadership of the party, and a deep and abiding sense of frustration at the failure of their long-cherished dream of perfect religious equality, protected and enforced by the state.

The close connection of political and religious reformism which had been apparent before the Rebellion of 1837 returned to prominence in the period of the Great Ministry. The personnel was largely new, but the ideals remained the same. The main difference in the Union was the absence of that political *lacuna* in the administration which had driven desperate Reformers to take up arms. Political change had become a constitutional possibility, thanks to Durham, but the moderation of the majority in Canada West enabled politicians to strike with fair success a compromise in the relations of church and state—that type of compromise so typical of Canada, which has robbed her of superficial colour while marking her with inherent stability.

APPENDIXES

COMPARATIVE GROWTH. OF DENOMINATIONS IN CANADA WEST
BASED ON CENSUSES 1842, 1851, 1861

A Number of adherents; B Percentage of total population; C Percentage increase or decrease over previous Census.

Denomination	1842 A	1842 B	1851 A	1851 B	1851 C	1861 A	1861 B	1861 C
Church of England	107,791	20.2	223,190	23.4	+3.2	311,559	22.3	—1.1
Church of Scotland	77,929	16.0	59,102	6.2	—9.8	108,963	7.8	+1.6
Church of Rome	65,203	13.3	167,695	17.6	+4.3	258,151	18.5	+ .9
Free Church	—	—	69,738	7.3	—	143,033	10.2	+2.9
Other Presbyterians	18,220	3.7	75,308*a*	7.9	+4.2	51,378*a*	3.7	—4.2
Wesleyan Methodist			108,502	11.3	nil	218,427	15.6	+4.3
Canadian	32,315	6.6						
British	23,342	4.7						
Episcopal Methodist	20,125	4.1	46,328	4.8	+ .7	74,616	5.2	+ .5
Other Methodists	7,141	1.4	58,607	6.1	+4.7	57,330	4.1	—2.0
Baptist	16,411	3.3	45,353	4.7	+1.4	61,559	4.4	— .3
Lutheran	4,524	1.0	12,089	1.3	+ .3	24,299	1.7	+ .4
Congregational	4,253	.9	7,747	.8	— .1	9,357	.7	— .1
Quaker	5,200	1.1	7,461	.8	— .3	7,383	.5	— .3
No denomination given	81,348	16.6	42,538	4.5	—12.1	25,500	1.8	—2.7
Total population*b*	487,053		952,004		+95.5	1,396,091		+46.7

a These figures obviously include many Free Church members who confused census-takers by giving their religious affiliation as "Presbyterian Church of Canada."
b Includes several small denominations not itemized.

[185]

DEVELOPMENT OF THE PRESBYTERIAN CHURCHES

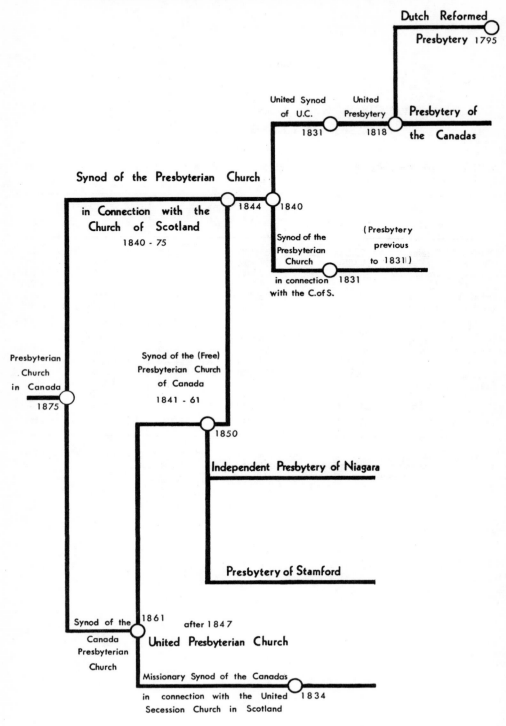

Dutch Reformed

Presbytery 1795

United Synod
of U.C.
1831

United
Presbytery
1818

Presbytery of

the Canadas

Synod of the Presbyterian Church

1844 1840

in Connection with the
Church of Scotland
1840 - 75

Synod of the
Presbyterian
Church

(Presbytery
previous
to 1831)

in connection 1831
with the C.of S.

Presbyterian
.Church
in Canada

1875

Synod of the (Free)
Presbyterian Church
of Canada
1841 - 61

1850

Independent Presbytery of Niagara

Presbytery of Stamford

Synod of the 1861
Canada
Presbyterian
Church

after 1847

United Presbyterian Church

Missionary Synod of the Canadas

in connection with the United 1834
Secession Church in Scotland

DEVELOPMENT OF THE METHODIST CHURCHES

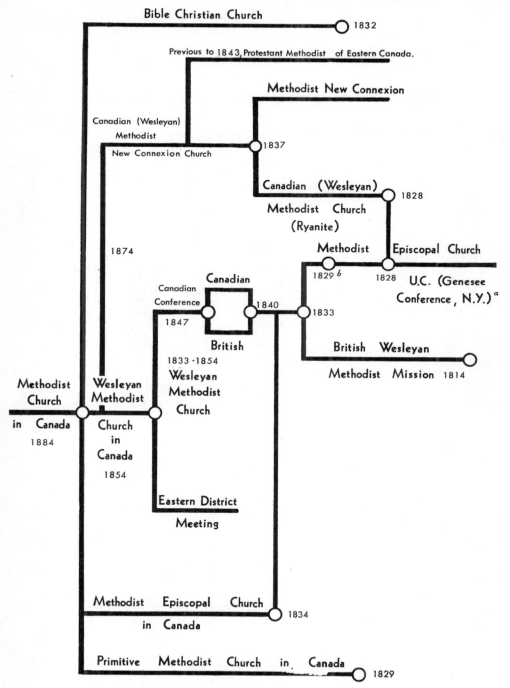

Bible Christian Church 1832

Previous to 1843, Protestant Methodist of Eastern Canada.

Methodist New Connexion

Canadian (Wesleyan) Methodist New Connexion Church 1837

Canadian (Wesleyan) Methodist Church (Ryanite) 1828

Methodist Episcopal Church

1829 *b* 1828 U.C. (Genesee Conference, N.Y.) *a*

1874

Canadian Conference Canadian 1840

1847 1833

British

British Wesleyan

1833-1854 Wesleyan Methodist Mission 1814

Methodist Church 1833-1854 Wesleyan Methodist Church

Methodist Church in Canada Wesleyan Methodist Church in Canada 1854

1884 1854

Eastern District Meeting

Methodist Episcopal Church in Canada 1834

Primitive Methodist Church in Canada 1829

a 1828 : Independence from American Body;
secession form Canadian Wesleyan Methodist Church.

b 1829 : Continuing independence, change of name to
Canadian Conference of Methodist Episcopal Church.

STATISTICS OF THE CLERGY RESERVES FUND, CANADA WEST

Year	Acres sold	Income		Disbursements to churches			
		Old Sales	New Sales	England	Scotland	Rome	Wes.Meth.
to 1841	528,245	£164,541	—	£55,599	nil	nil	nil
1841	2,666	4,940	—	8,941	£2,600	£1,667	£778
1842	1,486	11,467	—	8,189	2,418	1,667	719
1843	613	8,192	—	7,913	2,235	1,667	662
1844	569	16,426	—	7,725	1,831	1,667	662
1845	40,602	16,273	£10,584	8,729	6,756	1,667	608
1846	179,271	13,720	35,433	12,067	2,016	1,667	608
1847	196,568	9,928	33,252	17,941	9,953	1,667	608
1848	81,373	5,970	18,940	9,766	8,728	1,667	608
1849	70,726	5,452	18,781	12,283	6,819	1,667	591
1850	93,246	8,315	28,304	15,663	8,508	1,667	1,722
1851	91,706	5,552	26,903	14,008	7,671	1,667	778
1852	94,942	4,784	28,303	15,110	8,232	1,667	778
1853	150,809	8,424	52,871	?	6,865	?	?
1854 Jan.-June	127,638	6,249	41,096	21,088	?	?	?
Total 1829-54	1,660,460	290,232	294,468				

STATISTICAL GROWTH OF SEPARATE SCHOOLS IN CANADA WEST

Year	Total number of Schools[a]	Roman Catholic	Protestant
1841	1	?	?
1842	?	?	?
1843	5	4	?
1844	7	2?	?
1845	10	2	?
1846	11	?	?
1847	41	?	?
1848	32	?	?
1849	31 [51?][b]	?	?
1850	46	21 (14)	25
1851	20	16	4
1852	46	21 (18)	25
1853	?	32	(4)
1854	53	49 (44)	4
1855	58	53 (41)	4
1856	81	(81)[c]	
1857	100	(100)	
1858	94	(94)	
1859	105	(105)	
1860	115	(115)	
1861	109	(109)	
1862	109	(109)	
1863	120	(120)	
1864	147	(147)	
1865	152	(152)	
1866	157	(157)	
1867	161	(161)	

Figures given are compiled from *D.H.E.* and Hodgins, *Separate Schools* (see Bibliographical Note), with supplementary figures (in brackets) from J. W. Edwards, *The Wedge* (Toronto [1923?]).

[a] Separate schools might be Roman Catholic, Protestant, or coloured, which accounts for the disparity between the total number of Roman Catholic and Protestant schools, and the total number of separate schools as given here. Available statistics are incomplete for this period.

[b] Cf. the figure given by Ryerson of fifty-one separate schools, *supra*, p. 144.

[c] These figures from Edwards which follow assume that all separate schools were Roman Catholic. There is no evidence either to support or contradict this assumption.

THE SETTLEMENT OF THE RECTORIES QUESTION

SINCE the creation of the forty-four Rectories in 1836 they had generally been regarded as part and parcel of the larger problem of Clergy Reserves. Indeed almost three-quarters of the glebe lands had been taken from the Clergy Reserves. All Reformers and many conservatives considered that the creation of the Rectories had been at best impolitic, at worst fraudulent. But the real issue was the legality of the patents. If, after the accession to power of the Great Ministry, less verbiage and time were devoted to the Rectories question, this condition stemmed from the popular belief that secularization of the Clergy Reserves would involve at the same time the dissolution of the Rectories. Both problems were but two sides of the same coin—church statism—and the Rectories were of less consequence but certainly not inconsequential. Editors and agitators invariably linked the two together, and this note is included with the intention of completing the discussion of the problem.

In 1851, as a sop to uneasy Reformers, the provincial Parliament passed an Act vesting the right of presentation of incumbents in the diocesan Church Society until such time as a judicial decision on the validity of the patents was obtained. The following year during his trip to Britain Hincks initiated proceedings to get a legal opinion on that question. The opinion offered by the English lawyers stated that the Rectories had been illegally established, just as the Reformers had always contended. But this statement was only an opinion and the Government was pledged by the Act which it had pushed through Parliament to refer the case to the courts for a final decision, instead of abolishing the Rectories by statute as the Grits and many advanced Reformers demanded.

As the wheels of justice grind infinitely slowly, the test case of *The Attorney General* v. *Grasett* was not closed in Chancery Court until 1856. In the interval, sporadic agitation for a statutory death to the Rectories continued in the left-wing newspapers, and George Brown introduced in the Assembly in 1852, 1853, and 1854, Bills to nationalize the glebes for common school use, only to have the Bills rejected by overwhelming majorities, thanks to skilfully whipped-in ministerial votes. In 1855 the same Bill introduced by the same individual came closer to success. It was defeated by the slim margin of five votes.

The judges in Chancery disagreed with the opinion of the English lawyers. The Rectories were declared legally established because Colborne had possessed the necessary authority. Though it was not the concern of the courts of justice, the judges added suggestively that if the policy of erecting Rectories was objectionable the Legislature possessed remedial power. The existence of this power had already been acknowledged by Francis Hincks during the debate in 1851, but he had consistently refused to act on this authority. Bitterly, George Brown expressed the hope that the Reformers who had preferred judicial to legislative action on the Rectories would now be satisfied with this conclusion, and that David Roblin, who had opposed Brown's latest Rectory Bill, would "keep his mouth shut for the future." Legal or not, the Rectories were unjust in Brown's eyes, and they must be abolished to complete the separation of church and state. He was by no means alone in this opinion.

The Coalition Government had allowed the case of Grasett's Rectory, which was situated in Toronto, to go to the Court of Error and Appeal, and here the judgment of the Court of Chancery was sustained. This was sufficient justification for the Government to announce that the case would not be appealed to the Judicial Committee of the Privy Council. But it was not sufficient for the indomitable George Brown who introduced again his favourite Bill for abolishing the Rectories, saving the rights of existing incumbents. It met the same fate as its predecessors.

If, as Brown insisted, a state church would exist in principle as long as the Rectories did, then Ontario still preserves vestigial remains of a religious Establishment. The Rectory patents signed by Colborne in 1836 are still valid, and the incumbents draw a drastically deflated annual stipend of a few hundred dollars, though their glebes have long since been sold and the proceeds invested. Two Rectory glebes had been sold before Confederation, and by an Act passed in the last session of the United Parliament (29 & 30 Victoria, C. 16), the Church of England was empowered to sell the remaining glebes within ten years. A subsequent Act of the Province of Ontario (39 Victoria, C. 108) extended this period for another ten years. Like the Clergy Reserves, the Rectory lands if they had been held would have produced a far greater return at a later date, but the impossibility of establishing a tenant system on these holdings forced their sale. The existence of legal Rectories in Canada today is an anachronism of which few are aware and which no one would care to disturb.

BIBLIOGRAPHIC NOTE

THE MATERIALS consulted for these studies are many and varied; the majority of them, however, are in printed form. As a reflection of public opinion on the various topics the unparalleled collection of provincial newspapers in the Ontario Archives is invaluable, and this has been supplemented by reference to the files of Kingston papers in the Douglas Library, Queen's University, to the irreplaceable volumes of the *Globe* and *Banner* in the Ontario Legislative Library, to denominational newspapers housed in the United Church Archives at Victoria College, and to scattered titles at the Public Archives of Canada. The studies on education could not have been written without J. G. Hodgins' monumental *Documentary History of Education in Upper Canada* (28 vols., Toronto, 1894-1910), which, despite the editorial liberties which Hodgins has taken with some of the material, draws together every document of any importance on the subject, and many which are no longer accessible.

The valuable collection of Bishop Strachan's papers in the Ontario Archives provides material for every phase of this volume. Also in that repository, the Macaulay Papers and the J. B. Robinson Papers supplement the Strachan Papers with material on the Church of England and politics. The Hodgins Papers in the Ontario Archives are mostly letters extracted from Egerton Ryerson's correspondence by Hodgins, his literary executor, but the bulk of the Ryerson Papers, which are in the United Church Archives, contain little of importance that has not already been used by C. B. Sissons in his two-volume biography of Ryerson. The Charles Clarke Papers in the Ontario Archives are particularly useful in explaining the Clear Grit position on church-state problems.

For the history of the Church of Scotland and its attitude towards the Clergy Reserves, and for the history of Queen's University, the William Morris Papers, the Presbyterian Church Papers, and the Queen's University Papers, in the Douglas Library are most valuable, and also almost the sole source. The Clergy Reserves Collection in that Library consists largely of copies of documents which are available elsewhere. All of these collections at Queen's can be supplemented by reference to certain portions of Isaac Buchanan's papers to be found in the Public Archives of Canada.

In the Public Archives the most important manuscript collections are the transcripts of certain series of papers from the Society for the Propagation of the Gospel and the additional microfilm materials recently acquired from that Society. These papers collectively give a clear picture of ecclesiastical policy and also offer insight into the everyday work in the dioceses. The Wesleyan Methodist Missionary Society records recently obtained on microfilm by the Public Archives, though valuable for denominational history, are disappointingly meagre in their references to church-state issues, thus confirming the impression that officially at least the Methodists as a body eschewed political entanglements during this period whenever possible. Extensive resources of printed materials including denominational periodicals and newspapers such as the *Christian Guardian*, the *Canada Christian Advocate*, and the *Church* can be found in the

United Church Archives to illuminate the attitudes of various Protestant churches, particularly of course those of the several Methodist and Presbyterian bodies.

Of Canadian government records the most important materials are to be found in the records of the Governor General's Office (G 1, 3, 5, 12, 14, 20, and 21) and in the Executive Council Papers (E 1) at the Public Archives, along with the printed Journals and Appendices of the Legislative Assembly and Council. British government policy is exemplified in the long series of Parliamentary Papers, and although few of these deal directly with education, they are most important for the Clergy Reserves which were an issue in Imperial policy. The most significant Parliamentary Papers are: 1839, 537; 1840, 148, 109; 1843, 314; 1851, [1306]; 1852, [1448]; 1852-3, [1588], 173.

Church histories in Canada are few in number and generally inferior in scholarship, and with the exceptions of John Carroll's *Case and His Cotemporaries* (5 vols., Toronto, 1867-77), and William Gregg's *History of the Presbyterian Church in the Dominion of Canada* (Toronto, 1885), were of slight value to these studies. In addition to the standard Canadian reference works of collected biography, many individual biographies were consulted. The most useful are C. B. Sissons, *Life and Letters of Egerton Ryerson* (2 vols., Toronto, 1937, 1947); A. N. Bethune, *Memoir of the Right Reverend John Strachan, D.D., LL.D., First Bishop of Toronto* (Toronto, 1870); J. E. Wells, *Life and Labors of Robert Alex. Fyfe D.D.* (Toronto [1885?]); H. G. McKeown, *The Life and Labors of Most Rev. John Joseph Lynch, D.D., Cong. Miss., First Archbishop of Toronto* (Montreal and Toronto, 1886); Francis Hincks, *Reminiscences of His Public Life* (Montreal, 1884); and G. P. Scrope, ed., *Memoir of the Life of The Right Honourable Charles Lord Sydenham, G.C.B.* (London, 1843). Two documentary sources of particular value are Paul Knaplund, ed., *Letters from Lord Sydenham, Governor-General of Canada, 1839-1841, to Lord John Russell* (London, 1931), and Sir A. G. Doughty, ed., *The Elgin-Grey Papers 1846-1852* (4 vols., Ottawa, 1937).

The pamphlet material on the politics of the period is so extensive as to preclude its inclusion in such a brief note. The most significant items are cited in the notes. Mention should be made of the excellent studies on specialized subjects which lie buried in graduate theses, especially the series of theses completed at the University of Toronto on the political attitudes of various denominations. Specialized works on the Clergy Reserves question include contemporary pamphlets such as A. N. Bethune, *The Clergy Reserve Question in Canada* (London, 1853); Charles Lindsey, *The Clergy Reserves* (Toronto, 1851); and John Strachan, *The Clergy Reserves: A Letter from the Lord Bishop of Toronto to the Duke of Newcastle, Her Majesty's Secretary for the Colonies* (Toronto, 1853); also Francis Hincks, *Religious Endowments in Canada* (London, 1869); and E. R. Stimson, *History of the Separation of Church and State in Canada* (2nd ed., Toronto, 1887). On the University question there is no monograph which deals directly with the problem, but all the standard histories of the colleges and universities of the province contain some references. The wealth of contemporary pamphlet material is cited in the notes to chapters IV and V, and much of it is reproduced in Hodgins' *Documentary History of Education.* The best work on the separate school issue is the recent book by F. A. Walker, *Catholic Education and Politics in Upper Canada* (Toronto, 1955). The older study by J. G. Hodgins, *Legislation and History of Separate Schools in Upper Canada, 1841-1876* (Toronto, 1897), contains little material that is not reproduced

in his *Documentary History of Education*. There are also numerous contemporary pamphlets, most of which are cited in the course of chapters VI and VII
and which are also noted or reproduced in the *Documentary History of Education*.

J. C. Dent's *The Last Forty Years* (2 vols., Toronto, 1881) remains the only
history to deal with the period of the Union in any detail, and despite the fact
that it is not well documented it is very reliable for facts and interpretation.
E. H. Oliver's *The Winning of the Frontier* (Toronto, 1930) is an attempt to
apply the Turner frontier thesis to Canadian religious history that makes stimu-
lating reading. H. H. Walsh, *The Christian Church in Canada* (Toronto, 1956)
is a later survey that provides general background for these three studies. More
recent publications relating to Canadian church development include W. H.
Elgee, *The Social Teachings of the Canadian Churches: Protestant, the Early
Period before 1850* (Toronto, 1964), which contains a chapter on the attitudes
of these churches towards church-state relations, and J. S. Moir, *Church and State
in Canada 1627–1867: Basic Documents* (Toronto, 1967) which includes primary
source material on the Clergy Reserves and Rectories. A masterly biography,
Alessandro Gavazzi, Clerc, Garibaldien Prédicant des Deux Mondes (2 vols.,
Quebec, 1962) by Robert Sylvain, gives extensive and intensive coverage of
Gavazzi's visit to Canada.

NOTES

Abbreviations used in these notes are as follows: P.A.C.—Public Archives of Canada; O.A.—Ontario Department of Public Records and Archives; Q.U.A.—Queen's University Archives; *D.H.E.—Documentary History of Education in Upper Canada,* edited by J. G. Hodgins (28 vols., Toronto, 1894-1910).

INTRODUCTION

1. W. S. Wallace, *The Growth of Canadian National Feeling* (Toronto, 1927), p. 41.
2. Ernst Troeltsch, *The Social Teaching of the Christian Churches,* trans. by Olive Wyon (2 vols., London, 1931), II, 996; H. Richard Niebuhr, *The Social Sources of Denominationalism* (New York, 1957), p. 31.
3. Sir C. P. Lucas, ed., *Report on the Affairs of British North America,* (3 vols., Oxford, 1912), II, 309.
4. Troeltsch, *Social Teaching,* II, 489.
5. Cf. Niebuhr, *Social Sources,* chaps. VI, VII, and S. D. Clark, *Church and Sect in Canada* (Toronto, 1948), chaps. V-VII.
6. These are specific examples of what Niebuhr terms "idealizing the cause of the state" on the part of the denominations and sects (*Social Sources,* pp. 210-11).
7. O. A., Clarke Papers, J. McNab to Chas. Clarke, Sept. 9, 1854.
8. This same development, or accomodation to the New World political environment and assimilation of a new culture, has been noted in the United States by Niebuhr, *Social Sources,* p. 211.

CHAPTER ONE

1. The numerical strength and growth of the major denominations will be found in tabular form in Appendix I.
2. O. A., Strachan Papers, Feb., 1850, memo re division of Toronto diocese; *ibid.,* Letterbook 1854-62, p. 141, Strachan to Bishop Skinner, July 5, 1856.
3. The correspondence can be found in two British *Parliamentary Papers,* 1856, 131, and 1857, [2256].
4. Great Britain, *Parliamentary Papers,* 1852, 355-II; *ibid.,* 1856, 131, pp. 9-12.
5. C. W. Vernon, *The Old Church in the New Dominion* (London, 1929), p. 104.
6. *Echo,* May 8 and 15, June 12, 1857.
7. *Ibid.,* Jan. 18, Feb. 1, March 21 and 28, May 2, 1856; Barrie *Herald,* Jan. 23, 1856; Strachan Papers, Letterbook 1854-62, p. 119, Strachan to J. T. Lewis, Feb. 12, 1856; P.A.C., S. P. G. Papers, D 14, p. 940, Strachan to E. Hawkins, April 8, 1854, and *ibid.,* pp. 1096-7, Jan. 26, 1856.
8. N. F. Davin, *The Irishman in Canada* (Toronto, 1877), p. 628.
9. The copies of the S.P.G. Papers in the P.A.C. contain numerous letters from backwoods clergymen complaining bitterly of the niggardliness of settlers who expected "free religion."
10. Strachan Papers, T. V. Short to Strachan, May 3, 1849; P.A.C., G 5, Vol. 37, 191-2, Grey to Elgin, Nov. 15, 1850.
11. Cf. H. Richard Niebuhr, *The Social Sources of Denominationalism,* p. 211.
12. These points were raised by the *Echo* as early as 1856, and the *Canada Christian Advocate* was frequently quoted.
13. William Gregg, *History of the Presbyterian Church in the Dominion of Canada* (Toronto, 1885), p. 437 *et sqq.*
14. Q.U.A., Morris Papers, W. Smart to W. Morris, July 13, 1840.
15. Q.U.A., Presbyterian Church Papers, W. Smart to [?], Oct., 1843.

16. Q.U.A., Queen's University Papers, W. Morris to F. A. Harper, Jan. 1, Feb. 12, 1841.

17. Morris Papers, Hugh Scobie to W. Morris, Nov. 7, 1843; R. B. Sullivan to W. Morris, Nov. 18, 1843; *British Colonist*, Nov. 9 and 14, 1843; *Examiner*, Nov. 22, 1843.

18. Morris Papers, H. Scobie to W. Morris, Nov. 7, 1843.

19. G. Smellie, *Memoir of Rev. John Bayne, D.D., of Galt* (Toronto, 1871), p. 19.

20. Ian Rennie, "The Free Church and Relations of Church and State in Canada, 1844-54," unpublished M. A. thesis, University of Toronto, 1954, pp. 55-61.

21. R. F. Burns, *Life and Times of the Rev. R. Burns, D.D., Toronto* (Toronto, 1872), p. 244.

22. *British Colonist*, July 12, 1843.

23. Presbyterian Church Papers, Overture of Hamilton Presbytery, signed by Wm. King, Moderator, and M. Y. Stark, Clerk, 1844.

24. *Draft of an Answer to the Dissent and Protest of certain Ministers and Elders who have seceded . . .* (Kingston, 1844).

25. Presbyterian Church Papers, various items, 1844, referring to disruption in Canada West.

26. Morris Papers, Isaac Buchanan to W. Morris, Aug. 17, 1844.

27. *Ibid.*, July 5, 1844.

28. P.A.C., Buchanan Papers, 1845, contains correspondence with various congregational officials regarding their application for his assistance.

29. *Ibid.*, Wm. Rintoul to I. Buchanan, April 7, 1845.

30. Presbyterian Church Papers, Thos. Liddell to Andrew Bell, Dec. 10, 1844.

31. *A Historical and Statistical Report of the Presbyterian Church of Canada. . . for the Year, 1866* (Montreal, 1868), pp. 128, 165-72; Gregg, *History of the Presbyterian Church*, p. 494.

32. Rennie, "The Free Church," pp. 66-7.

33. Gregg, *History of the Presbyterian Church*, p. 494.

34. Anna Ross, *The Man with the Book or Memoirs of "John Ross of Brucefield"* (Toronto, 1897), pp. 76-81.

35. C. B. Sissons, *Life and Letters of Egerton Ryerson* (2 vols., Toronto, 1937, 1947), I, 152-91.

36. Paul Knaplund, ed., *Letters from Lord Sydenham, Governor-General of Canada, 1839-1841, to Lord John Russell* (London, 1931), p. 49.

37. *Christian Guardian*, Dec. 2 and 9, 1846.

38. G. W. Brown, "The Formative Period of Canadian Protestant Churches," in R. Flenley, ed., *Essays in Canadian History* (Toronto, 1939), p. 364.

39. J. E. Wells, *Life and Labors of Robert Alex. Fyfe, D.D.* (Toronto, [1885?]), p. 178.

40. Brown, "The Formative Period," p. 364.

41. A. N. Bethune, *Memoir of the Right Reverend John Strachan, D.D., LL.D., First Bishop of Toronto* (Toronto, 1870), pp. 174-5; C. W. Robinson, *Life of Sir John Beverley Robinson* (Toronto, 1904), pp. 237-63.

42. Strachan Papers, Letterbook 1839-43, p. 59, Strachan to J. H. Newman, May 23, 1840.

43. O.A., Letterbook of Mrs. R. D. Cartwright, p. 339, Mrs. Cartwright to Mrs. C. Dobbs, March 12, 1840.

44. *Christian Guardian*, Oct. 9, Nov. 13, 1839, April 1 and 15, 1840.

45. O. A., Macaulay Papers, J. Macaulay to Ann Macaulay, Dec. 24, 1839.

46. *Christian Guardian*, Dec. 11, 1839, April 1 and 8, 1840.

47. Knaplund, *Letters of Lord Sydenham*, p. 54.

48. P.A.C., G 5, Vol. 31A, 24-30, Stanley to Bagot, Oct. 8, 1841.

49. Strachan Papers, Letterbook 1839-43, p. 261, Strachan to J. S. Cartwright, Nov. 10, 1843.

50. *British Colonist*, Oct. 31, 1843.

51. O.A., Hodgins Papers, J. Scott to E. Ryerson, March 13, 21, and 25, 1844, copies; see also *Christian Guardian*, Feb. 7, 1844.

52. John Carroll, *Case and His Cotemporaries* (5 vols., Toronto, 1867-77), IV, 424.

53. Hodgins Papers, copy of resolutions passed at Toronto district meeting of the Wesleyan Methodist Church, May 30, 1844.

54. *Christian Guardian*, June 19, 1844.

55. Carroll, *Case and His Cotemporaries*, IV, 476.

56. Kingston *Herald*, April 23, 1844.

57. P.A.C., G 3, Vol. 1, Stanley to Metcalfe, Sept. 25, 1844, private and confidential.

58. G 5, Vol. 34, 353, Gladstone to Cathcart, Jan. 29, 1846, enclosure.

59. Kingston *Herald*, Jan. 19, 1848.

60. Cobourg *Star*, Oct. 17, 1849.

61. F. A. Walker, "Protestant Reaction in Upper Canada to the 'Popish Threat'," *Canadian Catholic Historical Association Report, 1951*, pp. 91-107.

62. John Strachan, *A Letter to the Right Hon. Lord John Russell, on the present State of the Church in Canada* (Toronto, 1851), pp. 14-15.

63. Alexander Mackenzie, *Life and Speeches of the Hon. George Brown* (Toronto, 1882), p. 33.

64. O.A., Clarke Papers, Wm. McDougall to Chas. Clarke, July 26, 1851.

65. *Globe,* Nov. 4, 1851.

66. *Christian Guardian,* June 15, 1853.

67. *News of the Week,* Aug. 13, 1853; *Protestant Guardian,* Oct. 7, 1853.

68. *Leader,* July 20, 1853.

69. *Catholic Citizen,* May 4, 1854.

70. *Ibid.,* Jan. 5, 1854.

71. *Ibid.,* May 4, 1854.

72. *News of the Week,* June 10, 1854, quoting the *Catholic Citizen.*

73. *Globe,* March 14, 1855.

74. *Ibid.,* Jan. 4, 1856.

75. *News of the Week,* March 1, 1856.

76. Bowmanville *Statesman,* Feb. 12, 1857.

77. *Mirror,* April 11, 1856.

78. *News of the Week,* July 18, 1856.

79. Guelph *Advertiser,* July 24, 1856.

80. Brampton *Weekly Times,* Aug. 1, 1856; *Mirror,* Aug. 1, 1856.

81. *Mirror,* July 18, 1856.

82. *News of the Week,* June 7, 1856.

83. *Mirror,* Nov. 14, 1856.

84. Robert Wallace, *Discourse delivered at Ingersoll before the Orange Association of the County of Oxford, Monday, 13 July, 1857* (Ingersoll, n.d.), p. 17.

85. *Mirror,* Jan. 8, 1858.

86. *Daily Colonist,* Jan. 7, 1858.

87. *Mirror,* Jan. 1 and 15, 1858.

88. *Ibid.,* April 16, 1858.

89. *Catholic Citizen,* May 13, 1858.

90. *Mirror,* June 18, 1858.

91. *Canadian Freeman,* Nov. 5, 1858.

92. *Ibid.,* Aug. 6, 1858.

93. *Daily Colonist,* Aug. 10, 1858; *Mirror,* Aug. 13, 1858.

94. *Canadian Freeman,* Aug. 27, Sept. 3, 1858.

95. *British Tribune,* Sept. 3, 1858.

96. *Mirror,* Feb. 25, 1859.

97. *Canadian Freeman,* Sept. 6 and 27, Oct. 11, 1860.

98. Quoted in the Toronto *Orange Herald,* Sept. 27, 1860.

99. D. G. Creighton, *John A. Macdonald, the Young Politician* (Toronto, 1952), pp. 304-7, 311.

100. *Canadian Freeman,* July 11, 1861.

101. Whitby *Chronicle,* May 1, 1862.

102. *Watchman,* Dec. 2, 1864.

103. *Canadian Freeman,* Dec. 15, 1864.

104. *Ibid.,* March 8, 1866.

105. *Ibid.,* June 7, 1866.

106. *Ibid.,* June 28, Oct. 11, 1866.

107. *Christian Guardian,* Aug. 13, 1851.

108. Egerton Ryerson, *A Few Remarks on Religious Corporations* (Toronto, 1851).

109. John Strachan, *Charge delivered at the visitation of the Clergy, 1856* (Toronto, 1856), pp. 27-8.

110. *Christian Guardian,* May 18, 1853.

111. *News of the Week,* Nov. 4, 1854.

112. *Christian Guardian,* April 20, 1853.

113. *The Good Templar,* May 26, 1863.

CHAPTER TWO

1. *Mirror of Parliament of the Province of Canada* (Montreal, 1846), p. 60.

2. *Journals of the Legislative Assembly of the Province of Canada* 1851, Appendix MM.

3. R. G. Riddell, "The Policy of Creating Land Reserves in Canada," in R. Flenley, ed., *Essays in Canadian History* (Toronto, 1939), pp. 296-317.

4. Sir C. P. Lucas, ed., *Report on the Affairs of British North America* (3 vols., Oxford, 1912), II, 173.

5. *Ibid.,* p. 176.

6. Great Britain, *Parliamentary Papers,* 1839, 537, pp. 3-4.

7. *Ibid.,* p. 5.

8. *Ibid.,* p. 7.

9. *Ibid.,* pp. 34-5.

10. Charles Lindsey, *The Clergy Reserves* (Toronto, 1851), p. 38.

11. *Parliamentary Papers,* 1839, 537, p. 35.

12. *Journals of the Legislative Assembly of the Province of Upper Canada,* 1839, p. 3.

13. *Parliamentary Papers,* 1839, 537, pp. 18-20.

14. Q.U.A., Morris Papers, Adam Fergusson to William Morris, May 2, 1839.

15. *Ibid.,* James Crooks to W. Morris, May 7, 1839.

16. O.A., Macaulay Papers, John Macaulay to Ann Macaulay, May 5, 1839.

17. Morris Papers, J. Crooks to W. Morris, May 2, 1839. See also C. B. Sissons, *Life and Letters of Egerton Ryerson* (2 vols., Toronto, 1937, 1947), I, 480-552.

18. P.A.C., G 12, Vol. 32, 34-5, Arthur to Normanby, May 14, 1839, confidential.

19. O.A., Strachan Papers, A. N. Bethune to J. Strachan, May 16, 1839.

20. Macaulay Papers, J. Strachan to J. Macaulay, May 21, 1839.

21. G 5, Vol. 27, 15, Russell to Thomson, Sept. 7, 1839.

22. G. P. Scrope, ed., *Memoir of the Life of the Right Honourable Charles, Lord Sydenham* (1st ed., London, 1843), p. 163.

23. *Ibid.,* p. 162.

24. G 5, Vol. 28, 122-3, Russell to Thomson, Dec. 16, 1839.

25. *Journals of the Legislative Assembly,* 1839-40, pp. 39, 73.

26. Scrope, *Lord Sydenham,* p. 168.

27. Macaulay Papers, J. Macaulay to A. Macaulay, Dec. 24, 1839.

28. Sissons, *Egerton Ryerson,* I, 546-51.

29. *Journals of the Legislative Assembly,* 1839-40, p. 120.

30. *Parliamentary Papers,* 1840, 148, pp. 7-11.

31. *Christian Guardian,* Jan. 8, 1840.

32. Strachan Papers, printed circular to the clergy and laity of the Diocese of Toronto, Jan. 15, 1840.

33. Macaulay Papers, J. Macaulay to A. Macaulay, Jan. 6, 1840.

34. Morris Papers, W. Morris to T. W. C. Murdoch, Chief Secretary, Government House, Jan. 4, 1840, draft.

35. *Ibid.,* Wm. Smart to W. Morris, Jan. 7 and 17, 1840.

36. *Parliamentary Papers,* 1840, 148, p. 2, Thomson to Russell, Jan. 22, 1840.

37. Paul Knaplund, ed., *Letters from Lord Sydenham, Governor-General of Canada, 1839-41, to Lord John Russell* (London, 1931), p. 41.

38. *Ibid.,* p. 43.

39. *Ibid.,* pp. 43-4.

40. *Ibid.,* pp. 44-5.

41. *Ibid.,* p. 44.

42. *Ibid.,* p. 48.

43. *Journals of the Legislative Assembly,* 1839-40, p. 385.

44. *Christian Guardian,* Feb. 12, 1840.

45. *Ibid.,* Jan. 29, Feb. 19, 1840.

46. *Ibid.,* March 18, 1840.

47. Knaplund, *Letters from Lord Sydenham,* p. 42.

48. Macaulay Papers, J. Macaulay to A. Macaulay, Jan. 28, 1840.

49. *Ibid.,* Wm. Macaulay to J. Macaulay, Feb. 5, 1840.

50. G 5, Vol. 29, 10-11, Russell to Thomson, April 14, 1840.

51. Knaplund, *Letters from Lord Sydenham,* p. 61.

52. R. S. Longley, *Sir Francis Hincks* (Toronto, 1943), p. 62.

53. *Christian Guardian,* Feb. 19, 1840.

54. Knaplund, *Letters from Lord Sydenham,* p. 53.

55. *Ibid.,* p. 54.

56. Strachan Papers, Letterbook to the Societies 1839-66, pp. 13-14, Strachan to A. N. Campbell, April 28, 1840, private.

57. *Ibid.*, Letterbook 1839-43, p. 60, Strachan to J. S. Pakington, May 22, 1840. In a letter to Campbell on May 1, Strachan covers the same points but specifically states that one-half of the Reserves' proceeds would be acceptable.

58. *Ibid.*, Strachan to the Bishop of Exeter, Feb. 20, 1840.

59. *Parliamentary Papers*, 1852-3, 160.

60. Strachan Papers, Sir Robert Peel to Strachan, July 7, 1840.

61. Charles, Earl Grey, *The Colonial Policy of Lord John Russell's Administration* (2 vols., 2nd ed., London, 1853), I, 253.

62. Strachan Papers, Letterbook 1839-43, p. 76, Strachan to the Bishop of Montreal, Nov. 3, 1840.

63. Strachan Papers, Sir Robert Peel to Strachan, July 7, 1840; W. E. Gladstone to Strachan, July 21, 1840.

64. John Strachan, *A Charge delivered to the Clergy of the Diocese of Toronto, at the Primary Visitation . . . 9th September, 1841* (Toronto, 1841), p. 14.

65. Knaplund, *Letters from Lord Sydenham*, p. 91.

66. Morris Papers, Robert McGill to W. Morris, Sept. 4, 1840.

67. *Ibid.*, Aug. 25, 1840.

68. Knaplund, *Letters from Lord Sydenham*, p. 95.

69. Morris Papers, W. Morris to Lord Sydenham, Oct. 2, 1840, draft.

70. *Ibid.*, Hugh Urquhart to W. Morris, Sept. 26, 1840.

71. *Ibid.*, Alex. Gillespie to W. Morris, July 31, 1840.

72. Q.U.A., Presbyterian Church Papers, "Memorial and Protest of the Commission of the Synod to Lord John Russell against the Clergy Reserves Settlement," Oct., 1840; letter of transmission, H. Urquhart to S. B. Harrison, Nov. 7, 1840, and reply, Nov. 27, 1840.

73. G 1, Vol. 51, 410-13, Russell to Sydenham, Jan. 30, 1841.

74. Sissons, *Egerton Ryerson*, I, 549 *et sqq.*

75. Knaplund, *Letters from Lord Sydenham*, p. 92.

76. *Ibid.*, p. 95.

77. Sissons, *Egerton Ryerson*, I, 563.

78. Cf. *Christian Guardian*, Oct. 14, 1840.

79. Sissons, *Egerton Ryerson*, I, 567-9.

80. *Parliamentary Papers*, 1843, 314, p. 3.

81. Morris Papers, W. Morris to the Synod assembled, June 27, 1842.

82. Strachan Papers, Letterbook to the Societies 1839-66, pp. 20-1, Strachan to A. N. Campbell, March 15, 1841.

83. *Journals of the Legislative Assembly*, 1846, pp. 90-1.

84. G 5, Vol. 31, 346, Stanley to the Officer Administering the Government of Canada, Oct. 7, 1841; *ibid.*, 368, Stanley to Bagot, Oct. 28, 1841.

85. Strachan Papers, Letterbook to the Societies 1839-66, p. 32, Strachan to Campbell, Nov. 18, 1841.

86. P.A.C., microfilm A211, S.P.G., "C" MSS, Box V/43, J. Strachan to Campbell, Dec. 24, 1841.

87. Strachan Papers, J. B. Robinson to Lord Stanley, endorsed by J. Strachan, Dec. 24, 1841.

88. G 5, Vol. 31A, 99-100, Stanley to Bagot, March 1, 1842.

89. *Ibid.*, pp. 272-3, Stanley to Bagot, April 2, 1842.

90. *Ibid.*, Vol. 32, 44-7, Stanley to Bagot, June 2, 1842.

91. *Ibid.*, p. 74, Stanley to Bagot, June 23, 1842.

92. Strachan Papers, J. B. Robinson to Strachan, Sept. 4, 1841.

93. O.A., Hodgins Papers, Francis Hincks to E. Ryerson, Dec. 22, 1842.

94. *Journals of the Legislative Assembly*, 1844-5, p. 278, and Appendix EE, Table I.

95. *Parliamentary Papers*, 1853, 173, p. 6.

96. Strachan Papers, Letterbook 1839-43, p. 257, Strachan to the Rev. Thos. Gale, for the information of the Church of Scotland Synod, Sept. 23, 1843.

97. G 5, Vol. 35, 238, Stanley to Metcalfe, March 22, 1844.

98. *Journals of the Legislative Assembly*, 1849, Appendix NNN, Gladstone to Cathcart, Feb. 28, 1846.

99. *Ibid.*, 1844-5, p. 60, p. 177, *passim.*

100. *Ibid.*, pp. 277-8, 427-8.

101. *Ibid.*, 1849, Appendix NNN.

102. *Mirror of Parliament of the Province of Canada* (Montreal, 1846), p. 178; *Journals of the Legislative Assembly*, 1846, p. 4, *passim.*

103. *Journals of the Legislative Assembly*, 1846, pp. 16 *passim*, 106-7; see also J. E.

Wells, *Life and Labors of Robert Alex. Fyfe, D.D.* (Toronto, [1885?]), pp. 111, 114.
   104. P.A.C., mf. A212, S.P.G., "C" MSS, Box V/44, Strachan to E. Hawkins, May 25, 1846.
   105. *Ibid.*, April 24, 1846.
   106. *Journals of the Legislative Assembly*, 1849, Appendix NNN.
   107. *Ibid.*, Cathcart to Gladstone, April 14, 1846.
   108. *Ibid.*
   109. *Mirror of Parliament of the Province of Canada* (Montreal, 1846), pp. 58, 156, 175-80, 186.
   110. *Journals of the Legislative Assembly*, 1849, Appendices NNN, IIII; Strachan Papers, Letterbook to the Societies 1839-66, p. 71, Strachan to Hawkins, Jan. 23, 1846.
   111. O.A., Baldwin Papers, printed letter to "Electors of the Fourth Riding of York, R. Baldwin, Toronto, 8 December, 1847."
   112. A. J. MacLachlan, "Baptists and Public Questions before 1850," unpublished B.D. thesis, McMaster University, 1937, p. 65.
   113. *Journals of the Legislative Assembly*, 1849, Appendix JJJJ.
   114. A. F. Kemp, *Digest of the Minutes of the Synod of the Presbyterian Church of Canada* (Montreal, 1861), pp. 413-14.
   115. *Journals of the Legislative Assembly*, 1849, Appendix JJJJ.
   116. *Ibid.*
   117. Sir A. G. Doughty, ed., *The Elgin-Grey Papers, 1846-1852* (4 vols., cont. pag., Ottawa, 1937), p. 140.
   118. Kingston *Chronicle & News*, Dec. 9, 1848, quoting *The Statesman*.
   119. *Globe*, Feb. 10, March 24, 1849.
   120. *Ibid.*, April 7, 1849.
   121. O.A., J. H. Price Letterbook 1842-65, Address of 900 Freeholders of the First Riding, York County, to J. H. Price, n.d.

CHAPTER THREE

   1. *Globe*, June 23, 1849.
   2. Sir A. G. Doughty, ed., *The Elgin-Grey Papers, 1846-1852* (4 vols., cont. pag., Ottawa, 1937), p. 604, March 11, 1850.
   3. *Examiner*, Sept. 26, 1849.
   4. *Globe*, Oct. 4, 1849.
   5. *Ibid.*, Nov. 10, 1849.
   6. *Ibid.*
   7. *Ibid.*, Dec. 25 and 29, 1849, April 11, 1850.
   8. *Ibid.*, Feb. 14, 1850.
   9. *Ibid.*, March 23, 1850.
   10. *Ibid.*, March 21, 1850.
   11. *Ibid.*, Jan. 19, 1850, quoting the Hamilton *Provincialist*, and from *Kent Advertiser*.
   12. R. S. Longley, *Sir Francis Hincks* (Toronto, 1943), p. 283.
   13. O.A., Clarke Papers, Chas. Lindsey to Chas. Clarke, Jan. 18, 1850.
   14. *Globe*, Jan. 26, 1850.
   15. *Ibid.*, April 27, May 9, 1850.
   16. *Ibid.*, May 11 and 16, 1850.
   17. *Christian Guardian*, May 22, 1850.
   18. Q.U.A., Morris Papers, W. Agar Adamson to W. Morris, March 13, 1850.
   19. O.A., Strachan Papers, A. N. Bethune to J. Strachan, April 24, 1850.
   20. Doughty, *Elgin-Grey Papers*, p. 623.
   21. *Globe*, May 16, 18, and 30, 1850.
   22. *Ibid.*, May 16, 1850.
   23. *Ibid.*, June 13, 1850.
   24. Doughty, *Elgin-Grey Papers*, p. 688.
   25. *Globe*, June 20 and 22, 1850.
   26. Doughty, *Elgin-Grey Papers*, p. 698.
   27. Great Britain, *Parliamentary Papers*, 1851, [1306], pp. 1-5.
   28. P.A.C., S.P.G. Papers, D 14, p. 129, Henry Patton to J. Strachan, July 12, 1850.
   29. Strachan Papers, J. B. Robinson to J. Strachan, June 21, 1850; *Globe*, July 13, 1850.
   30. *Globe*, July 13, 1850; Cobourg *Star*, May 15, 1850.
   31. *Watchman*, July 1, 1850.
   32. *Christian Guardian*, May 22, 1850.
   33. *Parliamentary Papers*, 1852, [1448], p. 1.

34. *Ibid.,* 1851, [1306], p. 6; *Globe,* March 8, 1851.
35. *Christian Guardian,* March 12, 1851.
36. Strachan Papers, E. Hawkins to J. Strachan, March 14, 1851, copy.
37. Morris Papers, Malcolm Smith, Moderator, to W. Morris, Feb. 4, 1851.
38. *Parliamentary Papers,* 1852, [1448], pp. 4-8, 21.
39. *Ibid.,* 1853, [1558], pp. 31-3.
40. John Strachan, *A Letter to the Right Hon. Lord John Russell, on the present State of the Church in Canada* (Toronto, 1851).
41. S.P.G. Papers, D 14, p. 276, J. Strachan to E. Hawkins, Feb. 18, 1851; Strachan Papers, Letterbook to the Societies 1839-66, p. 119, J. Strachan to E. Hawkins, March 4, 1851.
42. Strachan Papers, E. Hawkins to J. Strachan, March 28, 1851, private, copy.
43. *Ibid.,* E. Hawkins to J. Strachan, April 25, 1851, private, copy.
44. S.P.G. Papers, D 14, p. 276, J. Strachan to E. Hawkins, March 18, 1851; *ibid.,* pp. 254-5, same to same, April 12, 1851.
45. Strachan Papers, Letterbook to the Societies 1839-66, p. 121, J. Strachan to [E. Hawkins?], May 12, 1851, private.
46. Morris Papers, Alex. Mathieson to W. Morris, March 22, 1851.
47. *Ibid.,* Robt. McGill to W. Morris, March 19, 1851, and Hugh Allan to W. Morris, March 19, 1851.
48. *Ibid.,* Hugh Allan to W. Morris, April 5, 1851. Morris recorded his disappointment at this turn of events in his diary (see Letterbook 1837-51).
49. *Globe,* March 23, 1851.
50. Morris Papers, Letterbook 1837-51, W. Morris to Hugh Allan, April 11, 1851.
51. *Ibid.,* May 12, 1851.
52. *Ibid.,* W. Morris to Lord Grey, May 15, 1851.
53. *Ibid.,* memo of interview, May 16, 1851.
54. *Ibid.,* Hugh Allan to W. Morris, June 2 and 9, 1851.
55. *Ibid.,* H. E. Montgomerie to W. Morris, May 28, 1851.
56. Q.U.A., Clergy Reserves Collection, "Observations respecting the Clergy Reserves in Canada."
57. Morris Papers, Letterbook 1837-51, W. Morris to the Duke of Argyll, June 26, 1851, and Duke of Argyll to W. Morris, June 27, 1851.
58. Morris Papers, Hugh Allan to W. Morris, April 28, 1851.
59. *Globe,* May 6, 1851.
60. Guelph *Advertiser,* May 22, 1851.
61. S.P.G. Papers, D 14, pp. 319-21, memorial of John Flood to the S.P.G., July 5, 1851.
62. *Globe,* July 10, 15, and 29, 1851.
63. *Ibid.,* July 15, 1851; *Record,* Aug., 1851; Guelph *Advertiser,* July 17, 1851.
64. *Globe,* July 15, 24, 26, and 29, 1851.
65. *Ibid.,* July 12, 1851, quoting Bowmanville *Messenger,* and July 22, 1851.
66. *Ibid.,* July 22, 1851; *Examiner,* July, 1851, *passim; Report of a Public Discussion at Simcoe, on Wednesday & Thursday, July 16 and 17, 1851 on the Clergy Reserves and Rectories* (Simcoe, 1851).
67. *Globe,* July 19, 1851.
68. *Parliamentary Papers,* 1852, [1448], pp. 9-10; *The Minutes of the Annual Conferences of the Wesleyan Methodist Church in Canada, from 1846 to 1857 inclusive . . .* (2 vols., Toronto, 1846, 1863), II, 158-60.
69. *Christian Guardian,* July 2, 1851.
70. *Journals of the Legislative Assembly of the Province of Canada,* 1851, p. 61 *et sqq.*
71. *Ibid.,* pp. 105, 128-9; *Church,* July 3, 1851; Doughty, *Elgin-Grey Papers,* p. 850.
72. Doughty, *Elgin-Grey Papers,* p. 832.
73. *Ibid.,* pp. 827, 834.
74. *Ibid.,* pp. 827-8.
75. *Ibid.,* pp. 815-6, 819-20, 829.
76. S.P.G. Papers, D 14, p. 341, J. Strachan to E. Hawkins, Aug. 8, 1851.
77. *Ibid.,* p. 336, S. F. Ramsay to E. Hawkins, Aug. 6, 1851.
78. *Globe,* Aug. 19, 1851, see quotations from Paris *Star,* London *Free Press, Bathurst Courier, Huron Signal.*
79. *Ibid.,* Aug. 30, 1851.
80. *Ibid.,* Sept. 16, 1851.
81. *Ibid.,* Nov. 4, 1851; Francis Hincks, *Reminiscences of his Public Life* (Montreal, 1884), pp. 254-8.

82. *Globe,* Aug. 14, Oct. 4, Nov. 4, 1851.

83. *Ibid.,* Oct. 18 and 21, 1851.

84. Doughty, *Elgin-Grey Papers,* pp. 935, 985; cf. *Globe,* Sept. 16, 1851, and Guelph *Advertiser,* Aug. 14, 1851.

85. *Globe,* Dec. 20, 1851.

86. Doughty, *Elgin-Grey Papers,* p. 933.

87. *Parliamentary Papers,* 1852-3, [1588], pp. 16-17; J. C. Dent, *The Last Forty Years* (2 vols., Toronto, 1881), II, 257-61.

88. S.P.G. Papers, D 14, pp. 614-15, J. Strachan to E. Hawkins, March 15, 1852.

89. *Parliamentary Papers,* 1852-3, [1588], pp. 12 *et sqq.*

90. *Ibid.,* p. 16.

91. G 5, Vol. 37, 510-11, Pakington to Elgin, May 21, 1852; see also Appendix VI; Dent, *The Last Forty Years,* II, 261.

92. *Parliamentary Papers,* 1852-3, [1588], p. 13.

93. *Globe,* June 3, 1852.

94. *Parliamentary Papers,* 1852-3, [1588], pp. 5-7.

95. *Globe,* June 24, 1852.

96. Guelph *Advertiser,* March 25, 1852.

97. *Christian Guardian,* Aug. 25, 1852.

98. *Globe,* July 8 and 29, 1852, replying to the Hamilton *Journal & Express.*

99. *Ibid.,* Aug. 5, 1852.

100. *Ibid.,* June 8, 1852, quoting the Hamilton *Spectator.*

101. *Ibid.,* Aug. 5, 1852.

102. *Ibid.,* Aug. 10 and 14, 1852.

103. *Ibid.,* Aug. 28, 1852; Guelph *Advertiser,* Sept. 2, 1852.

104. W. Buckingham and G. Ross, *The Honourable Alexander Mackenzie, His Life and Times* (Toronto, 1892), p. 110.

105. *Globe,* Sept. 2, 1852.

106. Guelph *Advertiser,* Sept. 9, 1852.

107. *News of the Week,* Sept. 11, 1852.

108. *Globe,* Sept. 7, 1852; Guelph *Advertiser,* Sept. 9, 1852.

109. *Globe,* Sept. 14, 1852.

110. *Daily Colonist,* Sept. 22, 1852.

111. Theodore Walrond, *Letters and Journals of James, Eighth Earl of Elgin* (2nd ed., London, 1873), p. 126, Sept., 1852.

112. *Parliamentary Papers,* 1852-3, [1588], pp. 8-9.

113. Strachan Papers, A. N. Bethune to J. Strachan, Oct. 22, 1852.

114. *Ibid.,* Dec. 2, 1852.

115. *Christian Guardian,* Dec. 15, 1852.

116. Strachan Papers, Arthur Palmer to J. Strachan, Nov. 26, 1852.

117. G 5, Vol. 38, pp. 10-11, Pakington to Elgin, Dec. 2, 1852. Both despatches bear the same date. Francis Hincks, *Reminiscences of his Public Life,* pp. 292-4, a draft despatch by Pakington, dated Dec. 16, 1852.

118. Barrie *Herald,* Jan. 5, 1853.

119. Guelph *Advertiser,* Jan. 6, 1853.

120. *Globe,* Jan. 8 and 11, 1853.

121. Strachan Papers, A. N. Bethune to J. Strachan, Jan. 6, 1853.

122. *Parliamentary Papers,* 1852-3, [1588], pp. 14-15, Newcastle to Elgin, Jan. 15, 1853.

123. O.A., Kirby Papers, James FitzGibbon to Wm. Kirby, May 3, 1855.

124. Strachan Papers, A. N. Bethune to J. Strachan, Jan. 21, 1853; A. N. Bethune, *The Clergy Reserve Question* (London, 1853), p. 11 *passim.*

125. Strachan Papers, A. N. Bethune to J. Strachan, Feb. 8, 1853.

126. Clarke Papers, John Rolph to Chas. Clarke, Feb. 4, 1853.

127. *Globe,* Jan. 25, 1853.

128. Barrie *Herald,* Feb. 9, 1853; Kingston *Daily News,* Feb. 8, 1853.

129. Clarke Papers, Geo. B. Thomson to C. Clarke, Feb. 16, 1853.

130. *Globe,* Feb. 17, 1853.

131. Strachan Papers, Petition of the S.P.G. to the House of Commons, n.d.; S.P.G. Papers, D 14, pp. 1023-35, Petition of the Clergy and Laity of the Church of England to the House of Lords, n.d.; *ibid.,* p. 823, J. Strachan to E. Hawkins, April 9, 1853; *Parliamentary Papers,* 1853, 141, Copy of a Letter from the Bishop of Toronto to the Duke of Newcastle (printed as *The Clergy Reserves: A Letter from the Lord Bishop . . . to the Duke of Newcastle . . .* Toronto, 1853).

132. S.P.G. Papers, D 14, p. 817, J. Strachan to E. Hawkins, Feb. 26, 1853.
133. *Ibid.*, p. 819, same to same, March 4, 1853.
134. Morris Papers, H. E. Montgomerie to W. Morris, Feb. 17, 1853.
135. Strachan Papers, A. N. Bethune to J. Strachan, March 11, 1853.
136. *Ibid.*, April 19, 1853.
137. *Ibid.*, May 4, 1853.
138. *Globe*, May 31, 1853, quoting from *British American* and *United Empire*.
139. Streetsville *Weekly Review*, May 28, 1853.
140. Strachan Papers, Letterbook 1854-62, p. 141, J. Strachan to Bishop Skinner, July 5, 1856.
141. *Globe*, June 4, 1853, quoting from *North American; Leader*, June 8, 1853.
142. *Record*, June, 1853; *Globe*, June 4, 1853, quoting from Simcoe *Norfolk Messenger*.
143. Barrie *Herald*, June 8 and 29, 1853.
144. *Globe*, Oct. 3, 1853, quoting from the *Orange Lily*.
145. *Ibid.*, Nov. 10, 1853.
146. *Ibid.*
147. Guelph *Advertiser*, Nov. 17, 1853, quoting from Hamilton *Canadian*. See also *Canada Christian Advocate*, Nov. 9, 1853, quoting from *Western Planet* and Hamilton *Spectator*.
148. *Globe*, Nov. 18, 1853.
149. Barrie *Herald*, Dec. 28, 1853.
150. Guelph *Advertiser*, Dec. 29, 1853; *Canada Christian Advocate*, Nov. 30, 1853.
151. *Canada Christian Advocate*, July 27, 1853, quoting *Examiner; Christian Guardian*, Oct. 5, 1853.
152. Guelph *Advertiser*, Dec. 29, 1853.
153. *Ibid.*, Jan. 27, 1854.
154. *Canada Christian Advocate*, Jan. 18 and 25, 1854.
155. *Ibid.*, Jan. 18, 1854.
156. *Globe*, Feb. 16, 1854.
157. *Protestant Guardian*, Dec. 23, 1853; *Canada Christian Advocate*, March 22, 1854.
158. *Globe*, March 6, 1854, quoting *Examiner; Catholic Citizen*, May 4, 1854.
159. *Globe*, March 6, 1854.
160. Guelph *Advertiser*, March 30, 1854.
161. Clarke Papers, Wm. McDougall to Chas. Clarke, April 4, 1854.
162. *Extracts from the Letters of James, Earl of Elgin, etc., etc., to Mary Louisa, Countess of Elgin, 1847-1862* (London, 1864), p. 6.
163. *Globe*, June 22, 1854.
164. *Ibid.*
165. *Canadian Free Press*, June 29, 1854.
166. *Globe*, June 29, 1854.
167. *Ibid.*, July 20, 1854.
168. *Ibid.*, July 24, 1854.
169. *Ibid.*, July 13, 1854.
170. *Ibid.*, July 24, 1854.
171. *Ibid.*, Aug. 7, 1854.
172. Clarke Papers, Geo. B. Thomson to C. Clarke, Aug. 26, 1854, private.
173. *British Colonist*, Aug. 11, 1854.
174. S.P.G. Papers, D 14, pp. 593-4, J. Strachan to E. Hawkins, Aug. 14, 1854.
175. *Canada Gazette*, extra, Sept. 6, 1854, p. 1.
176. Guelph *Tri-Weekly Advertiser*, Sept. 18, 1854.
177. Francis Hincks, *Documents relating to the Resignation of the Canadian Ministry in September, 1854* (Quebec, 1854), p. 20.
178. Bradford *Chronicle*, Sept. 27, 1854.
179. Guelph *Advertiser*, Sept. 14, 1854.
180. Barrie *Herald*, Sept. 27, 1854.
181. *Globe*, Oct. 18, 1854.
182. O.A., Buell Papers, Alex. Cameron to A. N. Buell, Oct. 30, 1854.
183. *Christian Guardian*, Oct. 25, Nov. 1, 1854.
184. Buell Papers, Alex. Cameron to A. N. Buell, Oct. 30, 1854.
185. *Christian Guardian*, Oct. 25, 1854.
186. Strachan Papers, Letterbook 1852-66, p. 11, J. Strachan to A. N. Bethune, Oct. 31, 1854, private.
187. *Ibid.*, pp. 11-12, J. Strachan to Hon. Geo. Boulton, Nov. 8, 1854.

188. *Ibid.*, p. 12, J. Strachan to A. N. Bethune, Nov. 15, 1854.
189. Dent, *The Last Forty Years*, II, 314.
190. Clarke Papers, Geo. B. Thomson to C. Clarke, Jan. 25, 1855.
191. *Globe*, Feb. 20, 1855.
192. *Canada Christian Advocate*, Feb. 21, 1855.
193. S.P.G. Papers, D 14, p. 1007, J. Strachan to E. Hawkins, Jan. 6, 1855, and enclosure, p. 1011.
194. *Globe*, Jan. 17, 1855.
195. *Ibid.*, Feb. 17, 1855.
196. *North American*, Feb. 14, 1855.
197. *Journals of the Legislative Assembly*, 1854-5, Appendix LL.
198. *Ibid.*, Appendix BBBB.
199. *Globe*, March 14 and 15, 1855.
200. *Ibid.*, March 20, 1855; Guelph *Tri-Weekly Advertiser*, March 19, 26, and 30, April 11 and 20, and May 2, 1855 quoting Brockville *Recorder;* Streetsville *Weekly Review*, June 2, 1855; *Canadian Free Press*, Aug. 16, 1855; *Record*, April, 1855.
201. Guelph *Tri-Weekly Advertiser*, March 19, 1855.
202. *Canadian Free Press*, Aug. 16, 1855.
203. *Canada Christian Advocate*, May 30, 1855.
204. Strachan Papers, Letterbook 1854-62, p. 78, J. Strachan to Francis Hincks, June 22, 1855.
205. *Journals of the Legislative Assembly, 1856*, Appendix 35.
206. Strachan Papers, Letterbook to the Societies 1839-66, pp. 175-6, J. Strachan to E. Hawkins, June 22, 1855.
207. As each new diocese was established in Southern Ontario a portion of the original commuted Clergy Reserves money was granted to the use of its clergy. These funds are generally known as the Clergy Trust Fund, and, augmented by gifts from individuals, the invested capital returned the following rounded sums in interest in 1956: Toronto, $125,400; Huron, $15,700; Ontario, $13,000; Niagara, $7,800; Ottawa, $5,000.
208. *Globe*, Jan. 2 and 3, 1856.
209. Sissons, *Ryerson*, II, 315, n. 1; *British Wesleyan Missionary Notices*, Dec., 1855.
210. *Journals of the Legislative Assembly*, 1858, Appendix 30.
211. *Ibid.*, 1856, Appendix 35; *ibid.*, 1858, Appendix 40.
212. D. G. Creighton, *British North America at Confederation* (*Royal Commission on Dominion-Provincial Relations*; Ottawa, 1939), Appendix No. 2, p. 69.
213. *Globe*, April 16, 1861.
214. G 12, Vol. 67, 20, Head to Labouchere, Jan. 17, 1857.

CHAPTER FOUR

1. *Christian Guardian*, March 27, 1844.
2. *D.H.E.*, I, 221-5; IV, 171, 280.
3. A. N. Bethune, *Memoir of the Right Reverend John Strachan, D.D., LL.D., First Bishop of Toronto* (Toronto, 1870), p. 110.
4. *D.H.E.*, I, 17, 20-3.
5. *Ibid.*, III, 88-9.
6. *Ibid.*, IV, 177; [John Macara], *Origin, History, and Management of King's College, Toronto* (Toronto, 1844), pp. 69-83.
7. Francis Hincks, *Reminiscences of his Public Life* (Montreal, 1884), p. 183.
8. Q.U.A., Morris Papers, F. A. Harper to W. Morris, Dec. 24, 1839.
9. *D.H.E.*, III, 235-8.
10. *Ibid.*, pp. 69, 195, 284 *et sqq*; IV, 93-102; Morris Papers, Robert McGill to W. Morris, July 16, 1840.
11. *D.H.E.*, IV, 57-61.
12. *Ibid.*, p. 25.
13. *Ibid.*, III, 80-1.
14. *Ibid.*, V, 194.
15. Morris Papers, F. A. Harper to W. Morris, May 25, 1842.
16. P.A.C., G 14, Vol. 58, Part I, W. Draper to J. Strachan, June 25, 1842, copy in Strachan's hand.
17. G 5, Vol. 32, 156, Stanley to Bagot, July 23, 1842.

18. Morris Papers, Thos. Liddell to W. Morris, June 1, 1842.
19. *Ibid.*, John Hamilton to W. Morris, Oct. 27, 1842.
20. *D.H.E.*, V, 2 *et sqq.*
21. *Church*, Oct. 13, 1843, *et sqq.*; *Patriot,* Sept. 19, 1843, *et sqq.*
22. *British Colonist*, Aug. 9, 1843, *et sqq.*
23. *Ibid.*, Aug. 19 and 30, Sept. 20, 1843; *Patriot*, Aug. 18, 1843.
24. *British Colonist*, Sept. 2, 1843.
25. J. E. Wells, *Life and Labors of Robert Alex. Fyfe, D.D.* (Toronto, [1885?]), p. 140.
26. *Ibid.*, p. 129.
27. *D.H.E.*, V, 18.
28. *Ibid.*, p. 88.
29. *Ibid.*, pp. 67-87.
30. *Ibid.*, IV, 232-44 *passim.*
31. *Ibid.*, V, 13-17.
32. *Christian Guardian*, Oct. 4, 11, and 18, 1843; *D.H.E.*, V, 21-3.
33. *Christian Guardian*, Nov. 1, 1843; *D.H.E.*, V, 23-5.
34. *D.H.E.*, V, 27-31.
35. *Christian Guardian*, Nov. 22, 1843.
36. *D.H.E.*, V, 32-3.
37. *Ibid.*, pp. 47-59.
38. *Ibid.*, pp. 34 n., 35-47.
39. Macara, *King's College; British Colonist*, Dec. 15, 1843; *Chronicle & Gazette*, Dec. 20, 1843.
40. *Chronicle & Gazette*, Dec. 16, 1843.
41. [Francis Hincks], "A Reformer of 1836," *The Ministerial Crisis: Mr. D. B. Viger and his Position: ... By a Reformer of 1836* (Kingston, 1844), p. 4; *British Colonist*, Dec. 26, 1843.
42. *Proceedings at the First General Meeting of the Reform Association ... Toronto, on Monday, 25 March, 1844* (Toronto, 1844), p. 34.
43. O.A., Hodgins Papers, E. Ryerson to J. Scott, Feb. 26, March 16, 1844, and enclosures; O.A., Strachan Papers, Letterbook 1844-9, pp. 39-40, J. Strachan to Dr. Harris, July 22, 1844.
44. *British Colonist*, March 22, 1844.
45. John Watson, "Thirty Years in the History of Queen's," *Queen's Quarterly*, X (2), Oct., 1902, 191.
46. Strachan Papers, Letterbook 1844-9, pp. 39-40, J. Strachan to Dr. Harris, July 22, 1844.
47. *D.H.E.*, V, 218 *et sqq.*
48. Strachan Papers, Letterbook 1844-9, p. 64, J. Strachan to W. B. Robinson and H. Boulton, Dec. 5 and 6, 1844.
49. *D.H.E.*, V, 170 n.
50. Morris Papers, Isaac Buchanan to W. Morris, March 3, 1845; *ibid.*, H. Scobie to W. Morris, Feb. 19, 1845.
51. *Christian Guardian*, Feb. 19, 1845.
52. Cf. the respective clauses, 73, 80-6, 95, and 22-7, *D.H.E.*, V, 81-5, 162-3. Note that the function of the colleges is not defined by either Baldwin or Draper.
53. *Toronto Periodical Journal*, April, 1845.
54. *Canada Christian Advocate*, March 20, 1845.
55. *Banner*, March 21, 1845.
56. *Church*, Feb. 28, 1845.
57. Strachan Papers, Letterbook 1844-9, pp. 77-8, J. Strachan to Henry Boulton, Feb. 17, 1845.
58. *D.H.E.*, V, 169-70, 191 n.
59. *Church*, March 7, 1845.
60. *Chronicle & Gazette*, March 26, 1845.
61. *D.H.E.*, V, 172, 174. The *Banner* speaks of Colborne's "treachery and disobedience" (March 28, 1845), the *Globe* of the "disgrace" (March 25, 1845).
62. *Globe*, March 25, 1845.
63. O.A., Robinson Papers, J. H. S. Drinkwater to W. B. Robinson, March 20, 1845; Toronto *Herald*, April 3, 1845.
64. Toronto *Herald*, April 3, 1845, citing its agreement with the *Examiner, Pilot,* and *Banner.*
65. *Ibid.*, March 31, 1845.
66. Morris Papers, W. B. Robinson to W. Morris, July 12, 1845.
67. Kingston *Herald*, March 25, 1845; *Globe,* March 25, 1845; *Examiner*, March 19. 1845.

68. *Christian Guardian,* Jan. 28, 1846.
69. *Globe,* Sept. 23, 1845, quoting *Pilot.*
70. *D.H.E.,* VI, 111-12.
71. *Christian Guardian,* Feb. 11, 1846.
72. *Canada Christian Advocate,* Feb. 12, 1846.
73. *Chronicle & Gazette,* Feb. 14, 1846.
74. *D.H.E.,* VI, 80-92, 95-100, 103-6, 109-11.
75. Hodgins Papers, W. H. Draper to E. Ryerson, March 23, 1846.
76. *Ibid.,* Ryerson to Draper, March 30, 1846.
77. *Argus,* March 31, 1846.
78. *Mirror of Parliament of the Province of Canada* (Montreal, 1846), p. 133.
79. *Ibid.,* pp. 166, 196-205.
80. Q.U.A., Queen's University Papers, Thos. Liddell to F. A. Harper, July 13, 1846.
81. *Globe,* May 22, 1847; Sir A. G. Doughty, ed., *Elgin-Grey Papers, 1846-1852* (4 vols., cont. pag., Ottawa, 1937), p. 40.
82. P.A.C., J. A. Macdonald Papers, Vol. 336, J. A. Macdonald to W. Morris, May 9, 1847.
83. *D.H.E.,* VII, 3-7.
84. *Ibid.,* pp. 13-21.
85. *Banner,* July 23, 1847; *Canada Christian Advocate,* July 20, 1847; *Christian Messenger,* Aug., 1847; *Examiner,* July 14, 1847.
86. *Globe,* July 17, 1847.
87. *D.H.E.,* VII, 6-9.
88. D. G. Creighton, *John A. Macdonald, the Young Politician* (Toronto, 1952), p. 123.
89. *Christian Guardian,* July 21, 1847.
90. See *Globe,* July 17, 1847.
91. *D.H.E.,* VII, 2, 40-1.
92. John King, *McCaul : Croft : Forneri* (Toronto, 1914), p. 61.
93. *D.H.E.,* VII, 52; Creighton, *The Young Politician,* p. 121.
94. King, *McCaul : Croft : Forneri,* p. 61.
95. Strachan Papers, Letterbook 1844-9, p. 246, J. Strachan to J. H. Cameron, July 19, 1847.
96. D. G. Creighton, "An Episode in the History of the University of Toronto," *University of Toronto Quarterly,* XVII (3), April, 1948, 245-56.
97. *D.H.E.,* VII, 20.
98. *Ibid.,* pp. 52-4.
99. *Globe,* Nov. 13, 1847.
100. *D.H.E.,* VII, 55-8.
101. *Ibid.,* pp. 59-65.
102. O.A., Baldwin Papers, printed letter to "Electors of the Fourth Riding of York, Toronto, 8 December, 1847."
103. *D.H.E.,* VII, 68-70, 247-58.
104. *Banner,* April 7, 1848, *passim.*
105. *Globe,* Nov. 17, 1847
106. *D.H.E.,* VII, 256-7.
107. *Ibid.,* 248-53.
108. *Christian Guardian,* Dec. 15, 1847.
109. *Chronicle & News,* Dec. 22, 1847.
110. *Banner,* April 7, 1848, *passim.*
111. *D.H.E.,* VII, 257-8.
112. *Globe,* Nov. 15, 1848.
113. *Canada Christian Advocate,* Nov. 28, 1848.
114. Quoted in *Chronicle & News,* Dec. 20, 1848.
115. Cobourg *Star,* Nov. 22, 1848.
116. *D.H.E.,* VIII, 110.
117. *Ibid.,* pp. 114.
118. *Ibid.,* pp. 119-21, 147-66.
119. *Ibid.,* pp. 129, 139; *Canada Christian Advocate,* Nov. 21, 1848, Jan. 2, 1849.
120. *D.H.E.,* VIII, 130-2, 195-6.
121. *Ibid.,* pp. 110-11, 115.
122. *Ibid.,* pp. 134-5.
123. *Ibid.,* pp. 123-7.
124. *Ibid.,* pp. 127-9.
125. *Ibid.,* pp. 185-6.

126. *Church*, May 17, 1849.
127. *Christian Guardian*, April 18, 1849.
128. *Canadian Free Press*, April 24, 1849.
129. *Record*, July, 1848.
130. *Canada Christian Advocate*, May 1, 1849.
131. Strachan Papers, Robert Peel to J. Strachan, Aug. 3, 1849.
132. J. Strachan to Robert Baldwin, April 16, 1850, quoted in R. MacQ. Baldwin, "Private Papers of Robert Baldwin," unpublished M.A. thesis, University of Toronto, 1933, p. 59.
133. G 5, Vol. 36, 528, Grey to Elgin, July 9, 1849.

CHAPTER FIVE

1. *D.H.E.*, VIII, 210-11; P.A.C., G 5, Vol. 37, 7-8, Grey to Elgin, Jan. 7, 1850.
2. *Record*, Sept., 1849, March, 1850.
3. Sir. A. G. Doughty, ed., *Elgin-Grey Papers, 1846-1852* (4 vols., cont. pag., Ottawa, 1937), p. 624.
4. *Record*, March and May, 1850; *Watchman*, April 15, 1850.
5. *Christian Guardian*, Feb. 13, 1850.
6. *D.H.E.*, IX, 53.
7. Doughty, *Elgin-Grey Papers*, p. 727.
8. *D.H.E.*, IX, 146-8, 151-4.
9. *Ibid.*, pp. 146-8.
10. *Ibid.*, pp. 92-5.
11. *Globe*, Feb. 16, 1850.
12. P.A.C., S.P.G. Papers, D 14, p. 62, A. N. Bethune to E. Hawkins, March 11, 1850.
13. *Ibid.*, p. 71, J. Strachan to E. Hawkins, March 25, 1850.
14. Doughty, *Elgin-Grey Papers*, p. 631; see also *Church*, Sept. 12, 1850, quoting Hamilton *Spectator*.
15. *Globe*, March 9, 1850.
16. O.A., Strachan Papers, letters, June 1850, various items.
17. *D.H.E.*, IX, 114.
18. Strachan Papers, J. Strachan to J. B. Robinson, May 24, 1850; *ibid.*, same to same, May 24 and 31, 1850.
19. *D.H.E.*, IX, 95-9.
20. Strachan Papers, J. B. Robinson to J. Strachan, June 21, 1850.
21. *D.H.E.*, IX, 99-102, 118-22; Doughty, *Elgin-Grey Papers*, p. 641.
22. *D.H.E.*, IX, 130-2.
23. *Ibid.*, X, 51-3.
24. *Globe*, Nov. 16, 23, and 26, 1850.
25. *Ibid.*, Jan. 14, 1851.
26. Doughty, *Elgin-Grey Papers*, pp. 714, 726-7, 736; *D.H.E.*, IX, 253-4.
27. P.A.C., G 5, Vol. 37, 249-50, Grey to Elgin, March 11, 1851.
28. *D.H.E.*, IX, 254-6.
29. *Ibid.*, pp. 263-5.
30. *Ibid.*, pp. 248-9.
31. Strachan Papers, Letterbook to the Societies 1839-66, p. 119, J. Strachan to E. Hawkins, March 4, 1851.
32. *D.H.E.*, X, 72-5.
33. *Church*, Jan. 30, 1851; *Christian Guardian*, Jan. 29, 1851.
34. *D.H.E.*, IX, 221, 232-6.
35. *Ibid.*, p. 232, n. 1.
36. *Ibid.*, X, 85-6.
37. *Ibid.*, pp. 80-3; *Christian Guardian*, Sept. 10, 1851.
38. *D.H.E.*, XI, 7, n. 1; *Pastoral Address to the Clergy and Laity of the Diocese of Toronto* (Toronto, 1852); Strachan Papers, abstract of A. N. Bethune's journal of trip to England, June 2, 1852, *passim*.
39. *D.H.E.*, X, 203.
40. S.P.G. Papers, D 14, pp. 613-16, J. Strachan to E. Hawkins, March 15, 1852; *D.H.E.*, X, 204, and n. 2; G 5, Vol. 37, 483-4, Pakington to Elgin, April 2, 1852.
41. Strachan Papers, E. Hawkins to J. Strachan, July 8, 1852, copy.
42. S.P.G. Papers, D 14, p. 743, Geo. Whitaker to E. Hawkins, July 8, 1852.
43. *D.H.E.*, X, 148.

44. *Ibid.*, pp. 203, 240.
45. *Ibid.*, pp. 146-56.
46. *Globe*, Oct. 2 and 7, 1852.
47. *D.H.E.*, X, 157.
48. Strachan Papers, J. B. Robinson to Inspector General, Sept. 7, 1852, draft.
49. C. B. Sissons, *Life and Letters of Egerton Ryerson* (2 vols., Toronto, 1937, 1947), II, 263.
50. *D.H.E.*, X, 158.
51. *Ibid.*, p. 159.
52. *Christian Guardian*, Oct. 27, 1852.
53. *Ibid.*, Oct. 6, 1852.
54. *Examiner*, March 9, 1853.
55. *Globe*, Oct. 2 and 7, 1852.
56. *Record*, Nov., 1852; Guelph *Advertiser*, Oct. 21, 1852.
57. *Globe*, Oct. 23, 1852.
58. *Ibid.*, Oct. 9, 1852.
59. *Ibid.*, Nov. 4, 1852.
60. *D.H.E.*, X, 106.
61. *Ibid.*, pp. 106-8.
62. O.A., Buell Papers, Alex. Cameron to A. N. Buell, March 1, 1853.
63. *Ibid.*, A. N. Buell to Wm. B. Richards, March 11, 1853, draft.
64. *D.H.E.*, X, 129.
65. *Globe*, March 1, 1853.
66. *Ibid.*, March 8, 1853.
67. *Christian Guardian*, March 16, 1853.
68. *Daily Patriot*, March 14, 1853; *United Empire*, March 14, 1853.
69. *D.H.E.*, X, 108-10.
70. *Ibid.*, pp. 117-29, cf. 146-56.
71. O.A., Hodgins Papers, J. G. Hodgins, "The University Question—A Retrospect," MS, [187-?].
72. W. E. Macpherson, *The Ontario Grammar Schools*, Bulletin of the Departments of History and Political and Economic Science in Queen's University, no. 21, Oct., 1916, pp. 13-15.
73. *D.H.E.*, XI, 132-3, 300, 302; XVII, 55-7; L. K. Shook, "The Coming of the Basilians to Assumption College: Early Expansion of St. Michael's College," *Canadian Catholic Historical Association Report, 1951*, pp. 59-73.
74. *Christian Guardian*, May 23, 1855.
75. *Canada Christian Advocate*, April 6, Nov. 9, 1853.
76. Buell Papers, printed circular, Toronto, Nov. 10, 1854, soliciting funds.
77. *D.H.E.*, XIII, 95-8, XI, 301-2.
78. Thomas Webster, *History of the Methodist Episcopal Church* (Hamilton, 1870), pp. 406-8.
79. A. L. McCrimmon, *Educational Policy of the Baptists of Ontario* (Toronto, 1920), p. 2.
80. *Woodstock College Memorial Book* (n.p., 1951), p. 25.
81. *D.H.E.*, XIV, 50-1.
82. *Ibid.*, XVIII, 142-3.
83. W. S. Wallace, *History of the University of Toronto* (Toronto, 1927), p. 72.
84. W. A. Langton, ed., *Early Days in Upper Canada, Letters of John Langton* (Toronto, 1926), pp. 277-97.
85. *D.H.E.*, XV, 173.
86. *Ibid.*, XIV, 205-6.
87. *Christian Guardian*, July 13 and 27, 1859.
88. *Globe*, June 13, 1859.
89. *D.H.E.*, XIV, 208-15.
90. *Ibid.*, pp. 224-5.
91. *Ibid.*, pp. 220-3.
92. Q.U.A., Queen's University Papers, S. Nelles to J. Paton, Sept. 17, 1859.
93. *D.H.E.*, XIV, 225-49.
94. *Ibid*, XV, 32-3.
95. *Record*, March, 1860.
96. *D.H.E.*, XV, 33.
97. *Ibid.*, pp. 27-9.
98. *Ibid.*, p. 26.

99. *Ibid.*, p. 179.
100. *Ibid.*, pp. 203, 206.
101. *Ibid.*, p. 161 *et sqq.*
102. *Ibid.*, pp. 217, 222-3.
103. *Ibid.*, pp. 121-31, 148, *passim.*
104. *Globe*, April 7 and 20, 1860.
105. *D.H.E.*, XV, 167-79.
106. *Ibid.*, p. 313.
107. Francis Hincks, *Reminiscences of his Public Life* (Montreal, 1884), p. 311.
108. *D.H.E.*, XV, 211.
109. *Ibid.*, pp. 103, 216.
110. *Globe*, July 25, 1859.
111. *D.H.E.*, XV, 107.
112. *Ibid.*, XVI, 66-75.
113. *Ibid.*, XV, 306-14.
114. *Ibid.*, XVI, 62.
115. *United Presbyterian Magazine*, April, 1860.
116. *Christian Guardian*, March 28, 1860.
117. Queen's University Papers, John Cook to Jas. Williamson, March 29, 1860.
118. *Christian Guardian*, Nov. 14, 1860.
119. *D.H.E.*, XVI, 42-3.
120. *Ibid.*, pp. 160-9.
121. *Ibid.*, pp. 54-5.
122. *Ibid.*, pp. 239-60.
123. *Christian Guardian*, May 1, 1861.
124. *Record*, April, 1861.
125. *D.H.E.*, XVI 178-80.
126. *Ibid.*, pp. 172, *passim.*
127. Sissons, *Ryerson*, II, 428-9.
128. Q.U.A., Williamson Papers, Jas. Williamson to J. A. Macdonald, April, 1861, draft, unsigned.
129. Sissons, *Ryerson*, II, 430.
130. P.A.C., E 1, State Book W, p. 239.
131. *Christian Guardian*, June 19, 1861.
132. *Ibid.*, June 26, July 3, 1861.
133. *British Herald*, Sept. 4, 1861.
134. Bowmanville *Statesman*, May 8 and 23, 1861.
135. Oshawa *Vindicator*, Aug. 14, 1861.
136. Richmond Hill *York Herald*, June 28, 1861.
137. Bradford *Chronicle*, June 26, 1861.
138. *D.H.E.*, XVI, 227-8.
139. *Ibid.*, pp. 300-3; Sissons, *Ryerson*, II, 431.
140. O.A., Hodgins Papers, J. A. Macdonald to E. Ryerson, Oct. 31, 1861.
141. *D.H.E.*, XVII, 57-75.
142. *Ibid.*, pp. 76-104.
143. *Ibid.*, pp. 154-6.
144. *Ibid.*, pp. 143-4, 150-4.
145. *Ibid.*, pp. 171-2.
146. Mrs. R. P. Hopper, *Old-Time Primitive Methodism in Canada* (Toronto, 1904), p. 251.
147. *D.H.E.*, XVII, 161-70.
148. *Canadian Independent*, Feb., 1863.
149. Bowmanville *Statesman*, Feb. 5, 1863.
150. Richmond Hill *York Herald*, Feb. 13, 1863.
151. Sissons, *Ryerson*, II, 438.
152. *D.H.E.*, XVII, 309.
153. *Ibid.*, pp. 308, 310-16; XVIII, 8, 16-17.

CHAPTER SIX

1. G. W. Spragge, "Elementary Education in Upper Canada, 1820-1840," *Ontario History*, XLIII (3), July, 1951, 107-22.
2. *D.H.E.*, III, 128-9.
3. *Ibid.*, IV, 4.

4. *Ibid.*, pp. 4-6.
5. *Ibid.*, p. 32.
6. *Ibid.*, p. 15.
7. *Ibid.*, pp. 20, 22.
8. John Strachan, *A Charge delivered to the Clergy of the Diocese of Toronto at the Primary Visitation, held in the Cathedral Church of St. James, Toronto, on the 9th September, 1841* (Toronto, 1841), p. 25 *et sqq.*
9. *D.H.E.*, IV, 35.
10. J. G. Hodgins, *Legislation and History of Separate Schools in Upper Canada, 1841-1876* (Toronto, 1897), p. 22.
11. *D.H.E.*, IV, 48-55.
12. H. C. McKeown, *The Life and Labors of Most Rev. John Joseph Lynch, D.D., Cong. Miss., First Archbishop of Toronto* (Montreal and Toronto, 1886), p. 287.
13. *British Colonist*, March 2, 1842.
14. *Catholic*, March 9, 1842.
15. *D.H.E.*, IV, 232-3.
16. *Ibid.*, p. 52.
17. *Ibid.*, p. 240.
18. Francis Hincks, *Reminiscences of his Public Life* (Montreal, 1884), pp. 175-7.
19. *Ibid.*, p. 176.
20. *D.H.E.*, IV, 242.
21. *Ibid.*, V, 111-13.
22. *Ibid.*, pp. 116-18.
23. C. B. Sissons, *Life and Letters of Egerton Ryerson* (2 vols., Toronto, 1937, 1947), II, 56.
24. O.A., Hodgins Papers, E. Ryerson to J. Scott, March 16, 1844.
25. Egerton Ryerson, *The Story of My Life*, J. George Hodgins, ed., (Toronto, 1883), xi.
26. *D.H.E.*, VI, 72-3.
27. *Ibid.*, pp. 151, 147.
28. *Ibid.*, p. 158.
29. *Mirror of Parliament of the Province of Canada* (Montreal, 1846), p. 87.
30. Hodgins, *Separate Schools*, pp. 27-8.
31. Hodgins Papers, E. Ryerson to W. H. Draper, April 30, 1846.
32. *Ibid.*, W. H. Draper to E. Ryerson, May 4, 1846.
33. *Ibid.*, E. Ryerson to W. H. Draper, May 14, 1846.
34. Hodgins, *Separate Schools*, p. 29.
35. *D.H.E.*, XII, 29, cf. wording in Hodgins, *Separate Schools*, p. 30.
36. Hodgins, *Separate Schools*, p. 30.
37. *Ibid.*
38. *D.H.E.*, VI, 237-8.
39. Hodgins, *Separate Schools*, p. 31.
40. Sissons, *Ryerson*, II, 113.
41. Hodgins, *Separate Schools*, p. 31.
42. Hodgins Papers, W. H. Draper to E. Ryerson, Jan. 1, 1847.
43. *D.H.E.*, VII, 165.
44. *Ibid.*, p. 164.
45. *Ibid.*, p. 188.
46. *Ibid.*, p. 27.
47. Hodgins, *Separate Schools*, p. 44.
48. *D.H.E.*, V, 158.
49. *Ibid.*, VII, 15.
50. Hodgins Papers, E. Ryerson to W. H. Draper, March 29, 1847.
51. *D.H.E.*, VII, 178.
52. Strachan Papers, Letterbook 1844-9, p. 242, J. Strachan to [?], June 29, 1847.
53. *D.H.E.*, VIII, 86 *et sqq.*
54. *Ibid.*, p. 142.
55. *Ibid.*, pp. 224-5.
56. Sissons, *Ryerson*, II, 180.
57. *Ibid.*, pp. 180-6; *D.H.E.*, VIII, 230-47.
58. Sissons, *Ryerson*, II, 185.
59. *D.H.E.*, VIII, 225.
60. *Report of the Ontario Royal Commission on Education* (Toronto, 1950), p. 834.
61. *D.H.E.*, IX, 11.

62. *Ibid.*, p. 38.
63. *Ibid.*, p. 25.
64. *Globe*, July 9, 1850.
65. *Watchman*, July 15, 1850.
66. *D.H.E.*, IX, 208.
67. Sissons, *Ryerson*, II, 205.
68. *D.H.E.*, IX, 240.
69. Sissons, *Ryerson*, II, 220.
70. John Strachan, *A Letter to the Right Hon. Lord John Russell, on the present State of the Church in Canada* (Toronto, 1851), p. 16.
71. Sir A. G. Doughty, ed., *The Elgin-Grey Papers, 1846-1852* (4 vols., cont. pag., Ottawa, 1937), pp. 848-50.
72. *D.H.E.*, X, 91-2.
73. *Ibid.*, pp. 6-9.
74. Doughty, *Elgin-Grey Papers*, p. 834.
75. *D.H.E.*, IX, 228, 221, 243.
76. *Ibid.*, pp. 229-30; *ibid.*, X, 93, 96.
77. *Globe*, June 24, 1851.
78. *D.H.E.*, IX, 240, 250.
79. Hodgins Papers, E. Ryerson to F. Hincks and John Ross, Aug. 1, 1851, draft. In *D.H.E.*, X, 90-1, Hodgins has erroneously addressed this letter to Dr. John Rolph who was not even in Parliament at this time.
80. *D.H.E.*, IX, 237-41.
81. *Ibid.*, p. 240, n. 1.
82. Guelph *Advertiser*, Nov. 20 and 27, 1851.
83. *Globe*, Oct. 9, 1851.
84. *Ibid.*, Dec. 11, 1851.
85. PAC, microfilm A 212, S.P.G., "C" MSS, Box V/44, J. Strachan to E. Hawkins, Dec. 1, 1847.
86. *D.H.E.*, XIII, 269.

CHAPTER SEVEN

1. *Copies of Correspondence between the Roman Catholic Bishop of Toronto and the Chief Superintendent of Schools on the Subject of Separate Common Schools, in Upper Canada* ... (Toronto, 1853), p. 7.
2. *Ibid.*
3. *Ibid.*, p. 10.
4. *Ibid.*, p. 12.
5. *Ibid.*, p. 15.
6. *Ibid.*, p. 26.
7. *Ibid.*, p. 27.
8. *D.H.E.*, X, 270.
9. *Ibid.*, p. 272.
10. *Ibid.*, p. 162. This document has been badly mutilated by Hodgins in the process of editing. Cf. *Copies of Correspondence between the Chief Superintendent of Schools for Upper Canada, and other Persons, On the Subject of Separate Schools* (Toronto, 1855), pp. 20-1.
11. *D.H.E.*, X, 163. A decade after Confederation permissive legislation allowed Roman Catholic separate school boards to use municipal machinery to collect separate school taxes.
12. H. C. McKeown, *The Life and Labors of Most Rev. John Joseph Lynch, D.D., Cong. Miss., First Archbishop of Toronto* (Montreal and Toronto, 1886), pp. 292-3, n.
13. *Ibid.*, p. 292 n.
14. *Ibid.*, p. 293 n.
15. *D.H.E.*, X, 100-17.
16. *Ibid.*, p. 171 *et sqq.*
17. *Globe*, March 31, 1853.
18. *D.H.E.*, X, 111.
19. *Leader*, June 7, 1853.
20. Francis Hincks, *Reminiscences of his Public Life* (Montreal, 1884), p. 312.
21. *Globe*, April 2 and 5, 1853; Hincks, *Reminiscences*, p. 312.
22. *D.H.E.*, XI, 79.
23. *Ibid.*, X, 295.

24. *Ibid.,* p. 296.
25. *Ibid.,* p. 300.
26. [John Strachan], *Triennial Visitation of the Lord Bishop of Toronto and Proceedings of the Church Synod of the Diocese of Toronto: October 12 & 13, 1853* (Toronto, 1853), pp. 12-13.
27. *Christian Guardian,* Oct. 26, 1853; see also *D.H.E.,* XI, 90.
28. *Report of the Ontario Royal Commission on Education* (Toronto, 1950), p. 854.
29. McKeown, *Lynch,* pp. 293-4 n.
30. *Copies of Correspondence between the Chief Superintendent of Schools for Upper Canada, and other Persons . . . ,* pp. 55-77.
31. *Ibid.,* pp. 55-231.
32. *Christian Guardian,* May 10, 1854; *Mirror,* May 5, 1854.
33. *Christian Guardian,* May 17, 1854.
34. *D.H.E.,* XI, 109.
35. *Dr. Ryerson's Letters in reply to the Attacks of the Hon. George Brown, M.P.P.* (Toronto, 1859), p. 34.
36. J. G. Hodgins, *Legislation and History of Separate Schools in Upper Canada, 1841-1876* (Toronto, 1897), p. 77.
37. *Ibid.*
38. *Dr. Ryerson's Letters in reply to . . . George Brown,* p. 32.
39. *D.H.E.,* XII, 9-10.
40. *Ibid.,* p. 15.
41. *Ibid.,* p. 8.
42. *Ibid.*
43. C. B. Sissons, *Life and Letters of Egerton Ryerson* (2 vols., Toronto, 1937, 1947), II, 280.
44. *D.H.E.,* XII, 36.
45. McKeown, *Lynch,* p. 296 and n; *D.H.E.,* XII, 16-19.
46. *D.H.E.,* XII, 37.
47. *Ibid.*
48. *Ibid.,* pp. 19-34.
49. *Ibid.,* p. 32.
50. *Ibid.,* p. 38 *et sqq.*
51. *Ibid.,* XIII, 252, 269.
52. Guelph *Tri-Weekly Advertiser,* June 20, 1855.
53. *Echo,* June 29, 1855.
54. *D.H.E.,* XII, 40.
55. Letter of Bishop de Charbonnel to Vicar General Cazeau, printed in Markham *Economist,* July 24, 1856.
56. *D.H.E.,* XII, 42-3.
57. *Mirror,* Aug. 24, 1855.
58. *News of the Week,* Feb. 2, 1856.
59. *Ibid.,* March 8, 1856, copied from *British Colonist.*
60. *Dr. Ryerson's Letters in reply to . . . George Brown,* p. 36.
61. O.A., Strachan Papers, Letterbook 1854-62, p. 124, J. Strachan to J. H. Cameron, March 10, 1856.
62. *Echo,* March 7, 1856.
63. *D.H.E.,* XII, 239 *et seq.*
64. *News of the Week,* May 10, 1856.
65. *Mirror,* June 20, 1856.
66. *Christian Guardian,* July 16, 1856. Cf. *Dr. Ryerson's Letters in reply to . . . George Brown,* p. 36.
67. *Echo,* July 25, 1856.
68. *Christian Guardian,* July 16, 1856.
69. *News of the Week,* July 11, 1856.
70. Markham *Economist,* July 3 and 17, 1856.
71. *D.H.E.,* XII, 318; XIII, 31; see comments of the Guelph *Advertiser,* June 26, 1856.
72. *D.H.E.,* XIII, 25-8.
73. *Ibid.,* XII, 334-6; XIII, 1.
74. *Catholic Citizen,* March 26, 1857.
75. W. A. Langton, ed., *Early Days in Upper Canada, Letters of John Langton* (Toronto, 1926), p. 271.

76. *D.H.E.*, XIII, 164.
77. *Ibid.*, p. 192.
78. *Daily Colonist*, Jan. 19, 1858.
79. Prince Albert *Ontario Observer*, Dec. 18, 1857.
80. *Mirror*, April 23, 1858.
81. *Ibid.*, Jan. 22, 1858.
82. *D.H.E.*, XIII, 251-7.
83. O.A., Hodgins Papers, J. A. Macdonald to E. Ryerson, April 28, 1858.
84. *D.H.E.*, XIII, 267-73.
85. Sissons, *Ryerson*, II, 352.
86. McKeown, *Lynch*, p. 303. This is the only authority for the whole statement.
87. *Globe*, Dec. 8, 1858; Alex. Mackenzie, *The Life and Speeches of Hon. George Brown* (Toronto, 1882), p. 35.
88. *Canadian Freeman*, July 16, 1858.
89. C. R. W. Biggar, *Sir Oliver Mowat* (2 vols., Toronto, 1905), I, 89.
90. Markham *Economist*, Aug. 12, 1858.
91. *Dr. Ryerson's Letters in reply to . . . George Brown*, p. 61.
92. *Ibid.*, p. 12.
93. *Globe*, Dec. 8, 1858.
94. M. W. Applegate, "The Hamilton *Spectator* in the Decade prior to Confederation," unpublished M.A. thesis, University of Toronto, 1950, pp. 166-70.
95. Bowmanville *Statesman*, Sept. 8, 1859, quoting *True Witness*.
96. This remark is sufficiently substantiated by later events. At that moment, indeed, the Free Church Synod, Congregational Union, Wesleyan Methodist Conference, and the evangelically minded Synod of the Diocese of Huron were severally expressing their approval of the national school system, and its provisions for religious instruction. (*D.H.E.*, XIV, 268-9.)
97. *D.H.E.*, XV, 24-6.
98. P.A.C., Scott Papers, IV, 1651-4, E. J. Horan to R. W. Scott, April 13, 1860.
99. *Ibid.*, pp. 1600-3, J. Farrell to R. W. Scott, April 15, 1860.
100. Sissons, *Ryerson*, II, 450-1.
101. *News of the Week*, April 5, June 28, 1860.
102. *Canadian Freeman*, Nov. 4, 1859.
103. Sissons, *Ryerson*, II, 452.
104. Toronto *Orange Herald*, Nov. 28, 1860.
105. Hodgins Papers, E. Ryerson to A. Morrison, M. P. P., Nov. 21, 1860.
106. *Canadian Freeman*, Dec. 6, 1860.
107. *D.H.E.*, XVI, 169-72, 183. Hodgins wrongly infers that this was the same Bill as in 1860 (*D.H.E.*, XVII, 1).
108. Scott Papers, V, 1748-51, Angus Macdonell, Administrator of Kingston Diocese, to R. W. Scott, April 24, 1861.
109. *D.H.E.*, XVII, 4-5.
110. *Ibid.*, p. 192 *et sqq.*
111. *Ibid.*, pp. 194, 196.
112. Scott Papers, IV, 1655-8, E. J. Horan to R. W. Scott, April 4, 1862.
113. *D.H.E.*, XVII, 217.
114. Sissons, *Ryerson*, II, 465.
115. *D.H.E.*, XVII, 198, 214.
116. *Ibid.*, p. 214.
117. *Ibid.*, pp. 194-5.
118. O.A., Colquhoun Papers, S. Ault to [Wm. Colquhoun?], May 2, 1862.
119. Sissons, *Ryerson*, II, 466.
120. Uxbridge *North Ontario Advocate*, May 8, 1862.
121. *Christian Guardian*, May 14, 1862; Stratford *Examiner*, May 15, 1862.
122. Richmond Hill *York Herald*, May 23, 1862.
123. *D.H.E.*, XVII, 175-80, 183-92.
124. Richmond Hill *York Herald*, July 11 and 25, 1862; Uxbridge *North Ontario Advocate*, July 10, 1862; *Canadian Independent*, Aug., 1862.
125. *Canadian Independent*, Aug., 1862.
126. *Canadian Freeman*, June 5, 1862.
127. *D.H.E.*, XVII, 44. Hodgins names George Brown as a member, but Brown was not in Parliament then (Mackenzie, *Brown*, p. 80).
128. *D.H.E.*, XVII, 219.

129.   *Canadian Freeman,* Feb. 12, 1863; Richmond Hill *York Herald,* March 13, 1863; *Globe,* March 16, 1863.

130.   Barrie *South Simcoe Times,* July 17, 1862; *Christian Guardian,* July 2, 1862.

131.   Richmond Hill *York Herald,* March 6, 1863; *Watchman,* March 13, 1863; Durham *Standard,* March 27, 1863; *Globe,* April 13 and 15, 1863; *D.H.E.,* XVII, 281. Hodgins has taken extensive liberties with Ryerson's correspondence of this period; cf. Sissons, *Ryerson,* II, 477 *et sqq.*

132.   Sissons, *Ryerson,* II, 481.

133.   *Globe,* March 6 and 16, 1863.

134.   Bowmanville *Statesman,* March 12, 1863.

135.   Barrie *Spirit of the Age,* March 25, 1863; *Canadian Independent,* April, 1863.

136.   Bowmanville *Statesman,* March 12 and April 2, 1863.

137.   *Watchman,* March 13, 1863; Prince Albert *Ontario Observer,* April 16, 1863; Cobourg *Sentinel,* April 18, 1863.

138.   *D.H.E.,* XVII, 273-4.

139.   Scott Papers, III, 1033, telegram, J. Lynch to R. W. Scott, May 6, 1863, copy.

140.   *Globe,* March 9, 1863.

141.   *Ibid.,* March 20, 1863.

142.   *Ibid.,* March 21, 1863.

143.   *Canadian Freeman,* March 19, 1863.

144.   *Canadian Freeman,* April 9, 1863; *Watchman,* April 17, 1863. Statistics of attendance ranged from 4,000 to 10,000; cf. Bowmanville *Statesman,* May 21, 1863, and *Canadian Freeman,* May 14, 1863.

145.   Cobourg *Sentinel,* June 27, 1863.

146.   Scott Papers, IV, 1452, R. W. Scott to J. A. Macdonald, June 12, 1863, copy.

147.   *Ibid.,* p. 1454a, same to same, June 27, 1863, copy.

148.   *D.H.E.,* XVIII, 198.

149.   *Ibid.,* p. 247.

150.   *Canadian Freeman,* Jan. 5, 1865.

151.   *D. H. E.,* XVIII, 247-9, 304, 311-16.

152.   *Ibid.,* XIX, 7.

153.   *Ibid.,* XVIII, 305-16.

154.   *Ibid.,* p. 308.

155.   *Ibid.,* pp. 308, 310, 314, 316.

156.   *Ibid.,* p. 316.

157.   *Parliamentary Debates on the Subject of the Confederation of the British North American Provinces* (Quebec, 1865), pp. 18, 95.

158.   *Ibid.,* pp. 144, 177, 335, 420, 490, 666, 1025-7.

159.   *D.H.E.,* XIX, 211, see above n. 11.

160.   *Ibid.,* pp. 278-9.

161.   St. Catharines *Constitutional,* Aug. 9, 1866.

162.   Bowmanville *Statesman,* Aug. 9, 1866.

163.   Markham *Economist,* Aug. 9, 1866.

164.   Bowmanville *Statesman,* Aug. 9, 1866; Prince Albert *Ontario Observer,* Aug. 9, 1866.

165.   St. Catharines *Constitutional,* Aug. 9, 1866.

166.   *Canadian Freeman,* Aug. 9, 1866.

167.   O. D. Skelton, *The Life and Times of Sir Alexander Tilloch Galt* (Toronto, 1920), p. 404.

168.   Sarnia *Observer,* Aug. 10, 1866.

169.   *Report of the Ontario Royal Commission on Education* (Toronto, 1950), p. 803.

INDEX

ABERDEEN, GEORGE HAMILTON GORDON, fourth Earl of, 69, 70
Adamson, W. Agar, 54
Albert College, 117
Alder, Robert, 31, 40
Allan, Hugh, 59
Ambery, John, 121
Annexation movement, 16, 52, 102, 106, 141
Anti-Clergy Reserves Association, 12, 54, 55, 61, 72, 73, 77, 78
Anti-State Church Association. See Anti-Clergy Reserves Association
Argyll, George Douglas Campbell, eighth Duke of, 59, 60, 70
Arthur, Sir George, 28, 48; and Clergy Reserves, 29, 30, 31, 32, 40
Assumption College, 116

BAGOT, SIR CHARLES, 14, 15, 42, 43, 85
Baldwin, Robert, xiv, 48, 62, 63, 64, 74, 110, 141, 153; and Clergy Reserves, 36, 47-8, 53, 55; his University Bill, 1843, 15, 85-90, 91-3, 99, 100; his University Act, 1849, 102-5, 106-7, 111-15 passim, 122, 142; his University Act, 1850, 107; and University question, 93, 97-114; and elementary education, 134, 135, 145, 169. See also Baldwin-Lafontaine ministry, 1842-3; Great Ministry, 1848-51
Baldwin-Lafontaine ministry, 1842-3, 15, 89, 133, 134, 135; 1848-51, see Great Ministry, 1848-51
Banner, 8, 10, 49
Banner of Faith, 12
Baptist Church, 11, 12, 25, 54, 61, 185; and voluntarism, xiii, 11, 30, 49; and Clergy Reserves, 45, 49; and University question, 88, 92, 95, 97, 100, 102, 104, 116, 117, 119; and elementary education, 169
Basilians, 116
Bayne, John, 6
Beatty, John, 125
Beaven, James, 102
Beecham, John, 80
Bell, Robert, 178-9
Bethune, Alexander Neil, 4-5, 77; and Clergy Reserves, 31, 54, 56, 67, 68, 69, 70; and University question, 90, 108
Bible Christian Church, 9, 104, 187
Bidwell, Marshall Spring, 48
Bishop's College, 108
Blake, Dominic Edward, 58
Blake, Edward, 127
Blaquière, Peter Boyle De, 24, 42, 109, 120, 131

Board of Education. See Council of Public Instruction
Bolster, Sarah, 18, 22
Boulton, George Strange, 64, 77
Boulton, William Henry, 47, 67, 91, 92, 93, 96, 98, 103, 110-11, 113, 136-7, 141
Bowes, John George, 162-5, 166
British American League, 52
British Colonist, 8
British North America Act, 1867: and separate schools, xv, 178, 181
Brown, George, 22-5 passim, 53, 59, 60, 61, 63, 64, 71, 73, 74, 75, 76, 124, 179, 190-1; influence in Free Church, 7, 49; and Protestantism, 17, 18, 20, 21, 60, 75, 117, 144-5, 164, 169; and Orange Order, 17, 21, 23; relations with Clear Grits, 17, 60, 66, 67; relations with Reform party, 17, 60, 62, 64, 67, 74, 112, 115, 153; and Clergy Reserves, 66-79; and University question, 114, 115, 120, 121, 168; and elementary education, 135, 144, 146-8, 154-6, 160-9, 172, 177, 179. See also Brown-Dorion ministry, 1858
Brown, Peter, 7, 8, 49
Brown-Dorion ministry, 1858, 22, 167
Bruyere, J. M., 143, 165, 167
Buchanan, Isaac, 7, 90, 91
Buell, Andrew N., 114
Burns, Robert, 54, 55, 61, 95, 100, 101, 137
Burwell, Leonidas, 174
Bytown College, 85, 103, 116, 118, 142

CAMERON, JOHN HILLYARD, 55, 64, 77, 80, 163, 165; on Corrigan's murder, 19; and Orange Order, 20, 22, 23; and University question, 93, 98
Cameron, Malcolm, 17, 54, 56, 63, 67, 72-3, 120, 122, 141-2, 147
Canada Baptist Magazine and Missionary Register, 11
Canada Christian Advocate, 10
Canadian Baptist, 11
Canadian Church Press, 5
Canadian Churchman, 5
Canadian Freeman, 13
Canadian Independent, 12
Canadian Literary Institute. See Woodstock College
Canterbury, archbishop of. See Howley, William
Carlisle, George William Frederick Howard, seventh Earl of, 108
Caron, René Eduard, 101
Cartier, Sir George Etienne, 164. See also

Macdonald (J.A.)-Cartier ministry, 1857-62

Casual and Territorial Revenues, 34, 38

Cathcart, Charles Murray Cathcart, second Earl of, 46, 95, 96

Catholic, 13

Catholic Citizen, 13

Cauchon, Joseph, 78, 114, 164

Cayley, William, 76, 94, 96, 120, 122

Cazeau, Charles Félix, 156, 159, 161, 173, 177

Census, religious, 1839, 38-9, 45

Central Committee at Toronto for Promoting University Reform, 100

Chalmers, Thomas, 6, 32

Charbonnel, Armand François Marie de, 17, 112, 116, 138, 144, 145; and separate schools, 146-8, 150-3, 155-69, 172, 179, 181

Chiniquy, Charles Paschal Télesphore, 22

Christian Brothers, Order of, 133

Christian Guardian, 9, 10, 14; and Metcalfe crisis, 9, 10; and Clergy Reserves, 54, 57, 72; and University question, 99

Christian Journal, 10

Christian Luminary, 12

Christian Messenger (Baptist), 11

Christian Messenger (New Connexion Methodist), 10

Christian Offering, 12

Christians (denomination), 12

Christie, David, 73

Church, 5, 14, 15

Church-state relations in Canada West: historiography of, 3; divisive effect on denominations, 8, 10, 26; as political issue, 17, 26

Church-statism, xi, xiii, 16, 27, 64, 78. *See also* Establishment

Clarke, Charles, 53, 70, 73

Clear Grits, 62, 63, 68, 73, 75, 79, 114, 162, 190; relations with Reform party, xiv, 17, 53, 63, 64, 110, 112, 141, 153, 157; policies, 53, 66; and Clergy Reserves, 53-6, 60, 62, 63, 70; relations with George Brown, 60, 66, 67; and elementary education, 147, 154, 162, 163, 166, 167, 168, 169, 174

Clergy Reserves, xiii, xiv, xv, 4-18 *passim*, 27-81, 102, 110, 112, 113, 120, 124, 126, 130, 140-50 *passim*, 157, 163, 164, 188, 190-1; and establishment, xiii, 27, 29; Act, 1840, xiii, 15, 37-41, 51-68, 74, 91; Act, 1854, xiv, 76-81; Bill, 1840, 14, 33-7; extent and value, 27, 28, 42-7 *passim*, 50, 80, 91; religious purpose of, 27, 30, 58, 59, 65; and Rebellion of 1837, 28, 29; application to education, 30, 35, 53, 55, 57, 61, 62, 73, 77, 83-4; Bill, 1839, 30-2; denominational division of, 33, 37, 44-7, 65-6, 73, 77; Fund, 34, 37-8, 44, 48-9, 51, 68, 74-80, 88, 95, 143, 188; movement for secularization of, 52-76; Price's resolutions

on, 55-6; Act, 1853, 57, 62-79; and commutation, 76-81

Colborne, Sir John, first Baron Seaton, 35, 69, 93, 190, 191

Colonist, 14

Common schools, 17, 129-80; Act, 1853, 70, 154-5, 171; Bill, 1839, 130; Act, 1841, 130-4, 140, 155; Acts, 1843, 133, 136, 137, 140; Act, 1846, 136-40, 147; Act, 1847, 139, 140, 144; Act, 1849, 141-2, 147; Act, 1850, 142-8, 153, 154, 171; Act, 1851, 147; Fund, 152-8 *passim*, 178

Congregational Church, 11-12, 52, 54, 61, 137, 185; support for voluntarism, xii, 30; and Clergy Reserves, 49, 61; and University question, 87, 92-104 *passim*, 113, 116, 123, 124, 125; and elementary education, 169

Congregational College, 117, 123

Connor, George Skeffington, 128

Conservative party. *See* Tory party; Liberal-Conservative party

Constitutional Act, 1791, 27, 29

Cook, John, 119, 122, 123

Corrigan, Robert, 18-19, 162, 164

Council of Public Instruction, 137, 145, 161, 165, 176, 178

Croft, Henry Holmes, 88

Cronyn, Benjamin, 4, 61, 123

Crooks, Adam, 127-8

Crooks, James, 30, 39

Crown Lands Department: and management of Clergy Reserves, 43, 46

DALY, SIR DOMINICK, 139. *See also* Sherwood-Daly ministry, 1847

Day, Charles Dewey, 131, 132-4, 155

Denominationalism: conflict with nationalism, xiii, xiv, 16, 26, 74, 81, 115, 127, 128, 181; growth of, xiv; and Clergy Reserves, 28, 51; and University question, 91, 94, 95, 100, 102, 104-5; and elementary education, 129, 130, 135-6, 141, 146, 153, 167-8, 174, 180, 181. *See also* Separate schools

Derby, Edward George Geoffrey Smith Stanley, fourteenth Earl of, 14, 15-16, 42, 43, 44, 59, 64, 70, 71; his first cabinet, 64, 66, 67, 68

Disciples of Christ, 12

Donlevy, Charles, 163

Dorion, Antoine Aimé, 167. *See also* Brown-Dorion ministry, 1858

Double majority principle, 72, 174

Draper, William Henry, 14, 35, 47, 48, 96, 139; and University question, 85, 87, 89-90, 101; his University Bills, 91-4, 95, 96, 104; and elementary education, 137, 138. *See also* Draper ministry, 1844-7

Draper ministry, 1844-7, 45-8, 93-4

Drummond, Lewis Thomas, 164

Durham, John George Lambton, first Earl of,

14, 181; *Report on British North America,* xii, 14, 32; and Clergy Reserves, 28, 32
Duval, Jean François Joseph, 18, 19, 162

Ecclesiastical and Missionary Record, 8
Ecclesiastical corporations, 6, 24-5, 45, 64
Ecclesiastical Gazette, 5
Echo and Protestant Episcopal Recorder, 5
Education: and church-statism, xiii, 13, 26; elementary, xiii, xiv-xv, 112, 129-81; and religious instruction, xiv, 129-32, 135-6, 138-9, 140-50 *passim,* 165; Commission, 1839, 130; and Irish school system, 133, 139, 145, 167. *See also* Common schools; Separate schools; Grammar schools; University question
Elgin, James Bruce, eighth Earl of, 16, 50, 52, 62-78 *passim,* 100, 101, 104, 159; and Clergy Reserves, 54-5, 56, 57, 67, 68, 72, 73, 75; and University question, 96, 106, 107, 108-12; and elementary education, 142, 145, 146
Elmsley, John, 152, 170, 171
England, Church of, xi, xii, 3-5, 9, 12, 14-33 *passim,* 37, 42, 47, 50, 65, 73, 107, 135, 137, 164, 185, 190-1; and establishment, xii, xiii, 4, 14, 15, 27, 34, 38, 41, 67, 103; and Anglican separate schools, xiv, 58, 131-2, 133-7, 139, 140, 143, 148, 159, 161, 164, 165, 168, 172-3; government of, 4-5, 24, 58, 60, 80; and Clergy Reserves, 4, 5, 24-80; and University question, 16, 58, 83-128; Temporalities Act, 24; and elementary education, 130, 135, 156, 169, 180. *See also* Low Churchism; High Churchism; Puseyism; King's College; Trinity College
 Huron diocese, 4, 79, 173
 Montreal diocese, 29
 Ontario diocese, 4-5
 Quebec diocese, 45
 Toronto diocese, 4-5, 125, 127, 172; Church Society, 24, 42, 44, 45, 47, 65, 81, 190; Theological College, 107
Ermatinger, Edward, 109
Establishment, xi, xii, xiii, 13, 26, 180, 181
Evangelist, 10
Evangelical Alliance, 9
Evangelical Pioneer, 11
Examiner, 10

FARRELL, JOHN, 20, 21
Farrell, John, first Roman Catholic bishop of Hamilton, 168-9
Felton, William Locker, 163, 164, 166
Fenianism, 23-4, 170
Ferguson, Thomas R., 167, 174
Fergusson, Adam, 115
Ferrier, Andrew, 52
FitzGibbon, James, 69
Flint, Billa, 50
Foley, Michael Hamilton, 120, 173

Free Church, 7-8, 22, 54, 90, 137, 185, 186; and voluntarism, 7, 52, 62; and Clergy Reserves, 42, 49, 56, 69; and University question, 92, 95, 97, 100, 101, 102, 104, 106, 113, 116, 119, 120, 123, 124, 125, 127; and elementary education, 164, 165
Fulford, Francis, 56, 58, 65
Fuller, Thomas Brock, 125, 127
Fyfe, Robert Alexander, 87, 100, 117, 124, 127

GALE, THOMAS, 44
Galt, Sir Alexander Tilloch, 75, 178, 179
Gamble, John William, 160
Gavazzi, Alessandro, 17, 18, 22; and riots in Quebec and Montreal, 17-18, 71, 156
General election, 1847: and Reform party policy, xiv; and Clergy Reserves, 48; and University question, 99-101, 125
Gladstone, William Ewart, 38, 46-7, 58, 59, 68, 71
Glenelg, Charles Grant, Baron, 29, 30
Glenmorris, Ont.: political meeting at, 69, 70
Globe, 10, 17, 78
Good Templar, 25
Gowan, Ogle Robert, 47, 137, 174
Grammar schools, 83, 93, 97, 116, 121
Grasett, Henry James, 137, 190, 191
Great Ministry, 1848-51, 16, 48-63, 141, 142, 190; an historical epoch, xiii, 13, 181; and Clergy Reserves, xiv, 50, 51; and University question, xiv, 101-4, 128
Grey, Henry George, third Earl, 58; and Clergy Reserves, 54-64 *passim;* and University question, 108-10
Guelph, Ont.: Orange riot near, 19; Reform dinner at, 52
Gwynne, William Charles, 88

HAGERMAN, CHRISTOPHER ALEXANDER, 96
Hall, George Barker, 96
Halton county, Ont.: crucial by-election in, 53
Hamilton, John, 85, 86, 87
Hamilton College, 116
Harper, Francis A., 85, 86
Harrison, Samuel Bealey, 137
Hartman, Joseph, 73, 160
Hawkins, Edward, 58, 64, 70, 110, 112
Head, Sir Edmund, 81, 166; and Orange Order, 19-20, 21
Head, Sir Francis Bond, 28, 29, 30, 48, 62
High Churchism, 4, 60, 90, 92, 96, 97, 106, 147, 153, 160, 164, 169, 172-3, 180
Hincks, Sir Francis, xiv, 4, 17, 36-7, 43, 53-74 *passim,* 141, 153, 154, 190; and Clergy Reserves, 65, 67, 68, 72-3, 74-6, 79; and University question, 84, 87, 88, 90, 122; and University Act, 1853, 110-15, 117, 118, 119, 121-2, 154; and elementary education, 133-4, 142-4, 145, 147, 148,

154-6, 157-9. *See also* Hincks-Morin ministry, 1851-4
Hincks, Thomas, 4
Hincks-Morin ministry, 1851-4, 25, 63-76, 113, 114, 147-8, 153-8
Hodgins, John George, 116, 135, 137, 139, 142, 159, 167, 173
Hogan, accused of murder of Robert Corrigan, 19, 20
Holton, Luther Hamilton, 163
Hope Commission on Education in Ontario, 129
Hopkins, Caleb, 53, 56
Horan, Edward John, 154, 168, 171
Howard, James Scott, 137
Howley, William, 32, 37, 38
Huron College, 4

INDEPENDENCE OF THE LEGISLATIVE ASSEMBLY ACT, 1844, 16
Ireland, Church of. *See* Low Churchism
Irish potato famine: and emigration to Canada, xiv, 12, 25, 148

JACKSON, SIR RICHARD DOWNES, 42
Jennings, John, 54
Jesuit Estates, 32, 100

KING'S COLLEGE, xiii, 42, 54, 82, 99, 109, 110, 118, 125, 126, 133, 135, 144; endowment, 83-4, 85, 91-102, 139; and University amalgamation, 85-8; and University Bills, 88-98; and University Act, 1849, 102, 103, 104
Kingston, Roman Catholic bishop of. *See* Horan, Edward John
Knox College, 90, 104, 116, 118, 120, 123

LAFONTAINE, SIR LOUIS HIPPOLYTE, xiv, 50, 53-64 *passim*, 143, 153. *See also* Baldwin-Lafontaine ministry, 1842-3; Great Ministry, 1848-51
Langton, John, 77, 117-25 *passim*, 160
Laval University, 118
Leitch, William, 123, 126, 127, 128
Lemieux, François Xavier, 164
Lesslie, James, 54, 55
Lett, Benjamin, 61
Lewis, John Travers, 5
Liberal party. *See* Reform party
Liberal-Conservative party, 19, 157, 170; and Clergy Reserves, xiv, 64, 69, 71-2, 74-5; and elementary education, 159, 164-73 *passim*. *See also* Tory party
Liddell, Thomas: on voluntarism, 7; and University question, 85-9, 96
Lillie, Adam, 54, 127
Lindsey, Charles, 53
London University, 82, 83, 94, 110, 111, 113, 122
Lount, Samuel, 21, 48
Low Churchism, 5, 79, 88, 123, 139, 169; and

politics, 4, 7; opposition to Strachan and High Churchism, 4, 5, 164
Loyal Orange Lodges. *See* Orange Order
Lutheran Church, 12, 49, 185
Lynch, John Joseph, 24, 132, 165, 170, 172, 174, 176

MACARA, JOHN, 87, 90
Macaulay, John, 14, 30, 31, 32, 33; on Clergy Reserves, 30, 31, 34, 36
Macaulay, William, 36
McCaul, John, 93, 98, 103, 114
McClure, W., 54
Macdonald, Sir John Alexander, 21, 23, 47, 154, 165, 167; his University Bills, 16, 48, 96-101, 104, 111, 113, 114, 139, 140; and University question, 103, 117, 120-2, 123, 124, 125, 126; and elementary education, 159-74. *See also* Macdonald (J. A.)-Taché ministry, 1856-7; Macdonald (J. A.)-Cartier ministry, 1857-62
Macdonald (J. A.)-Cartier ministry, 1857-62, 120, 123, 126, 170, 171, 172, 173, 177
Macdonald (J. A.)-Taché ministry, 1856-7, 22
Macdonald, John Sandfield, 20, 63, 75, 128, 174, 177. *See also* Macdonald (J. S.)-Sicotte ministry, 1862-3
Macdonald (J. S.)-Sicotte ministry, 1862-3, 126, 173-7
Macdonell, Alexander, 84, 130, 131
Macdonell, Angus, 49, 143, 147, 173, 177
McDougall, William, 55, 73, 78, 179
McGee, Thomas D'Arcy, xii, 13, 21, 24, 166-78 *passim*
McGill, Robert, 38-9
Mackenzie, Alexander, 67, 174
Mackenzie, William Lyon, xiv, 48, 60, 67, 147, 153, 154, 160
Maclean, T. A., 127
McMaster, William, 117
McNab, Alexander, 107
MacNab, Sir Allan Napier, 19, 74, 76, 159. *See also* MacNab-Morin ministry, 1854-5; MacNab-Taché ministry, 1855-6
MacNab-Morin ministry, 1854-5, 75-6, 78, 159, 191
MacNab-Taché ministry, 1855-6, 19, 78, 79
McNaughton, Peter, 79
Maine Law, 25, 67
Matthews, Peter, 27, 48
Melbourne, William Lamb, second Viscount: his second cabinet, 36
Mennonites, 12
Merritt, William Hamilton, 77, 93
Metcalfe, Charles Theophilus Metcalfe, Baron, 15, 16, 44, 45, 48, 89, 90, 94, 135; and constitutional crisis, 1843, 9, 15-16, 44, 48, 89, 90, 133, 135, 141
Methodism, 3, 10, 12, 25, 169; support for voluntarism, xiii, 10, 30, 49; and University Question, 92, 113, 125
Methodist Episcopal Church, 8, 9, 10, 52, 54,

61, 79, 117, 185, 187; and Clergy Reserves, 72, 79; and University question, 92, 97, 100, 101, 104, 116, 117, 119
Miller, William, 20
Millerism, 9
Mirror, 13
Molesworth, Sir William, 68
Monck, Sir Charles Stanley, fourth Viscount, 126-7
Montreal, bishop of. *See* Fulford, Francis
Moravian Church, 49
Morin, Augustin Norbert, 67, 74, 76, 78, 133, 153, 154, 159, 160. *See also* Hincks-Morin ministry, 1851-4; MacNab-Morin ministry, 1854-5
Morris, James, 127
Morris, William, 30, 32, 38, 40, 47, 54, 59; and United Synod, 6, 34-5; and Clergy Reserves Act, 1840, 39, 42; defends Clergy Reserves settlement of 1840, 57, 59-60, 70; and Queen's University, 84-7, 91; and elementary education, 131
Morrison, Joseph Curran, 50, 63, 137
Mountain, George Jehosaphat, 58, 65, 67
Mowat, Sir Oliver, 23, 167
Municipal Corporations Act, 1849, 141
Municipal Loan Fund, 80
Municipalities Fund, 76, 80
Murray, Robert, 134-5

Nationalism, xi-xii, 19, 45, 126; and education, xii, xiv-xv, 129, 135, 152, 177, 180; conflict with denominationalism, xiii, xiv, 3, 16, 26, 28, 81, 115, 181; and Clergy Reserves, 28, 41, 74; and University question, 104, 105, 120-8 *passim*
Nelles, Samuel Sobieski, 107; and University question, 119, 123, 126, 128
Newcastle, Henry Pelham Fiennes Pelham Clinton, fifth Duke of, 22, 69, 70
New Connexion Methodist Church, 9, 10, 54, 144, 187; and University question, 92, 97, 100, 104
New South Wales system, 29, 30, 32, 35
Normal school, 138, 146, 176, 179
Normanby, George Augustus Constantine Phipps, Marquis of, 30, 31, 32
Notman, William, 50, 52
North American, 55, 78

O'Brien, M. T., 139
Orange Order: and nationalism, xii, 13, 15; relations with Church of Rome, xii, 15-24; and Rebellion Losses Bill riots, 16; growth of, 17, 18, 20; and politics, 17, 19; educational policy, 17, 162, 164, 170, 174, 175; and public disturbances, 19, 20-1, 22; incorporation of, 20, 21; and University question, 106
Ormiston, William, 61
Osler, Edward, 16
Ottawa University. *See* Bytown College

Oxford Movement, xi, 4

Pakington, Sir John, 64-70 *passim,* 112
Palmer, Arthur, 68
"Papal Aggression" controversy, xi, 13, 16-17, 60, 116, 132, 144-5, 148, 156, 164
Papin, Joseph, 163
Party Processions Act, 1843, 15
Paton, John, 119, 125
Patriot, 5
Patton, Henry, 56
Patton, James, 125, 128
Peel, Sir Robert, 37, 38, 46, 68, 71, 104, 108
Perry, Peter, 53
Pinsonnault, Pierre Adolphe, 165
Pius IX, xi, 144, 145
Plain Folk: and voluntarism, xiii
Power, Michael, 17, 137-8, 139-50 *passim*
Presbyterianism, 14, 35, 79, 169; and voluntarism, 7, 30
Price, James Hervey, 63, 64; and Clergy Reserves, 47, 50, 52, 53, 60, 62; his Clergy Reserves resolutions, 55-7, 58, 64
Primitive Methodist Church, 9, 10, 92, 127, 187
Prince, John, 55
Privy Council, Great Britain: and Clergy Reserves, 29, 37
Protestant Alliance, 18
Protestantism, xv, 13, 18, 25, 81; antipathy to Church of Rome, 13, 17-26, 72, 145, 162-80 *passim;* and Orange Order, 19, 23; and elementary education, 131-46, 150-80
Puseyism, xi, 4, 39, 108, 132, 135
Pyper, James, 54

Quakers, xiii, 12, 185
Quebec, bishop of. *See* Mountain, George Jehosaphat
Quebec Conference, 1864, 175-6, 177
Queen's College, 6, 84, 90, 108, 109, 111, 112, 142; endowment, 84, 85, 97, 98; and university amalgamation, 85-96 *passim;* and University Act, 1849, 103, 104, 106; and University Act, 1850, 107; and university affiliation, 118-28. *See also* Scotland, Church of

Ragged schools, 172, 173
Ramsay, Septimus, 63
Rebellion Losses Act, 1849, 16, 50, 55, 102, 104, 106, 141; and Montreal riots, 16, 50
Rebellion of 1837, xi, 9, 43, 53, 75, 181
Record. See Ecclesiastical and Missionary Record
Rectories, xiv, 27, 28, 32, 50-67 *passim,* 143, 154, 181, 190-1; and establishment, xiii, 30; legislation on, 63, 65, 66, 190-1
Reform Convention, 1859, 120, 169, 170
Reform party, 48, 62, 75-6, 90, 94, 96, 135, 141, 143, 153, 157, 181, 190; and nationalism, xii; and general election, 1847, xiv,

16, 48; and Clear Grits, 17, 52, 153; and Protestantism, 18; and Clergy Reserves, 48, 51, 72-9; and University question, 88-90, 96, 100, 101, 116; and elementary education, 130, 134-5, 140, 148, 164, 166, 169

Regiopolis College, 49, 84-5, 91, 95-103 *passim*, 116, 118, 126, 142

"Rep. by Pop.," 20, 125

Responsible government, 16, 18, 45, 68, 94, 99, 106, 109, 139, 181

Ribbonmen: blamed for murder at St. Sylvestre, 18

Richards, Sir William Buell, 113, 114, 115, 152, 153, 154

Richardson, James, 54, 61

Richey, Matthew, 33

Rintoul, William, 7

Roaf, John, 54, 61, 95

Roblin, David, 190

Robinson, Sir John Beverley, 14, 22, 31, 42, 43, 58, 108, 109, 110, 113

Robinson, William Benjamin, 16, 91, 92, 93-4, 103, 160

Rolph, John, 17, 63-76 *passim*, 113, 156

Rome, Church of, xiii, 4, 12-13, 21, 22, 23, 46, 66, 83, 144, 185; relations with protestantism, xi, 4, 9, 13-26, 32, 58, 60, 71, 168, 175, 179-80; and separate schools, xiv-xv, 17, 18, 20, 129-81, 189; and Clergy Reserves, 13, 41, 49, 56, 58, 60, 74-80, 165; and University question, 13, 16, 97-105, 116-17, 125, 128; political views of, 14, 15, 16, 20, 21-4, 98, 105, 156-9; incorporation Acts, 24-5; government aid to, 29, 33, 38; endowments, 58, 63, 68-76, 79, 89; Toronto Catholic Institute, 73, 156-8, 159

Ross, John, 147

Rouge party, 75, 163

Russell, Lord John, 9, 14, 32, 39, 40, 54, 64, 68, 140, 145; and Clergy Reserves, 32-8, 58, 62

Ryerson, Egerton, 15, 30-6 *passim*, 90, 92, 138, 144; and elementary school system, xiv, 116, 134-74; and Clergy Reserves, 30, 31, 36, 40; and union of Wesleyan Methodists, 39-40; and University question, 82-128; and University Act, 1853, 112-15; and common school Acts, 136-56; and separate school legislation, 159-74. *See also* Common schools; Separate schools; Wesleyan Methodist Church

Ryerson, William, 172

SABBATARIANISM, xv, 24, 25, 67

St. Ignatius College, 116

St. Jerome's College, 116

St. Michael's College, 85, 116, 117

St. Sylvestre: murder at, 18-19

Scobie, Hugh, 6, 8, 88, 90, 91, 92, 98, 137

Scotland, Church of, 5-8, 12, 15, 29, 37, 42, 64, 69, 135, 137, 185, 186; disruption of, xi, 6-7, 42, 44, 90; and establishment, xii, 5, 14, 27, 29, 66; and voluntarism, xiii; and use of Bible in schools, xiv, 130-1; and church union, 5-6, 34-5, 80; Temporalities Bill, 6, 24; relations with Church of Scotland in Britain, 6-7, 39, 58, 59, 60; and Clergy Reserves, 6, 27-80; and University question, 16, 84-7, 90, 95-109, 116, 119, 123-5, 127. *See also* Queen's College

Scott, Jonathan, 14, 15

Scott, Richard William, 168-75, 179, 180

Seaton, John Colborne, first Baron. *See* Colborne, Sir John

Secret Societies Bill, 1843, 15

Seignorial tenure, 74, 75, 76, 77, 157

Semi-voluntary scheme. *See* New South Wales system

Separate schools, xiii, xiv, 23, 64, 67, 105, 110, 112, 126-81, 189; Act, 1863, 129, 168, 174-80; Act, 1855, 160-71; Bill, 1856, 162-3; Bill, 1860, 168-9, 170; Bill, 1861, 170; Bill, 1862, 171-4; Bill, 1866, 178-9. *See also* England, Church of; Rome, Church of

Separation of church and state, xi, xii, 16, 61, 181. *See also* Voluntarism

Sheedy, Matthew, 21

Sherwood, George, 47, 64

Sherwood, Henry, 47, 64; and Clergy Reserves, 45, 46, 47, 55, 96; and University question, 91, 93, 98, 110-11, 113. *See also* Sherwood-Daly ministry, 1847

Sherwood-Daly ministry, 1847, 96, 98, 99

Sicotte, Louis Victor, 74, 75. *See also* Macdonald (J. S.)-Sicotte ministry, 1862-3

Simcoe, Ont.: Clergy Reserves debate at, 61

Smart, William, 6, 35

Society for the Propagation of the Gospel in Foreign Parts, 31, 37, 42, 43, 46, 58, 60, 63, 70, 75, 108, 110

Sons of Temperance, 25

Stanley, Edward George Geoffrey Smith. *See* Derby, Edward George Geoffrey Smith Stanley, fourteenth Earl of

Starr, Miss, "abducted", 22

Stinson, Joseph, 31, 33, 119, 122

Strachan, James McGill, 59, 65, 73

Strachan, John, 4, 14, 16, 24, 25, 37, 46, 47, 54-68 *passim*, 73, 82, 114, 160; attitude to Church of Rome, 15, 17, 27-32, 137, 145-6; and Clergy Reserves legislation, 30-48, 70-9; and Clergy Reserves settlement, 1840, 58-65, 145; and King's College, 83-98, 103; and University legislation, 89-106 *passim*; and Trinity College, 107-17, 126-31; and separate Anglican schools, 114, 131-40, 145-6, 153-6, 163-9; and elementary education, 137, 138. *See also* England, Church of

Stuart, George Okill, 56
Sullivan, Robert Baldwin, 43, 84
Sydenham, Charles Edward Poulett Thomson, first Baron, 9, 14, 32, 48, 84, 88; and Clergy Reserves, 32-43, 51, 130; and elementary education, 130, 134, 135

TACHÉ, SIR ETIENNE PASCHAL, 144-5; his separate school Act, 1855, 160-71 passim. See also MacNab-Taché ministry, 1855-6
Temperance, xv, 24, 25
Thomson, Charles Edward Poulett. See Sydenham, Charles Edward Poulett Thomson, first Baron
Thomson, George B., 70, 75, 77
Three Rivers Cathedral Bill, 25, 70
Toronto Periodical Journal, 10, 92
Toronto School of Medicine, 113
Toronto, University of, 88, 102, 106-15, 116, 117, 119-28, 131
Tory party, 16, 35, 45, 55, 56, 62, 73, 74, 89, 90, 91, 101, 102, 114, 115, 162, 164; decline of, 14, 64, 66; connection with Church of England, 14, 47, 61, 66
Tractarianism, xi, 4, 9
Trinity College, 4, 69, 107-17, 173; and University affiliation, 113, 118, 121-8. See also King's College; England, Church of
True Witness, 13
Tunkers, 12
Turgeon, Pierre Flavien, 153, 154

UNION OF UPPER AND LOWER CANADA, 1841, xi, xii, xiii, 9, 14, 36, 46, 68, 120; Act, 14, 43, 132, 150
United Presbyterian Church, 8, 54, 61, 186; and Clergy Reserves, 49, 61, 72; and University question, 113, 123, 125
United Presbyterian Magazine, 8
United Secession Church. See United Synod
United Synod, 186; union with Church of Scotland, 6, 29, 34-5; and Clergy Reserves, 6, 29, 35, 38, 39, 66, 79
University College, London University, 82, 83, 88
University College, University of Toronto, 110, 115-18
University question, xiii, xiv, 9, 16, 64, 82-128, 140, 142, 152, 166, 168; and university endowment, xiii, 13, 83-108, 110, 113, 118-28; and University Bill, 1843, 15, 85-94, 97, 101, 102; and University Bill, 1847, 16, 48, 94-104, 111-15, 139, 140; and University Act, 1849, 52, 101-4, 106, 112, 114, 116, 122, 142; and religious tests, 83, 88, 102, 107-13 passim; and university amalgamation, 85-105; and University Bills, 1845, 91-8, 102, 104;

and University Bills, 1846, 94, 95, 96, 114; and university affiliation, 102, 110-28; and University Act, 1850, 107, 112; and University Bills, 1851, 110-11, 113; and University Act, 1853, 110-25, 154; and University Commission, 1861, 124-8
Upper Canada College, 84, 118
Urquhart, Hugh, 39

VAN DIEMAN'S LAND SYSTEM, 32
Victoria College, 9, 33, 43, 61, 84, 90-117 passim, 142; and University Bills, 88-92, 97; and University Acts, 103-7; and university affiliation, 118-28. See also Wesleyan Methodist Church
Viger, Denis Benjamin, 90
Voluntarism, xii-xiii, 41, 61, 77; denominational support of, xiii, 12; conflict with church-statism, xii, xiii, 27, 52

WAKEFIELD, EDWARD GIBBON, 90
Wallace, Robert, 20
Watchman (New Connection Methodist), 10
Watchman (Orange), 10, 23
Wellington, Arthur Wellesley, first Duke of, 108
Wesleyan, 10
Wesleyan Methodist Church, 8-10, 12, 35, 37, 61, 73, 117, 135, 185, 187; relations with British Wesleyan Methodist Church, 8-9, 10, 30-1, 33, 39-41, 43, 98, 185; and politics, 8, 9, 14, 15, 30, 92; and voluntarism, 9, 10, 30, 31, 62, 66, 68; and Clergy Reserves, 9, 14, 30, 33, 34, 38, 39, 41, 43, 49, 50, 54, 57, 61-2, 66, 72, 74, 76-7, 79, 80; and University question, 9, 16, 84, 86-92, 95, 98-104, 106, 109, 115-20, 123-5, 128, 168; and "Papal Agression," 17; and benevolent societies incorporation, 24; and elementary education, 157-69, 180. See also Victoria College; Wesleyan Methodist Church, British
Wesleyan Methodist Church, British, 8-9, 31, 185, 187; and establishment, 8-9, 31, 33; government aid to, 29, 30, 66; and Clergy Reserves, 33, 40, 43; London Missionary Committee of, 40, 80
Westminster Conference, 1866, 179
Wetenhall, John, 45, 50, 53, 102
Whitaker, George, 112, 118, 121, 126
White, John, 70, 73
Williamson, James, 123, 124
Willis, Michael, 54
Wilson, Daniel, 120-1, 122, 123
Witness of Truth, 12
Woodstock College, 117
Wycliffe College, 4

DATE DUE

FEB 2 4 2006			

GAYLORD PRINTED IN U.S.A.

WITHDRAWN